THE SYMBOLIC QUEST

The Symbolic Quest

Basic Concepts of Analytical Psychology

Edward C. Whitmont

PRINCETON UNIVERSITY PRESS
Princeton, New Jersey

Acknowledgments

I WOULD like to express my gratitude to those pioneer workers who carried forward and developed Jung's theories, especially Erich Neumann and Esther Harding, upon whose efforts much of the present volume is based; to Anneliese Aumüller for her helpful advice in going through the manuscript; and to Patricia Spindler for assistance in editing the original lectures which were the basis for this book.

Acknowledgments are also due the following publishers, institutions and individuals who have very kindly given permission to quote from copyrighted material:

To the Princeton University Press in Princeton, New Jersey, the Bollingen Foundation in New York and Routledge & Kegan Paul in London for the passages from *The Collected Works of C. G. Jung;*

To Basic Books and to Sigmund Freud Copyrights Ltd., Mr. James Strachey and the Hogarth Press Ltd. for permission to quote from the Standard Edition of *The Complete Psychological Works of Sigmund Freud;*

To Bantam Books for material from *The Dybbuk and Other Great Yiddish Plays;* to Clarkson N. Potter and Anthony Blond Ltd. for Erwin Schrödinger's article in *On Modern Physics,* to the Dial Press for *Another Country* by James Baldwin; to Harcourt, Brace & World for Jung's *Modern Man in Search of a Soul* and *Psychological Types;* to Harper and Row for Mircea Eliade's *Myths, Dreams and Mysteries* and for the Koestler passage from Crossman's *The God That Failed;* to Holt, Rinehart & Winston and Laurence Pollinger Ltd. for the poem "Snow" by Robert Frost, to the Humanities Press Inc. and Routledge & Kegan Paul for Jean Piaget's *Language and Thought of the Child;* to the Macmillan Company and A. D. Peters and Company for *The Invisible Writing* by Arthur Koestler; to International Universities Press for *A Genetic Field Theory of Ego Formation* by René Spitz and for the Üxküll material from *Instinctive Behavior;* to Alfred A. Knopf for Kahlil Gibran's *The Prophet;*

To W. W. Norton for *Thought Reform and the Psychology of Totalism* by R. J. Lifton; to Pantheon Books, a Division of Random House, for Jung's *Memories, Dreams, Reflections,* and for Esther Harding's *Women's Mysteries;* to the Philosophical Library for Martin Buber's *Hasidism,* Ananda Coomaraswamy's *Hinduism and Buddhism,* and *The Analysis of Dreams* by Medard Boss; to Princeton University Press for the *I Ching* and for Jolande Jacobi's *Archetype/Complex/Symbol.* To Sheed and Ward and the Harvill Press for *Images and Symbols* by Mircea Eliade; to Simon & Schuster for *The Legends of the Bible* by Louis Ginzberg; to the University of North Carolina Press for *Cell and Psyche* by E. W. Sinnott; to the Yale University Press for Ernst Cassirer's *Essay on Man;*

To the Cambridge University Press for *Science and Humanism* by Erwin Schrödinger and for Michael Fordham's article in *The British Journal of Medical Psychology*; and to Routledge & Kegan Paul for Jung's *Psychological Types*; To Verlag Hans Huber for *Seelenkunde im Umbrich der Zeit* by G. R. Heyer; to Ernst Klett Verlag for *Meditation in Religion und Psychotherapie* and for the *Antaios* article "Pharao und Jesus als Söhne Gottes" by Emma Brunner-Traut; to Kösel-Verlag for Romano Guardini's *Rainer Maria Rilkes Deutung des Daseins*; to Rascher Verlag for *Studien zur Analytischen Psychologie C. G. Jungs* and for Aniela Jaffe's *Der Mythus vom Sinn*; to Rhein Verlag for *Der Schöpferische Mensch* by Erich Neumann and for Adolf Portman's *Biologie und Geist*; to Julius Springer Verlag for *Kulturelle Bedeutung der Komplexen Psychologie*;

To *The American Psychologist* for "The Misbehavior of Organisms" by Keller and Marian Breland; to *Look Magazine* for "The Tense Generation" by Samuel Grafton; to *Spring* for the passages from "The Interpretation of Visions" by C. G. Jung, for "The 'I' in Dreams" by Sonja Marjasch, and for my own material published in "The Role of the Ego in the Life Drama"; and to H. K. Fierz for permission to use the passages from *Psychologische Betrachtungen zu der Freskenfolge der Villa Dei Misteri in Pompeji* by Linda Fierz-David.

I am also grateful to a former patient for his permission to use the drawing which appears as a frontispiece to this volume.

E.C.W.

Contents

Preface to the 1991 Edition

WHEN I SET OUT to review the text of this book, twenty years after the original publication, I wondered how many changes would be needed to bring it up to the ways in which the practice of analytical psychology has evolved. Many contributions in the fields of preoedipal dynamics and feminine psychology have enriched our clinical scope.

Under the impact of the sexual revolution and the drug culture, formerly rigid persona and superego-determined ego structures have softened and, at times, even vanished. In Freud's and Jung's days the repression of sexuality and spirituality by an overrigid ego accounted for the majority of psychopathology. Nowadays the problems lie more frequently with insufficient ego structuring, confusion and borderline pathology and the difficulties of finding new forms of I-Thou relationships in a world no longer regulated by viable collective standards.

During Jung's lifetime the main analytic thrust was toward opening a too rigidly structured ego to a dialogue with the nonpersonal psyche. His stress was on the necessity of the ego's confronting and coming to terms with the world of archetypes. Today, perhaps owing to the dissolution of traditional standards, and the consequent weakening of persona support as well as the influx of often inadequately understood Eastern religious and cult influences, we encounter many more instances of inadequate egos being "lost" in the world of archetypes. An adequate personal ego structure has to be built before the transpersonal unconscious can be faced. To this end, introversion alone does not suffice. Working on one's relationships to partners, group and community is an equally important aspect of ego building and individuation.

In response to this situation various "schools" of Jungian practice have developed. The "developmental" school (Andrew Samuels, *Jung and the Post Jungians*, London: Routledge & Kegan Paul, 1985, p. 15) tends to promulgate the "clinical" approach that emphasizes the reductive dealing with personal traumatic, early childhood causation over the a priori archetypal data of the structuring and guiding Self. The "classical" and "archetypal" schools, in turn, tend to concern themselves more with archetypal than developmental dynamics and with the analysis of transference and countertransference. In their extreme forms both positions tend to identify with one aspect of what is in fact an interdependent field of complementary dynamics.

From this interdependent field perspective I see transformation and healing brought about through actualizing the guiding impulses from the archetypal world and the Self. They operate in terms of one's personal difficulties and emotional and relationship problems and in the effects of past traumatizations. From this perspective individual life can be seen as a dramatic story or "myth" which "stages" dramatic performances in phases that involve "quantum leaps" of creation and breakdown: birth, death and rebirth. Such a model can include *both* the "clinical" causal view of problems and pathology as "caused" by traumatic "accidents" that interrupted a purportedly "normal" state; and we can also see these traumatic cause-and-effect relations as subordinated to and "necessitated" by the "intents" of the play staged by the individual Self. To be an actor in one's life's drama without understanding its dramatic thrust, the action's place and function within the overall intended order which is both "because" and "in order to," makes it meaningless at best and chaotic at worst. Yet in order to grasp the crisis and its possible resolution, we must understand the meaning of the action as it unfolds as well as the impasse out of which it arose. The dramatic action evolving from the original difficulties must be reconstructed by reductive analysis to make the repressed traumatic conditionings adequately conscious. They must be actualized in the experiences of transference and countertransference. Their meaning or significance, however, arises through archetypal and mythological understanding.

What has meaning can be better borne. When we can forge our experiences of pain into a meaningful pattern, they can be seen as functional elements of our destiny. Chaotic suffering is unbearable. From this perspective we can understand the apparent paradox that digging up and reactivating old and even forgotten misery can have healing effects. And we can also appreciate the experiences of negative as well as positive transference.

A lack of relation to the archetypal dimension results in spiritual impoverishment and a sense of meaninglessness in life. But insufficient anchoring of the archetypal in the personal realm results in mere "head trips" and narcissistic preoccupation. There we merely speculate about archetypal meaning rather than try to discover this meaning through living concretely the prosaic and "trivial" problems and difficulties of everyday feelings and relationships—including those that arise in the transferential interaction with one's therapist. Then the symbol fails to heal and may, indeed, insulate us from the unconscious rather than connect us to it.

While the original edition of this book did not yet explicitly deal with the questions arising from these shifts of accent, its basic viewpoints by and large happen to do justice to them. However, I feel that in addition to minor textual changes, there are three areas in which, under the pressure of clinical experience, our concepts have evolved since their original formulation.

One concerns the definitions of the gender archetypes in exclusively contrasexual terms. These have been found to be too limiting by some therapists, this author included. Evidence seems to be accumulating that anima and animus may be seen as archetypal gender potentials, both of which apply to both sexes.

The prime emphasis of early analysis upon an introverted understanding of psychodynamics in terms of a predominantly verbally oriented interpretative method needs to be amplified. While these factors most certainly continue to be of basic significance, they must be balanced by active and guided imaginal work that is nonverbal and bodily. Increasingly we also find that extroverted relationship experiences require attention in order to build an adequate ego structure that eventually may be relativized with respect to the shadow, archetypal world and Self.

Finally, a clear distinction must be made between projection that is a potentially pathological misperception of reality and symbolic experience that mediates our relation to the spirit.

In order to avoid confusing those readers for whom this book serves as an introductory guide, restatements of these subject matters are offered as appendices at the end of the book.[1]

[1] My thanks are due Sylvia Perera for her helpful comments on the proposed changes.

Introduction

ANY ATTEMPT to present a systematic survey of the theory and practice of analytical psychology—that approach to depth psychology which is based upon the discoveries of C. G. Jung—is from the very outset confronted with a paradox. On the one hand, a theoretical presentation is vitally necessary in view of the fact that many interested readers have experienced great difficulties in appreciating the meaning of Jung's contribution to modern thought. On the other hand, an adequately logical and systematic presentation is next to impossible because of the nature of the subject matter. The psyche does not operate along the lines of our accustomed rationality. This paradox is perhaps appropriate, however, since one of Jung's major themes is the paradox and its reconciliation.

We hear many of Jung's terms in current speech daily—*extravert, introvert, thinking type, archetype*—but what Jung really meant to convey is rarely understood by most of the people who use them. It must be admitted that his approach, which is so foreign to the mental training of the twentieth century as to be dubbed "mystical" by many, is difficult to comprehend; also, this difficulty is compounded by the fact that Jung's psychological terminology, coined as it was to fit particular empirical findings, sometimes turned out to be at cross-purposes with general word usage and current philosophical definitions, and the door was opened to endless misunderstandings. Therefore, a certain amount of epistemological clarification and redefinition seems in order.

On the philosophical level, we find that past formulations are not appropriate for the new evidence we have before us because they lack adequate awareness of the workings of the unconscious psyche. They apply to a stage of science which is already outpaced, both by Jung's discoveries and by those of nuclear physicists. We cannot put new psychological wine into old philosophical bottles; new bottles need to be made by us and by coming generations. This task, however, will demand no less than a radical revision of our intellectual attitudes if we are to succeed in integrating into our view of the world those facts and findings which defy our rationalistic and positivistic frames of reference.

On the practical level, we run into difficulty in presenting our subject matter because the practice of analytical psychology consists of a dialectical encounter between two unique individuals, analyst and analysant, who are both unpredictable in their individual variants, hence unknown inasmuch as they are unique human beings and to an extent even unknowable; that is, their functioning is determined not only by conscious but also by unconscious factors—and we cannot ever completely uncover the total depth of the unconscious. The encounter of these two unknown variables results in a third variable: the therapy process itself. This, since it rests on unconscious more than on conscious interaction and dynamics, constitutes an equally unpredictable synthesis of the encountering two. It is an autonomous pattern of unfoldment which is different from and more than the sum of its constituent parts.

Hence it may safely be assumed, indeed even hoped, that analytical psychology in its practical application varies in as many different ways as there are different therapists and analysants who react in individually different ways to the ideas of the original discoverer. Thus also the presentation in this book necessarily represents my own individual way of comprehending and applying Jung's original findings. It may differ from the viewpoints of other analytical psychologists and even from Jung's own, to varying degrees and in various areas. This, however, is in agreement with Jung's own desires: he wished for followers who would see and think for themselves instead of being "parrots," as he once jokingly remarked. It is also imperative for the understanding of the psyche and the dynamics of the unconscious that we have direct experience of them, rather than that we merely think about them. Hence Jung's insistence—which subsequently was seconded by Freud—on the analysis of the would-be therapist.

The relative scantiness of specific information concerning applications of the principles set forth is therefore quite intentional; I am not attempting a didactic exposition of the practice of analysis but am endeavoring to convey a general feeling of its *modus operandi*. Although I shall give examples of dreams and their interpretation, I am not trying to teach the reader how to interpret dreams himself. Such an attempt would obscure more than enlighten and would lead the reader to the assumption that he can understand them without concrete, actual personal experience.

Yet, in spite of these barriers to understanding, there *are* certain basic concepts and working principles that can be conveyed as a groundwork for further investigation. In my attempt to state some common denominators, I shall try to adhere as closely as possible to Jung's own formulations, which are the basis for all subsequent elaborations and practical applications by his followers. Only where I feel there are gaps or a need for greater clarification (for instance in the sections on the actualization of archetypes, archetypal presentations of male and female, and ego development) shall I attempt to reformulate and to present versions of my own.

I find, moreover, that I must limit my presentation solely to Jung's ideas and their elaboration in analytical psychology and renounce comparisons and concordances with other schools of psychotherapy. This is not meant as minimizing the relevance of other schools or disregarding the contributions of their founders, but rather to express the conviction that such an attempt is premature. The frame of reference of analytical psychology presents such a unique world that any adequate interdisciplinary comparison would create more confusion than clarity at this juncture and goes beyond my present intent.

Finally, the nature of the material necessitates a text written on two levels and consequently presupposes two classes of readers. The more substantial portion is addressed to the general reader who may or may not have some prior knowledge of the principles of analytical psychology. But the text also contains several sections designed less for the general than for the professional reader. Chapters 1, 7 and 14 are among those more directly relevant to the work of the therapist, psychologist, analyst and psychiatrist. The general reader may find these chapters less readily comprehensible than others in the text, and he may avoid them if he so desires. However, a little patience and close attention will prevent even these chapters from falling outside the general reader's province.

The major theme of this book is the quest for symbolic experience, a quest which has urgency and meaning for our time and which finds its most useful and comprehensive expression in the discipline of analytical psychology.

Cease to seek after God (as without thee), and the universe, and things similar to these; seek Him from out of thyself and learn who it is, who once and for all appropriateth all in thee unto Himself, and sayeth: "My god, my mind, my reason, my soul, my body." And learn whence is sorrow and joy, and love and hate, and waking though one would not, and sleeping though one would not, and getting angry though one would not, and falling in love though one would not. And if thou shouldst closely investigate these things, thou wilt find Him in thyself, one and many, just as the atom, thus finding from thyself a way out of thyself.

—Monoïmus: Hippolytus, Elenchos (*Refutatio omnium heresiarum*) in Hippolytus Werke, ed. Paul Wendland, Vol. 111, Leipzig 1916. Referred to by Jung, CW 11, p. 264–65.

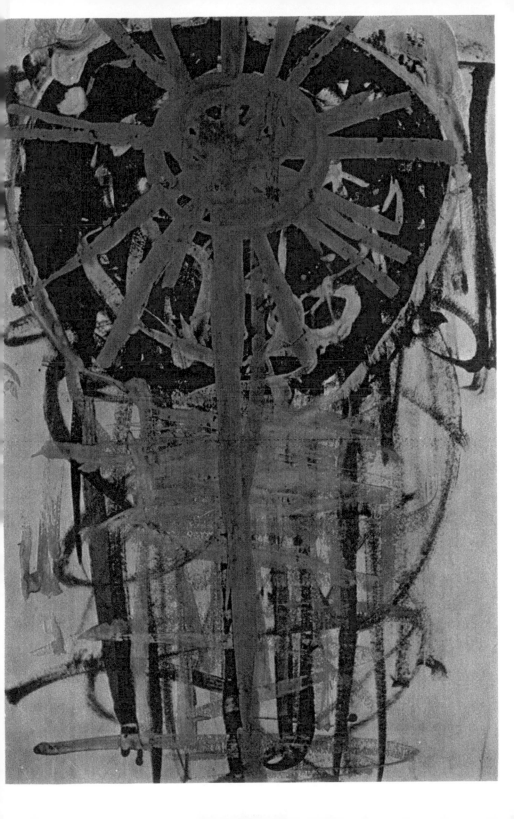

1. The Symbolic Approach

TWENTIETH CENTURY PSYCHOLOGY, in its concern with depth analysis, and twentieth century physics have begun to direct man's attention toward the use of symbols as a helpful means of comprehending and making use of the non-rational and intuitive realms of functioning. In analytical psychology, Jung's development of new symbolic categories can be compared with a similar approach initiated by the modern physicist. In both cases the subject matter defies comprehension in accustomed rational categories; hence symbolic "working models" or working hypotheses, such as the archetype or the atom, had to be set up in order to describe as adequately as possible the way an otherwise indescribable unknown acts in the world of matter. Thus the structure of the atom can be represented by the construction of an orderly arrangement, in model form, of its theoretical components—nucleus and electrons—whose existence can be deduced from observable data. In a similar manner, the totality of the human psyche, of which consciousness is but an aspect, can be dealt with scientifically through the formulation of a system of postulated elements whose existence can be deduced from observable data. We will return to this subject later when discussing the scientific acceptability of the symbolic approach.

Like the atom the psyche and its elements are not physical objects that can be seen or touched, but unlike the atom they cannot even be made to fit the conditions of laboratory testing and statistical evaluation. We cannot speak of the psyche as a thing that *is* or *does* this or that. At best we can speak of it indirectly by describing human behavior—the behavior of others and also our own subjective experience—*as if* it expressed aspects of a hypothetical pattern of meaning, *as if* a potential, encompassing wholeness were ordering the action of the parts. For instance, we can recognize that an autonomous impulse or a hitherto hidden personality pattern has emerged and behaved as if it intended a certain action which was meaningful in relation to that total personality. The most basic hypothesis about the human psyche with which we deal here, then, is that of a pattern of wholeness that can only be described symbolically.

To illustrate: a woman who buys everything she can find in the shape of a butterfly or decorated with butterflies is caught by an urge that calls for symbolic understanding. In this case, a butterfly may be expressive of her strong inner need to emerge from a confining cocoon, perhaps a cocoon of old protective attitudes. Or a young man whose unrecognized urge is to exercise great power over people may want to become an analyst and he may be able to give all kinds of exemplary, conscious reasons for wanting to. If the symbolic nature of his urge—namely to gain power over himself rather than over others—is not discovered, his influence will be most unfortunate. (This is also one of the reasons why an analyst must himself be analyzed.) Or a humanities student may suddenly change his field to regional planning. His urge to "save" the world, to reorganize and order society, can be understood *as if* it expressed his own inner need for rescue and for organization. Whether this "choice" of occupation is also valid on the outer plane will be discovered as it is lived. If it is *only* symbolic of an unrecognized inner state, it will eventually run into snags in the concrete world. The student is likely to be a more effective planner if he becomes aware of this kind of meaning in his choice of profession and if he can separate the two endeavors, although he may first have to work the problem through in terms of the form in which he sees it in the outside world. In this way he can test his ego strength against something concrete and thus prepare himself to have some voice in the optimum development of his own inner regions.

This symbolic approach can mediate an experience of something indefinable, intuitive or imaginative, or a feeling-sense of something that can be known or conveyed in no other way, since abstract terms do not suffice everywhere. While to most people in our time the only comprehensible approach to reality lies in defining everything by means of literal, abstract, impersonal conceptualizations, it is this challenge to and reliance upon the intuitive and emotional faculties that constitute the fundamentally new character of Jung's approach. Indeed he held these faculties to be indispensable for an adequate experiencing of the psyche, for it is only by means of all its elements that we can attempt to understand the psyche. This approach opens new doors, but it also raises potential obstacles for the newcomer to these concepts who has as yet no personal experience in the depths of the unconscious areas of the psyche.

The difficulties that the average contemporary encounters in attempting to grasp the symbolic approach rest upon the fact that, in response to the mystical introverted trend and the later ecclesiastical obscurantism of the Middle Ages, recent Western development has overstressed abstract, rational thought. It has concerned itself predominantly with the practical utilization of external things and external needs and has in our day culminated in fact- and logic-oriented positivism. It has largely disregarded—or at least relegated to a position of lesser importance—the emotional and intuitive sides of man. Hence the capacity to feel (which is the capacity to experience a conscious relationship to emotion—emotion itself being the impulse, an autonomous force) and the capacity to intuit (that is, the capacity to perceive through other means than our five senses) have not been given adequate moral value or conscious scrutiny; feelings are regarded as something that can be dispensed with, intuitions are not considered as "real." This is an approach which fails to help us toward the understanding of basic motivation; for ethos, morality and meaningfulness of existence rest basically upon emotional and intuitive foundations. These areas may be secondarily rationalized, but mere reason alone never touches or moves them; were it otherwise the scientists and philosophers would long ago have reformed mankind. We see in all the lives around us how ineffective rational appeals are in comparison with emotional ones. Our culture is logic-oriented but in dealing with our most fundamental problems rational logic fails to offer us adequate answers to the understanding and living of life.

In our time this extraverted rationalism has gone to such an extreme that it has been remarked that "not only the occidental Western world but the whole of humanity is in danger of losing its soul to the external things of life. Our extraverted forces of the intellect are so much concerned with adequate feeding and hygienic care of the underdeveloped parts of the world, as well as with raising our standard of living, that the irrational functions, the heart and the soul, are more and more threatened with atrophy." [1]

Some of the results of this one-sided emphasis are the individual and mass neuroses of our time, with the ever-latent danger of explosive eruptions. Addictions to alcohol, narcotics and the "mind-expanding drugs" also express a search for emotional experiences which in the course of our extreme intellectualization have become lost. But it is not only the drug- and alcohol-addiction; "work-addiction," the "manager disease," the compulsive need of always having to do something in order to appear busy, also indicates the inability of modern man to find a meaning in life.

This traditional devaluation and neglect of emotion and intuition in favor of outer world-directed reason has left Western man without an adequate cultivation of conscious modes of orienting himself in the inner psychic world of emotion, ethos and meaning; for what is not consciously developed remains primitive and regressive and may constitute a threat.

Consequently most of our contemporaries have no way of recognizing intuitive or feeling responses, either in another person or in themselves. It is very difficult for today's typical intellectual to discover a way out of the unbalanced psychic state in which he eventually finds himself, for even the most intense experiences can appear to the "thinking man" to be meaningless. As James Baldwin has put it: ". . . the occurrence of an event is not the same thing as knowing what it is that one has lived through. Most people have not lived—nor could it, for that matter, be said they had died —through any of their terrible events." [2]

In the face of this impasse it was Jung's concern, and indeed the very point of parting with Freud, to show that intuition and emotion and the capacity to apperceive and create by way of symbols are basic modes of human functioning, no less so than perception through the sense organs and through thinking.

A genuine symbol in Jung's terms is not a freely chosen, abstract designation attached to a specified object by convention (such as verbal or mathematical signs) but is the expression of a spontaneous experience which points beyond itself to a meaning not conveyed by a rational term, owing to the latter's intrinsic limitation. Jung defines a symbol as "the best description, or formula, of a relatively unknown fact; a fact, however, which is none the less recognized or postulated as existing." [3] "(It) is not an arbitrary or intentional sign standing for a known and conceivable fact, but an admittedly anthropomorphic—hence limited and only partly valid—expression for something suprahuman and only partly conceivable. It may be the best expression possible, yet it ranks below the level of the mystery it seeks to describe." [4]

These definitions indicate that the full range of functioning rests not merely upon the need to answer rational, logical questions such as "How?" "Wherefrom?" and "What for?" but also upon a search for significance: "What does it mean?" Therefore it is important to differentiate between a true symbol, in the sense of our definition, and an allegory or metaphor that may point to rationally conceivable facts or to dynamics of the personal unconscious.

> Every view which interprets the symbolic expression as an analogue or an abbreviated design for a *known* thing is *semiotic*. A view which interprets the symbolic expression as the best possible formulation of a relatively *unknown* thing, which cannot for that reason be more clearly or characteristically represented, is *symbolic*. [5]
>
> An expression that stands for a known thing always remains merely a sign, and is never a symbol. It is, therefore, quite impossible to make a living symbol, i.e., one that is pregnant with meaning, from known associations. [6]

In the following quotation, Heyer expresses the unique importance of the symbol (in this case, the symbol of creative potency) and comments on the ease with which we can misunderstand or ignore it:

> Let us assume someone dreams of so-called phallic objects. The old method of psychoanalysis would have seen in this only repressed, and [in other words] disfigured images for the penis. This *can* . . . very well be the case, but it *need* not. The tower, the obelisk, the church steeple, the sword, the lance, the knife, etc., can represent for the dreamer the not yet dared male potency, *sensu strictiori*, that is, sex. This then would become the object of analysis.
>
> But we do not want to forget that the genital function and the members of the body assigned to it are not the only emanations of the manly and masculine, the brave, the constant, upright, aggressive, etc.
>
> The genital potency is only *one*, namely a *personal* actualization of this principle—that is, of the masculine pole in the sense of both mundane and cosmic total being; as represented, for instance, in towers.
>
> Whoever recognizes in the dreamed or actual tower, obelisk or sword *only* the "repressed" *membrum virile*, is actually blind to the fact that the inner world of man in a state of trouble produces these images of the *potentia erecta* because only thereby can those larger, more powerful and all-inclusive and—in the truest sense—significant entities and realities be evoked, which mediate to us the *meaning*, the inner being of these qualities rife with symbolism.
>
> Whoever reduces the image to a disfigured substitute for something else degrades it, and misunderstands the secret indications; better, neglects them or rather neglects to perceive the potent symbol hidden under private covers. If, however, one extracts the real core of the image, one thereby helps to make contact with that power inherent and living within the symbol—a power that "can move mountains."
>
> For symbols are not merely representational forms which serve our cognition, but rather they are highly potent powers. This becomes clear at once when we consider what effects symbols can produce, as for instance flags, with their symbolic signs—the cross or the crescent —what world-shaking deeds are connected with these! [7]

In practical terms, Jung's method of interpreting spontaneous symbols of the unconscious never attempts to say that a human situation *is* such and such, but rather that these images describe the situation itself in the form of analogies or parables. The symbolic approach by definition points beyond itself and beyond what can be made immediately accessible to our observation. While this approach is not abstract or rational, neither can it be regarded as irrational; rather it has laws and a structure of its own which correspond to the structural laws of emotion and intuitive realization.[8]

Perhaps before discussing the symbolic experience further in its epistemological, philosophical and practical terminological implications, an example of the symbolic approach to a dream might be given to illustrate how this approach functions in a therapeutic situation. This patient had undergone previous psychotherapy which had not been based on Jung's symbolic approach but. upon the traditional symptomatic approach. I do not, of course, mean to imply that a failure of psychotherapeutic efforts proves that the approach has been wrong. There are many factors involved, to be discussed in later chapters, foremost among them the personal relationship between therapist and patient. However, this case was unique, didactically classical, as are most of those I shall use here as examples. It is rare for a sudden dramatic change in a patient's attitude to occur through a single insight; however, this patient did experience immediate release from his neurotic impasse. Thus his case appears particularly suitable for demonstrating the concrete effects of a different line of therapeutic approach.

The symptomatic approach of which I spoke—as opposed to the symbolic one—viewed the patient's reaction pattern merely as a deviation from normal sexuality, falling into a certain classification, in need of correction and presumably caused by specific disturbances. While all of this was quite correct, namely in terms of an abstract system of classification, it nevertheless omitted to ask what in practical terms turned out to be the most important question, namely the question of the meaningfulness of the unknown message which was inherent in his strange compulsion.

There are two possible approaches to the problems and disturbances which life presents. We can see them as symptomatic deviations from a desired normalcy of "what things should be like," caused by some wrongness and hence the expressions of trouble or illness. We can on the other hand suspect that the known facts may attempt to point further and deeper, to a development still called for and a meaningfulness so far unrealized. Only then do we think or live not merely symptomatically but also symbolically. The realization of that meaning which has so far been missed might then point toward a cure.

The patient was a businessman in his middle thirties who came to me in a state of panic; he had been plagued since the beginning of sexual maturity by what had been diagnostically classified as fetishism, with a masochistic component. He was unable to function sexually with any woman except through first licking or kissing her feet. In order to accomplish sexual arousal he had to prostrate himself before his partner, caress and kiss her feet and gradually, as it were, work his way upwards. Any attempt to avoid this path of approach would always result in sexual impotence. During one of his initial analytic interviews, he told the following recurrent dream:

"I saw a dagger, sickle-shaped and silvery, and I was told that this was the weapon that would kill or had killed Siegfried, and there was the implication of a threat that this weapon might also kill me."

As this man became more and more worried about his "perversion" and his neurotic tensions, which made adequate relationships with women rather impossible, his impotence increased. The interpretation he had been given previously was in terms of a masochistic tendency, a wish to punish or humiliate himself for his aggressions, based on a serious conflict situation with his parents, notably his mother. The recurrent dream could be made to fit fairly well with this interpretation, namely as an urge to self-destruction or self-castration. Of course, one might ask further questions. Why the worshipping just of the feet? Why the fancy image of the dagger? Why did these insights and the previous therapy based upon this interpretation do nothing to help him?

If one interprets the patient's manifestations symbolically, in Jung's fashion, one might assume that his symptoms reveal a psychic demand requiring that he worship at the feet of women; also that the dream warns him of a situation in which the hero is felled by the moon-shaped weapon. We read these situations *as if* they were real facts—as indeed they are, the "best possible expressions of a relatively unknown, highly potent power," presented in the symbolic language of the psyche. Thus, his compulsion is seen not only as a deviation from normalcy, as we believe we know it, but also as a path, which the psyche attempts to show him, toward his own individual normalcy. The dream, therefore, does not distort or censor what we presume to know as a standard reaction—in this case a castration wish—but points toward an as yet unknown psychic fact which is most adequately depicted through the image of the hero threatened by the moon-dagger. But how can we comprehend a meaning in these images when they are regarded in this fashion?

Our patient was a very aggressive man, independent, self-reliant and overly rational. He expected every situation and every person to yield to his driving will and he insisted on his own way in everything. While very successful in business, he was impoverished in terms of feeling and of interpersonal relationships, and especially in terms of orientation toward a higher meaning in life. His lack of ability to express feeling and relatedness apparently constituted a highly-charged energy potential in spite of their repression—or rather because of their repression, since such repressed psychic contents tend to build up pressure—and they presented themselves in this bizarre imagery.

When regarded symbolically, his dream would show him that the hero attitude or hero aspect in him which expresses his need to fortify his ego position (formed in reaction to his early experience with his overpowering

mother), namely that attitude which expects to vanquish through reliance
upon aggressive courage, is not invulnerable. It may succumb to an element, a force, which is likened here to the moon or to a sickle-shaped
weapon. The moon crescent and the sickle-shaped sword occur repeatedly
in mythological imagery. The significance of mythological symbolism will
be dealt with subsequently,[9] but we may state here that the crescent moon
refers to the rising power of what may be intimated as the world of the
feminine: the crescent moon is Selene, Artemis, Diana; the virginal, as yet
unopened mystery of emotion, of love, generativeness, renewal and change;
the mystery of the womb, the feminine as yet unrevealed. Incidentally, the
image of the sickle-shaped dagger constitutes a deviation from the traditional version of the Siegfried myth with which the dreamer happened to
be familiar. Siegfried is killed by a spear, not by a dagger. Whenever a
dream repeats a consciously-known context, the areas of departure from or
variations of this context are especially significant for interpretation.

The symbolic significance of the moon weapon thus points to the fact
that the force of the moon, the force of the cyclic tides of life, of emotional
rather than rational functioning, represents an energy not to be disregarded. It may destroy when it is disregarded and provoked into opposition
by a one-sided attitude of hero-identification, that is, by an exaggerated,
exclusive reliance upon one's will-power, upon that virtue expressed by
"where there's a will there's a way," and upon an over-rational planning
that disregards the intangibles. Our dreamer is warned that it is an aspect of
life itself which his attitude is offending, which comes back at him and
castrates him—indeed may threaten him even further. Siegfried is the hero
who expresses a trust in light (which equals consciousness) and a belief in
conscious ideals; he is killed at the instigation of Brunhild, the maiden he
has betrayed. This means that the exclusively heroic attitude is bound to
perish if it disregards the power of the feminine realm. The dreamer is in
psychic danger if he cannot find a way of balancing the one-sidedness of his
approach to life.

We may now look further and understand the meaning of his obsessive
state in the light of its symbolism. What seems to express itself here is an
unaccountable urge to humble himself, to worship at the feet of the woman
—of any woman—for we may say as do the Hindu Tantras that every
woman incarnates, represents and incorporates or symbolizes what is called
the Shakti power, the world of feminine energy. In his obsessive symptoms
this breaks through involuntarily, this world of the feminine to which he
refuses to give voluntary homage by delimiting his one-sided emphasis on
the masculine will-attitude. It is a quasi-religious dedication that is asked of
him, a yielding to that aspect, that mystery of life which is forever beyond
our control, which has a meaning, a purpose and a power of regeneration of

its own: the "eternally feminine," the world of what Chinese philosophy calls Yin, compensating and complementary, different from the merely rational, conscious and will-determined, driving, straight-to-the-point Yang world of the male.

In this particular patient's case, the acceptance of a different attitude toward life and everyday living, a greater respect for and relatedness to the mystery of existence and the intangibles of feeling and instinctual involvement did result in the easing of his compulsive syndrome. A better sexual adjustment accompanied his new life- and relationship-adaptation, and he began to glimpse the new horizons opening to him.

But—and this I wish to emphasize—this opening of new horizons through what formerly appeared as mere illness or perversion was made possible by a change of viewpoint, namely by taking the images as pointing to a reality beyond themselves and not just as symptoms of a problem which is nothing but disturbed normalcy. Such a view may change illness and difficulty into something from which new life may spring. The "illness" can become a source of renewal when it pressures us into another life meaning.

Our patient's images—of the hero-felling dagger, of the worship of what we may call the feminine potency—came from unconscious depths, charged with power and meaningfulness. They were not invented or intended by him to explain or hide or rationalize something he knew about, but rose into consciousness in order to connect him with a dimension of being from which his life had become separated at the price of sterility. The symbolic experience thus is not *made by* us, rather it *happens to* us. We may choose to disregard it, or we may be unconscious of it, and indeed our time has repressed the symbolic function and the instinctual urge for meaning which it serves, no less than the Victorian era repressed the sexual instinct. But like every basic function it continues to operate, whether consciously or unconsciously; and like every function it may, when so repressed, give rise to difficulties and pathological expressions, degraded or degenerated mythologems and obsessive impulses.

What are the chief objections to the acceptance of the revelatory capacity of the symbolic experience and how can they be answered?

Heyer regards the depreciation of the symbol as stemming from the tendency in psychiatry—and shared by traditional psychology and psychoanalysis—to base the evaluation of normalcy upon the observations of disturbed psychology. This has tended to fortify the traditional rationalistic bias toward asserting the *concept* as the basic psychic product or form element, whereas the *image* is regarded as a mere secondary distortion, the result of repression of the concept. Heyer[10] quotes Ernest Jones' statement that only repressed material is symbolized and in need of symbolization. He further notes the speculations of Rank and Sachs that symbolization is the result of a primitive adaptation to reality which would become superfluous —a mere hindrance—as development progresses, and thus belongs to the junk-heap of civilization.

In a somewhat less radical form, the following description by Piaget also expresses this attitude. His characterization of the problem with which we are faced is brilliant and perceptive, and is at the same time instructive in illustrating the bias which has so far prevented traditional psychology from reaching an adequate appreciation of the dynamic importance of the symbol and of symbolic thinking. This passage is from *The Language and Thought of the Child*:

> Psycho-analysts have been led to distinguish two fundamentally differ-ent modes of thinking: *directed* or *intelligent thought*, and *undirected* or, as Bleuler proposes to call it, *autistic thought*. Directed thought is conscious, *i.e.*, it pursues an aim which is present to the mind of the thinker; it is intelligent, which means that it is adapted to reality [namely to external reality] and tries to influence it; it admits of being true or false (empirically or logically true), and it can be communi-cated by language. Autistic thought is subconscious, which means that the aims it pursues and the problems it tries to solve are not present in consciousness; it is not adapted to reality, but creates for itself a dream world of imagination; it tends, not to establish truths, but so to satisfy desires, and it remains strictly individual and incommunicable as such by means of language. On the contrary, it works chiefly by images, and in order to express itself, has recourse to indirect methods, evoking by means of symbols and myths the feeling by which it is led.
>
> Here, then, are two fundamental modes of thought which, though separated neither at their origin nor in the course of their functioning are subject, nevertheless, to two diverging sets of logical laws. Directed thought, as it develops, is controlled more and more by the laws of experience and of logic in the stricter sense.
>
> Autistic thought, on the other hand, obeys a whole system of special laws (laws of symbolism and of immediate satisfaction) which we need not elaborate here. Let us consider, for instance, the completely different lines of thought pursued from the point of view of intelli-gence and from that of autism when we think of such an object as, say, water.
>
> To intelligence, water is a natural substance whose origin we know or whose formation we can at least empirically observe; its behavior and motions are subject to certain laws which can be studied, and it

has from the dawn of history been the object of technical experiment (for purposes of irrigation, etc.). To the autistic attitude, on the other hand, water is interesting only in connexion with the satisfaction of organic wants. It can be drunk. But as such, as well as simply in virtue of its external appearance, it has come to represent in folk and child fantasies, and in those of adults of subconsciousness, themes of a purely organic character. It has in fact been identified with the liquid substances which issue from the human body, and has come, in this way, to symbolize birth itself, as is proved by so many myths (birth of Aphrodite, etc.), rites (baptism the symbol of a new birth), dreams and stories told by children. Thus in the one case thought adapts itself to water as part of the external world, in the other, thought uses the idea of water not in order to adapt itself to it, but in order to assimilate it to those more or less conscious images connected with fecundation and the idea of birth.[11]

Autistic thinking (non-conceptual image-thinking, which is associatively rather than causally logical) is here implicitly devalued by Piaget. He regards it as inferior or pathological—the term *autistic* implies pathology since autism is a schizophrenic pattern—because such thinking is "not adapted to reality but creates for itself a dream world of imagination . . ." and so on. His value judgment appears to be that reality is found *only* in the world of external objects; therefore, the only reality adaptation rests in that sort of mental attitude described as directed thought, which is concept-based, will-directed and causality-oriented and thus is suitable for making the external world usable. The experience of one's own inner world which occurs through image-thinking is not granted the character of reality, and is regarded as nothing but primitive, inferior and pathological. This is the bias of extraverted positivism.

This bias seems to find evidential support by pointing to the pathological states of neurotic or psychotic individuals, and by showing clinically autistic states in which external reality adaptation has indeed suffered or broken down and has been replaced by a hypertrophy of non-directed thinking, of day-dreaming or the flooding of consciousness by a non-rational image world. Also, in cases of neurotic repression, the unacceptable thoughts and wishes are replaced with images which can frequently be recognized as variations on, or even distorted images substituting for, the repressed concepts. But must we jump to the conclusion that because they show this distortion and replacement the images are *nothing but* distortion? And to what extent and under what safeguards is it justifiable to accept the testimony of pathology as a standard for normalcy?

I would suggest that certain phenomena may be first or even most readily observed in abnormal states, and yet this does not necessarily justify the conclusion that they are in themselves nothing but abnormal. Abnormal states may exhibit phenomena which in themselves are parts of normal functioning. For instance, the accumulation of white blood cells as pus in states of inflammation does not prove that white cells are themselves abnormal products. Even their accumulation in inflammation is not abnormal but is rather a healthy defense reaction, a compensation for the noxious invasion of germs. And indeed a failure of white cell production and accumulation would threaten the organism with breakdown.

Thus it is inadmissible to base one's understanding of human functioning of supposed normalcy only upon one's observations of the pathologically disturbed. To do so would be equivalent to attempting to understand walking, posture, the human gait by regarding and trying to understand it as nothing but prevented falling. Walking is a function of its own, subject to its own form elements, rhythms, laws, etc., which in turn also may be interfered with, be in conflict with other functions or become subject to exaggeration, thereby exhibiting what we may call pathology. This may result in falling as a result of disturbed walking. But walking is more than merely prevented falling; our understanding of its functioning cannot be derived from its own pathology. The normal—namely the broad spectrum of general human tendencies and possibilities in its balanced state—has to be our standard of understanding even though it does not lend itself to a definition in rigid terms and even though, by virtue of the polarity of all functioning, it carries within itself the possibility of abnormal functioning without which there could be no concept of normalcy. As Goethe expressed it:

> Nature fashions in normalcy when it encompasses the many details in a rule and an order, when it determines and qualifies. Phenomena are abnormal when the single details gain a preponderance in an accidental or arbitrary fashion. However, since both tendencies are closely related to one another, and the regulated as well as the non-regulated are inspired by the same spirit, a fluctuation ensues between the normal and the abnormal, formation alternates with reformation, so that the abnormal appears to become normal and the normal to become abnormal.[12]

It fell to Jung to correct the error of early psychiatry and to point out that the attitude of the introvert (for whom adaptation to outer reality is secondary and decidedly inferior in development compared to his concern with inner experience) is not necessarily autistic, *i.e.*, pathological. Nor are the means for such inner self-experience—non-conceptual experiencing in terms of images and undirected thinking—pathological. Quite the contrary. Not only is the presence of the image not pathology but the loss of awareness of the image dimension (which is the loss of contact with inner reality, as we shall see) gives rise to pathology, just as conversely the loss of external adaptation (the fixation in early fantasy states which is not compensated by logical thought) gives rise to pathology. While the latter leads to the loss of external reality adaptation as seen in the familiar clinical psychoses, the former results in a loss of connection with one's emotions and imaginative faculties, a dissociation between the now isolated intellect and the emotional world of meaning—hence of the very source of life—which validates transpersonal reality. Lastly, the one-sided hypertrophy of merely extraverted and intellectual thought has led to depersonalization; for abstraction (Latin *ab-trahere*, to pull away, namely from object or emotional reality) is an attempt to "objectify" by leading away from emotional, psychic reality.

> In every causal . . . explanation there is . . . an effort to adapt one-self to the external world, an effort to objectify, and, one might say, to depersonalize one's thought.[13]

On the other hand the symbolic mode of experiencing approaches that area which Kant called the forever unknowable "thing in itself" by sensing an ultimate trans-logical meaningfulness that is not bound by time, space and causality, to be only hinted at or intuited. Indeed, in his statement, "A signal is a part of the physical world of being; a symbol is a part of the human world of meaning," [14] Cassirer suggests that man may be defined as *animal symbolicum* rather than *animal rationale*.

A question now arises as to the origin and functional importance of perception in symbolic images. If their appearance in pathological states is not to be taken as evidence of the primitiveness, inferiority and pathology of image experience *per se*, why are we served images and not concepts? And what is the functional relation between image and concept?

The example of the patient previously given can readily answer the latter question. The renewal of psychic life which followed his acceptance of what the images portended—the need for reverence toward the world of the feminine and the danger of identification with the heroic self-will which disregards the power of the scorned world—shows that the images function in a *compensatory* or *complementary* way.

The images arise as carriers of messages which are lacking—at times dangerously lacking—in consequence of the one-sided views and convictions of consciousness. The rising pressure of images is the defense reaction of a self-regulating, balancing psychic system which is quite analogous to the biological process of the accumulation of white blood cells. Just as the blood cells are normal and basic constituents of the biological functioning, so are the images basic constituents of the psychic functioning.

But why images rather than concepts? Why, if the one-sided or exaggerated positions of consciousness are formulated in conceptual terms, is the compensating reaction not couched in similar terms? Why do we usually dream images rather than logical thoughts? Why does the psyche bother us with seemingly irrational or at least difficult-to-comprehend symbolic fantasies if it wants to help us overcome our impasses? Might the purpose not be accomplished more easily if dreams and fantasies were expressed in plainly understandable, logical, everyday language?

To understand this we must renounce another cherished prejudice, namely that consciousness and its concept-based, abstract frame of reference *is* the totality of the psyche, or even the standard pattern or standard unit for psychic functioning. It is merely a late-coming upstart. Not only are the conscious concepts partial aspects of the psychic totality, but consciousness based upon conceptualized mental functioning is a relatively late, secondary form of mental development. The basic or original unit of mental functioning is the image. Concepts are fashioned out of images through the activity of abstraction which is a thought process. One abstracts, or pulls away, one's awareness from the original psychic reaction which is emotionally charged, towards de-emotionalized concepts. The unit of basic psychic operativeness is the emotionally-charged image. Conceptualization can be compared to the creating of safety islands which consciousness has to build for itself in the midst of the cross traffic of emotionally-charged image-centered impulses in order to establish a seemingly independent stand.

This activity of consciousness—the establishment of control in the world of things through conceptualization, rational thought, and the development of discipline and the abstractive repression of emotions—is an utterly vital and indispensable phase of psychic development. It leads from psychic primitive infancy to adulthood. Mythological tradition likens this development to the creation of the world from the original chaos to the establishment of a foothold on dry land away from the threat of drowning in the flood waters. Yet it is not the "dry land" of rational consciousness that contains and supports the ocean but conversely: the waters of the ocean contain the dry continents, and life upon them depends upon the waters. Similarly, it is the unconscious organism, the unconscious psyche, that gives rise to and maintains the world of consciousness. Consciousness with its concepts is a relatively minor part of the total psychic functioning, and in terms of dynamics certainly not the most powerful one. It establishes fixed points of rational reference—but at the price of a loss of emotional connection. Images, on the other hand, constellate emotional and imaginative qualities and thus reconstitute a connection which the abstractive process has severed.

The first elementary form of conscious perception occurs through the merging of sense perceptions into comprehensive images. As we see most clearly in the mental processes of children, unconscious psychic functioning first reaches a conscious state in terms of the images of external forms with which we have experience. The object world gives us our vocabulary and our only means of approaching the transcendental reality of Kant's "things in themselves." What these things in themselves are we cannot know, for we are limited to our typical human modes of experiencing. Indeed the concepts of "things in themselves" and of human capacities are in themselves expressions of typical human mental functioning, that is, of abstraction and rational thought, tending to be arranged in a cause-effect order and determined by the questions: wherefrom? why? whither?

The structuring of our minds, then, makes us experience existence in the dualistic form of a world of "outer" objects which we are able to organize, and of "inner" impulses which we find hard to master. But in both dimensions we perceive by way of images. The same images which present themselves to us as representatives of the outside world are subsequently used by the psyche to express the inner world. For the realization of the existence of one's inner world as an entity of its own comes to consciousness relatively late. When this begins to occur, consciousness has already established itself in terms of abstract conceptualizations based upon but also separated from the original outer images. These images of outer objects, then, are the first and only units, the points at which the conscious mind touches or reaches back to the basic experience of its being, which is prior to the separation of conscious and unconscious, hence to its source-ground, the unconscious psyche. (The unconscious itself, since it *is* unconscious, is imageless, conceptless: it is unknowable—as Kant's "thing in itself." We can at best speculate about it in terms of energy currents, dynamisms, etc., but even these are abstract concepts gained from the observed external images.)

Since these original units have become established in relation to the experiencing of "outer" objects, they are likely to be regarded invariably as pertaining only to these outer objects by a consciousness that lacks adequate awareness of the inner dimension. The image of water, for instance, is assumed to refer to drinkable H_2O, even when it arises, not from an external percept stimulus, but from an inner state *like* water. Whenever the psyche attempts to present us with an awareness of an inner dimension for the experience of which there is no precedent (since we have so far learned only to orient ourselves to external things), this can occur only through linking this new, unknown inner territory with or expressing it in terms of the image of some outer object. In the case of the dream or fantasy image of water, we are really being confronted with an outer image which now means inner water: "water of life," "fountain of youth." When interpreted as representations of exterior objects, images in this context are obviously meaningless.

We begin to see that the way in which the mind experiences the outer world is made to serve a different purpose at this stage of development, a relatively novel purpose, namely the experience of the inner, hitherto unconscious world. This requires, for its adequate functioning and integration, a novel means of perception, namely that of intuiting inner meaning. This intuiting of meaning, beyond what the external object (whose form the image wears) *per se* represents, we have called the symbolic mode of comprehension. When this mode is absent or is not sufficiently available to consciousness, the psychic images are, as they arise, naively referred to as merely pertaining to outer reality. Then they seem as meaningless and absurd as melodies would be to a tone-deaf person, or pictures to someone who has no sensitivity to form or color. Such a person would also be inclined to regard melodies as pathological deviations of the simple straightforward monotone, or pictures as pathological deviations from a straight line. It may be assumed that the emergence of images from the depths of the psyche tends to complement the isolated standpoint of the abstracting consciousness not only in terms of content—by raising up themes and subject matter which the conscious mind has disregarded—but also in terms of quality—by doing it in images rather than concepts, thus attempting to reconnect us with a mode of experiencing from which we have become separated, to our greatest peril.

When the symbolic sense has not been consciously developed, the associative interconnections, such as linking water with eternal life and rebirth, appear as insults to intelligence and seem to leave no alternative between renouncing rational thought for the sake of blind faith or refusing even to consider them worthy of intelligent consideration.

But now a last serious question arises. Does this symbolic mode of subjective experiencing have a claim to be admitted into the sanctuary of scientific concern? Is the symbolic approach, relating as it does to "mere" inarticulate intuition and feeling dimensions, scientifically respectable?

I believe that the answer has to be that by its own definition science concerns itself with knowing and with needs of knowing; hence it has to utilize whatever means can serve knowing rather than renounce the ability to know because means might be required for the purpose of knowing which hallowed tradition has tended to frown upon. The means of scientific approach are appropriately dictated only by practicability, not by tradition and prejudice. For a dimension that can be comprehended only symbolically, the symbol will have to do. Whatever is accessible to direct outer physical observation and can be made understandable and meaningful to rational thought is indeed in no need of the symbolic approach. But for those areas of experience which respond only to intuitive and emotional approaches—and this covers a very large and fundamental part of human experience—the symbolic approach is appropriate because it is the only practical approach. As we progress from the world of simple external facts into the more intimate dynamisms of life, into the intimate functioning of the unconscious psyche, we find ourselves reaching domains in which our logical understanding no longer suffices; it can help us no further. Our investigation finds itself confronted with a difficulty that is quite analogous to the one which, in our own time, has had to be faced and overcome by the reputedly most exact of all sciences, that of nuclear physics.

We have already taken cognizance of the fact that nuclear physics also found itself confronted by a situation in which the traditional ways of description and explanation were insufficient to convey any meaning. Thus, like depth psychology, modern nuclear physics had to find a new mode of perception and description, which would be suitable for the world of microphysical intra-atomic events which behave so differently from the macrophysical world of observable things and objects. Thus also nuclear physics had to accept a method of classification and description which is quite akin to what we have here characterized as the symbolic approach.

Erwin Schrödinger characterizes this step as follows:

. . . the attitude of that time [of the 19th century, looking for precise description] . . . was different from what it is now, it was still a little too naïve. While asserting that any model we may conceive is sure to be deficient and would surely be modified sooner or later, one still had at the back of one's mind the thought that a true model exists—exists so to speak in the Platonic realm of ideas—that we approach to it gradually, without perhaps ever reaching it, owing to human imperfections.

This attitude has now been abandoned. The failures we have experienced no longer refer to details, they are of a more general kind. We have become fully aware of a situation that may perhaps be summarized as follows. As our mental eye penetrates into smaller and smaller distances and shorter and shorter times, we find nature behaving so entirely differently from what we observe in visible and palpable bodies of our surrounding that *no* model shaped after our large-scale experiences can ever be 'true'. A completely satisfactory model *of this type* is not only practically inaccessible, but not even thinkable. Or, to be precise, we can, of course, think it, but however we think it, it is wrong;

not perhaps quite as meaningless as a 'triangular circle', but much more so than a 'winged lion'.[15]

And speaking of the atom models:

> The . . . shapes displayed in these pictures are not anything that could be directly observed in the real atoms. The pictures are only a mental help, a tool of thought, an intermediary means, from which to deduce, out of the results of experiments that have been made, reasonable expectation about the results of new experiments we are planning. We plan them for the purpose of seeing whether they confirm the expectations—thus whether the expectations were reasonable, and thus whether the pictures or models we use are adequate. Notice that we prefer to say *adequate*, not *true*. For in order that a description be *capable* of being true, it must be capable of being compared *directly* with actual facts. That is usually not the case with our models.[16]

What Schrödinger describes here is a method of dealing with empirical material in terms of "as if." Something acts *as if* it could be pictured as certain particles called electrons juggling around a central nucleus, for instance. No claim is made that the model literally and accurately pictures the situation. It merely represents the best possible formulation of a reality that cannot adequately be described in any other way because the facts of the situation are admittedly outside the domain of direct literal comprehension or observation.

There are areas in which nature behaves "so entirely differently from what we observe in visible and palpable bodies of our surrounding that *no* model shaped after our large-scale experiences can never be 'true' " or even thinkable, be it the concept of a limited universe that continues to expand (we may ask into where or into what?) or be it the concept of a particle of anti-matter or of pure shape without matter (to quote a few examples from physics); or whether it is a matter of psychic energy configurations called archetypes that behave like personalities and give rise to phenomena which transcend consciousness and space and time as we know them. Confronted with such phenomena, which defy comprehension in terms of everyday rationality, we may choose to disregard them and deny their very existence, or to explain them away, or to try hopefully to make them fit into already existing thought categories which express a narrower range of knowledge, thereby distorting their meaning. All this has been largely the approach of 18th and 19th century positivism. Or we may seek an appropriate new frame of reference which is capable of integrating them into our capacity for comprehension. Thereby we would fill a void not only in scientific knowledge but also in man's self-understanding and self-realization, and would in that way satisfy the human need for a meaning in existence.

Of course, this means renouncing the claim that our mind can always understand what it deals with. We have to renounce the concepts of things that *are* this or that and can be manipulated at will, like external objects. We cannot claim that we understand, for instance, what (in Jung's terms) the objective psyche, animus, anima and the Self *are*; for that matter we even doubt they *are* anything, for they are not things or objects in our usual sense. In like fashion Schrödinger remarks:

> If you ask me: Now, really, what *are* these particles, these atoms and molecules? I should have to admit that I know as little about it as where Sancho Panza's second donkey came from. However, to say something, even if not something momentous: They can at the most perhaps be thought of as more or less temporary creations within the wave field, whose structure and structural variety, in the widest sense of the word, are so clearly and sharply determined by means of wave laws as they recur always in the same manner, that much takes place *as if* they were a permanent material reality.[17]

But in accepting the images that present themselves as adequate "as if" representations and in accepting that they are adequate, though insufficient, representations of a reality that has existence and transcends what we can think, we may acquire the ability to comprehend a different dimension of existence and of functioning. This is a dimension that is certainly no less, and is perhaps more, real than our familiar world of directly observable, classifiable objects.

Like the energy of the atomic nucleus, the energy of the psychic "nucleus" of the unconscious constitutes a dimension of so far unfathomed and terrifying elementary energy potential, equally capable of destroying as well as of aiding us, depending upon whether we become its victim owing to our continuing lack of comprehension or whether we acquire the capacity to relate to it adequately and turn its energy potential to our benefit.

By way of summarizing the implications of the symbolic approach, we will consider its relevance for us as to philosophy and terminology. The theoretical methodology and the actual practical approach to the suffering person will be dealt with subsequently, in Chapter 2 and Chapter 18 respectively.

Philosophy

We admit the fact that our observation of the dynamics of unconscious psychic phenomena leads us into a border situation: to the limits of competence of our thing-oriented minds. Thus we are forced to resort to a cognitive mode which our rational development has tended to by-pass: the symbolic mode, which in the historical development of the human mind is found to be the active element in the formation of recurrent mythological images (mythologems). Eliade[18] characterizes the myth as disclosing "a boundary situation of man, not only a historical situation. A boundary situation is one which man discovers in becoming conscious of his place in the universe."

This mythologem-forming symbolic approach is thus an approach to reality, especially to psychic or transpersonal or cosmic reality, which concedes our inability to know this reality in intellectual terms. In this sense it may be characterized as an agnostic approach. Nevertheless the images do transmit knowledge of a sort; not through the intellect but through the effect of the image upon feeling and intuition, thus mediating another, perhaps deeper or more profound, kind of knowing than the intellectual one. The intellect is useful to the extent that it adapts and resigns itself to dealing not only with directly observable things and facts but also, like the atom physicist, with models of reality subject to alteration according to the requirement and contingencies of the ever-changing psychic reality.

This, however, requires the renunciation of a certain naive realism which regards the world as a world of simply knowable things, and the substitution of a world of best possible pictures or expressions of the unknown and unknowable. We then become aware of energy configurations, or energy "fields" or energic action potencies—*Wirkungspotenzen* (Heyer)—and we admit that we do not even know what energy "is," as little as we can know what matter is or what anything "is." These descriptions do not refer to directly observable things, but are images or models, descriptive in terms of "like," "as if," pointing at or hinting, intimating "something" that is accessible to our cognition in no other way. This way is just as unique and necessary to our total functioning as is the sensory approach to some reality we know not what (like Kant's "thing in itself"), which we experience as "objective" through the perception of our five senses; this too is a particular way of approaching experience which cannot be replaced by any other. Thus we would accept different approaches to different aspects of reality, each valid and useful, even essential in its own right, and not interchangeable but complementary to each other, and all of them the expression of a mysterious organism—world unity correspondence.

Terminology

We must understand that whatever terms have to be introduced and used for the sake of communication about scientific and psychic facts between therapist or counsellor and client, patient or advisee, as well as among therapists and researchers themselves, should be regarded as no more than code words agreed upon in order to denote certain areas of symbolic experience. They "are" not that experience, they do not refer to fixed, definable "things": objective psyche, animus, anima, Self, shadow or archetype are not things, but they are fixed terms or code words (since communication necessitates a relatively fixed code) to point to basic experiences in symbolic "as if" terms, hence to image, emotional and drive experiences which must touch upon corresponding actual individual experiences if the code words are to have any meaning at all. Moreover, these terms refer to images which, because they are symbolic, are merely the "best possible expression for something essentially unknown and unknowable" and may at any time be replaced by other images or other terms if those should prove more adequate or suitable for the psychic experiences as they offer themselves. In this sense all terminology is merely temporary and tentative. Thus all psychological terms and theories that are taken for established facts become hindrances rather than aids toward psychological understanding.

Jung himself remarked that "theories in psychology are the very devil. It is true that we need certain points of view for orienting and heuristic value; but they should always be regarded as mere auxiliary concepts that can be laid aside at any time." [19] We should also remember that in a theoretical presentation such as this we have to resort to language, concepts and abstractions in order to describe something that actually presents itself as an intuitive or emotional image or dynamic experience. We therefore have to atomize and systematize and separate something that is actually encountered as unitary experience or as polar aspects of unitary fields. In this connection we must also remember that no theoretical, didactic presentation—the present one not excluded—can do full justice to the actual facts nor can it replace individual experience of the dynamics of the unconscious psyche.

2. The Approach to the Unconscious

WE HAVE SEEN that in contradistinction to generally prevailing thought, which regards rational, conceptual experiencing as the standard of normalcy, and dream and fantasy activity as primitive, regressive and abnormal,[1] Jung views spontaneous image productions, dreams, fantasies and artistic expressions as vitally indispensable sources of information and guidance supplied by the healthy—not the pathological—aspect of the psyche. According to his view, the dream (and this applies as well to fantasy and artistic expression to the extent that they are not contrived) "as the expression of an involuntary, unconscious psychic process beyond the control of the conscious mind . . . shows the inner truth and reality of the patient as it really is: not as I conjecture it to be, and not as he would like it to be, but *as it is*." [2]

Jung does not distinguish between manifest or latent dream content in the same manner that Freud does. The dream does not censor or distort. Seeming distortion, condensation and replacement phenomena do occur in dreams, but they do not necessarily serve the purpose of disguising an unacceptable wish. Although there are dreams which on the surface do look like disguised wish-fulfillment, a more profound understanding will invariably be gained if even these dreams are approached with the hypothesis that dreams do not hide but reveal, that they invariably point to something as yet unknown which they express in the vocabulary of the known, rather than merely disguising or censoring what one already presumes to know, namely the fulfillment of a consciously unacceptable wish.

For instance, if a woman dreams that a strange weird-looking man who faintly reminds her of her father or her analyst hands her a pen which makes her feel joyfully satisfied, this would be interpreted in psychoanalytical tradition as the fulfillment of an incest wish. She is sexually drawn to her father and/or her analyst—the well-known Oedipus (or in this instance Electra) complex—but cannot admit it. This interpretation would almost be a foregone conclusion. For the father's penis or that of the analyst, the dream censor is presumed to have substituted the unknown man's pen. But we all—including this dreamer—are perfectly capable of, indeed do dream of the sex organs of our parents and of other people, our therapist not excluded, and of many other objects and events that make us blush and even recoil before the shameless bluntness of their images. The insistence upon censored wish-fulfillment as the invariable dream content is thus scarcely substantiated by the facts. Rather it rests on an *a priori* conviction, a foregone conclusion, that the unconscious is concerned only and invariably with nothing but pleasure, sexuality and wish-fulfillment.[3] If therefore one approaches this dream with the hypothesis that it does not hide but tries to reveal a hitherto unknown but vitally important content, then the merging or substitution of the strange unknown man with father and analyst might be taken as pointing to some qualities shared by father and analyst which, in the role they play in her own masculine potential,[4] are unknown to the dreamer and which strike her as weird when experienced in herself. Thus the dream would not be concerned with the actual father or analyst but with this analogue within the dreamer. In this instance those unknown qualities with which she could not credit herself but which she regarded as mere weirdness were the capacity for independence and originality. Thus rather than receiving her father's penis in the dream, her potential for independence and originality offers her a phallic—not sexual but creative—means for expression. The pen, being a pen, not a sensored penis, refers to her ability as a writer. Far from expressing an infantile incest wish, the dream conveys the message that what she regards as merely a strangeness in herself is really a capacity for creative expression which can be realized once she accepts and develops such creativity as an expression of her own independence and originality.

So we see that the dream speaks in the archaic symbol-language of the objective psyche. It means what it says and expresses, in symbolic terms, the unknown side of the life situation as it is apprehended and mirrored by the unconscious. Dreams, therefore, are not symptomatic but symbolic. They are symbolic inasmuch as the objective psyche does not conceptualize; it does not speak English or French or German or Chinese; it speaks *images*, which are the aboriginal forms of perception and expression. Language and concepts are the concomitants and products of ego development. The nonego does not speak concepts, except intermittently here and there when sentences or words or sometimes short treatises (which quite often present rationalizations) appear in our dreams. The deeper layers speak in images. These images are to be viewed *as if* they presented us with descriptions of *ourselves*, or our unconscious situations, in the form of analogies or parables. We must translate the dream statements into some sort of conceptualization that is at least accessible to us, even though this translation can never be a completely adequate one, because a dream image always points to much more than can be put into an abstract concept. The translating is done by putting the dreamer's associations and explanation into the context of the images. *Associations* are the contents which happen to come to mind when the dream image is considered, whether they be rational or irrational. If I have dreamed of a fountain pen, I might recall that I always become angry when a certain person uses this pen: this is an association. An *explanation*, on the other hand, is a more rational description of what the dream image means to me. The explanation regarding the fountain pen could be, for instance, that it is a tool for writing, with the addition, perhaps, that to me it is obsolete; I have given it up because I now use a ballpoint pen. Ordinarily, this is about as far as association or explanation go; they are not spun out by *free association*. It is not practical to use free association except in special situations. It is usually more fruitful to mark out the immediate circumference of a dream motif by direct association and amplification of the image on the assumption that it does not conceal but expresses. Since the image holds the meaningful content within its immediate context, the method of free association which tends to lead away from this immediate context may also lead us away from the most immediate expression of the meaning of the dream. However, free association is helpful when there appears to be an associational block, when nothing comes, when no associations can be elicited to the immediate dream context because the dreamer is too bound to rational thought. An overly rational person whose fantasy is stifled may try so hard to figure out what the dream symbol could mean that he is unable to express his spontaneous associations. They seem to him too stupid or irrelevant. In such a situation free association can help to overcome the rational shyness or resistance and to free the fantasy.

When the dreamer's personal associations and amplifications do not seem to suffice, when mythological motifs occur, the analyst's *amplification* (but not the analyst's associations) may be added—namely what the analyst happens to know about the historical context and meaning of the symbolism. This is justified inasmuch as a certain amount of material, as we shall see in the following chapter, comes not merely from the dreamer's own personal life but also from the collective storehouse of mankind, from the mythological layer of the objective psyche. The understanding and awareness of what a mythologem has meant historically, what themes are pointed to or touched by these motifs, can then be usefully added in order to widen both the context and the overall meaning.

A dream represents the dreamer's situation *as it is*, externally or internally or both; and it compensates the one-sidedness of the conscious view, that is, it relates a message which is unknown to the dreamer but is potentially vital and in need of being known. Thus every dream interpretation may pertain either to what we call the object level or to the subject level. If the dreamer sees himself or someone else cutting recklessly into traffic and being knocked down, it may point toward a tendency—of which he is unaware—to behave this way in traffic. On the object level, he should be alert to the possibility that such behavior might lead to an actual accident. But the dream may also point to the relationship of his ego attitude to the "psychic traffic," that is, to the current of life. He may have an overbearingly manipulative or recklessly controlling power attitude; this is interpretation on the subject level. In terms of practical psychology, however, these two interpretations are frequently synonymous, because it is precisely such a reckless ego orientation that will lead to this particular type of behavior in actual traffic. Hence this dreamer may be an accident-prone person who is being warned of the likelihood of an accident, and he may also be a person who will meet with an accident in his total living.

To take another example: A patient's dream of being threatened by her sister could be interpreted first on the object level as a warning against her sister's behavior, if the dreamer happened to be unaware of the true situation and could see only the friendly side of her sister. However, should the dream's message seem to repeat a conviction already held by the dreamer, indeed possibly constituting what may amount to an obsession with a persecution idea, then the dream's message would be truly compensatory only when interpreted on the subject level. In this case it would confront the dreamer with her own projection.[5] On this level it would refer to the "sister within," her shadow, namely to those qualities which the dreamer happens to associate with her sister but probably tends to minimize in herself (jealousy or cynicism, for instance), or perhaps also positive qualities such as imagination or artistic talents which the dreamer devalues.

Often it is quite obvious that on the object level the dream would be irrelevant or trivial. If the dreamer's dead grandfather converses with the candy store man from the dreamer's childhood, this will hardly bear an interpretation on the object level. In such a case the dream refers directly to subjective states: it expresses a personification of unconscious partial aspects, partial personalities, drives, qualities, etc.

This mode of dream interpretation as descriptive of the inner partial personalities is not only unique but is perhaps also one of the most important practical contributions that Jung has made to analysis. It is a diagnostic tool that could be likened to an X-ray of the psyche; it offers us a direct view of the situation and is in need of interpretation by the experienced, skilled specialist.

In the following chapters we will make use of much spontaneous imagery of the objective psyche, interpreting its symbolism and using it for illustration and evidential support whenever possible. For the objective psyche's statements about itself and how it "sees" the various aspects of existence represent the only first-hand empirical evidence available on which to base theoretical conclusions.

We will use dreams for the most part, rather than waking fantasies, for dreams have a more autonomous character and thus lend themselves less to tampering by the conscious convictions or prejudices of either therapist or dreamer.

3. The Objective Psyche

THE PSYCHO-PHYSICAL totality, as previously stated,[1] experiences its world in endogenous as well as exogenous images. The latter are those images originating from without the organism and refer to the factual, material world of external things; the former are images originating from within and refer to the meaningful, spiritual aspect of existence. (The term "spiritual" has become somewhat suspect through indiscriminate usage.) Both types of images, however, are first experienced, through the sense organs, as being "outer directed" forms of perception. The individual must learn how to conceptualize the exogenous images and how to experience the endogenous images symbolically.

Jung has suggested the term *objective psyche* for that totality of the psyche which generates concepts and autonomous image symbols. Hence the ego-centered, subjective consciousness is a partial rather than a complete manifestation of the psyche. In the views of the psyche which were prevalent until Jung's studies became known, psychological functioning was a meaningful organization only in and through the activity of the ego. The drives themselves which constitute Freud's id were regarded as merely irrational, chaotic and senseless, not even related to a balance which keeps the organism alive but only striving to satisfy their own innate needs. Any meaning to be attached to the psychic organism could therefore be viewed solely in terms of ego rationality. The unconscious was quasi-attached to the ego as a general receptacle for that which the ego must repress because it is culturally or personally unacceptable. The psyche was thus "my" psyche, a part of my subjectiveness. In Jung's view this unconscious is the *personal subjective unconscious*, as distinguished from what may be regarded as an objective unconscious—hence his choice of the term *objective psyche*. The personal unconscious then is only a small part of the whole.

The term *objective psyche* replaces and enlarges the earlier concept of the *collective unconscious* originally used by Jung to denote a dimension of the unconscious psyche that is of an *a priori*, general human character, rather than merely the precipitate of personal repressed material. Because this term gave rise to many confusions and misinterpretations—such as the seeming advocacy of collectivity or of a mass psyche—he substituted the term *objective psyche* in later writings.

This image-producing stratum, this objective psyche, is also manifested in emotions and drive impulses. The correspondence between images and emotion or action patterns will be discussed in a later chapter.[2] All of these psychic energy expressions have been classified as *libido*—a term used by Freud to include only sexual drive. We prefer to regard libido simply as all the diverse expressions of psychic energy in any of its manifestations or, to borrow a concept from modern physics, its "field" activities.[3] A field is an energy pattern or configuration that becomes perceptible to the experienced observer only through the patternings of directly observable elements susceptible to its influence. To give a simple example, under the influence of a magnetic or electric field, invisible *per se*, iron filings will arrange themselves in a specific pattern which thereby makes the field effect visible. What Jung calls the objective psyche may then be likened to an encompassing energy stratum from which arise varying field activities discernable to the experienced observer through the patternings of image, emotion and drive configurations. These psychic field expressions Jung has called *complexes* and *archetypes* of the objective psyche. They are typical energy configurations which are activated by situations and problems, both outer and inner, by people, emotional conflicts, maturational needs, etc. They impress their force-patterns upon the totality of happenings within their scope. The objective psyche exists independently of our subjective volition and intent. It operates independently of the ego, but can be experienced and comprehended to a limited extent by the ego. That which, lacking understanding, we would view as merely chaotic imaginations, urges and impulses, can disclose meaning when we are capable of interpreting its image manifestations symbolically.

I would like to emphasize again that to Jung libido is not just chaos-producing pleasure, satisfaction-seeking sexual energy or mere power drive, but embraces every manifestation of psychic expression including the urge toward a spiritual or religious search for meaningful existence.

When the expressions of the objective psyche are interpreted symbolically and are then put to the test of reality in living experience, we find that they not only function autonomously but that this functioning also appears to have a definite interactive relationship with the rational, conceptualizing, conscious mind. This relationship is one of complementation or compensation, inasmuch as it tends to counterbalance vital deficiencies or critically one-sided tendencies of the conscious standpoint.

Such unconscious complementation or compensation implies, however, an inherent direction or goal. Complementation or compensation for something missing or exaggerated presupposes a totality-configuration or wholeness pattern, even though this may manifest itself in a distorted or deficient way. This purposive wholeness pattern which Jung postulates and calls the *Self* (at variance with the general usage of the term as synonymous with ego) is conceived—and here again we use symbolic language—to be a superordinated personality which encompasses and meaningfully directs conscious as well as unconscious functioning.

A number of years ago I was asked to see a girl about seven years old who suffered from a bronchial asthma which had thus far proved resistant to treatment. The question of a psychogenic factor had been raised but to all appearances there was no conflict anywhere in the harmonious family life. The girl did very well in school, was extremely intelligent, rational and well-adapted—indeed, as we shall see, a bit too well-adapted and controlled. She was closely attached to her mother, was a model of perfect behavior and obedience, a bit quiet, and became more quiet whenever mother was about to speak. She was already a miniature replica of mother.

The mother was a school teacher, intelligent, controlled, poised, educated and well-read. She seemed to have read almost everything that was ever mentioned to her; or so, at least, she felt. She lived in a small town, was a regular church-goer and adhered to sane, well-balanced, middle-of-the-road convictions; everything in her life was intelligently planned and put into its proper place. Her marriage seemed to be without a flaw. The husband was a small-businessman, the more yielding of the two, who readily deferred to his wife's judgment in all domestic matters, since mother obviously knew best. She was deeply concerned for the child's welfare. Thus the family life appeared to be quite harmonious.

After the surface evaluation of the scene, which offered some possible clues but nothing very definite to go by, I saw the mother alone and asked for dreams, either her own or the child's, in order to get an objective idea of the meaning of the situation. The mother remembered two dreams, both recurrent, one of her own and one of the child's. The fact that dreams recur, presenting repeatedly the same or similar motives, marks them as particularly important. Through them an evidently vital message is attempting to reach consciousness.

This was the mother's dream:

"*I am with a group of women, all masquerading as angels. A man is trying to break into the house, even though all the doors and windows are barred and shut tight. He is an Eastern potentate, and he says that if I do not let him in he is going to kill the child.*"

In her own dream, *the child is trying to get onto an island from the water, but the "goat people" or sometimes "a huge great goat-man" will not let her onto the land, but always pushes her back into the water.*

Asked for associations, the mother said that Eastern potentates exploit the people for their own personal advantage. She thought of King Farouk of Egypt, who had just been deposed, and of some Asiatic rulers. The child had no comment on her dream, except that it frightened her. Both dreams, if we put them side by side, seem to agree on one point, namely that the child is threatened. This threat arises from the mother's refusal to admit some sort of inner power. In her own dream, the child is threatened by the goat people or the great goat, who will drown her by pushing her off the dry land, and in the mother's dream she is threatened by the Eastern potentate. Hence one may tentatively assume that the statements of the two dreams are synonymous, that the dream images coincide by something more than mere chance, and we may perhaps be justified in equating the Eastern potentate with the goat people. Also, with some experience one recognizes that such dream images are mythological; they do not allude to any part or person of the dreamer's own life. To make a short cut in interpretation, we may now ask: Is there such a thing in mythology as an Eastern, Egyptian or Asiatic potentate or power who is also a goat-like person or a great goat? And indeed there are several such figures that fit this image. There is for one the Great Goat in Western mythology who was worshipped by the witches in the Sabbath rite, who has been called Satan by the church, and is actually a variation on the figures of Dionysus and Pan, the powers of ecstasy and all-nature in Greece and Asia Minor. There is also a horned god in Egypt—Ammon.[4] (Horned gods are always gods of power. For example, we have reproductions of Alexander the Great with horns; also Michelangelo's statute of Moses with horns. The horns represent the radiating power which they emanate.) Ammon is described as having the head of a ram, or a plumed crown. He is the king of the gods, the phallic power of reproduction, fertility and creation. Interestingly enough he is the father of Pharaoh, who was regarded as the Son of God born of a virgin mother. Ammon is the "Holy Ghost" by whom the virgin begets the savior who rules the land of Egypt. The Pharaoh is therefore the Son of God, hence god incarnate on earth, ruling by the power of the great God. This myth, with all the essential details of the Christian myth, antedates the latter by about 2000 years.

Pan and Dionysus, who were demoted to the nether regions of hell by the Medieval church, point to the realm of the orgiastic experience of natural and instinctual life. They represent "divinities"—namely autonomous creative drives, independent of man's volition—which are related to the lunar or earthly world of generativeness, joy, lust, sexuality, growth and renewal through life and death cycles of nature, rather than through rationality and mental discipline. (The world of discipline, order and harmony was represented in Greece by Apollo, who was brother and partner to Dionysus—they shared the sanctuary at Delphi—as well as his antithesis.) Dionysus was also worshipped at Eleusis as Hades, the lord of the underworld, of the unconscious and of death, and in Egypt as Osiris, who suffers, is dismembered and rises from the dead; therefore he has to do with the power of the mystery of life's renewal.

When we return to the dreams and view them in terms of the foregoing mythological images, they point to the kind of power which the mother is keeping out of her life. It appears as if mother's angelic attitude (in the dream she masquerades as an angel) is based upon rejection of instinctual urges and results in a danger to the child. She is a "good" woman in the traditional Christian sense and her angelic pose masks her refusal to "let in," to grant a place to, the powers of her natural drives and impulses towards pleasure, joy and sexuality, towards accepting the unforeseen and the spontaneous. These forces could bring about a renewal and a widening of her life scope; they represent a potential for the inspiring and renewing power of the spirit, the *logos spermatikos* (Ammon). In their repressed form, however, they represent what Jung called "sexuality through the head," a ruthless power-ridden dogmatism and domineeringness, a devil of opinions, quite unconscious as far as their owner is concerned, and all in the name of righteousness and truth and angelic goodness. This creates the mother's atmosphere which, unknown to her, prevents the child from gaining a foothold on the island, a *terra firma* in the ocean of unconsciousness. The child cannot reach firm ground because the energy which the mother has failed consciously to assimilate creates a "field," an atmosphere of dogmatic, oppressive restraint, a disabling barrier, so to say, which keeps the child from establishing a conscious individuality of her own.

When the personal situation was investigated it bore out the message of the dreams. Mother had a tremendous potential that she had not realized in her life. Her frame of reference was far too small and narrow for the power and impulse that, as it were, worked through her and upon her. While liberal and deliberately tolerant in her conscious intellectual convictions she was quite rigid and tyrannical in her unconscious emotional demands and reactions which permitted no deviations from the way in which she planned, arranged and reasoned every detail of the child's life. Very subtly, it was *her* way or the wrong way. Everything had to be just so, and the result was that the child was not able to "catch her own breath." (Breath in Greek is *pneuma*, in Hebrew *ruach*, both meaning spirit.) The child's impasse was acted out in the form of body symbolism through the asthmatic oppression. The unlived creative power of the mother was indeed threatening to destroy the individuality and life of the child.

But what a strange representation, what far-fetched imagery, for such a simple personal problem! We are, however, not yet through with strangeness. The first interview was rather unsatisfactory because, as was to be expected, the mother knew better than the analyst, and very little of what I tried to convey really struck home (although she began to sense that she had a problem). The child, I must add, knew nothing of that interview or of what had been discussed. Nevertheless, her asthma, up to then quite persistent, stopped suddenly and unexpectedly and did not recur. All that one could say was that the conscious awareness of the mother had been struck by something. It would have been far too optimistic to assume that she treated the child differently in any radical fashion. Nor is it probable that the asthma was permanently cured. I lost contact with mother and child after a while and cannot tell whether or not it recurred. But even a temporary remission, coinciding as it did in such a dramatic fashion with mother's confrontation with the message of the unconscious, is significant enough.

Admitting that theories are "the very devil," let us nevertheless consider some theoretical assumptions which seem to be permitted on the basis of this material.

(1) The expression of the unconscious takes a very peculiar, nonrational and illogical, or rather prelogical, form. The dreams do not say: the child is mistreated, therefore such and such. They say: an Eastern potentate . . . goat people . . . water . . . *et cetera.* They present images linked by associational bonds of similarity and contiguity, rather than by rational cause-and-effect concepts.

(2) The images thus represented are images that are more or less regularly found to correspond to what we may call mythological themes.

(3) A connection, a bridge, can be established between this nonrational, mythological imagery and our logical concepts, but *only* by analogy and symbolic understanding, not by direct deduction. We must look for something in the psychology of the mother and the child which is analogous to the Eastern potentate and to the goat people. We cannot simply say, because a goat person is there, you are sick. This would of course be absurd.

(4) The images refer to a stratum of high-powered dynamic energy which has the capacity to compel the ego against its will, to derange and distort rationality and hence to destroy the personality. We deal here again with energy configurations which we have seen to be analogous to the dynamic field in physics. They can also be described as vortices of psychic energy which suck everything in—conscious intention included. In other words, we are dealing with energy accumulations of a compulsive quality. The mother's affects are destructive to the child, in spite of the mother's best intentions and regardless of her serious concern for the child's well-being. She cannot help but destroy the child's individuality which she consciously wishes to preserve.

(5) As these energic configurations become fixed, they form what we call pathogenetic complexes, that is, highly-charged—even explosive—non-

rational patterns of feeling and behavior. Ten years from now this girl will have a mother complex: "Mother knows best" and also "I, her daughter, (aping her views) know best." She will be highly sensitive and will over-react to anyone and anything that behaves or appears like mother. She will turn red and purple at the sight of any similar approach, yet will be as dogmatic and as convinced of having a hot line to the Holy Ghost as her mother was. She will have identified with her mother's complex; both will be certain that they know *the* truth, *the* ultimate answer, and heaven help you if you challenge it.

(6) We see demonstrated again the dynamic unity of these energy fields, an interaction which precludes subject-object separation. This unity expresses itself here in the psychic identity, or telepathic identity, between mother and child, for they dream essentially the same dream. Coinciding with the mother's emotional realization that something is amiss, the child reacts favorably, without conscious knowledge of the situation, and we can-not establish a causal relationship between mother's and child's reactions. We may say that in this dimension space, time and causality as we know them are relatively invalidated.

The subject and object non-separation will also express itself in the mut-ual identities of complexes and projections which we may find quite clearly developed a few years later. The child might begin to resist the mother because she will sense that mother's dogmatism interferes with her freedom of expression; and mother is likely to assert that the child has a veritable devil, for otherwise why would such a "nice" child begin to be so obstreper-ous and to resist her loving mother? They both suffer from the same com-plex now; mother's devil has inadvertently trained the child (and of course mother had a mother too). It is even questionable whether the child was trained or simply grew into this atmosphere and became what the atmos-phere expressed. In other words, children live the unconscious problems of their parents, and there is no avoiding this, regardless of good intentions and "angelic" efforts.

Again, we can formulate this by saying that a dynamic field is established which encompasses mother and child equally and simultaneously—in this case, the field of the "horned power." Both are contained in it, fatefully bound to it and to each other, without their knowing or choosing. Obvi-ously any real relatedness between them would depend upon an awareness of what it is that encompasses them. Without this awareness they are pulled hither and thither, never knowing what has them by the neck. Hence relatedness and freedom of choice always depend on—and are an illusion without—an awareness of the "field" power or archetypal power within which we move.

(7) Dream images appear as if purposive. They provide vital informa-

tion which is necessary for an appropriate evaluation of the actual life situation and which is unavailable to consciousness through logical channels. Therefore they complement or compensate for the one-sided, limited nature of the conscious viewpoint. When consciousness is so limited that it has angelic standards, the rejected creative power becomes a devil. The psyche compensates any extreme with its opposite. If the mother only knew what was trying to get into her angelic masquerade, she would understand the situation in which she found herself. In the child's case, of course, we cannot yet say, "If the child knew"—the child cannot yet know. Nevertheless, those images warn the child at least emotionally that she has to fight hard. The result is that of making her lower *her* horns, which she needs to do!

In thus complementing and compensating, the images seem as if bent upon altering and widening consciousness. We may say that they represent contents and impulses which demand to be allowed into conscious life. The one dream even says it literally: Unless you let me in, unless you open the doors and windows (the "outlooks" of your consciousness), I will destroy your child. The child, in this dream, may indeed be taken to refer to her daughter; but the child motif can have a wider meaning. Taken on the "subject level" as referring to an element of the dreamer's psyche—the child within—it refers to her own developing individuality, her potential for future growth. Hence also the mother's individual development is threatened by her refusal to allow the intruder into her house.

The threatening intruder is, incidentally, a dream motif which is met innumerable times in various versions. It may be a burglar who tries to get in, or a tramp, or a salesman, or a soldier—in any case it is a suspect person —and the dreamer, who is afraid of him, tries desperately to shut him out. Yet when he is let in he usually turns out to be helpful.

What is asserted by all these variations of the same theme is that new life and developmental possibilities always tend to approach us in a form which is suspect to our conservative orientation. When these suspect forces are not let in they may threaten destruction; as the old Roman proverb expressed it: *"Fata volentem ducunt, trahunt nolentem"* ("Whoever is willing the Fates will lead, the unwilling they will drag along"). Jung remarked that human freedom rests essentially upon the choice to walk upright on our appointed path,[5] namely when we consent to walk it, or to be dragged "like cattle to the slaughterhouse" when we attempt to refuse.

We may say that one's unrealized potential, one's undeveloped growth needs, may become one's fate. Seemingly, life demands not only adaptation to external reality but, equally, adaptation to inner reality, to what one is "meant to be" in terms of the force patterns of the objective psyche. There appears to be a compelling urge to adapt to what one is meant to be—to one's inner truth—which may have little or nothing to do with one's conscious ideas or purposes. Jung has called this the individuation urge.[6]

In sum, the study of dreams can show us a dimension which operates prior to and regardless of conscious subjective ego functioning, in terms of typical, age-old, highly dynamic, unitive configurations. If we do not keep up with the inner pressure to assimilate them into conscious life, these configurations can become disturbing complexes.

We have now to clarify the relationship between objective psyche and ego. As we have seen, the objective psyche, on the one hand, functions independently and regardless of the ego's intentions; in fact the ego is gradually formed by the objective psyche as its focal point (as the child rises out of the waters in her dream). On the other hand, the objective psyche appears to insist on a continuous dynamic relationship between itself and its focal point in the ego. The conscious ego must make the effort to relate to the unconscious, its maternal source-ground, in order to maintain adequate, healthy functioning.

Such a conscious relationship does, however, require an effort—as anyone who attempts to become aware of unconscious drives quickly discovers—for it appears as if the unconscious would put every possible obstacle in the way of that very relationship which it ostensibly insists upon (as the hero in the fairy tales is always beset with difficulties he must overcome almost as if by previous arrangement): the paradox of the objective psyche.

It takes a great leap of imagination to conceive of this ego position. We are so much in the habit of taking our conscious selves for granted that our sense of ourselves seems to us the primary fact from which all other experiences arise merely secondarily. We find it difficult to regard the subjective experience of "I" as in any way secondary, as something through which some objective "other"—namely, a "not-I," an objective psychic stratum—brings itself to experience as consciousness, as a focal point of the total field in terms of space and time.

Such an *a priori*, unconscious, yet well patterned, functional organization, which can become in part subject to conscious control, is not a novel phenomenon, however. Let us consider the physical organism of both men and animals—as an analogy, not as a causal explanation.

The physical organism is also a self-balancing but unconscious functional system, organized and directed by a central nervous system, centered in the brain stem and the spinal cord. Only secondarily—phylogenetically in the differentiation of the animal species into the human organism, and ontogenetically in the development of embryo, infant and child into a conscious person—do the consciousness centers of the brain cortex develop and superimpose a consciously controlled functional system upon the autonomous unconscious organism. But while we may deliberately and consciously will our legs and arms to move, we cannot directly, by sheer will, influence the workings of our stomach or our liver or spleen. Indeed, unless we are told so we are not even aware of the existence of the spleen or of adrenal glands. Yet all of these unconscious organs and organ-systems do continue to function in an organized, meaningful fashion prior to and regardless of our awareness of them. Hence, for the sake of our health we have to take into account not merely our own wishes and desires, not only the facts of our external existence, but also the needs and requirements and "intents" of our unconscious physical inner organism which thus constitutes an independent system of its own.

Similarly, as Jung has described it:

> Our consciousness does not create itself—it wells up from unknown depths. In childhood it awakens gradually, and all through life it wakes each morning out of the depths of sleep from an unconscious condition.[7]

> Consciousness grows out of an unconscious psyche which is older than it, and which goes on functioning together with it or even in spite of it. Although there are numerous cases of conscious contents becoming unconscious again (through being repressed, for instance) the unconscious as a whole is far from being a mere remnant of consciousness. Or are the psychic functions of animals remnants of consciousness? [8]

> I have always been greatly impressed by the character of dissociated fragments as personalities. Hence I have often asked myself whether we are not justified in assuming that, if such fragments have personality, the whole from which they are broken off must have personality to an even higher degree. The inference seemed logical, since it does not depend on whether the fragments are large or small. Why, then, should not the whole have personality too? *Personality need not imply consciousness. It can just as easily be dormant or dreaming.*[9]

We see now how this other *a priori* personality may appear very negative, threatening or even evil to the ego which thinks of itself as *the* personality. And if not granted a right to exist in reality, it may indeed turn out to be quite destructive. On the other hand, the objective psyche has its positive aspects as well. It contains all of our potential creativity, developmental abilities and goals of life. It may have, if properly channeled, a constructive and enriching effect. The objective psyche is not merely the cesspool of rejected conscious material but is also the clear spring of future development and growth. We see here how Jung's approach puts the whole situation entirely outside the realm of pathology and focuses upon the "normal" adult's potential need to come to terms with the unconscious as a means of developing into what he *could* be in the full expansion of his powers!

It follows then, that what makes us ill need not be our worst, it may also be our best. But if the power is not admitted, if doors and windows are barred, if it has to force its way in, a whole life may be damaged in the process.

Analytic experience has shown that there seems to be a general law which decides between psychic health and psychopathology. The balance is tipped by the ego's strength, capacity and willingness to unbar the doors and windows to the unconscious and to receive the stranger; that is, to confront and channel the inner world of images and affects while, at the same time, retaining its own grasp upon external reality.

The more consciousness refuses to or is incapable of concerning itself with the non-ego contents of the objective psyche, either in their personal or archetypal aspects, the more likely are these elements to disrupt, invade and threaten consciousness with the compulsive, obsessive power of their weird imagery. Complexes that are not granted reality by consciousness and are not dealt with as "powers" to be taken seriously, but are dealt with by repression, tend to take hold in an unadapted, primitive, regressive, compulsive and destructive fashion. This results in what we call neurotic or psychotic disturbances. In neurosis the ego's function is merely interfered with. When the grip of the complex is serious enough to shatter also the fundaments of the ego's reality adaptation, we speak of psychosis. In these more serious invasions the non-personal, that is archetypal, elements of the central cores (see Chapters 4 and 5) tend to inundate consciousness with their bizarre imagery.

On the other hand, the ego's effort to confront the personal distortions—the "shells"—of the complexes and finally to comprehend their archetypal cores has a constructive effect. Capacities which may have been lacking before and whose unavailability was compensated for by neurotic exaggeration of available capacities as well as by compulsive, obsessive pressure of the barred energies, may now become accessible to the conscious personality. Thereby not only is psychopathology relieved, the creative potential is enhanced also. But of course, as we have already remarked, the greater the energic charge of the unconscious capacities and drives, the greater also their conflict potential and their disruptive threat when not assimilated. The difficulty in assimilation is caused by the greater degree of "otherness" which they bring into the ego's accustomed frame of reference.

In the paradoxical way typical of unconscious functioning, the objective psyche, besides straining the ego's strength to the utmost, also appears to shape and determine the ego's capacity to deal with what is in store for it. Of course, serious emotional deprivation during the early years of life decidedly tends to undermine or even to destroy the firmness of the ego structure. Nevertheless, there is apparently an *a priori* variability of resistance to such undermining influences and at times a rather weak ego to begin with, even in the absence of such undermining influences. There seems to be such a thing as constitutional ego strength or weakness, determined by the structuring which the ego receives as it is "born" of the objective psyche.

In that game of interaction which the ego plays with the objective psyche, it appears as if the cards were dealt by the unconscious, since it is the unconscious which gives rise to and shapes the strength or weakness of the ego. The ego's responsibility is to do the best it can with the hand it is dealt.

However, the unconscious appears to be concerned with conscious progress, to the extent that a sort of foreknowledge is often evidenced through dreams and visions. Here we confront a puzzling space-time transcendent dimension of a quasi-absolute knowledge from within, which is not, however, directly accessible to the rational ego. In dreams the unconscious dimension operates as if it encompassed unknown events outside of space and time (and to the dreamer often enough unknowable) and also subjective problems which lie ahead in the dreamer's development. This dimension includes information about the dreamer's probable reaction to these events as well as about his capacity to deal with them. Here we encounter the so-called anticipatory dreams which the experienced analyst has come to look forward to, so as to utilize them for diagnosis, prognosis and information about the nature and cause of the problem, the conduct of the therapy process and the intrinsic ego strength. Our judgment of ego strength, based on manifest behavior only, can be quite erroneous. A seemingly weak ego may have an intrinsic capacity for growth, and a seemingly firm structure may actually be a pseudoego which maintains an artificial front and is ready to crumble at the slightest threat. Then a very practical use of the space-time transcendents of the objective psyche can be made.

The following dream material offers examples of this use for prognosis and diagnosis.

A young man came to see me because he was greatly disturbed by a fear of approaching insanity. He had lately begun to experience a great intensification of his fantasy life, of almost visionary character, and had become concerned about his ability to hold onto reality. He brought the following dream: "*I saw a strange horse which frightened me. But then I was told that the horse's name was Chrysalis.*"

Now the chrysalis, the pupa state, opens into a butterfly, and the Greek name for butterfly is *psyche*. In the butterfly is seen an image-likeness of the psyche. Thus the dream says: The horse, the animal energy of the unconscious which confronts and frightens you, is but a developmental stage of the psyche; your state is not an illness leading to death or insanity, it is a developmental stage; there is no need to be afraid. This dream hands us not only a diagnosis, but a prognosis as well.

In another example *the dreamer goes down into an underground chamber in order to find access to the treasure hidden there. He comes to a big iron door that is closed, but from behind it a tremendous pressure makes itself felt; the dreamer can see how the door bulges with it. Two guardian figures stand in front of the door and say, "This door is closed, never to be opened."*

In another dream, *a young man finds a bottle which contains a life-giving, life-assuring fluid. But the bottle has no opening and no stopper. In order to get at the fluid, he would have to break the bottle, and this would destroy it.*

These two latter dreams show situations in which no development is possible. The energies of the unconscious cannot be tapped; to attempt it might invite a flooding of the ego or a break. Both images express the danger of psychotic break; the relative ego strength is insufficient.

In viewing such dreams it is important to remember what has already been stressed (Chapter 2), that dreams are not disguised wish-fulfillments but show the situation exactly as it is. For one might wonder, in circumstances such as these, whether it is not resistance to the analysis that is the problem. And indeed the dream with the bulging door shows a resistance, but also, like the latter dream, it warns that in this case the resistance is to be respected or at least that it cannot be overcome without grave risk, at least for the present. On the other hand, no dream is final unless it expressly "says" so. Hence one must beware of rigid standpoints. Life can be a great teacher and it is quite possible that at a later stage the situation might be different; we might then encounter a dream of a bottle with a cork that *can* be pulled out.

Neither—and this is a warning to the inexperienced reader—must one generalize about the meanings of like images; symbolism is not fixed. The same images may present different meanings in different contexts, as expressed in the differing details of the dream, in the character of the life situation to which it relates, as well as in the different associations which they evoke.

At times the anticipatory foreknowledge of the objective psyche expresses itself through what may be regarded as truly prophetic dreams. A woman who had discovered a questionable knot in her breast, about which the diagnosis at the time was unclear, dreamed: *"I met my husband who told me that everything would be all right and that I need not worry. I then bade him goodby and found myself at the seashore. The beach was lonely and the light was darkening; the shore was empty except for some barges."*

To the barges she associated the Egyptian barges of the dead which she had seen at the Metropolitan Museum of Art. To the husband she associated a silly ostrich who never could face up to reality and who was always over-optimistic. This dream, then, said: Your over-optimistic, silly ostrich side tells you not to worry, but you are bound for the journey of the dead. The knot turned out to be an inoperable cancer, of which she subsequently died. Her further analysis was able to prepare her for the experience of death.

A dream which illustrates the complete transcendence of space, time and rational knowledge is described in *The Analysis of Dreams* by Medard Boss:

[Bishop Joseph Lanyi of Grosswardein, Hungary] had been the teacher and afterwards a friend of Archduke Franz Ferdinand, assassinated in 1914. In this dream he was informed of the future murder of his previous pupil. He recorded this dream on the morning of the assassination. This is what he wrote:

"On the 28th of June 1914 at a quarter to four in the morning I awakened from a terrible dream. I had dreamt that in the early hours of the morning I had gone to my desk in order to look through my letters. Right on top there was a black-bordered letter bearing a black seal with the coat of arms of the Archduke. I immediately recognized his writing. I opened it and on top of the letter I noticed a light blue picture, like those on a picture postcard, on which there appeared a street and a narrow passage. Their Highnesses were sitting in a motor-car, facing them was a general, and next to the chauffeur there was an officer. On both sides of the street there was a large crowd. Two young fellows suddenly jumped out from the crowd and fired at Their Highnesses. The text of the dream letter itself was, word for word, as follows: 'Dear Dr. Lanyi, I herewith inform you that today my wife and I will fall victims to an assassination. We commend ourselves to your pious prayers. Kindest regards from your Archduke Franz, Sarajevo, the 28th of June, 3:45 A.M.' Shivering and in tears I jumped out of bed, and saw from my clock that it was a quarter to four. I rushed to my desk immediately, and wrote down all that I had read and seen in the dream. I even copied some of the Archduke's writings as I had seen it in the dream. My servant entered my study at 5:45 A.M. and noticed how pale I was and that I was telling my beads. He asked me if I felt ill. I said: 'Please call my mother and our guest. I wish to say mass for Their Highnesses for I have had a terrible dream.' I then went to our chapel with them. I passed the day in fear and trembling until at 3:30 P.M. a telegram brought news of the assassination."

We owe an important addition to this written record of the Bishop to K., a reporter of the *Wiener Reichspost*. In a personal conversation he had learnt from the Bishop that after the latter had recorded his dream he had also drawn a sketch of the assassination just as he had dreamed it, since he had felt that there had been something peculiar about this particular dream vision. Still on the 28th of June, he had had his drawing certified by two witnesses and had then sent an account of this dream to his brother Edward, a Jesuit Father, to which letter he had appended a sketch of the narrow passage, the motor-car, the crowd, and the murderer at the moment of jumping towards the car and firing the fatal shots. These drawings were in complete agreement with the photographs published in the press some days afterwards.[10]

These examples illustrate the hypothetical concept or "model" of the objective psyche as a "concealed personality," a pattern of existence, space and time transcending, with an awareness and function-potential of its own, touching upon and yet quite remote from our rational conscious functioning.

An analysis conducted with an openness to this dimension is bound to be different from one which rationalizes it away. An investigation which takes heed of the objective psyche will over and again take heed of evidence of some inner authority, some entity, which knows, directs, insists, plans, wills and threatens if need be, but which can also be approached and dealt with, and which can provide sustenance and creative power.

To sum up: Jung's concept of the "objectiveness" of the psyche hypostatizes it as an independent autonomous fact, prior to and regardless of consciousness, with a meaning of its own, one particular aspect of which is represented by ego consciousness. The objective psyche is viewed as not a part of "my" subjective being which I call "I." Rather my subjective experience of myself is seen as a part and indeed usually a rather incomplete and inadequate part of a wholeness of psychic existence. In order to reach wholeness of being, this "other" has to be confronted by me as an independent fact, as another personality to which I am tied, an inner "Thou." Its laws cannot be derived from my subjective rationality but operate on autonomous terms of their own, irrespective of and at times contrary to and in opposition to consciousness, able to overrule and even to submerge the ego.

At first Jung's hypothesis may appear very startling and at variance with seemingly obvious facts. It is a step comparable to the transition from a geocentric to a heliocentric view in astronomy. As a symbolic working model the heliocentric view, which was set forth in the sixteenth century through the writings of Copernicus and which could not be readily visualized at that time, eventually proved of greater practical usefulness for the understanding of empirical facts than the earlier, seemingly obvious pre-Copernican model. Similarly, the concept of a subjective ego revolving around a central objective Self may in the long run prove its practical usefulness.

4. The Complex

The term *complex* denotes the basic structural element of the objective psyche, and the central element of the complex is the *archetype*. We shall see more clearly how complexes manifest themselves if we again turn to an actual case.

A young man came for help because of pervasive difficulties with people, with anyone who challenged his compulsive need to dominate any situation, especially, of course, with his superiors at work. His eagerness to lead and to dominate others worked fairly well until he felt that his leadership was somehow called into question. He would even construe an attempt to get to know him better as a threat to his authority. Anyone having a semblance of authority over him seemed immediately to insult him, and therefore he constantly found it necessary to change jobs. He had not been able to finish college because he was intolerant of the required discipline. He plainly had a problem with authority and discipline and reacted violently to them, yet he had the potential for becoming an excellent leader. He was very sensitive to the feelings and needs of others—even though at this point his sensitivity worked against him by making him the more ready to recoil.

He was at the same time repelled and fascinated by authority; he could neither accept it nor exert it in any appropriate way. In simple psychological language this young man had an authority complex. He always got hooked on authority. He would make a beeline for it, he would fight it and defy it, he always felt impelled to exert it. Yet he was unable to fit into any ordinary situation in which the exercise of authority would have been appropriate, much less to meet a real challenge that called for it.

Here we have a situation in which it was *as if* a split-off authority personality were driving and taunting the individual in question, leading him toward meeting the authority problem everywhere, regardless of his better judgment—or his "worse" judgment for that matter—and what is more important he did not know he was being driven.

Anything even remotely associated with authority, especially paternal authority, set this force into motion, and set it into motion in a rather destructive fashion, because whether he met it in others or exerted it himself trouble was bound to arise; he would either antagonize people or be antagonized by them, and he invariably put the blame on the others. It always appeared to be the other person who did not recognize his beneficial effect, and it was always the other who fenced him in or wanted to pull him down or who challenged and antagonized him.

In psychological language we would say that this person was *identical* with his authority impulse. He was *compulsive* about it, and he *projected* it onto others. This is the nature of a disruptive complex. It is an autonomous set of impulses grouped around certain kinds of energy-charged ideas and emotions; it is expressed in *identity, compulsiveness* and *primitivity, inflation* and *projection*, for as long as it remains unconscious.

A state of identity is a lack of differentiation. In such a state one cannot separate oneself from the driving elements, hence one is deprived of a conscious choice between ego motivations and the driving elements. For example, we tend to do things which we later regret—and even at the time know to be destructive—whenever a sensitive area, namely a complex, is aroused. We then wonder "what got into us." We do not seriously entertain the thought that indeed a split-off "other personality" has taken over.

When we are identical with a drive there is no difference between our conscious reactive capacity and the impulse of the drive. We usually discover a thousand reasons why it had to be that way and could not have been otherwise; these reasons always seem perfectly logical and convincing —and we are sure that as far as they are sensible and good they obviously pertain to ourselves, whereas the negative reasons could only pertain to the other person.

Since identity means that the ego is identical with the drive, identity also means total unawareness of the existence of the drive as something separate from our own reasoning capacity. We notice the result *after* it has occurred.

The possibility of choice and relationship depends fundamentally upon getting out of this state of identity. As long as this unconscious identity with a drive or impulse persists there is no possibility of choice, for we act like helpless puppets and we never know what strings have pulled us. There is no possibility for any personal conscious relatedness because neither of two people who are identical with their impulses knows what is moving him or what, if anything, this has to do with the other person. Separation from the original state of identity is fundamental for any psychological development and for personal differentiation.

A point of warning here: *Identity* is readily confused with *identification*. In the usage of analytical psychology, however, identity has a very different meaning. *Identification* is imitation, conscious or unconscious. When we admire a person and knowingly or unknowingly emulate him, we identify with him. When we admire a goal or a purpose and try to adjust ourselves to it, we identify with it. This is not identity. *Identity* with unconscious impulses, as Jung saw it, is an *a priori* state; it is not made but is the original condition of man, and of course of the animal. In this sense unconsciousness and identity are practically synonymous.

We all start out in a state of more or less complete identity with the objective psyche; this is the state of the infant. As we develop, the ego gradually separates and emerges from this identity with the original unstructured drives. Indeed what is generally called ego development is the separation of a center of consciousness from the world of drives. We will explore this process in detail in Chapters 7, 15 and 17.

Wherever there is identity, as we have seen, there is compulsiveness. When we are identical with a drive we never question why we are moving or where we are going: there is only automatic response to an impulse. This state of compulsiveness, moreover, gives us the feeling of being carried by a tremendous force of energy, in much the same way that an automobile going at the speed of eighty miles an hour may give us a feeling of exhilaration: We are really going fast now! This exhilaration, this unquestioning feeling of assurance that "I'm really going, and I'm going fine and well" is called *inflation*.

Inflation then describes a feeling of power in which we are blown up by an unknown force that is not our own, not of our own judging and choosing. However, it feels as if it were and we claim it as our own. It makes us feel cocksure and self-righteous: "I am really going to show him, because he has it coming to him . . . and nobody can stop me, and nobody can tell me anything . . . and I don't care what the consequences are for I am right!" This feeling might give us pause for thought, but it usually does not. Only after it is all over we may wonder, "What came over me?" Unless, of course, it was "entirely his fault" and "I could not possibly have acted otherwise!"

In this inflated, compulsive state of identity, we and the drive are at our most harmful; the drive will unfold and we will act out its extreme, inappropriate and destructive side. In the process we get the worst of it, along with the other people involved. The wrong thing usually happens at the wrong time and in the wrong place. A capacity for moving toward differentiating and transforming the drive will not arise until the state of identity has been dissolved. This requires a confrontation of the drive as a *Thou*, as something that is not *I*, as something separate from ourselves. Only at this point can the inner dialogue begin. Until then the drive remains unconscious, primitive and destructive. Only after the identity has been dissolved by learning to experience the drive as an autonomous entity that is separate from the ego, despite its tendency to engulf the ego, do we get a chance to choose a right time and place and to develop the positive potential of the drive.

The drive or complex always reveals itself initially, in the primitive stage, as though it came from the other person, because whatever is unconscious, whatever we are identical with, is projected.[1] We use the term *projection* here in a different sense than it is ordinarily used in psychological language. Its common meaning is that one blames somebody else for what one is doing in order to defend oneself. Projection, as Jung uses the term, is not a deliberate defense maneuver but a choiceless original state, and is the avenue by which the unconscious complex attempts to reach our consciousness. This has to do with the fact that fundamental primary orientation and psychological differentiation are achieved through the sense perceptions, which are derived from the outer world. Our original frame of reference is wholly in terms of images of the outer world, or of thought pertaining to them, or emotions reacting to them: our own nature reaches us first in terms of the outer world. Projection is therefore the first stage of awareness —albeit an inadequate one—and is the actualization of a psychic content or of a complex *as if* it adhered or pertained to an external object, be it a thing or a person. We might describe a projection as a vision or inner image which is evoked by outward elements that correspond to the energy field of a complex and is as yet experienceable only in terms of these outward elements. Complexes therefore operate not only as sets of inner tendencies and drives but also as expectations, hopes and fears concerning the outward behavior of people and objects. Philosophically speaking, since all our perceiving occurs in terms of our psychological predispositions we may regard all perceptions as projections upon the object, the "thing in itself," but in our clinical usage we limit the term to those situations in which the reality perception is distorted by the compelling power of a constellated complex or archetype.

The question now arises: If everything unconscious is projected, and every projection—for example, something that annoys us about another person—pertains to a content of one's own psyche, how may we know the difference between perceiving a fact adequately and projecting?

It is the emotional coloring that will tell us whether or not we are caught in a projection. Since a projection is always the visualization of a complex, it makes itself felt by a strong affect charge. In plain English, whenever a projection is involved, it "gets" us, it "gets under our skin." Our reaction is affect-determined and we are therefore unable to react adequately to a person or situation; we can neither accept nor modify nor leave that person or situation. This is one of the few basic laws of the psyche which is, without exception, one-hundred-percent foolproof.

As a rule of thumb, when such an uncomfortable situation occurs, when somebody really "gets under your skin" and you want to know in what way you are responsible, verbalize what "gets" you in the other person. Say: "He is a dogmatic authoritarian (or as aggressive as a bulldozer, or an opinionated old bat . . .) and I can't stand that!" Then take out the "He is" and put in an "I am" or "My complex is like" and you will have a description of the complex at work.

However, complexes are not necessarily only negative; they cause attraction as well as repulsion. We are involved in a positive projection when what gets under our skin attracts us, fascinates us, arouses our admiration—when we "fall in love" with a person or idea. Whenever this happens we have met a positive potential of our own with which we are identical—i.e., undifferentiated from and unaware of—even if this positive potential is clothed in an obviously negative garb. For instance we may be attracted by a quality which on closer acquaintance we recognize to be thoroughly destructive, yet since we have failed to develop this quality in ourselves and since it is destined to be a vital and creative capacity when constructively used it will attract us even in this inappropriate form for so long as we are unaware of it; yet it can become constructive of course only when consciously developed. Again, when we compulsively hate and resent, we have met a negative complex, a potential for the worse, or at least a tendency *of our own* to which we would attach a negative value judgment if we were aware of it.

Furthermore, we may be attracted and repelled by the same person. Usually attractions and repulsions refer to distinctly different qualities or sets of qualities in the person. In such a case the thing which attracts us is a projection of our positive potential; the thing which repels us is a projection of our latent negative traits. However, it may not be so simple. The very same thing may attract and repel. This is a more extreme form of the instance described above. Our value systems are involved here; that is to say, particular individual qualities which we have learned to regard as negative and are fearfully trying to repress will cause the repulsion, but if these qualities could be of constructive capacity when properly integrated they would at the same time attract us. This could, for example, refer to sexuality. A certain element may arouse profound disgust and yet we are unable to refrain from constantly seeking it out; every day we have to spend half an hour of offense-taking on that! This is, then, something which we regard in terms of our upbringing as bad, wicked and awful; however, in its profound archetypal meaning it contains something which might very well be essential for the total growth process and therefore fundamentally constructive. We can say this also in another way. We can be attracted by something which "wants to be known" even though it now works against us because it is unconscious. We cannot get away from it; its pressure to be known will not let us go. It requires that we say to it, like Jacob, "I will not let thee go, except thou bless me!" It is the intruder, the stranger, who wants to be let in.

The call to individuation is contained within this dynamism; if we want to know the next step along the path toward what we are "meant to be," we can look for the thing that attracts and frightens at the same time. That which merely attracts or merely repels is also something to be dealt with, but in a slightly more peripheral way.

We may well ask at what point, if any, our feelings of attraction or repulsion cease to be projections of our own inner unconscious disruptive complexes and become a true awareness of the qualities of the other person. Are we ultimately solipsistic and isolated—all values being simply projections? Our previous characterization of projections as visualizations of an affect-charged complex, hence as expressions of compulsiveness, gives us the answer. Where we are not projecting, we cease to be compulsive. Where we *may* rather than *must*, we are relating to and appreciating. Again, this theoretical formulation refers to an ideal state. Remember that we defined projection as the first stage on the way to consciousness; if we were to cease all projecting we would cease all development toward consciousness. Such a completely projection-free state is unthinkable, unless we postulate that it is possible to reach absolute and complete consciousness, but this, as Jung once remarked, is an idea like the notion of drying up all the oceans. We can only speak of degrees. To the degree that we are free and may go or stay and choose to move or not to move we have ceased to be under the spell of a projection which pulled and pushed us against our will.

Where we do not project, we may see something which displeases us but we can decide for ourselves whether it is necessary or important or relevant that we go and do something about it. We may choose to do so for reasons of our own. However, when we see something which displeases us and are compulsively involved in how we feel about it and can neither take it nor leave it, then we are projecting. Projection denies us freedom of choice. To the extent that projection recedes we can choose the appropriate time and place for action or nonaction, even for relationship or no relationship. We can, for instance, be deeply in love and decide to renounce. However, to the extent that we love someone even if it kills him—"I'd rather kill you than lose you and kill myself in the process too"—there is a projection. There we are in love with our anima or animus as the case may be. That feeling has very little to do with the other person as a person.

Of course the carriers of projection are not limited to people. Fetishism, for instance, is an example of object projection. The fetish has a compelling attraction; therefore it holds compelling psychic content. All forms of animism, anthropomorphism, and religious imagery can be contaminated with projection. The projection aspect accounts for the impassioned, literalistic, and dogmatic certainty of fundamentalist convictions and doctrines. The genuine symbolic perception, on the other hand, is of a nature with a tentative "as if" statement. It apprehends a reality that is experienced as impossible to define or even put into words.

The carrier of the projection and the projected content must, of course, have some intrinsic correspondence. There is an associational connection. We can say that every projection needs a "hook" to "hang" itself onto. Such a hook is usually more readily attached to a person but, as we have said, it may also be attached to an object. It is the associational relationship which arouses and places the emotional charge; we can get into a "state" when we meet a person who acts like our resented father; equally we could react to seeing a pair of spectacles or a pair of pants that looks like father's.

The intrinsic correspondence may vary between an almost unnoticeable semblance to a full-sized likeness. In the extreme of the former, we may be dealing with a practically paranoid state; in the latter, with a true representation on the outside of that very psychic content which strives for realization within. In between we have all the various shadings. The effect of the projection, therefore, is independent of the "hook." In other words the intensity of the projection does not depend so much upon the magnitude of the hook, the degree of likeness, but rather upon the intensity or charge of the projected content. We can never know what we really meet on the outside until we have some notion of the complexes which may color our view. If we wear red spectacles and look at a traffic light, the red that we see may be there but it may also only be in our spectacles.

So far we have given an account of the manner in which complexes make us behave. How does the complex itself operate and what is its structure? Jung describes it in this way:

> It appears as an autonomous formation intruding upon consciousness. Of consciousness one might say that it is our own psychic existence, but the (complex) has *its* own psychic existence, independent of ourselves. This statement seems to formulate the observable facts completely. If we submit such a case to an association experiment, we soon discover that man is not master in his own house. His reactions will be delayed, altered, suppressed, or replaced by autonomous intruders.[2]

The association experiment, which was Jung's first major research project [3] and upon which the polygraph (lie detector) is based, works approximately as follows: A person is given random words—*tree, flower, bush, father, mother*—and has to answer with the first word that comes into his mind (tree—*green*, flower—*lily*, etc., whatever it happens to be). When certain words are thrown out, a "blocking" is found to occur, reaction is delayed; sometimes no reaction occurs. Or, at times, a reaction will be distorted, in that responses are strangely irrelevant, and this is what Jung is describing above. Instead of the expected ready-reacting capacity, something seems to interfere, to distort and alter it, and to push it into a different direction.

> There will be a number of stimulus-words which cannot be answered by (the subject's) conscious intentions. They will be answered by certain autonomous contents, which are very often unconscious even to himself. . . . Whenever a stimulus-word touches something connected with the hidden complex, the reaction of the conscious ego will be disturbed, or even replaced, by an answer coming from the complex. It is just as if the complex were an autonomous being capable of interfering with the intentions of the ego. Complexes do indeed behave like secondary or partial personalities possessing a mental life of their own.
>
> Many complexes are split off from consciousness because the latter preferred to get rid of them by repression. But there are others that have never been in consciousness before and therefore could never have been arbitrarily repressed. They grow out of the unconscious and invade the conscious mind with their weird and unassailable convictions and impulses.[4]

These invasions include not only stereotyped behavior and uncontrollable affect-reactions, like those of our young man who flew into a rage whenever discipline was mentioned, but they also include physical responses (a rise in blood pressure, an increase in circulation, changes in the functioning of inner organs: the whole host of "psychosomatic" reactions). The lie detector is based on such measurable physiological responses. When something pertaining to the complex—in this case, the lie —is mentioned, a block and an affect reaction occur. The blood pressure goes up and the pulse rate and skin temperature change as a result of the affect-tension of the complex. In other words, another psychic entity takes over, altering and taking possession of even the most profound physical reflexes.

Jung says that

> while complexes owe their relative autonomy to their emotional nature, their expression is always dependent on a network of associations grouped round a center charged with affect. (In the association experiment) the central emotion generally proved to be individually acquired, and therefore an exclusively personal matter. Increasing experi-

ence showed, however, that the complexes are not infinitely variable, but mostly belong to definite categories, which soon began to acquire their popular, and by now hackneyed, designations—inferiority complex, power complex, father complex, mother complex, anxiety complex, and all the rest. This fact, that there are well-characterized and easily recognizable types of complex, suggests that they rest on equally typical foundations, that is, on emotional aptitudes or *instincts*. In human beings instincts express themselves in the form of unreflected, involuntary fantasy images, attitudes, and actions, which bear an inner resemblance to one another and yet are identical with the instinctive reactions specific of *Homo sapiens*.[5]

This behavior may be compared directly to Wagnerian music. The leitmotiv, as a sort of feeling-tone, denotes a complex of ideas which is essential to the dramatic structure. Each time one or other complex is stimulated by something someone does or says, the relevant leitmotiv is sounded in one of its variants. It is exactly the same in ordinary psychic life: the leitmotivs are the feeling tones of our complexes, our actions and moods are modulations of the leitmotivs.[6]

Jung saw in every complex two aspects. The first he called the *shell* of the complex, the other the *core*. The shell is that surface which immediately presents itself as the peculiar reaction pattern dependent upon a network of associations grouped around a central emotion and individually acquired, hence of a personal nature. In our patient these associations were linked with resentment of authority or anything connected with authority: discipline, forcefulness, exploitation and above all everything that reminded him of the behavior or attitudes of his father. An intense affect response, namely resentment, hate and abrupt withdrawal, was always elicited by any of these associational elements. The connection with father proved to be the crucial point. It was put into depth perspective by a dream the young man had in which *he was in his childhood home and asked his father for money to buy clothes. The father said, "Yes, of course," reached into his pocket and handed him some paper bills. Looking at the bills the dreamer saw that they were worthless pieces of scrap, whereupon he became angry and pulled out a gun and threatened his father. Father then pulled out his gun and threatened the son, wherupon the dreamer ran and father ran after him. He ran over hill and dale with father behind, pursuing him. Wherever he hid, his father would threaten to kill him. He could never find peace or rest from the threatening father, until finally he came to a pool of water that was being restored, and there he found refuge.* Thus ended the dream. When the dream was discussed the young man said, yes, this was exactly how father was. He would always seem to be helpful, to do something for you (and of course in return you had to do something for him), but you could never rely on him and he always would get the best of you. He would always ruthlessly exploit you. Father, according to his picture, was a regular slave driver, tricky and sly.

We can see why this man had a father-authority complex; to father and paternal authority he associated breach of faith, exploitation, heartlessness and the exercise of a ruthless discipline (the fruits of which would never accrue). Anything that reminded him of the form in which he had experienced authority aroused terror in him, pursued and threatened him; naturally he could never accept discipline or leadership, even when it was appropriate.

The associative shell or structure in which the complex confronts us consists of the sum total of childhood conditioning pertaining to the particular instinctual pattern in question. It always points toward personal experiences and is a network of emotionally-charged associations made up of one's personal history and conditioning grouped around certain affect-arousing situations. In Jung's words: "The individual ideas are combined according to the different laws of association (similarity, coexistence, etc.), but are selected and grouped into larger combinations by an affect." [7]

These "shells" of complexes are largely shaped by childhood events, childhood traumas, difficulties and repressions and so can always be reductively traced to one's personal past and explained in terms of cause and effect. In fact they should always be experienced in this light first, for these associational patterns are the concrete manifestations of the complex in the here and now. They explain and express the complex as an autonomous pattern of behavior and emotion, and this shell, or the totality of these shells of complexes, are the constituents of what in Chapter 3 has been referred to as the personal unconscious. The personal unconscious is equivalent to what most people ordinarily call *the* unconscious.

Up to this point, there is no essential disagreement between Jung's analytical psychology and conventional psychoanalysis. However, here their ways diverge. For at this stage we understand the complex but we still have it, or rather it still has us. Moreover, we are stuck with the confusing fact that we can trace our complex to a particular childhood patterning, and that although our cousin and even our brother were subject to the very same influences, the effect on them was not the same. So, even though it is true that childhood conditioning had an effect in shaping our complexes and in forming their mode of expression, it cannot be said that this conditioning explains everything. There must also be differences of individual basic predisposition that determine what sort of complexes develop or fail to develop in response to this environment.

Understanding merely in terms of past environmental factors does not prevent the complex from operating. After our patient, for example, understood why he ran away from discipline and authority, all he could do then was to avoid the state of identity. This meant only that he recognized its occurrence, he could not prevent it. And the recognition of what "gets" us unfortunately all too often comes only after the damage is already done; our vision is clear only through hindsight.

At this stage we still have to use a maximum effort of watchfulness and painful discipline in our efforts to undo the damage. We may hope to achieve a certain measure of relief through *sublimation*, which merely means that the energy which flows into the troubled area is drained away by a conscious effort toward applying ourselves elsewhere. This state falls far short of what is possible through the transformation of the core of the complex, and this is the ideal goal of Jungian analysis. In transformation *the drive itself* becomes changed and ceases to trouble us, because it has turned its other face, has been made into a constructive and helpful impulse. Sublimation is a conscious attitude, a conscious effort. Transformation indicates a change in the unconscious itself.

This transformation is not accomplished through understanding the shell of the complex or through emotional integration of the why and how of the past, though such emotional recognition and acceptance of full responsibility for our own past in our own present is absolutely essential for further progress. Apparently the energic charge of the complex which accounts for its disturbing field effect originates elsewhere, not in the personal layer, since the effect does not cease when met by consciousness on this level only.

It is usually at this point that what Jung calls the *mythological core* of the complex makes its appearance. In the case of our young man, his dream had ended by stating that running from father would not solve his problem, but that a refuge was to be found at the rather mysterious pool of water then being restored (perhaps to its rightful place in the dreamer's conscious value system). The pool or spring of renewal and healing is a widespread mythological motif, for instance the pool of Bethesda in John 5 or, in modern dress, the clear source of the *Virgin Spring* in the film of that name. Some time after the dream of the persecuting father had been discussed and understood, the young man dreamed that *he was trying to rob an ancient king's grave of a television set. A very old man appeared, a majestic figure, apparently the guardian of the grave, and warned the dreamer that he did not have the proper approach to this sacred place. He was told that he needed patience and reverence, and that he must humbly await whatever the powers should decree.*

Another patient with an equally serious father complex had a dream in which *a wicked magician priest put a spell on the dreamer*. Also, the little girl in Chapter 3 did not dream of her mother but of the goat people, and the mother dreamed of an Eastern potentate.

Such images as these are met in mythological and religious representations over and again. Jung has written:

> (The complexes) have a dynamic and a formal aspect. Their formal aspect expresses itself, among other things, in fantasy images that are surprisingly alike and can be found practically everywhere and at all epochs, as might have been expected. Like the instincts, these images have a relatively autonomous character; that is to say they are "numinous" [8] and can be found above all in the realm of numinous or religious ideas. . . . I have chosen the term "archetype" for this formal aspect of the instinct.[9]

The core of the complex, then, consists of the nucleus of a universal human pattern which is called an *archetype* of the collective unconscious or of the objective psyche. These typical foundations or archetypes in turn are regarded as corresponding to instincts, namely basic aptitudes or preformed tendencies toward typical reaction modes. They are expressed in terms of fantasy and dream images (Jung calls these images the formal aspect) and of emotional attitudes and action responses. While originally limiting the term archetype to the formal image aspect as in the above quotation, Jung later expanded it to include the dynamic as well as the formal expression. Here we may see what Jung meant by his early use of the term "collective unconscious." The archetypes are collective in the sense that they are no longer purely personal contents belonging to this or that person in terms of individual associations and histories, but belong rather to the trends toward certain types of symbolic representations inherent in all of us.

Jung's concern with the mythological core of the complex, the archetype, has given rise to a great deal of misunderstanding about his supposed tendency to disregard personal history in favor of mythological background. Freud expressed himself on this matter as follows:

> I fully agree with Jung in recognizing the existence of this phylogenetic heritage [namely the mythological patterns]; but I regard it as a methodological error to seize on a phylogenetic explanation before the ontogenetic possibilities have been exhausted. I cannot see any reason for obstinately disputing the importance of infantile prehistory while at the same time freely acknowledging the importance of ancestral prehistory.[10]

This would seem to pose the question of either/or, either collective or personal, and this point of misunderstanding is common among non-Jungians, and indeed not quite clear among Jungians themselves. Jung's attitude was, however, that it is not a matter of personal history versus universal ancestral history, but rather a question of first the one and then the other, or the two interwoven. Neither of the two is sufficient.

Only when the personal (the ontogenetic) is fully explored can the archetypal core of the complex effectively be reached, because the personal shell of the complex is the form in which the eternal mythological motif incarnates itself and makes itself felt in our personal life and our personal nature.

Unless we can deal with the mythological core in personal terms we have nothing *real* to deal with. Unless, however, we deal with the personal history in mythological terms we do not touch its driving power and *meaning*, nor do we reach that which is to be transformed; we do not reach the source of its energy, the "pool of water," or the wellspring of renewal, in order to be able to restore or rechannel this energy. The personal association patterns, in other words, give us the manifestations of an illness, if it be an illness, but not yet the misdirected function or meaning itself. And this is indispensable for redirection and healing.

Moreover, what is experienced only in terms of a personal impasse can seem quite hopeless until and unless it receives a general human meaningfulness by being recognized as one's individual and perhaps discordant share in, or variation of, a general theme of human striving and seeking.

Consequently, in Jung's view the complexes *per se* do not necessarily represent pathology. Everybody has complexes. They are, in Jung's terms, "focal or nodal points of psychic life which . . . must not be lacking, for otherwise psychic activity would come to a fatal standstill." [11] Complexes contain the driving power of psychic life. "Suffering is not an illness; it is the normal counterpole to happiness. A complex becomes pathological *only when we think we have not got it.*" [12] Because then it has us. Thus it would seem that the unawareness of one's complexes favors their tendency to become sources of pathological disturbance.

A distinction apparently needs to be made between "morbid" and "healthy" complexes, as Jacobi calls them. "Clearly this inference cannot be rejected," she explains, "especially if we . . . recall that Jung draws a certain distinction between the complexes of the personal unconscious and those of the collective unconscious." [13]

"Certain complexes," he writes, "arise on account of painful or distressing experiences in a person's life. . . . These produce unconscious complexes of a personal nature. . . . But there are others that come from quite a different source. . . . At bottom they are irrational contents of which the individual had never been conscious before, and which he therefore vainly seeks to discover somewhere outside him." [14]

What Jung expresses in these lines, which may appear a bit confusing in this form, is his earliest expression of a distinction between what he later termed the shell and the nuclear core of the complex. And it is the shell, the structure of the personal unconscious, which determines whether the total complex acts as a morbid or a healthy element. The way in which the "core" elements—the "potentials"—are actualized in early childhood experiences determines whether the energy content of the complex can be harmonized with conscious ego dynamics and the rest of the drives or whether this energy is forced to operate as if it were a disturbing intruder. Such a disturbing complex can be brought nearer to integration when it is possible to go past its conflict-ridden shell and reach its archetypal source or core. In our patient's dream this is expressed in terms of coming to the source or pool of water; that is to say, the original meaning, understood and freed from its distortions, can be rechannelled into more suitable personal channels.

Jacobi says further:

> Complexes belong to the basic structure of the psyche. If we think them through, these views of Jung have vast implications. They imply that the complex actually constitutes the structure of the psyche, or in other words that the complex *in itself* is a healthy component of the psyche. Material deriving from the collective unconscious is never "pathological"; it can be pathological only if it comes from the personal unconscious, where it undergoes a specific transformation and coloration by being drawn into an area of individual conflict. When a complex is "divested" of the superimposed contents from the personal life of the individual, as occurs in the course of analysis when this repressed material of conflict is raised to consciousness, the true nucleus of the complex, the "nodal point" in the collective unconscious, [15] is freed from all these contents in which it has been cloaked. The individual, who hitherto has been caught in his personal entanglements, is then confronted with a problem which no longer represents solely his personal conflict but gives expression to a conflict that it has been incumbent on man to suffer and solve from time immemorial. True release will never be achieved by too concretistic an explanation of the content of the complex, precisely because such an explanation always stops at the personalistically toned material that caused this disorder. Only an interpretation on the symbolic level can strip the nu-

cleus of the complex from its pathological covering and free it from the impediment of its personalistic garb.

If a complex embedded in the material of the personal unconscious seems to stand in inexorable conflict with consciousness, its "nucleus," once laid bare, may prove to be a content of the collective unconscious. For example, the individual is no longer confronted with his own mother, but with the archetype of the "maternal"; no longer with the unique personal problem created by his own mother as a concrete reality, but with the universally human, impersonal problem of every man's dealings with the primordial maternal ground in himself. Anyone who has ever been through such a psychic experience knows what an immense relief this can be, how much more bearable, for example, it is for a son to conceive the son-father problem no longer on the plane of individual guilt—in relation, for example, to his own desire for his father's death, his aggressions and desires for revenge—but as a problem of deliverance from the father, i.e., from a dominant principle of consciousness, that is no longer adequate for the son: a problem that concerns all men and has been disclosed in the myths and fairy tales as the slaying of the reigning old king and the son's accession to his throne.

Accordingly, if a complex remains only a greater or lesser nodal point in the collective unconscious, if it is not swollen and overgrown by too much personal material, then it is not harmful but extremely fruitful, for it is the energy-giving cell from which all further psychic life flows; but if it is overcharged and becomes autonomous, or if it invades the realm of consciousness, it may take on any of the forms that generate neurosis and psychosis. And if the conscious mind cannot "cope" with these contents, the result, in peoples as well as in individuals, is the same: disorganization and disintegration. Thus it is solely the state of the conscious mind, the greater or lesser stability of the ego personality, that determines the role of the complex. Everything depends on whether the conscious mind is capable of understanding, assimilating, and integrating the complex, in order to ward off its harmful effects. If it does not succeed in this, the conscious mind falls a victim to the complex, and is in greater or lesser degree engulfed by it.[16]

Whether or not a complex is an energy center that enhances or disturbs psychic life depends upon the nature of the personal association materials which constitute the "shell" of the complex and upon the ego's strength and ability to assimilate them. If we use our patient's case for illustration we may say that everybody has a father complex, namely a sensitive, emotionally potent area of fantasy images and action and reaction potentials in respect to relating to and enacting authority, leadership, etc. In the case of our patient this general, eternal—hence mythological—theme was experienced as, and thus became associated with, a way of behavior, namely that of his particular father, which rendered it unassimilable to the ego's general adaptation. When authority becomes identified with treachery and exploitation, the ego is forced to reject rather than accept it if it is not to lose its basic sense of integrity. But this rejection means that authority—the whole complex of emotions, fantasies and reaction potentials—becomes an overcharged, problematic and unacceptable element, like a foreign proliferating and disturbing cancer which causes illness in the psychic organism.

The father complex is pathologically constellated, as the dream showed. And the resolution of this dangerous situation can be found not by mere running away from the problem through repressing it, but by confronting it, by seeking the healing or renewing pool or source ground from which its energy originates: the mythological or archetypal core from which all psychic life flows—in our patient's dream, the pool of water that is in the process of renewal.

We may say that our complexes are the cards that fate has dealt us; with these cards and with no others we either win or lose the game, and if we behave as though we did not have them or if we ask for different ones we are beaten before we start.

The form, then, in which our complexes confront us is the form in which the fundamental materials of our human structure come into our here-and-now existence. Like crystals they are always imperfect to some extent and often unrecognizable or grossly disfigured in comparison with the "ideal" shape, the shape that would represent the "pure" incorporation of the crystal scheme. But we have to meet them in this more or less imperfect or distorted form and out of this form we have to transform them into something that may be more akin to the aboriginal "intent" inherent in their archetypal cores.

This undertaking, this process, is what Jung calls *individuation*.

5. Archetypes and Myths

IN ORDER TO effect a constructive and lasting change in our lives we must strive toward a transformation of the potentially disturbing or disruptive complexes by reaching their archetypal cores. Such a transformation can occur only when we have gone beyond the personal dimension to the universal. This process is sustained by guidance from the objective psyche through dreams and fantasies.

The archetypal core can best be described in terms of its dynamic and formal aspects. The dynamic aspect refers to energy, to expression *per se*— actions, reactions, patterns of emotion and behavior—which are brought into play through the forms of the personal shell of the complex. The formal aspect involves percepts—representational experiences—usually in the shape of dream or fantasy images, but sometimes in the form of auditory experiences and occasionally of experiences of one of the other senses. All of these manifestations can be seen to correspond to mythological motifs.

Thus the nuclear core of a complex characteristically presents itself in the form of mythological representations and images, such as the horned power and the renewing pool of water referred to in the preceding chapters. We call these images mythological because we are familiar with them through their appearance in myths, stories, fairy tales and traditional religious forms of all ages, locales and epochs, and we refer to these recurring motifs as *mythologems*. They occur in the dreams and fantasies of contemporary men, and do so under three types of circumstances:

(1) Mythologems appear in the analytic situation when complexes have been understood and dealt with but when a step beyond the understanding of their personal genesis is required. An example of this is the dream of the patient who stood before the grave mound of an ancient king from which he intended to steal a television set and was confronted by a guardian figure who admonished him to wait patiently and see what developed in his life through gradual growth rather than trying to force ready-made "views" (television views). The figures of the ancient or dying king and of the guardian of the sanctuary are found frequently in myths and fairy tales.

Another example is found in the second of Jung's *Two Essays on Analyt-*

73

ical Psychology,[1] in which he describes the case of a patient with a severe transference problem: Jung was to this young woman father, beloved, teacher, physician all in one. Even after she had understood this she continued to feel exactly the same way about him and finally dreamed that *her lover grew to superhuman size and became a vegetation god, striding over the fields and holding her in his arms.* The personal carrier of the projection here changed into the mythological representation of the archetypal power which stood behind the person of the therapist and which had been actualized at first through the transference.

(2) Archetypal images may appear spontaneously when inner or outer events which are particularly stark, threatening or powerful must be faced, when there is a state of psychic or physical emergency. In such cases the raw, archetypal core may present itself very suddenly. An example of this is the emergency situation of the asthmatic child. In her dream she was not confronted with her mother but with goat people who threatened her. The unconscious presented her with the nature of the non-personal power itself, a power which threatened her life through the personal mother.

(3) In cases of imminent or acute psychosis and in cases of demonic or religious "possession," the objective psyche takes over. Such extreme situations serve as excellent textbooks on the strange time- and space-transcending nature and the overpowering quality of the mythologem. The concrete, rational personal frames of reference are about to be or have been swept away.

An example of this strange time- and space-transcendent quality of the mythological or archetypal motifs is offered by one of Jung's earliest cases in which he describes the hallucinatory fantasy of an uneducated schizophrenic who at that time was hospitalized in Zürich. The patient used to call the hospital physicians to the window and inform them that if they looked at the sun and moved their heads from side to side they could see a tail or penis coming down from the sun and moving to and fro. This, he said, was the source of the wind.

After the patient's death Jung happened to be studying a German philologist's translation of a Mithras liturgy, from the original Greek papyrus which was then accessible only to a few scholars. In this obscure work dealing with Mithraic initiation it was stated that the initiate saw a pendulous tube coming down from the sun, from which arose the wind. The initiate was then asked to move his head to see the tube moving, producing the east and west winds. Jung added that there were other details in the text, as well as in the schizophrenic fantasy, and that his study of the fantasy helped him to understand some difficult passages in the text. (He also pointed out that analogous representations of such a phallic tube appear in medieval pictures of Mary, in which she is impregnated by a tube coming down from heaven and going up underneath her skirt; through the tube comes the Holy Ghost.)[2] There was, of course, no possibility that the schizophrenic patient could have heard of or read this material. We have here an example of mythological representations, almost literally alike, which appear in an unexplained fashion over a period of about 2000 years.

The scope of correspondence does not end here. An article on the front page of *The New York Times* for October 11, 1962, attracted my attention —it was a year after Jung's death:

MARINER 2 DATA DISCLOSE A CONSTANT SOLAR WIND
Washington, October 10, 1962. The Mariner 2 spacecraft bound for a December 2 rendezvous with Venus has discovered that there is a steady wind of charged particles blowing off the boiling surface of the sun into interplanetary space. The experimental determination of the existence of the continuous solar wind provides a new insight into interplanetary weather and the manner in which solar energy is transported to earth.

The same newspaper on November 11, 1963, p. 33, reports further:

COMET WAGS TAIL IN 4 DAY RHYTHM
Regular Movement May Be Linked with Solar Wind, Astrophysicists Assert/ Cyclic Action Puzzles/ Nothing is Known About Sun that Would Account for it/ There is a comet which slowly wags its tail. The wags have a rhythm, each taking about 4 days and covering a 15 degree arc. Nobody knows why they occur. . . . By wagging its tail, the comet may be telling scientists something about the solar wind, a cloud of electrons and atomic fragments spewed out continuously in all directions by the sun. The solar wind causes the comet's tail to stream outward always away from the sun, regardless of which direction the comet is moving.

The foregoing connections do not prove anything about the solar wind or a solar appendage; but they demonstrate the meaningful reality of the space- and time-transcendent mythologem as a universal, transcendental form-principle.

There is a further epilogue to this coincidence of archetypal manifestations. About a year after the *Times* stories one of my patients in a severe anxiety state spontaneously painted the picture reproduced as the frontispiece to this volume. It also shows the sun with a tail- or phallus-like appendage which reaches down to earth. The patient had no associations to it and needless to say had not heard of Jung's previous research. Nor had she paid any attention to the observations of the solar wind. (I had forgotten about them also.) Without understanding her picture the patient was calmed by painting it, for the conscious expression of archetypal fantasy material in such forms as clay, paint or body motion usually has the effect of transforming and thereby relieving the pressure from the unconscious.

The correspondence between the mythologem from 100 B.C., the two patients' visions—the one in the early 1900's, the other in 1964—and the configuration of stellar matter all point to an energy configuration that encompasses the structure of psyche and matter, object behavior, personal and transpersonal events. Rationally we cannot comprehend these connections. Only the symbolic experience can give us a sense of their meanings. In the case of this particular mythologem the symbolic image points to an entity that could be described as a central spiritual principle which reaches down, which makes itself accessible to us. It is as if the life-giving, light-bringing force were connected with earthly reality and thus would stimulate, create, fertilize and inspire.

On a less grandiose scale but not on a less dramatic one, the spontaneous emergence of space- and time-transcendent mythologems is a fact that can be observed quite routinely and regularly in his daily practice by any psychotherapist sufficiently familiar with mythology to be able to spot and recognize the recurring images in the unconscious material of his patients.

This is not to say that dream and myth are the same thing. Dreams are not coherent myths, but rather flash-pictures, as it were. In dreams mythological pieces are fitted into a great deal of personal material in an apparently irrational arrangement. The dream is thus a fragmented or personalized myth. On the other hand the myth (and we include also the fairy tale) could be regarded as a consciously molded or depersonalized dream. There are, however, instances when the unconscious presents a myth directly, when, for example, fantasy production takes place, not under conditions of an absolute exclusion of consciousness but in a half-awake or trance state, or under hypnosis, or by use of the technique which Jung called *active imagination*. Myths also appear naturally and spontaneously in yarn-spinning and storytelling—especially by children.

The world of myth has its own laws and its own reality. The myth has often been dismissed as something invented or untrue, as a primitive, pseudo-scientific attempt to rationalize astronomical, seasonal, sexual or historical facts. In ordinary language a myth carries the meaning of something untrue. Taken literally, namely as a description of external things or people, it is certainly not true. The question, however, is whether this is the only way it can be viewed, that is, whether there are not different kinds of truth: the truth of object behavior, and what Jung called *psychic truth* which is the adequate, that is, symbolic, description of inner psychic dynamics and experiencing. The myth's truth is accessible only to the symbolic view.

As we have ample evidence to demonstrate, the dream, our source of current mythological representation, describes a situation in terms of psychic inner truth and reality. The myth follows the same sort of inner law, and the element of conscious shaping by the community results in a coherent symbolic description of the eternal truth of psychic existence. The myth, as Coomaraswamy says in *Hinduism and Buddhism*, is

> the penultimate truth, of which all experience is the temporal reflection. The mythical narrative is of timeless and placeless validity, true nowever and everywhere. . . . "In the beginning" . . . or rather "at the summit," means "in the first cause": just as in our still told myths, "once upon a time" does not mean "once" alone but "once for all." The Myth is not a "poetic invention" in the sense that these words now bear: on the other hand, and just because of its universality, it can be told, and with equal authority, from many different points of view.[3]

Eliade says the following:

> Myths and rites always disclose a boundary situation of man—not only a historical situation. A boundary situation is one which man discovers in becoming conscious of his place in the universe. . . . As is generally admitted today a myth is an account of events which took place *in principio*, that is, "in the beginning," in a primordial and nontemporal instant, a moment of *sacred time*. This mythic or sacred time is qualitatively different from profane time, from the continuous and irreversible time of our everyday, de-sacralised existence. In narrating a myth, one reactualizes, in some sort, the sacred time in which the events narrated took place. [A myth may not be told by everybody and at any time, but only under the proper ceremonies.] . . . In a word, the myth is supposed to happen—if one may say so—in a nontemporal time, in an instant without duration, as certain mystics and philosophers conceived of eternity.[4]

Emma Brunner-Traut speaks of the sources and of the inner laws of the myth:

> In our rational approach to the world of the spirit which distinguishes between physics and metaphysics, we try to comprehend religious phenomena through logical causal thinking; and our theology based on this frame of reference concerns itself with the doctrine of God by

carrying on a discussion or dispute *about* God. Mythical understanding, however, arises from a common experienced realization *of* God himself; out of the experience, it is shaped into image and event.

However, as with everything that comes from the gods, even when it is imprisoned within the limits of solid material forms of space and time, it still in reality rests within itself in timelessness and so without a history; so too that which is described or rather circumscribed by the myth creates a history with action, characters and a time; but yet mythical time is not scientific time and allows the vision of the timeless to shine through.

It is their relationship to time that divides the mythically oriented and the historically minded man (and this is decisive for the understanding of the Gospels). He who only measures and calculates finds no access to that which cannot be grasped by the space-time concept. For mythical understanding does not aim at the known order but relates to that which in itself creates, contains, and presents question and answer.

Whereas the nature of rational judgment requires that man provide his own frame of reference, his set of conditions for his questioning of things, in the myth the objects have their own inner relation to each other; they meet and interact in a world of their own, hidden and unmindful of the questioner. They are sufficient and attuned unto themselves thus constituting their own truth in the dimension of the boundless.

As much as they are in need of each other, myth and logical knowledge are also in opposition, but the myth lies closer to the gods. All characters and tales relate to certain representations of mythical thinking and for the attuned can call forth the intended image without fail. We call these figures and tales *patterns* and may compare them with the *concepts* of rational thinking.

There is, then, a kind of terminology also in the mythical statement, even though the nature of the myth is playful, forever finding new forms and transforming the accustomed and established ones. With this incomparable playfulness and changeability, it is able to adapt to ever new situations in a living way. As with a concept, also in the pattern, the concretization can reach the limit of the absurd in its quest for realization. Many patterns stand side by side and they do not want to be connected or interrelated to one another in the eye of the observer; they are bound together by association but they are not interconnected by rational order. Hence the logical mind finds them full of contradictions.

He who has not himself met the gods will not believe the myth,

and for him myths become fairytales, fantastic stories or even carica-
tures. Moreover, he who thus tells these myths without belief becomes
a liar. But one who has been intimate with the gods knows the children of the gods as well as the Son of God and what he tells of them
can only be expressed in the language of the myth.

In the ancient past the idea of faith in the sense of belief did not
exist; for them it was a matter of "knowing." For those who "know,"
the unspeakable can be uttered without being misunderstood. But already where the smallest distrust creeps in and hidden meaning must
be explained, there an integrity is endangered, especially so when the
secret becomes a dogmatic formulation. It is placed into the light of
critical doubt and demand for proof, and in this light it appears false.
Myth is not definition, nor is it proof. It is self-evident. It is endowed
with dignity and majesty, perfect in its inner power and validity, and
the only adequate language for that which we can grasp only through
faith and through our action in the physical world.

Even in us it is still alive, albeit drowned out by the clamor of fact-
fascinated science. For the myth, which is a kind of symbolic language,
shares with the sign its silence. That which cannot be grasped by the
intellect strives toward realization in the symbol, the mythical sign and
the myth itself.[5]

The body of religious traditions, the collection of mythologems or archetypal images received from unconscious sources as "revelations" from the
objective psyche, consists of revelations of an unfathomable entity, ap-
proachable only through the living symbolic experience. The images of God
do indeed arise, as Buber says, out of the meeting of the divine and the
human. And for exactly that reason and in the sense of this definition the
images are not belittled by being regarded as expressions of myth-making
fantasy—the experience of divinity is not psychologized away—since we are
able to become aware of the presence of that which cannot be grasped by
direct rational cognition but *only* through symbol and myth.

The symbol, as Jung has defined it, "always ranks below the level of the
mystery it seeks to describe." [6] And the objective psyche, in Jung's view, is
far from a product of man's subjectivity. God is not reduced to a drive or a
psychological function. The objective psyche, as an *a priori* datum, imposes
upon our subjective selves the forms and limitations which determine the
quality of our experiences. Thus it follows that religion is not and never can
be invented by man's subjectiveness; rather it is "suffered" as the intrusion
of something objective and *per se* unfathomable. It is transmitted, as it
were, through the objective psyche in the form of its own typical (i.e.,
archetypical) imagery, which makes us experience it as a transpersonal

"Other," as a "Thou." Also a meaning in existence cannot be invented but only discovered.

Particular mythological images represent a living, collectively valid religious force for as long as they are in accord with the essence and forms of the psychological currents arising from the objective psyche for the majority of individuals of a particular period and cultural setting. Whenever the traditional mythologem loses its adequacy as a symbolic representation, it appears to be "dead." It is not "God" who has "died" then in our time, but a particular image or mythologem. The myth-forming force does not die; newly valid mythologems may be expected to arise.

Myths or archetypes and the driving forces which they represent are neither constructive nor destructive *per se*. They may be either, depending upon how they are fitted into the life of the community or of the individual and how they are lived in terms of the here and now. If they are consciously related to and reconciled with ethical requirements they will be constructive because they are the elements through which life receives its impulse.

> The archetype . . . as well as being an image in its own right . . . is at the same time a *dynamism* which makes itself felt in the numinosity and fascinating power of the archetypal image. The realization and assimilation of instinct [drive] never take place . . . by absorption into the instinctual sphere, but only through integration of the image which signifies and at the same time evokes the instinct.[7]

Integration of the archetypal image comes about through recognizing and experiencing it as a "picture of meaning" (*Sinnbild*), as a symbol. Its integration involves also a conscious realization of the underlying drive as a powerful impulse toward a meaningful activity or experience which has to be made real in terms of what is rationally and ethically possible. If we remain unaware of the autonomous power of the mythologem and maintain an uncritical identification with our drive or vision, we risk being inundated by its force or carried away to destruction by an *idée fixe*. As Eliade puts it:

> Modern man is free to despise mythologies and theologies but that will not prevent his continuing to feed upon decayed myths and degraded images. The most terrible historical crisis of the modern world—the second world war and all that has followed from it—has effectually demonstrated that the extirpation of myths and symbols is illusory.[8]

We have seen what can happen when the disregarded myth arises compulsively and hence irresponsibly: The German hero myth invaded modern history and wreaked havoc. And because of the over-optimistic and materialistic outlook of our era, the power of the myth was disregarded until it was too late.

The German version of the hero myth has been "spooking about" in the German psyche for the last two centuries, and the fact that the dark well was stirring had become apparent to Jung as far back as 1922 when he published an essay called "Wotan," [9] in which he warned that the world would find itself confronted with inconceivable events if the myth were not heeded.

According to the *Voluspa*,[10] the myth of the world goes from the golden age to the great corruption, with the death of Balder, the light hero, and the punishment of his evil adversary. This is followed by *ragnarök*, the destruction of the world. The Nordic version of the hero myth appears to be complemented and given a new possibility by the Christian myth; after the hero has suffered his dark side (personified by Judas), has suffered on the cross and descended into hell, he rises up to heaven, and renewal of life occurs. The turning point is the conscious acceptance of mortification and voluntary suffering. The story of deliverance through voluntary acceptance of suffering is also told in *Parsifal*, one of Wagner's versions of the hero myth.

Adolf Hitler was caught in the Nordic myth by an inadequate awareness of it, and by naïvely identifying with the hero-messiah he brought about a sort of rational *ragnarök*. He was caught to such a degree that he even stated in his final mania that if National Socialism had to go it would bring the world down in ruins with it. Here a myth became destructive due to the fact that it was not rationally and appropriately confronted and reconciled with personal and communal moral requirements.

Karl Marx, too, was affected by the repressed energy of a myth—that of the Golden Age—with many elaborations. Eliade says:

Whatever we may think of the scientific claims of Marx, it is clear that the author of the Communist Manifesto takes up and carries on one of the great eschatological myths of the Middle Eastern and Mediterranean world, namely: the redemptive part to be played by the Just (the "elect", the "annointed", the "innocent", the "missioners", in our own days by the proletariat), whose sufferings are invoked to change the ontological status of the world. In fact, Marx's classless society, and the consequent disappearance of all historical tensions, find their most exact precedent in the myth of the Golden Age which, according to a number of traditions, lies at the beginning and the end of History. Marx has enriched this venerable myth with a truly messianic Judaeo-Christian ideology; on the one hand, by the prophetic and soteriologi-

cal function he ascribes to the proletariat; and, on the other, by the
final struggle between Good and Evil, which may well be compared
with the apocalyptic conflict between Christ and Antichrist, ending in
the decisive victory of the former. . . .

In comparison with the grandeur and the vigorous optimism of the
communist myth, the mythology propagated by the National Socialists
seems peculiarly inept; . . . above all because of the fundamental pessimism of the Germanic mythology. . . . From the point of view of
the depth-psychologists, such an effort was, in effect, an invitation to
collective suicide; for the *eschaton* prophesied and expected by the ancient Germans was the *ragnarök*—that is, a catastrophic *end of the
world*.[11]

The invasion of this "inept" Germanic myth bathed in blood a world
that was unconscious of the moving power of the myth. Today the attempt
at literal enactments of the myths of the Messianic Age and the New Jeru-
salem through Communist and Western ideologies once again threatens
the annihilation of modern civilization, this time in a bath of radioactiv-
ity and ecological destruction.

Human libido is powerfully motivated, not only by biological drives but
by spiritual urges. The one can never be understood and integrated without
the other, and neither may be disregarded or explained away in terms of
something else.

The attempt to explain unconscious mythological representations in
terms of something else, the meaning of which we confine within our rational frame of reference and assume we can know beforehand, is actually a
denial of the unconscious dimension as an independent entity; it assumes a
psyche which can simply be deduced from consciousness. In this sense the
Freudian reduction of everything unconscious to wish fulfillment is also a
denial of the unconscious. Jung formulates his own view in this way:

> The spiritual appears in the psyche also as an instinct, indeed as a real
> passion. . . . It is not derived from any other instinct, as the psychol-
> ogists of instinct would have us believe, but is a principle *sui generis*, a
> specific and necessary form of instinctual power.[12]

The one thing we can under no circumstances tolerate is lack of meaning. Everything, even death and destruction, can be faced so long as it has
meaning. Even in the midst of plenty and fullness the lack of an inner
sense of meaning is unbearable. In Jung's terms:

> Ordinary reasonableness, sound human judgment, science as a com-

pendium of common sense, these certainly help us over a good part of the road, but they never take us beyond the frontier of life's most commonplace realities, beyond the merely average and normal. They afford no answer to the question of psychic suffering and its profound significance. A psychoneurosis must be understood, ultimately, as the suffering of a soul which has not discovered its meaning. But all creativeness in the realm of the spirit as well as every psychic advance of man arises from the suffering of the soul, and the cause of the suffering is spiritual stagnation, or psychic sterility.[13]

Thus the confrontation with the myth is actually a confrontation with religious meaningfulness in the sense in which Jung defines religion.

Religion, as the Latin word denotes, is a careful and scrupulous observation of what Rudolf Otto aptly termed the *numinosum*, that is, a dynamic agency or effect not caused by an arbitrary act of will. On the contrary, it seizes and controls the human subject which is always rather its victim than its creator. The *numinosum*—whatever its cause may be—is an experience of the subject independent of his will. At all events, religious teaching as well as the *consensus gentium* always and everywhere explain this condition as being due to a cause external to the individual. The *numinosum* is either a quality belonging to a visible object or the influence of an invisible presence that causes a peculiar alteration of consciousness.[14]

The religious attitude is

a peculiar attitude of mind which could be formulated in accordance with the original use of the word *religio*, which means a careful consideration and observation of certain dynamic factors that are conceived as "powers": spirits, daemons, gods, laws, ideas, ideals, or whatever name man has given to such factors in his world as he has found powerful, dangerous, or helpful enough to be taken into careful consideration, or grand, beautiful, and meaningful enough to be devoutly worshipped and loved.[15]

When we are in touch with universal meanings, with the powerful archetypal expressions which we have observed as being inherent in basic human nature (not mere constructions of the conscious mind), we find that new impulses enter our lives. Psychic development can be initiated anew, the energy at the center of the complex can be redirected, and we discover ourselves, in the process of discovering the "other," who attempts to enter through the myth, that is, to find its actualization in our individual lives.

6. Archetypes and
the Individual Myth

What we are to our inward vision, and what man appears to be *sub specie aeternitatis,* can only be expressed by way of myth. Myth is more individual and expresses life more precisely than does science. Science works with concepts of averages which are far too general to do justice to the subjective variety of an individual life.[1]

JUNG FELT THAT the central meaning of our lives can be grasped only through a realization of our own individual myths. These myths demand to be realized and translated into actual living, in terms of what is rationally possible. They must not remain mere fantasy or daydreaming. For "everything in the unconscious seeks outward manifestation, and the personality too desires to evolve out of its unconscious conditions and to experience itself as a whole." [2] When we confront the myth—the mythical (archetypal) core of our complexes—we confront the ultimate border line of our place in transcendental meaningfulness. We confront that utterly essential and indispensable element of meaning in our lives which had hitherto clothed itself in personal experiences and associations in the form of the shells of our complexes. Owing to adverse personal circumstances or traumatic conflicts which result in unacceptable forms of personalization—in pathological complexes, as in the case of the patient in Chapter 4 for whom authority came to mean personal exploitation—an archetype may find no channel for the conveyance of meaning; the meaning may be distorted and unassimilable. A confrontation with the germane "intent" at the basis of what has become a disturbing complex can give us a new direction; our personal lives can be regenerated. But the myth must be confronted with a full realization of its import in terms of personal impasses and problems; only then is there a channel for the new flow of life.

The individual who works seriously with the products of the unconscious finds symbols and images arising within himself which have occurred over and over again in the religious experience of all peoples—whether within the framework of an organized religion or not. Since religion and a religious attitude arise spontaneously from the unconscious as mythological presentations, they are not, from the Jungian point of view, to be identified with any specific belief or doctrine, nor for that matter with any teaching or conviction of the analyst. They are exclusively concerned with the individual's personal relation to ultimate reality, under whatever aspect it appeals to him most deeply. What they demand of him is not only abstract consideration in philosophical terms but psychological reorientation in terms of his concrete everyday problems, based on the symbolic understanding of these images which the objective psyche presents to him.

Again, this does not reduce God to "nothing but an archetype." Whoever objects to a psychological approach to religion fails to differentiate between the "what," namely the object of experience, and the "how," the type or quality of the experience. While the former is unknowable, the latter is psychological like any and every human experience. Although we can characterize "how" we experience that which has traditionally borne the name of God, we can never attempt to say "what" it is, what constitutes its nature. We are forced by our human limitations to remain within the confines of our psychological structure and this structure constrains us to use the symbolic "as if" approach. Thus we speak of a transpersonal "power" which expresses itself to our subjectivity "as if" it were personal guidance, and as if it confronted us, individually as well as collectively, with a need for meaning in our personal lives and destinies, and demanded of us that we strive toward the fulfillment of an inherent wholeness of personality and life expression.

Moreover, an approach to analytical therapy that concedes an objective reality to what we experience subjectively in psychological symbolism can do far more than merely relieve overt neuroses and psychoses. It can unfold the deepest meaning of life and bring us face to face with the creative sources of our very existence.

The dreams which follow will suggest something of the manner in which this unfolding occurs in analysis. It must be borne in mind that we deal with typical examples in an isolated fashion; that in fact these dreams occurred in connection with other dreams and discussions which referred to specific details of each dreamer's personal psychological problems, of his illusions, shortcomings, repressions and difficulties in relationship. This fact cannot be sufficiently stressed, for only in terms of concrete personal problems does the archetypal material fulfill its function of psychic renewal. But as we have noted, the conflicts between ego values and unacceptable drives, when seen as personal problems *only*, produce meaningless and hopeless suffering. It is by placing them in a wider transpersonal pattern of evolution and growth that the experience of the archetype gives a new impulse to the flow of psychic energy. Psychic life is then rekindled and takes a new direction; difficulties and problems that heretofore seemed insurmountable can now be dealt with or accepted. Jung puts it thus:

> If you sum up what people tell you about their experiences, you can formulate it this way: They came to themselves, they could accept themselves, they were able to become reconciled to themselves, and thus were reconciled to adverse circumstances and events. This is almost like what used to be expressed by saying: He has made his peace with God, he has sacrificed his own will, he has submitted himself to the will of God.[3]
>
> To the patient it is nothing less than a revelation when something altogether strange rises up to confront him from the hidden depths of the psyche—something that is not his ego and is therefore beyond the reach of his personal will. He has regained access to the sources of psychic life, and this marks the beginning of the cure. . . . As a religious-minded person would say: guidance has come from God.[4]

Quite frequently, in the later phases of life no cure can be accomplished unless a new religious attitude is found. This means nothing less than that the source of revelation is not closed for the individual who is in a deadlock, even though he may not be able to find a way in terms of the traditional religious representations which have somehow lost their meaning for him.

The following examples describe some of these unexpected "theophanies," these spontaneous intrusions of religious elements that demand a *metanoia*, a change of attitude (which the traditional New Testament translation of the Baptist's teaching as *repentance* fails to convey).[5]

A patient dreamed: "*I was in a place surrounded by old buildings. Suddenly there were explosions on all sides, the buildings began to crumble and fall, steel beams and molten steel were falling all around—a most dangerous, deadly situation. The only relatively safe spot was a small area with a floodlight shining on it. But there I was a slave and prisoner of the Nazis and death from their hands would be my lot. The only ones to whom the Nazi regime permitted free travel and who would not then be killed by beams of steel were pilgrims and beggars traveling to the Holy Land. As it was obvious that we were meant to assume that role we began to crouch and limp like beggars and, though I could hardly believe it, I saw that we were actually leaving that evil place and no harm was befalling us.*"

And again: "*I was in a classroom and Dr. W was the teacher. He seemed to ask riddles in a foreign tongue with which I was not familiar though the others understood it. I was about to give up, but just at the end of the period the answer came to me and I was the first to raise my hand. I said hesitantly: 'It is the crucifixion.' He said: 'That's right. Why?' I said: 'Because the tree represents the tree of life and the other symbol therefore represents Christ on the Cross.' He nodded, yes."*

This dreamer was a woman in her late thirties who came from a Jewish Polish immigrant background. She sympathized strongly with the goals and methods of communism, and nothing could be more remote from her consciousness than a religious outlook, least of all the Christian form of symbolism. Entirely concerned as she was with her own narcissistic and egotistical demands, utterly frustrated, disgruntled and haunted by the obsessive and paranoid impulses of her projected aggressive hostility, she did indeed find these dreams to be "riddles in a foreign tongue." For they informed her that while a first temporary island of safety from a destructive breakdown of her old orientation (the crumbling of old buildings) could be found through conscious insight (the intensely lighted area), much more was still necessary. There was still a mortal danger to her mental health from the Nazis, the ruthless and egotistical dictators within herself. Salvation could come only through humility and a submission to life as it is, through an attitude of patient searching, symbolized in the dream by the humble mendicants or pilgrims seeking the Holy Land. The Holy Land is also the place of crucifixion. There the selfish ego-demand yields to voluntary sacrifice. To accept voluntarily the suffering incurred by conscious living, by the realization of one's conflict-ridden nature (the cross), to yield to life's demands rather than to insist only on personal satisfaction, this, the dream asserts, is what furthers life. The answer to the riddle of life is the crucifixion. The cross is the tree of life.

The dreams alluded to a number of mythical motifs which were totally unknown to the dreamer: the story of the "Great Riddle" which, if it is not answered correctly, claims the life of anyone who attempts an answer (found in such diverse forms as that of the Sphinx, the Chinese tale of Turandot, Hans Christian Andersen's "Traveling Companion," and the East Indian story of "The King and the Corpse"); the paradisal tree of life which in Gnostic legend formed the Cross on which Christ was crucified; the dangerous pilgrimage, Great Trek or Great Journey which many myths say must be taken if a lost value is to be recovered; the representation of life as a learning process. Hence what was asserted in these dreams was that to live and learn is to live the "riddle," the paradox of existence, for which there are no simple or definite final answers—for in the myth each answer is followed by yet another riddle.

In Guardini's words:

These are secrets in the sense in which a great interpreter of difficult poetry texts juxtaposes "mystery" and "problem": the latter must be solved, and when that happens, the problem as such disappears. The former, however, must be experienced, revered and made part of one's own life. A mystery that can be explained was never a real one. A mystery resists explanation and not just because it eludes our investigation by ambiguous tricks of pseudo-truth but rather because it cannot of its own nature be rationally solved. However, it belongs to the same reality that the explainable does and relates to it in an absolutely honest way. It challenges the attempt at explanation and the purpose of this attempt lies mainly in showing up what is truly unexplainable.[6]

But that which supports life also crucifies us; salvation and the fullness of life may also come through loss or renunciation of what had appeared to be the only life—the life under the ego's conscious will, devoted to the satisfaction of its demands.

Thus the unconscious offered an image pattern of meaning to the dreamer whose conscious existence was at that time meaningless and frustrated. The emotional impact of the image pattern was as unexpected as it was disturbing in its paradoxical message, for this message constituted a direct contradiction of all her conscious convictions and values. It required that she relate to her existence not so much by asking, "What may I get out of life?" and "How can I protect myself so as best to further my own ends?" but rather, "What do I owe to life?" and "Where have I failed to live up to those sacrifices that life requires of me?"—in short an acknowledgement, in terms of concrete, practical life values, of a reality and existence above and beyond her own. And indeed only when it was possible for her to accept and test the message in the reality of living did her life begin to change, to take a turn for the better.

The necessity for acknowledging this debt to life is shown even more clearly in the following dream. It was brought by a man living in modest circumstances, who had decided to leave his wife and children in order to marry a wealthy girl many years his junior. He dreamed that *he was about to take a trip to a rather out-of-the-way destination.* "*Rushing off hurriedly, I passed a group of respectable-looking elderly men who disapprovingly shook their heads. Disregarding them, I pushed on, when suddenly from out of the clouds a huge hand appeared, took hold of me and shoved me right back where I started from.*"

This dream frightened him so much that, knowing a bit of depth psychology, he sought analytical advice. The dream indicates that what he sets out to do is "out of the way" and contrary to generally accepted moral standards (the disapproving elders: Freud's superego). It shows that he may disregard these considerations with relative impunity and still manage to get by. Something else, however, will not be disregarded. A power that reaches from heaven to earth does not allow him to proceed. Whether we call this power the inner judge or conscience, the moral integrity of the personality, the will of life or—like the symbolic image of this dream—the hand of God, we merely substitute various words and varying symbolic representations which all express the same thing: that is, an entity both unknown and unknowable, yet objectively real, transpersonal and supreme, which has been instinctively acknowledged by mankind throughout the ages in the form of many symbols and under many names.

Another example is the dream of a young man with a rather happy-go-lucky outlook who thought he knew all the answers and could afford to play forever. In his dream *he was in a boat, in a flooded market place, where everybody was hurriedly trying to rescue whatever they could. But instead of helping in the rescue work, he amused himself with picking up driftwood wherever he could find a pretty piece. While so doing he inadvertently touched a high tension wire and was electrocuted.*

The dream says to the young man something like this: You are living in a serious emergency situation, but instead of applying yourself to the job at hand you only want to have fun; in so doing you are forfeiting your life. And in fact about four months later the man suffered a sudden and inexplicable emotional breakdown and really went to pieces.

The archetypal motif here is the intervention, or *deus ex machina,* through the lightning bolt. Here Zeus presents himself in the disguise of kilowatt power, but he does his job just as efficiently as in the days before electricity.

This dream brings into focus a question often raised in connection with Jung's approach. Is this kind of dream analysis not a form of fatalism? Here is a picture of power, absolute power, represented as dominating one's life and demanding serious consideration. Does this not infringe upon human freedom? But let us look carefully at what this dream demands. Here the power demands that this man take personal responsibility. This man *was* a fatalist who said: What does it matter? I might as well play. It is the transpersonal power which demands that fatalism be abandoned, that personal responsibility and freedom of choice be accorded a place.

Another dream of this sort is one of a young girl who dreamed that *while she was lying in bed all of her belongings were being moved away at her mother's behest.* (This mother, of course, is not a personal mother, it is the Great Mother, the Mother of all existence; Life itself.) *Finally, however, she bestirred herself, realizing that if she did not do so she would lose everything she had. As she began to get busy with the few poor tools at her disposal, from every direction unknown people came to help her and what she could not accomplish alone was accomplished with their help.* This dream also says in effect that unknown psychic elements come to her rescue once she begins to make an effort. God helps those who help themselves— the very opposite of fatalism!

Following is another example which quite clearly illustrates that the acceptance of the need to relate to a power or powers beyond our personal control and rational comprehension does not necessitate, indeed does not even permit, abandonment of our personal responsibility but rather requires of us that in the domain of the personal life assigned to us our own responsibility must be exerted to its limits.

The patient who had dreamed of the pilgrimage and the crucifixion upon the tree of life later dreamed that *she was in an automobile with a frivolous chatterbox of a friend. While they were having a wonderful time, she suddenly noticed that their car was pursued by a madman in a truck who seemed intent on running them down and destroying them. They tried to escape but to her terror the dreamer realized that the driver of her own car seemed to have a secret understanding with the murderous pursuer and that she would be destroyed unless she herself took the wheel.*

Only by assuming responsibility for her life herself, that is, by "driving," incompetent as she was, would she be able to escape her pursuer.

These dreams speak a clear language. Our own efforts must be strained to the limit of our personal capacities; only the earnest assertion of responsibility and consciousness determines whether the pattern of force in the unconscious will help us toward growth and unfoldment or threaten us with danger and destruction; divine providence is no excuse for inertia; the will of the providential powers can be explored only through active living, never through fatalistic passivity.

But where is our freedom? If we are up against necessity, is freedom just a matter of intellectual choice? The answer might be attempted in this way: Freedom seems to lie in the capacity for conscious choice and voluntary commitment to the use of our faculties within the limitations of what is necessary and possible. This means that we have to be able to find out where and when we may or must choose and when we are up against delimiting insuperable necessity. Or, in terms of a frequently encountered dream: *You are on a stage and you are to improvise a poem or script and everyone knows the contents of the script but you. There you are on the spot and you have to give. Your freedom lies in the way you improvise the required action.*

In terms of the myth, here is an old cabalistic legend describing the "Formation of the Child."

God ordains that at the moment of creation the seed of the future human being shall be brought before Him, whereupon He decides what its soul shall become: man or woman, sage or simpleton, rich or poor. Only one thing He leaves undecided, namely whether he shall be righteous or unrighteous, for, as it is written, "All things are in the hand of the Lord, except the fear of the Lord." The soul, however, pleads with God not to be sent from the life beyond this world. But God makes answer: "The world to which I send thee is better than the world in which thou wast; and when I formed thee, I formed thee for this earthly fate." Thereupon God orders the angel in charge of the souls living in the Beyond to initiate this soul into all the mysteries of that other world, through Paradise and Hell. In such manner the soul experiences all the secrets of the Beyond. At the moment of birth, however, when the soul comes to earth, the angel extinguishes the light of knowledge burning above it, and the soul, enclosed in its earthly envelope, enters this world, having forgotten its lofty wisdom, but always seeking to regain it.[7]

Without consciousness of one's potentials, limitations and necessities, freedom is a fancy concept. This is why we find in our present age so much talk of freedom and so much compulsiveness and herd-instinct and lack of freedom, in consequence of the disregard of the innate "providential" necessity, the "individuation" necessity, which requires that we become what we are "meant to be." This of course may also mean that we meet with a deadlock in our lives when we attempt to travel a road which is not for us. Sometimes this deadlock may even in itself be insuperable, as in the dream of the bulging door. The message there was that the door was not to be opened; the eternal sources were not to be tapped.

We all too readily assume that a happy ending should always be possible if we behave "normally" and if everyone does what is "right." But the unfolding life pattern does not always seem to care for what we consider to be good or right. ("For my thoughts are not your thoughts, neither are your ways my ways, saith the Lord" [8] already expresses the fact.) Often what is asked is renunciation.

This was poignantly shown in the analysis of a highly gifted young girl who wanted to be a musician. One of her dreams was as follows: "*A bird descended from the sky and defecated upon my head; I felt that the excrement penetrated my head and made me slightly dizzy.*" Here the bird is the spirit, but behaves in a very awkward fashion; it does not cooperate creatively. Rather, as the drastic image says, it makes a "mess" in her head. Her high-flown ideas about herself are unrealistic inflations. Another of her dreams concerned *a field in which immense treasures were buried, but her mother would not allow these treasures to be dug up. Mother had decided that the field was to be used for a cow pasture. And so it was.* The dreamer's life evidently had to be lived in renunciation of her gifts. This was an instance in which the analyst saw and did not behold. I refused to accept the judgment, I was tempted to put my judgment ahead of the dream's, and the work continued. But whatever she undertook misfired. In fact, her neurosis grew worse and worse. She found it impossible to play for an audience. Eventually she became involved in an affair and had a child. That gave content to her life and the neurosis was relieved. This life, at least in its immediate phase, was indeed to be lived as a cow pasture. In other words, domestic life was the thing that eventually held her, in spite of her convictions and the convictions of her analyst. Only then could the destructive forces come to a standstill and perhaps a further development become possible.

Another kind of life-myth, quoted by M.-L. von Franz,[9] is shown in the last dream of a young woman who was about to be executed by the Nazis for her part in the student uprising. She dreamed that *she had in her hands a beautiful child and was to carry this child across a chasm to be christened. As she stepped across the chasm she realized that she would fall, and she did fall to her death. But as she fell she was able to reach the child across, and another hand picked it up.* This dream before her execution seems to sum up the myth of her life. Even as it showed life's termination, it bestowed meaning. The fact that the dream was recorded and published means that it must have had a deep impact on her—and on those who kept it for her.

The myth of one's life does not ordinarily appear in a single installment. There is a "to-be-continued" element and no single dream or situation is *the* myth. Each dream sees the myth from a new angle. As we go on the story unfolds and may even change direction. The myth for each individual is to be intuited from the total tableau as it reveals itself in time and space. The actual development is one of a constant dialogue which interacts between conscious and unconscious. We react to the dream, the dream reacts to our reaction to the dream, and so on.

As consciousness takes responsibility and makes its painful choices and accepts the risks inherent in them, those elements which may at first appear to be discouraging or seem to be closing the door may change their character. What we encounter as denial need not necessarily be final. A dream always speaks to the situation as it is. Hence it may show a threatening or hopeless situation under the currently prevailing circumstances, which, however, may be changed by the very realization of the existing situation, by means of the dream. For example, there is the woman who dreamed that *she stood before a forest and saw that it was completely dead. She was afraid to enter because she was sure something terrible would happen to her if she did. However, she decided to enter, and in doing so came upon a beautiful pasture where she found a white shepherd.* The dream says: As things are now everything is dead and sterile, but if you have the courage to enter, it may open up.

During the interplay in this kind of dialogue a new picture may unfold, sometimes from meaningless, negative or even quite destructive pieces. And it unfolds only as it is put to the test of living.

When he began to realize the extent to which the objective transpersonal patterns must be taken into account, one patient asked, "But aren't you afraid when you know that there is such a power over your life?" And, indeed, awe and fear are common reactions to the confrontation with the transpersonal. On the other hand—a seeming paradox—we find just as often that anxiety is alleviated once the will of a superordinated directing principle is acknowledged and consciously confronted.

This apparent paradox becomes more understandable when one remembers that awe and fear are presumably basic characteristics of human nature; they are part of our instinctual realization of the disproportion between the limited power of man and the immense, overwhelming might and grandeur of the forever incomprehensible Absolute in nature, life, death and infinity. One of the oldest images of the mystery of life, death, transformation and return is the labyrinth (the individuation path is also like a labyrinthine spiral) in which we fear to lose ourselves. Dread is, as Kierkegaard puts it, an intrinsic element of humanness; what it expresses is the fear of life and the fear of God.

This basic existential fear is governed by the same laws that govern all psychological activity. Repressed and rationalized, it retains a primitive, compulsive character and because of its unconsciousness is subject to displacement and projection. Thus, when the "fear of God" is not faced consciously we may become subject to "free-floating anxieties," or to fears projected upon sexuality, parental figures, authorities, enemies, etc. Any vague anxiety may, it is true, be the expression of repressed instincts, repressed sexuality, but it may equally well be a repression and projection of "primordial fear," of awe before the irrational, ultimate power of life which we call God. This is particularly likely when we try to substitute for this ultimate power a rational, mechanistic universe, or to replace a genuine religious attitude with a dogmatized code of moral behavior in the name of "true religion." Only by realizing the repressed fear and its implications can the compulsive anxiety be allayed. It is by relating to the will of life, rather than by trying to manipulate it, that freedom is obtained.

The following dream of a patient with obsessive anxiety illustrates this:

"I was at my usual place of work. Everything looked plain and friendly as usual, but I became aware of an inexplicable fear, as toward something unknown. I made sure that all the doors were locked. Then I heard a pecul-

iar noise in the adjoining room of what was now a castle and I remembered that the former inhabitants of the castle had lived there. Now only a curtain separated me from them and suddenly it parted and there arose the colored shadow of a ghost suspended in the air. He had the head of a Jew with a sharply hooked nose and fiery red hair and was dressed in medieval garb. The apparition was surrounded by a bright halo of light. I was dreadfully afraid of the immobile apparition and also realized that I was ashamed of the Jew. I thought, 'I shall pray that he may be allowed to return to his grave.' But as I prayed he became threatening and moved nearer as though to kill me and I realized that he did not want to return to his grave."

This patient was of Jewish background and had grown up in an atmosphere of well-educated, rationalistic enlightenment with a superficial Christian church affiliation, which to her was devoid of any deeper meaning. Suddenly now, she saw this world of "business as usual" haunted by the Jew, the ghost in the castle: something which the modern "enlightened" point of view considers "dead and buried," a mere environmental factor or a prejudice. But what is the Jew to mean to her? No doubt she had to become aware of her suppressed sense of shame over belonging to a minority group which is discriminated against. But the atmosphere of the dream, the halo, the medieval garb, makes us feel that it involves more than a modern social problem of group adaptation. It confronts her with an archetypal challenge, a spiritual issue.

Another similar dream growing out of a like situation makes this still clearer. *"Abraham stands before God who is Adonai. Sternness is his countenance and he says he is to be taken as a reality."*

In contradistinction to JHVH, the name not to be spoken, and Elohim, the Hebrew title of God, the name Adonai means "Our Lord." It therefore represents that aspect of the divine which is experienced as a personal lord and ruler. Both dreams express equivalent demands coming from the unconscious. To accept the Jew would be equivalent to accepting the archetypal Jewish attitude toward the divinity as "Adonai," an attitude which has actually been one of the germinal elements underlying all of Western culture. It means to accept a relationship to the transpersonal "as if" to a lord, "Our Lord"—not a vague ethical principle but a personal "Thou"— from whom directions, commands and decisions flow. By "careful consideration" of the reverberations from the unconscious objective psyche which come to us as the will of "Our Lord," we may find release from the obsessive fears which are due to a disregarded need for inner religious adaptation.

Is this, however, the best we may ever hope for? Are we always to remain slaves to that "Other" to whom we must adapt, or may the "fear of God" ever be transcended? Is there, beyond the experience of the Lord of Awe, also a divinity in whom love and grace may be experienced? An idea of the

direction of this inner development is given in the dream which follows:
"*I was in a room with a woman analyst. With great solemnity she said; 'I
give you a Buddha for your protection so you may carry it with you and
incorporate it into yourself.' Out of her bosom she took a little statue which
she had carried there and which had lived there. It was a statue of a little
boy in modern dress. I viewed the figure with great doubt and scepticism.
How could a dead statue help me? But suddenly it came alive, looked at me
with half-opened eyes and said something very important. Then I began to
trust it a bit more. And suddenly a new feeling of indescribable strength
penetrated me; it felt like wine. Also I had a dish of fruit in my hands
which I offered to other people.*"

The patient's personal associations to Buddhism were, "inner peace
through inner realization" and a relationship to the ultimate which arose
from an experience of a union with God within one's soul rather than
through a theological doctrine or an external creed. In the dream, therefore,
something is given to her which embodies liberation through growth within
her own soul. The experience comes in a form adapted to the mentality of
our time (in modern dress), in a phase of development not yet fully matured, still young and growing (the boy). By dreaming of her analyst as a
woman the dream seems to emphasize the emotional rather than the intellectual quality of the source from which the redeeming element is to come;
it is given by the "analyst within," the archetype of the *psychopompos*, the
inner guide. That which would be like a dead statue if it were a mere
intellectual concept, now has the power of life and "says something very
important" when it comes from the bosom of real feeling.

Finally the dream illustrates a mysterious transformation. Contact is
made with new sources of vibrant strength. The dreamer is able to give of
her "fruits" rather than merely to receive. That her experience felt "like
wine" hints at a resemblance to the ecstatic Pentecostal onrush of the Holy
Spirit upon the disciples, of whom the crowd said, "These men are full of
new wine." [10]

What does all this mean psychologically? When one has learned to live
with the manifestations of the "not-I" in an attitude of concrete acceptance, bearing one's seemingly inferior personal characteristics as a burden
rather than identifying with them and at the same time humbly remaining
open to the demands of hitherto unrealized transpersonal powers, a new
phase of psychological transformation is initiated. The instinctual drives
themselves may change character and consequently the needs for suppressive discipline or sublimation can be lessened. Much of what formerly
seemed evil, or at least compulsively disturbing, reveals itself as merely
primitive and therefore capable of constructive growth. The instinctual
drives thus transformed and matured cease to be sources of moral danger,

temptation or sin; instead they become the originators of new creative impulses and possibilities of expression which eventually widen the scope of the personality and with it the whole life.

A dream typical of this phrase of moral deliverance is the following:

"*I was given an ugly filthy rag. At first I would not even touch it. But finally after long hesitation I accepted it. As soon as I touched it, it turned into a beautiful snow-white shining cloth.*"

Subjectively, this transformation is felt to be a gift of redemption. Because it is spontaneously fulfilled through the changes in the transpersonal level of the unconscious, the constraining limitations of our merely conventional standards of right and wrong can be transcended. It is as though within one's own soul a new life had been experienced, which connects us with a new source of ethical decision that comes from an indestructible core of being which surpasses one's ordinary ego limitations. Moreover, although the experience is entirely individual and thoroughly personal, all those who have undergone it have usually used similar terms and images, again and again, throughout the ages, to describe the nature of the transformation. They say it is like the unfathomable mystery of grace and redemption, forever beyond our human grasp yet entering miraculously into our limited human lives. Symbolically, it is represented in the imagery of individuation, such as finding the elixir of life, drinking the draft of immortality. The holy marriage, the incarnation of the Holy Spirit, the birth of the Divine Child or the Redeemer all depict it.

The function of the analysis is to bring about the change of conscious attitude, the *metanoia*. This is the indispensable prerequisite for the transformation which itself, however, occurs spontaneously in the unconscious and cannot be brought about directly by any deliberate effort of will, or by any urging or suggestion on the part of the analyst. It is like a free gift of grace which is experienced by the soul in the course of living devotedly, in an attitude of dedication to one's life and one's difficulties.

Thus, another patient dreamed: "*After He has preached the Sermon on the Mount, He goes and tills the ground. He is the Green One, the Ancient One and the Young One. Now He holds a huge circular bowl filled with fruits. It all happens in an open church-like space and from every side people press and crowd in to see and receive their share. I do not crowd in. I know I do not have to see it closely. I can receive it from within, without physical proof or pressure. Triumphant joyous music pervades everything.*"

In this dream the Redeemer does not merely teach new ways (the Sermon on the Mount) but, as "He who tills the ground," shows Himself as a force actively involved and concerned with the troubles and labors not only of spiritual but of physical living. This tilling of the ground of earthly existence prepares for the growth of the "fruits" of this life. These are then contained in a circular bowl which, because of its shape, can be likened to the mandalas which are frequently encountered as symbols of an organizing center, that is, symbols of the Self, the totality encompassing both the personal life and the transpersonal life.

We also see that the redeeming force is experienced as quite independent of any particular creed or doctrine. Christian, Mohammedan, Jewish and Buddhist symbolism appear interchangeably in our examples of the spontaneous productions of the unconscious. In the last dream mentioned, the Christian Jesus, whose symbolism was familiar, is specifically equated with the (to the dreamer rather remote) Mohammedan figure of Khidr, the "Green One," who as the greenness of ever-renewed life on earth is Allah's messenger. In the preceding material, the same patient dreamed of the apparition of the Jew and the gift of the Buddha; it is as if the acceptance of the Jew, the submission to Adonai, had led to the inner peace which the Buddha symbolized. For the Ultimate reflects itself in any and every religious experience; what appears to us in the various symbolical presentations which we call God is and is not Jewish, Christian, Mohammedan, Hindu, Buddhist, Taoist or pagan. It is all of them and yet none of them, for it "is" not any "thing" but may appear "like" this or that, independent of theological preconceptions.

Regarded in this way, the outer forms of creeds, "the many-hued reflections," reveal themselves as symbols, as the "best possible expressions for a superhuman and thus only conditionally comprehensible content." Yet, when genuinely "realized," this content is, as the above dream puts it, "received from within, without proof or pressure."

Here is an example of a rather unorthodox revelation that set a new direction for an individual's religious reorientation. It is the dream of a young man of a strictly virtuous, puritanical, disciplined, self-possessed and scientifically-trained outlook. His religious background had become meaningless to him. Yet it had unconsciously retained its hold on him (as on so many of us) in the form of an overdisciplined, overrational, strictly legalistic do-or-don't, black-or-white virtue—a moralistic frame of reference which had stifled his capacity for spontaneity and authentic expression of feeling, as well as his capacity for love. He dreamed:

"*I prayed to have my God revealed to me. Then like a huge panorama opening up I beheld the deity in a cave, sitting in radiant light: a hare holding its baby in its arms. Awestruck, I fell on my face and worshipped.*"

This dream was profoundly moving to the dreamer, as the description of it conveys to us. For him it had the character and impact of a genuine theophany. But what a strange and—to our sense of traditional religion—blasphemous notion of God and the Mother of God! Surely, a few hundred years ago such a "revelation" would have been suspected as the work of

Satan and would have brought its recipient perilously close to the stake. Yet, whereas in terms of Christian theology such an image would rank as heresy or as Satanic, it is by no means absurd or blasphemous when apprehended as an eruption of archetypal imagery which has found a place in Christian symbolism only in a very marginal way. The hare is mythologically associated with the moon almost all over the world, in China, India, North America, ancient Egypt, among the Hottentots, and even in eastern Europe, namely in the Easter Rites and the spring and full moon festivals. As such it has to do with fantasy life, intuition, the life of the unconscious and of the feminine world, instinctuality, feeling, love, sexuality, even promiscuity—the hare, for example, is the animal of Aphrodite, of the Dionysian orgies, of Freya, the Norse goddess of beauty and love. Finally the hare is associated with regeneration through the unconscious—the hare as Buddha sacrifices itself by leaping into the fire. Hence the hare also has to do with the sacrifice through which the fleshly instincts are transmuted into the spirit.

This dream then would seem to be nothing less than a new experience of the divine, giving a new—and unexpected—sense of direction and meaning to the dreamer's life. It implies that renewal and redemption would come to him not only through the feminine values of intuition, feeling and love, but indeed through experiencing and accepting them in an ethical frame of reference other than the traditional Judeo-Christian morality. The reference to the promiscuous orgiastic rites of the spring festivals of Freya, Aphrodite or Dionysus cannot be overlooked; it has even crept into our own culture in the image of the Easter rabbit bringing eggs—of all things. As a symbolic statement of an eternal mythical truth regardless of the limitations of a specific dogmatized creed, this imagery carried a most important message to the dreamer. Once its meaning was comprehended, it constellated a renewal of life which to his individual eixstence was like the birth of the Savior in the cave to which the image alludes. What this person had to experience was nothing less than the. "divinity" of Aphrodite or Venus; to know that the instincts no less than the spirit are "of God," and to accept and to find a devotional attitude to the pleasures of the senses in sexuality *per se*. In Tantrism sexuality is the expression of the power of Shakti, the manifesting divine life-energy. For us Westerners, even in our "modern" outlook, sexuality is at best admissable when serving love or procreation. It is also fun, but it is regarded as "nothing but" fun when not serving love or procreation. It is not seen as divine in itself, revealing and leading to the unfathomable, to union with and a vision of the eternal. We forget that whatever is not offered up to the gods is likely to fall into the gutter. Aphrodite and Ishtar, made into the "Witch Venus" and the "Great Whore of

Babylon" by Christianity, take their revenge by drying up our capacity for relating to our instincts, for freely experiencing our feelings, and even for loving.

It seems that "man is free to despise mythologies and theologies but that will not prevent his continuing to feed upon decayed myths and degraded images." [11] Thus the sexual crisis of our time with all its confusion, smut and frivolousness, private orgies and drug addictions, may be regarded as a result of the loss of the divine meaning of sexuality, of the repression of the archetypal numinous majesty of Dionysus and Aphrodite. We must again remember that whatever basic archetypal impulses are not consciously integrated threaten to invade us through our "barred doors and windows" in a destructive fashion.

An impressive—indeed tragic—example of this fact has been demonstrated to us in the life and suicide of Marilyn Monroe, described here in some detail since it is a case history which is publicly accessible.

Miss Monroe is reported as having said: "I dreamed I was standing up in church without any clothes on and all the people there were lying at my feet." [12] Few of her early experiences correspond to this manner of relating to the world. Her mother had nothing of this spell over men nor did she have collective prominence, and Marilyn's own childhood partook of the sexual restrictions of a Catholic orphanage, the attendants of which are generally indisposed to such behavior. On the other hand, the problem takes on a certain intelligibility if we assign this pattern of behavior to archetypal sources. Even the most superficial of inquiries will reveal a correspondence between Marilyn Monroe's life and the archetype represented by Aphrodite.

Of course, this is not to claim that Marilyn derived this image from an esoteric study of mythology or from any other extraneous source. The objective psyche confronted her not only with the image but with the affectivity of Aphrodite. Granted, she probably believed that her dream and her way of life belonged to her personally. Yet this only confirms the contention that she was grasped unconsciously and compulsively by the transpersonal element.

How completely she was under the sway of the archetype we cannot say, although society's response would indicate that she carried the image without rival and therefore must have been closely identified with it. Also the world related to Marilyn in an archetypal way. Without awareness of the mythological tag of Aphrodite, our nation simply regarded her as its sex symbol and as a "Love Goddess." [13] Her own breezy response to this designation indicates its non-personal character. She said, "I never quite understood it—this sex symbol. I always thought symbols were those things you clash together." [14] It is evident on many scores that she was not a real "I" to the public; one had only to witness the singular insensitivity with which reporters swooped upon her following her miscarriage.

Even without a knowledge of the actual circumstances, one might further speculate that her captivity by the "not-I" affected all of *her* relations to the world as well. Embodying Aphrodite, could she be expected to see men in any position other than prone, in adoration? Her identity with the archetype and its consequent compulsiveness made her the companion of many male figures, to the exasperation of her various husbands. Finally, there was the inflation of being "MM" for a whole society, the individuals of which she could hardly have related to as persons, even had they been willing. She saw these people at her feet and they in turn felt this; so that the average man, while fascinated by her spell, would probably not have dared to touch her. In the grip of the archetype, all her personal qualities were relegated to a state of insignificance and undifferentiation.

Apparently Marilyn was invaded, possessed, by the power of the Love Goddess without being able to find in this force an adequate meaning which was ethically and morally acceptable since there was evidently no understanding of the profound religious importance for her of that which her dream portended. It is quite probable that the compulsive power of this archetype was enhanced by the lack of warmth and protective love in her childhood; for, as we shall discuss later in more detail, to the extent that there is an absence of adequate channelling, primarily through parents or parental figures capable of mediating the archetypal functioning in a personal form or context, the archetypal power cannot be integrated into an adequate way of living, especially in terms of emotional experience. It becomes a pathological complex, an obsessive danger. Thus the deity of love, not related to meaningfully, became an obsession, evidently driving Marilyn Monroe from one sordid affair into another and perhaps, since no relation to personal love and meaning could be found, finally into suicide.

This example of MM's individual existence foundering under the impact of an unrealized mythologem I consider no less significant than the example of the collective catastrophe of National Socialism. Both are illustrations of the destructive capacity of the archetypes when they are not consciously realized and constructively channelled. The effects are the same whether they occur collectively or individually and whether the invading power happens to be love, heroism, the search for the promised land or any other great human ideal.

The energy which is conveyed through the eternal images is *as such* neither constructive nor destructive, neither healthy nor pathological. Health or disease, growth or decay, depend upon whether or not consciousness is ready and able to confront, mold and integrate the archetypal energies into a concrete personal life-style, to offer a concrete life as material for the expression of the creative impulse of the mythologem—albeit within the restrictions imposed by the material at its disposal, namely by the particular personal capacities and limitations. Thereby the Logos, the Word, would be "made flesh" as the image of St. John expresses it.[15]

But we must also keep in mind that no absolute or invariably valid predictive standard pattern can be found for the way in which an individual life demands to be lived in order to be meaningful. The archetypal action patterns show an endless variety of possibilities, each applying to a particular situation. Nowhere can this be seen more clearly than in the immense diversity of fairy tales, which like the myth could be regarded as mankind's store of archetypal patterns.

In one fairy tale the hero comes to the witch's house and has to go in and kill her or he is done for. The next fairy tale tells him: Come to the witch's house, but as soon as you see her you had better turn around and go away or she will kill you. The next tells him: You have to come to the witch's house, and you have to go in and sit with her and eat with her and be nice to her.

One time the hero has to kill the beast, another time he has to avoid it—it may be the same animal. Once the wolf eats him and he comes unscathed out of the wolf's stomach; another time the wolf eats him because he is asleep and that is the end of him because he should not have been sleeping. Another time his life is saved by the fact that he was asleep. There is no standard solution.

There is, however, one thing about which all the tales and myths and stories seem to agree, and it is the only point of common consent of which I am aware. It always pays to be good to the animals and to pay attention to what they have to say—but with a grain of salt, for they may also trick you if they can. But never disregard them. This means, never disregard the instinct life. Never fall for the hybris of consciousness which tells us that the contingencies of ever-changing life can be successfully met by relying exclusively on conscious rationality and sensible rules, and that it might be safe to disregard the transpersonal dimension of existence which we have here symbolically termed the objective psyche. We may even go so far as to say that some dreams are ignored only at our peril.

But the fact is, we no longer understand mythological significance and have repressed the myths which characterize our time and our present-day religious tradition. This situation is no less catastrophic than that which existed in pre-Freudian days when instincts were repressed and their significance denied. It is no accident that schizophrenic fantasies (for example, the sun phallus) consist essentially of primitive sexual and religious motifs.

The loss of the mythological context results in the feeling of meaningless existence which lurks everywhere today as the result of our positivistic out-look and education. We have discovered that the highest suicide rates exist in those countries which are most highly developed both technically and rationally. We are beginning to be aware of the deep pessimism and sense of meaninglessness in our youth. In an article in *Life* magazine[16] this prob-lem is reported to be found in some of America's finest prep schools. A seventeen-year-old boy at Andover is quoted as saying: "I have no values because there is no basis for them. I haven't any goals because I don't know what to aim for."

The law of the preservation of energy applies also to the psyche. What-ever is repressed, while then lost to consciousness, still does not disappear. It becomes an unconscious compulsive force which then has primitive and potentially destructive characteristics. Repression of sexuality leads to hys-terical (*hystera* means womb in Greek), exaggerated pseudospirituality, typical of Victorianism and of Freud's days. But repression of the religious myth leads to the neurosis of our time, to a primitive mythologization of secular values, to a pseudoreligion of material prosperity, monetary greed and sexual thrills. Finally, the repressed energy of the myth contains also the threat of collective no less than individual psychosis, which those who can become aware of the situation have the awesome responsibility to at-tempt to transform.

7. Archetypes and Personal Psychology

THUS FAR IN our consideration of psychological response patterns we have given exclusive attention to the intrinsic factors of predisposition, general and individual. We must now turn our attention to the undeniable effects of environment, of parental influences, of conditioning and learning upon the structuring of personality. In short, we have to investigate how the archetypes are actualized in terms of and in response to given environmental data; that is, how the archetypes express themselves in actual personal ideational, feeling and behavioral patterns. It is important to keep in mind that Jung's concept of the archetype includes both the typical image as well as the typical automatic—that is, instinctual—emotion and drive pattern. If the emotion and drive patterns were not considered parts of the archetypal expression no direct connection could be conceived between the archetypal core and the personalized shell of the complex. Such a connection can be understood only when the personalized emotions and behavior patterns of the shell are regarded as special, namely conditioned, instances of general emotions and behavior patterns comparable to the conditioned reflex which is a special modification of a general species-typical reflex pattern.

To the student of Jung's earlier writings the interconnection between archetypal images and patterns of behavior and emotions would not seem obvious, for he would be under the impression that Jung defined archetypes merely as images (*Urbilder*). This was true, but Jung developed his concepts heuristically rather than dogmatically; he revised them again and again to fit empirical facts as he found them, without much regard for terminological consistency. Jacobi remarks, "At first the notion of the archetype was applied by Jung primarily to psychic 'motifs' that could be expressed in images. But in time it was extended to all sorts of patterns, configurations, happenings, etc., hence to dynamic processes as well as static representations. Ultimately it came to cover all psychic manifestations of a biological, psychobiological, or ideational character, provided they were more or less universal and typical."[1] Consequently, archetypes "are systems of readiness for action and at the same time images and emotions." [2]

> The term (archetype) is not meant to denote an inherited idea, but rather an inherited mode of psychic functioning, corresponding to the inborn way in which the chick emerges from the egg, the bird builds its nest, a certain kind of wasp stings the motor ganglion of the caterpillar, and eels find their way to the Bermudas. In other words, it is a "pattern of behavior." This aspect of the archetype is the biological one. . . . But the picture changes at once when looked at from the inside, that is from within the realm of the subjective psyche. Here the archetype presents itself as numinous, that is, it appears as an experience of fundamental importance. Whenever it clothes itself in the appropriate symbols, which is not always the case, it puts the individual into a state of possessedness, the consequences of which may be incalculable. [3]

In a further attempt to clarify his concept, Jung later distinguished between "the archetype as such," that is, "the nonperceptible, only potentially present archetype, and the perceptible, actualized, 'represented' archetype." [4] We may compare his concept of the "archetype as such" with the physicist's concept of "pure shape, nothing but shape," devoid of and prior to any material substratum but underlying actual forms. [5]

The "archetype as such" becomes archetypal image, typical emotional attitude and action pattern when actualized into complexes through the channels of personal experience and conditioning, predominately during childhood. We have discussed the manner in which the actualized archetypes—in the form of complexes—can affect our lives and have seen that their power can be either constructive or destructive, depending on the form of actualization and the attitude taken by consciousness.

In the process of being actualized into the individual human situation, not only individual and personal but also typical or general human attributes are to be distinguished. We do not realize this distinction in ourselves unless we make an effort to do so, but it is easy to document the spontaneous appearance of mythological images in children's dreams—such as the goat person (see Chapter 3)—or of totally unknown or even unknowable motifs in the material of adults—such as the tail or penis of the sun.

Mutual communication and social organization would be impossible without the existence of images and concepts shared by all. On the other hand, until we consciously set out to separate what is typical and what is individual in ourselves, we are constantly mixing up the two in inappropriate ways: trying to solve individual problems in collective terms and to deal with nonpersonal collective impulses as if they were individual reactions. For instance, let us say that someone's notion of mother is that she is a woman who always interferes, who never gives the child a chance to go his own way, who smothers his whole life and poisons all his relationships, and who by sheer magical power always knows how to interfere mysteriously at the critical moment. This "experience" of mother and mothering very likely is based upon a personal experience with an over-protective mother; thus it is a precipitate of a distorted actualization of the archetype of protective sheltering in one's personal experience. But when we look carefully into this personal history and get to meet mother, we may find that the picture is rather exaggerated, even distorted. Instead of a malignant witch there may be merely an average, concerned and anxious woman, devoid of the magical capacities which the son or daughter's vision has ascribed to her. Whence then the magical terror of the witch? This aspect is a precipitate of the general human experience of overwhelming magical power which every child experiences in regard to its mother. The incorporation of the power of life in its mysterious terror in the figure of a mother who thus inevitably is seen as a good or bad witch is generally human. Behind the individual mother and our emotional reaction to mothering—the shell of our mother complex—stands the archetypal core, namely the typical or archetypal mother, the mythological witch or Great Goddess. In relating to her or to any woman upon whom this archetypal quality (see Chapter 12) becomes projected we may all too easily fail to distinguish between an actual person and our personal and mythological projections.

The "archetype as such," the invisible ground plan, precipitates an archetypal mythological core and a personalized shell. Yet the images, emotions and behavior patterns—expressed in both core and shell—lack clear distinction as we experience them. The reason is that the typical, archetypal *core* material has a more general range of meanings than the personal *shell* material. For instance, the dream image of an eagle, hawk or raven, if without personal associations—i.e., simply as fast or aggressive birds—can be related to the feeling realm of spiritual uplift, of soaring to the heights through awareness. As such generally-known birds, these three are associated in mythology with the transcendental general human experiences which have been called gods: Zeus (eagle), Horus (hawk) and Odin (raven). If the dream bird appears as a parakeet or a lamed sparrow which was one's pet in childhood, rather than as a typical mythological bird, the motif has become personalized into an emotionally-toned individual modification of the general pattern. Instead of soaring to the heights, one's individually modified bird may merely babble or be lame; it will take the form of whatever image would most suitably express what happened to one's aspirations during the formative childhood years. In the personalized shell of a complex, the typical becomes varied, accentuated, fragmented, inflated or distorted. Both general and personal images and patterns can be called symbolic when we experience them as pointing beyond the concrete thing, person or situation which they purport to reflect (one's mother or bird) to an energy field which is in itself unfathomable except as it is thus represented and manifested. The image of the mother becomes a symbol when we do not (or do not *only*) take it as referring to a real or imagined person, when we see it as referring to a dimension of psychic experiencing, to the area of the "motherly," the carrying, nurturing—and destroying—energies in life and in ourselves. The unknown and unknowable "void," the "pure shape without material substratum," the pregnant energy potential thus actualizes itself in the materials of physical experience and becomes perceptible in images of what is knowable. The typical and personal complexes are the focal points, the forms of actual psychic experiencing, and through them we can reach back and touch the general and even the source ground of the void.

The terms *actualization, symbolization* and Neumann's *evocation*[6] refer to essentially the same process, through which an intrinsic core of meaning imprints itself in matter by becoming expressed in images, emotions, behavior patterns—experiences that are available, or at least accessible, to consciousness.

The term *actualization* expresses simply the fact that the incorporation of the potential into some form of the actual has (as such and *per se*) taken place, either unconsciously or in conscious and rational awareness; it need not have been experienced symbolically by the person in whom it took place. "Whether a thing is a symbol or not depends chiefly upon the attitude of the consciousness considering it,"[7] that is, upon whether or not consciousness can intuit a meaning toward which the concrete image or experience points.

Symbolization refers to a particular differentiation of consciousness. It expresses an attitude toward the manifestations of the actualization process which regards the available experience as a semblance of or a correspondence to an otherwise inaccessible source-ground, lying beyond that very experience.

The archetypal factors which form the cores of complexes are the general motifs of human functioning, the ways in which the motive powers of existence are experienced by mankind. They cannot be matched up with certain predictable environmental factors. In forming the personal shells of complexes (namely of our own emotional vulnerabilities and behavioral predispositions as modifications of and variations on the general themes) any archetypal factor may interact with any environmental element.

The environmental, associated circumstances can more or less harmonize with or oppose the general themes, constellating varying degrees of constructive or destructive aspects, or in the case of a missing parent, for instance, may activate them relatively little. The relative tension between personal and archetypal factors in a complex will determine the degree of its dynamic or disruptive effect in the total personality.

Parents and other personifications of archetypal energy fields can be viewed as if they were partial representatives, actualizing and mediating the hypothetical totality, and thus be seen as part of a wider meaning. Our relationships to the archetypes thus constellated and represented affect our relationships not only to the persons who carry the images for us but also to the whole world. The dynamic range of their functioning includes: as father—spirit, Logos, order, law, activity; as mother—life, emotionality, receptivity; as hero—daring, initiative, etc.[8] Inasmuch as ordering activity and emotional receptivity are felt as belonging to the masculine and feminine principles respectively, the first life contacts with father and mother set the basic patterns for the development of our assertiveness and our feeling. When there are problems in these areas they must be confronted and consciously re-examined in terms of these original encounters before a further development can become possible.

In terms of these typical human constellations of attributes, anything repressed or lacking in the individual will make itself felt sooner or later in some manner if it is at all vital to his development. The objective psyche tends to compensate for the one-sidedness of our personal histories. If properly approached it can show us our present situation and the areas which need further actualization; moreover it also tends to provide the pressure which eventually may force us to some kind of reaction and reassessment. This pressure may force us into a neurotic state when it is necessary for us to move and we do not know which way to go or cannot accept or channel the urges that arise in us. Psychosis may threaten when the energy of the rising images, emotional forces and behavior patterns is strong enough to overwhelm the conscious, rational frame of reference.

The conscious viewpoint is therefore of decisive importance. The more we deny or try to rationalize the complex, either in its personal or archetypal aspects, the greater the risk that it may disrupt, invade or disturb consciousness with its compulsive power. If on the other hand we "sell out too easily" to the archetypal urges by failing to take the limitations and needs of concrete existence into rational consideration, if we identify with the archetypes in their irrational manifestations, then we usually fail in the task of providing adequate channels for their constructive expression; also we may pay for this with psychopathology. An illustration of this is Kazantzakis' novel *The Greek Passion,* in which the actors chosen for the Passion Play fail to discriminate between archetypal drama and personal life and, in consequence of regarding themselves as Judas, Christ and Mary Magdalene, indeed become these figures. The result is madness and destruction. There is a third possibility however. The patterns of the typical human capacity for relating to life, representing our spontaneous talents and creative possibilities, mediated by the archetypal urge to manifestation, can be made available to consciousness. The prerequisite is that consciousness, while maintaining its stand in external reality and its awareness of personal limitations, not be afraid to confront the inner powers as realities and to experiment with their urgings in terms of what is realistically possible.

Archetypes as Patterns of Emotion and Behavior
In preceding chapters we have attempted to show how mythological images which express underlying patterns tend to set what might be called patterns of life for individuals as well as culture groups. These images function as leitmotifs, expressing basic undertones of meaning in terms of what ideally would unfold as a religious connection with ultimate reality. This mode of human functioning has become problematic today, especially now that our traditional religious forms and symbols are losing their expressive power. At the same time, many individuals are beginning to discover powerful images in dreams or fantasies which are at variance with traditional beliefs—those beliefs which they may still hold consciously and which determine the orientation of their culture group. Most people either rationalize these images away and disregard them or sentimentalize them in new faiths and cults. In neither case can they provide guidance toward a meaningful redirection of the emotional and instinctual urges. Thus our present situation is characterized by a split between symbolic images that are not adequately understood —or are disregarded—and the urges, which then run their own course in a seemingly chaotic and destructive fashion. Furthermore, failure to understand the images leaves a vacuum that is filled by ineffectual moralistic rationalizations. Even more important, we miss the fact that these images express not merely more or less abstract eschatological or mythical ideas, they give us symbolic keys for an understanding of the way the archetypal energies of which they are the representational aspects tend to motivate us as patterns of emotion and of behavior.

The following presentation of three actual cases which developed in similar environments may throw some light on the complex growth and interaction of archetypal and environmental factors and give us a glimpse of the ultimate mystery which surrounds individual manifestations of the eternal.

Three young men grew up in essentially similar childhood circumstances. Each had a domineering, bossy mother and a weak, over-rational, legalistic father who failed to provide adequate guidance, so that the strong masculinity in the family situation came from the mother.

Of the three, the first had a very weak ego structure, was subject to day-dreaming and impractical escapism, was over-emotional and in no way capable of standing his ground. His dream was as follows:[9]

He is in his childhood playroom, playing with a toy soldier. As he does so he happens to see the moon through an open window. At that moment he chops a stick, or (as it appears to him as he recounts the dream) the penis, off the soldier. The toy soldier turns into the stick. He breaks the stick and throws it under a tree. Then he sees blood spurt out of the stick and he is deeply shocked.

The second man was of a different caliber. He would have been a bit rebellious but was not quite sure how to rebel or whether he really should. Whenever he did, he found himself plagued by a bad conscience, because everywhere he ran up against *oughts, shoulds* and *shouldn'ts,* and rational obstacles. He had the following dream:

A soldier in ancient armor beckons to him; as he follows he comes to a place where an old man in white garments is seated. The soldier gives him a sickle; with his weapon he must chop off the old man's genitals. He is rather hesitant, but as he hesitates the old man becomes quite impatient and tells him to get busy with his job. After he has performed the task, the old man examines the results and expresses his satisfaction. The dreamer is struck by the fact that no blood flows.

The third example is the case mentioned in Chapter 1. This man had become quite rebellious in opposition to his domineering mother; he had rejected feeling and emotional values in a rather summary fashion and had come to rely exclusively on his own rational judgment and will power. His was not ego weakness but rather a cocky ego hypertrophy. It was he who dreamed of a sickle or moon-shaped sword or dagger and a voice which said, "This is the sword with which the hero (Siegfried) was killed" (see page 21).

These dreams present us with three different archetypal-environmental interactions. Similar environments here seem to have activated different formulations of the hero archetype. At the time of his dream each man had realized his personal impasse; the first knew that his ego was weak, the second realized that some action or activity was required, and the third had a remote inkling of the fact that he was too rebelliously self-willed. Moreover, each recognized that his childhood relationship had formed his attitudes. Now what, if anything, do these dreams contribute? When they are interpreted in the traditional psychoanalytic way, that is, merely "symptomatically," pointing to nothing but personal distortions, the answer would seem rather negative; they appear to restate what is already well known, namely the presence of a castration fear and/or an urge to self-destruction. This explanation may or may not be valid. At any rate it is of no help at this point toward a further therapeutic development; it does not add anything practically useful to the patient's or therapist's insights. The situation changes at once, however, when we recognize the mythological or archetypal character of the dreams. When we view them symbolically we can understand them not merely as statements of limited personal wishes, or fears or symptoms, but as "objective" statements of the psyche pointing to archetypal, *general*, human reaction patterns which, regardless of and even contrary to the dreamer's personal ideas, happen to be activated in each instance. We can then attempt to channel the flow of psychic energy in the specific direction it needs to take. For this purpose we have to recognize the mythological motifs expressed in these dreams, motifs which span hundreds of years from antiquity to the present. As is often the case with mythological material, our patients' personal associations were sparse. At such times the analyst has to draw on his own knowledge of mythology.

The first dream reads startlingly like the myth of Attis and Cybele.[10] Cybele was the Great Mother Goddess of Asia Minor. She was a moon goddess and her son Attis was her lover. When he undertook to marry a human princess, the Mother appeared at the wedding feast and struck everyone present—foremost her son—with madness. In his madness Attis castrated himself under her tree; or, according to another version, he hung himself upon the tree and died to be reborn the following spring. He was a god of vegetation. The celebrations of the festival of Attis included a "Day of Blood" when his worshipers would castrate themselves and throw their genitals at the feet of the altar image of Cybele, thenceforth to be her devotees and priests.

In this dream the dreamer, as the moon rises, carries out the castration ritual. He breaks, destroys and castrates the soldier—the figure of his manhood, his own hero potential—who has turned into a mere stick or phallus, and the blood, the real life energy, is lost. The dream says: The myth in terms of which you respond to your life situation is the myth of the son-lover, of the one who is hopelessly in the clutches of the overpowering mother and is thereby not a person but a mere means of instinctual satisfaction, a phallus; and in agreeing to this you yourself destroy your phallus, your manhood, in the service of the mother.

In what fashion is this psychologically true? In what way does such a person live his personal life *as if* he were a devotee of mother, a mere phallic satisfaction and victim of mother? He does so in the first place by continuing to function as if he were still her baby, by escaping from the realities of life and by indulging in an inertia of daydreaming and ruminating fantasy. For we must remember that archetypes take shape not only in dream images and personal relationships but in the way we experience life as such. So the dream says: As long as you are caught by and in love with the world of the Mother, in a fashion which breaks the soldierly attitude of will and initiative, you castrate yourself and you cannot become a real person; you belong to Mother, to the world of the moon, to the unconscious. Your male capacity for ego strength and controlled rationality and independence is lost in the endless cycle of the matriarchal world of mere vegetative, unconscious functioning. As a man and a person, the individual degenerates unless he awakens from this matriarchal enchantment. (The dream does not say that this state is final, as dreams sometimes may also do.)

There is a castration motif in the second dream also. But here no blood flows, there is no sense of tragedy or destruction but rather of accomplishment. Approval is expressed when the dreamer fulfills the command of the soldier and succeeds with the castration. This dream refers to Uranos as well as Kronos.[11] Uranos was the father of Kronos and had the uncanny habit of hiding his children away in the womb of Gaea, the Earth Mother, but Kronos overthrew and castrated Uranos with a sickle sword. Kronos in turn devoured his children until one of them, Zeus, in turn castrated his father and threw the genitals into the sea. Out of the union of Uranos' genitals and Mother Sea arose Aphrodite. In this set of myths, also, something is depotentiated but out of this depotentiation comes the potential for love. Both Uranos and Kronos, as fathers who do not permit their sons to live and become men, represent a principle which limits and would restrain growth by its hard, rigid, conservative power. It is a false spirituality, a rigid traditionalism, which forever prevents development of the individual by keeping it on the level of the potential (in the womb). It is phallic power, aggressive male energy, which in its rigid one-sidedness hinders development.

The dream of the second man therefore informs him that he must use the power of his imagination (the moon sickle) to overthrow the constraining rational tradition, the false limiting ideals, and to strike out with the help of imagination to find new paths. He is called upon by the heroic instinct in himself (the soldier) to overthrow, to depotentiate, to castrate the archetype of the paternal principle in order to come into his own. The patriarch himself approves; the archetype of the spirit demands this act for its own redemption in this modern form of the myth.

The third dream which we have already discussed in Chapter 1 warns the dreamer that the extreme position of hero identification arouses the counterforce of the maternal pole in a dangerous compensatory fashion. Siegfried, the sun-hero identified with consciousness, is killed in the Germanic myth because he insults the dark warrior woman of the fire-ringed castle, to whom he forgets he is betrothed. He forgets the unconscious, thus is felled by his own unrealized dark double (Hagen). This dream merely points cryptically to the moon sword. The disregarded world of the mother can kill; it must not be disregarded but must be propitiated.

All three dreams reveal that an overbalance must be redressed. However the reaction of the objective psyche is shown to occur in terms of quite different archetypal patterns in each case (in the son-lover, the son who overthrows the father, and the dragon-slaying hero who may himself be slain) even though all three men had been exposed to essentially the same kind of personal environmental problems. The dreams reveal this information in terms of universal human situations which have inherent universal answers applicable to these particular personal predicaments. All three patients came from environments dominated by overbearing mothers but they—or rather their unconscious predispositions—reacted in different ways, in terms of individually different archetypal programing.

The first was crushed as an individual and he reacted in terms of the son-lover pattern, whereby individuality is suffocated through emotionality. He would need to apply more practical sense and discipline of will in order to overcome his fascination by the unconscious and his emotional dependence on mother. The second was called upon to react in terms of the hero myth. He was endangered not so much by the world of emotions as by his inappropriate reaction to it in terms of patriarchal rigidity. He had to use emotional initiative and fantasy, the powers of the mother archetype, to free himself from the paralyzing effects of conformism, authority and tradition. The third was endangered by the force that would have aided the other two; too much hero attitude—along with too little reverence for the world of the "Mothers"—threatened to undermine the adequacy of his human functioning.

In all three cases an integration of the emotional capacities is demanded. But the manner in which this is to be accomplished is quite different in each case. The archetypal patterns indicate to therapist and patient alike the direction which psychological development is to take and the natural gradients, the lines of force, the structuring of the "energy fields" which are constellated. These, rather than the therapist's or the patient's ideas, are to be followed if the development is to lead to a fulfillment of the patient's true individuality. They indicate the frames of reference within which an organic development is possible.

Archetype and Environment
Our examples have shown us that environmental factors do not simply train a stereotyped adaptation pattern upon the *tabula rasa* of the individual, as the strict behaviorist might tend to assume. The environmental factors give variations of actual shape to specific, preformed patterns that are typical for the species; and more than this, there appears to be a highly

specific pattern for each individual, exhibited in the varied selection of the particular facets which are actualized. The development of the three different individuals illustrates three different interactions between given elements in the environment and given elements in the psyche; similar environments seemed to evoke different variants and modifications of the hero, father and mother archetypes. The universal manifests in individual forms —a given personality seems "called" to incarnate highly specialized facets of the total range of human archetypes. He will live these forms whether he knows about them or not, but their more constructive aspects can be contacted if he does know and can understand them.

It is interesting to note here that even behaviorist experimental work has already led to the recognition of preformed typical patterns specific for the species. In an article entitled "The Misbehavior of Organisms," [12] Keller and Marian Breland describe their experiments with pigs. They attempted to condition these animals for advertising purposes—for instance, to train them to pick up coins and put them into piggy banks. They report that the pigs conditioned very rapidly.

> . . . they have ravenous appetites . . . and in many ways are among the most tractable animals we have worked with. However, this particular problem behavior developed in pig after pig, usually after a period of weeks or months, getting worse every day. At first the pig would eagerly pick up one dollar, carry it to the bank, run back, get another, carry it rapidly and neatly, and so on, until the ratio was complete. Thereafter, over a period of weeks the behavior would become slower and slower [in spite of continuing rewards]. He might run over eagerly for each dollar, but on the way back, instead of carrying the dollar and depositing it simply and cleanly, he would repeatedly drop it, root it, drop it again, root it along the way, pick it up, toss it up in the air, drop it, root it some more, and so on.[13]

What came through was archetypal pig behavior! The article does not use the term archetypal; it simply states that the pig began to behave like a pig. This broke into the conditioning. The same kind of thing happened with chickens and with raccoons. The article concludes:

> Three of the most important . . . tacit assumptions seem to us to be: that the animal comes to the laboratory as a virtual *tabula rasa*, that species differences are insignificant, and that all responses are about equally conditionable to all stimuli.

It is obvious, we feel, from the foregoing account, that these assumptions are no longer tenable. After 14 years of continuous conditioning and observation of thousands of animals, it is our reluctant conclusion that the behavior of any species cannot be adequately understood, predicted or controlled without knowledge of its instinctive patterns, evolutionary history, and ecological niche.[14]

It is now recognized by leading biologists that there is a high degree of correspondence between specific predispositions and specific aspects of the environment. "All animals, from the simplest to the most complex, are fitted into their unique worlds with equal completeness. A simple world corresponds to a simple animal, a well articulated world to a complex one." [15]

Thus the "inner" predispositions, reaction patterns, urges, perceptive possibilities do not just accidentally fit and interact with "outer" environmental factors—the animal does not develop hunger or sexual urges and then just luckily happen to find food and sexual partners in the world—but the inner structuring of the animal is, in an *a priori* fashion, directed to corresponding elements in his own particular outer world; he forms a functional whole with them. Thus also psychic predispositions are not isolated "inner" factors that could be separated from the "outer" world but world and archetype correspond to each other and "that which our consciousness calls world and that which it calls psyche are not just two aspects of the one total reality but two paths of development of the whole which belong together." [16]

But in man the specificity is not only one of the species but also of the individual. Hence it cannot be sufficiently emphasized that neither archetypal predispositions nor personal environmental conditioning factors can be determinative *apart from* each other. There is no doubt from the clinical standpoint that childhood experiences and the relationship with the parents have profound effects upon the emerging personality of the child. We know from such cases as the "wolf children" that no human personality develops if an infant lacks an environment of human relationship. Children who have been totally rejected by their parents (there have been instances of children locked away in a room for years) fail to develop humanly. In other words, the archetypal determinants do not unfold when they are not actualized by the appropriate corresponding environment.

But the correspondences are so individually and uniquely specific that simple schematizations are impossible. Just as what would appear to be identical environmental factors may evoke differing archetypal responses, so may varying environmental elements evoke the same archetypal response. The conquering hero, for instance, may be called forth either in response to a very weak father or in rebellion against an overly repressive father. There is no simple linear, one-to-one, predictable relationship between environmental stimulation and archetypal response or between archetypal patterning and environmental unfolding. We can, however, discover a very individual kind of key-to-lock fitness and correspondence in the dynamism of the archetypal and personal factors as the dialogue between consciousness and the objective psyche unfolds in an analysis.

Stages of Actualization
It is important to know as much as possible about the way the actualization process occurs, how the phenomenal world interacts with the archetypal response capacity and gives rise to perceiving, feeling and acting—in other words, how the innate human mode of experiencing the "archetype as such" becomes actualized into images, emotions and actions.

The child develops at first in terms of sensory and intuitive (presymbolic) experiences. Between the child's percepts and the mature adult's symbolic intuition there evolves a graded spectrum of actualizations, an expansion of conscious experiencing, which could be described in three stages. In respect to the outer world, we have, first, percepts, then abstract concepts and lastly intuitive symbolic experiences; in respect to the inner world, we are first in identity with reflex-like automatic responses, then we develop conscious, rational, purposeful understanding and a rationalization of our emotions and drives, and lastly we can develop the capacity to experience symbolic meaning.

The first phase, that of perceptual functioning and total reflex automatism in a magical identity of the outer and inner worlds of early childhood, sets the stage; the initial and basic actualization of archetypes now occurs in terms of an infant's environmental identity interaction. The complexes, the units of manifest psychic functioning, are thus formed.

In the second phase, which spans approximately the ages from five through middle life (45–50) and indeed for many people the whole of their adult life, the archetypes enact themselves through shaping our rational frame of reference which we mistakenly regard as consciously or deliberately acquired. Yet our conscious ideas and convictions are but creations of the unconscious psyche, archetypal structures "filled in" with conscious ideational material. Subsequently we can become aware of the discrepancy between conscious ego ideals and the unconscious functioning of those deeper layers from which the ego has differentiated itself. Then we may attempt to correct the one-sidedness of the original actualizations by a rational understanding of the environmental factors that determined them. We then confront ourselves as objects and, in terms of Freud's *reductio ad primam figuram*, are capable of understanding the childhood influences that shaped us and that so often distorted our reactions. Through conscious re-education some of this imbalance may then be redressed. In the third phase, that of symbolic intuition, a glimpse may be attained of the element of meaning in the life drama which is being enacted through childhood impasses, adult inner and outer conflicts and the potential, mature vision of the transpersonal themes and actors of that drama which, with its unavoidable conflicts, is the mystery of existence.

In order to comprehend the whole range—from the simplest imprinting to the most evolved actualization pattern, that of the symbolic apperception of meaning—we have to see that the evolution has been in relation to the most elementary one which we share with animals and with which we begin as children: the reflex-like, instinctive, unconscious *behavior pattern*, in which perception, emotion and action still operate within the unitary field, undisturbed as yet by consciousness.

The zoologist Portmann[17] describes the mating flight of the Kaisermantel butterfly in which recognition of the female by the male occurs optically. The male is sometimes misled by a falling leaf or by another butterfly, although never by a yellow or white one. A patterned sensory stimulus is the attraction and olfactory stimuli prepare the butterflies for mating, while resting on flowers or leaves. A new state takes over when the eggs begin to mature in the female butterfly's body. She begins a search for violet leaves, because violets are the food of this species. She does not lay the eggs on the perishable leaves but under the bark of the nearest tree. Soon the caterpillars emerge and spin themselves into their cocoons. In the spring they are near the new greening violets; the unconscious knowledge of the mother insured this survival measure.

The important elements in the behavior of these butterflies are the varying inner states or "moods," inner urgings requiring different expressions. The searching is a compulsion to look for something specific, the nature of which is predetermined in the inner expectation of the animal, in a fashion unknown to us.

> The Kaisermantel has never smelled nor seen either itself or its kind; its caterpillar has never tasted a violet leaf. Nevertheless the experience of the sexual mate and of the particular plant which is to be its food is prepared in a pre-arranged fashion in its nervous structure, similar to the way in which a radio receiving set is attuned to and prepared for a specific broadcast. The individual's new and vital experiences are not really new for the super-individual system of the species. The "recognition" of that which "belongs" to it is prepared.[18]

These inborn response "patterns" have at times a most definite, specific shape. In such instances only a sharply defined correspondence of the environmental factor will activate them. In other instances the inborn schemata appear to be much more "open" and can be imprinted by quite a few variable stimuli. For instance the gosling will follow as its protector the first living creature it sees after emerging from the egg. Usually this will be its own mother, at times a chicken, but even a human being can fill the part.

Further, this imprintability presupposes a structural pattern which is waiting to be activated. In the gosling's instance, the required Gestalt qualities (form qualities) are relatively vague. In other instances they can be very precise. It is also of great interest that not only the fulfillment of relationship needs to others of its own kind is performed in this fashion, but also the image of the typical enemy can be inborn, inherited. Thus ducklings will crouch when the model of a bird of prey is held over their cage. The important constituents of this image are merely a short neck and a long tail. If one moves the model inversely, tail first, it has no effect. This illustrates how definitely such patterns are preformed in the central nervous system. Here is imprinted something truly *a priori* that corresponds to the image of an archenemy never yet encountered by the individual in his own experience.

In describing the behavior of the young cuckoo, which seeks and succeeds in finding others of its own kind even though it was raised in a nest of strange birds, Portmann uses the phrase: "the search for the external object never seen before." [19] His examples illustrate response-readiness of behavior and emotional states, structural patterns "waiting to be activated," or, as we term the process, to be actualized. Portmann stresses that he does not disregard the many situations in which experience and habit determine an animal's behavior, but that he is here demonstrating the existence of such "preformed patterns of behavior" in the sensory and nervous systems of animals which are oriented toward expected elements of the environment —the structural patterns that make possible the recognition of something "never seen before." The actualization of these patterns occurs through "enactment" in a unitary field where perception, emotion and action are one and without consciousness in our sense. This is also the first actualization form in infants and young children.

The analogous processes on a higher level are described by Jung as those of conceptual and symbolic experiencing, where image, idea and symbol are actualization forms of archetypal preformed structures.

> The organism confronts light with a new formation, the eye, and the psyche meets the process of nature with the symbolic image, which apprehends the Nature-process just as the eye catches the light. And in the same way as the eye bears witness to the peculiar and independent creative activity of living matter, the primordial image expresses the

unique and unconditioned creative power of the mind.

The primordial image, therefore, is a recapitulatory expression of the living process.[20]

And Jacobi says:

When the archetype manifests itself in the here and now of space and time, it can be perceived in some form by the conscious mind. Then we speak of a *symbol*. This means that every symbol is at the same time an archetype, that it is determined by the nonperceptible "archetype *per se*." In order to appear as a symbol it must, in other words, have "an archetypal ground plan." But an archetype is not necessarily identical with a symbol. As a structure of indefinable content, as a "system of readiness," "an invisible center of energy," etc. (we have previously characterized the "archetype as such" in these terms), it is, nevertheless, always a potential symbol, and whenever a general psychic constellation, a suitable situation of consciousness, is present, its "dynamic nucleus" is *ready to actualize itself and manifest itself as a symbol*.

The psyche "is, in fact, the only immediate experience we can have and the *sine qua non* of the subjective reality of the world. The symbols it creates are always grounded in the unconscious archetype, but their manifest forms are molded by the ideas acquired by the conscious mind. The archetypes are the numinous, structural elements of the psyche and possess a certain autonomy and specific energy which enables them to attract, out of the conscious mind, those contents which are best suited to themselves." "The unconscious provides, as it were, the archetypal form, which in itself is empty and therefore irrepresentable. But, from the conscious side, it is immediately filled out with the representational material that is akin to it or similar to it, and is made perceptible."

For as soon as the collective human core of the archetype, which represents the raw material provided by the collective unconscious, enters into relation with the conscious mind and its form-giving character, the archetype takes on "body," "matter," "plastic form," etc.; it becomes representable, and only then does it become a concrete image —an archetypal image, a symbol. To define it from a functional point of view, we might say that the archetype as such is concentrated psychic energy, but that the symbol provides the mode of manifestation by which the archetype becomes discernible. In this sense Jung defines the symbol as the "essence *and* image of psychic energy." Consequently one can *never* encounter the "archetype as such" *directly*, but *only indirectly*, when it is manifested in the archetypal image, in a symbol, *or in a complex or symptom*. As long as something is unconscious, no statement can be made about it; hence any statement about the archetype is an "inference." [21]

Thus, in archetypal actualization the empty but pre-arranged Gestalt-schema—the pure shape without material substratum[22]—manifests in material substrata, namely images, emotions and actions that are capable of being conscious inasmuch as they are part of the frame of reference of material existence, the phenomenal world.

But let us remember that the form of experiencing this material substratum tends to emerge in terms of the three stages enumerated previously—infant-environmental identity, rational frame of reference and symbolic intuition. Thus it may be a simple, unconscious, automatic life-expression comparable to the animal's instinctual responses. It may be conscious, in the form of concepts or ideas, feeling and rational actions. These two levels of actualizing substrata may also be in conflict or at least at variance with each other in varying aspects and degrees. This usually is the situation which underlies our conflicts in adulthood when we find that an aspect of an archetype has been actualized and habit-fixed in a complex but is excluded from or in conflict with rational ideas, feelings or actions. Then it is likely to break through as a pathogenetic complex or symptom. For instance, we may have been trained into an actualization of the hero archetype, into an ego-ideal of Christ-like good will to all men, only to discover that when as adults we are expected to hold our own and act aggressively and independently we are prevented from doing so by seemingly irrational phobias and guilt. Finally, when consciously experienced as symbol, as pattern of "transrational" meaning, archetypal actualization reaches its highest level. Here the material substratum points beyond itself, as it were, beyond the material time-space limitation of consciousness, to a "third" position, that of meaning which can reconcile the conflicts between the first and the second, the nonrational (instinctual) and the rational actualization.

But what is most important at this point is that we can begin to understand that all such diverse phenomena as instinct-responses, ideas, affects, emotions, behavioral habits, complexes, symptoms and symbolic experiences are aspects or manifestations of the same process: *the actualization of archetypes*.

Laws of the Actualization Process
The material network crystallizes around the "vehicle of meaning" through the laws of association, the basic ordering principles of the mind as it con-

ceives the world of the senses. These laws take two forms: (1) *similarity*, or correspondence, in shape, appearance or function; and (2) *contiguity*, or coexistence in time or space, that is, simultaneity or sequential order. The evocative effect of similarity, its capacity to evoke identical reactions to merely similar situations, is something with which we are relatively familiar. Less well known, however, and perhaps more important are the effects of contiguity.

Through contiguity, any quality which happens to coincide with a strongly affect-toned, archetypal pattern or situation becomes a functional part of it even though it is not essential to its meaning. For instance, the mustache which father wore, or the color of his favorite necktie, may evoke the memory, the feeling and the behavior patterns associated with father and may make one react "as to father" whenever and wherever a similar black mustache or necktie or even the necktie color is seen in later life, regardless of whether or not it appears in connection with father-like men. The intensity of the reaction will depend upon the emotional impact of the original conditioning situation and the amount of conflict between the emotion and what one might regard as the germane "intent" of the archetype.

Association by contiguity thus includes the phenomenon of *conditioning* as originally described by Pavlov. When a dog is fed and a bell rung simultaneously, and when the subsequent ringing of the bell alone is sufficient to activate the secretion of digestive juices, then the archetypal expression of nourishment in its actualization as a typical general feeding instinct and feeding reaction pattern has included the bell in its associational network as an individual modification through contiguity. Or a typical defense instinct will be activated and modified when the sight of meat has become associated with an electric shock; subsequently the sight of the meat alone initiates a defense reaction. Conditioning is thus an associative modification of the typical representational, emotional or behavioral aspect of "universal" complexes, making them individual, and possibly even pathological, if too much at variance with the typical basis or functional intent.

The likelihood of a pathological complex is strongest when contiguity overrules correspondence in the conditioning process, when the forms of actualization do not merely modify but are directly antagonistic to the fundamental archetypal pattern. In Pavlov's experiments, dogs strapped in a harness in uncomfortable positions fell asleep when they were tired enough. Eventually they fell asleep as soon as their "torture" was applied. Torture and sleep then became associated. But in another kind of experiment a whipping administered to an animal along with the feeding would not only make it afraid of the whip but also of the food; it would provoke inhibition and anorexia at the sight of food. The feeding reflex then became estranged from its own fulfillment capacity through the particular conditioning in which fear and the defense reaction became associated, by contiguity, to the satisfaction of appetite.

Extreme forms of such pathological conditioning are described by Werner Engel in his paper on the psychological effects of concentration camp experiences.[23] When work and torture were unavoidably connected, the positive values of work and authority were annulled through this conditioned union of incompatible elements. Two different response patterns—namely the urge to express oneself through work and the urge to avoid danger and torture—became inextricably associated and thereby formed a pathogenic complex. It often happened that a person subjected to this conditioning was forced into permanent inertia; after liberation from the camp he would continue to react with panic to the necessity for work. Also, for some, the camp experience in which survival meant continued suffering fused life and suffering into one complex and resulted in an unwillingness to live, even after liberation. Serious childhood traumas have similar effects.

All conditioning in humans and in animals cannot be unlimited and arbitrary, as behaviorism in its rather extreme form would claim; we have seen this most distinctly in the pig experiment. The *a priori* dispositions set limits and mark out channels of expression in animals as well as in humans.

Psychic Induction

It is important to bear in mind that the functioning of association is the expression of more than a merely mental event (as it is usually regarded). It also points to an energic process whereby a mental image or a formulation of the lines of energy—the actualization fields of the archetypes—becomes apparent. Like the iron filings in a magnetic field the associations point out the directions toward action of the motivating emotion and compelling drives. The association experiment has demonstrated that the two associative channels, similarity and contiguity, are actual "transmitting lines" for psychic energy; for in a triggerlike fashion, associated elements, whether they are images, concepts, emotions or actions, will invariably activate the libido charge of the total complex to which they are attached. Therefore, to touch a point of the association connexus is always like touching a high-tension wire that invariably connects to the source of the charge, namely to the archetype and the complex and their image, emotion and behavior patterns.

We deal here with a phenomenon which may be called *psychic induction*, comparable to the induction observed when a particle of iron is caught and arranged in the force field of a magnet and becomes itself a source of magnetic energy. And it is as if not only iron filings but wood shavings which happened to be scattered around also become charged (these being analogous to the contiguous elements). The part thus carries the energetic charge, the libido of the whole—*pars pro toto*, the law of the magical dimension of the unconscious, which is constantly demonstrated in primitive and psychotic psychology.

All elements associated with archetypal energy fields both express and activate the *total* archetypal affect core, as clinical experience demonstrates again and again. This means, for example: To the extent that our experience of the fatherly has been limited to an actualization only of a dictatorial despot, it may result in a pathogenetic father complex which will express itself in fear and resentment of any such person encountered in later life; yet we will also feel drawn to such a person, attracted to him in our unknown and unrealized search for the "never seen before," the unactualized other part of the archetype—the stability and protection, let us say. Thus our search for stability and protection will be made in precisely the wrong places, where it can never be found, either from the overly dictatorial man or from a merely overbearing person who features a black mustache resembling father's. A profound conflict of ambivalent emotions is the result, usually producing a "double bind." Yielding to the attraction increases fear and anxiety; resisting the attraction results in depression and unfulfillment, with attendant anxiety and vague fears. Moreover we find ourselves involved unwittingly and unwillingly and contrary to our rational judgments and intents.

This means that our contact with the actualized aspect of the archetype in any form associated with the real father tends to trigger not only the response of its corresponding, actualized complex but also the total archetype; the parts which have *not* been actualized but which strive for actualization are touched through the channels which are already available, although they are insufficient and inadequate for appropriate expression. There is a sort of vacuum effect, with a compensatory suction toward the unexperienced portion, the "search for the external object never seen before." Then we are drawn by a longing for the "ideal" father, mother, lover, etc., which is the more unattainable or unrealistic as the discrepency increases between the actual experience or lack of it and the unrealized elements.

When actualization is grossly insufficient, the drive toward incarnation inherent in the unactualized archetypal dynamism creates a correspondingly powerful compensating unconscious attraction; involvement in any situation which corresponds to the unactualized form elements takes place again and again with its accompanying double bind. We may then forever search for the ideal stability-giving father or the warm protective mother who was never experienced in childhood and thus find ourselves involved with the most unlikely men or women, notably those who are actually similar to the weak playboy we had for a father or the dragon we knew as mother. Deceived again and again by surface appearance, we expect from this kind of person what was never experienced, and we are bound to meet with disappointment.

In turn, when the actualization failure has been relatively partial, there is simply an effort to pour new wine into old bottles; the inertia principle leads to an attempt to put the unknown into familiar containers which sour the new experience.

Psychic Inertia

Newton's law of inertia—the fundamental law of bodies—that every body perseveres in its state of rest, or of motion, unless it is compelled to change that state by forces impressed thereon, seemingly affects not only "bodies" but anything which appears in time and space. In the psyche inertia is seen as a tendency toward habit formation and ritualization.

An impressive example of psychic inertia is described by the zoologist Lorenz.[24] Lorenz had a goose, Martina, which he raised from the egg. As geese do not care for human handling, he tried to train her to climb the stairs to his bedroom where she slept. He let her in by the front door but there she panicked and, instead of following him directly to the stairs on the right, she raced to a large window to the left in order to reach the light, just opposite the door. After she had calmed down she waddled obediently to the stairs after him. On subsequent evenings she continued to repeat this pattern, going first to the window before climbing the stairs, but each time she hesitated a little less at the window until finally she cut the angle to a diagonal and approached the stairs from the left instead of directly from the door. One evening Lorenz forgot to let the goose in at the usual time. When he did open the door for her she impatiently shot between his legs, straight to the stairs, instead of diagonally from the left. At the first step she stopped in alarm, stretched her neck, honked and seemed about to take off. However, she paused and, turning, retraced her path to the door almost in a panic. Then she started afresh on her accustomed course on the diagonal. This time, upon reaching the fifth step, she halted, shook herself and "greeted"—both signs that all was well—then proceeded to the bedroom door. Thus Lorenz discovered that a habit had become a ritual which could not be broken without causing deep fear.

This law of inertia, which is characteristic of all complexes, not only makes us try to put new wine into old bottles but is also essential for the sense of stability and permanence which is the basis of consciousness. Consciousness after all occurs in terms of permanence in time and space. In fact it would appear that consciousness and the sense of an ego rest upon this inertia principle, which guarantees a constancy and a fixity of experiencing;

it provides a set of standards for judgment and comparison. Only with constant values can we build and structure a world in which we are able to orient ourselves. Our sense of identity requires an established framework of memories, images and experiences in terms of which we can feel and express ourselves as "I." Hence the actualization of archetypal potential in the form of permanent images and habit patterns shaped from personal experiences would seem to serve as the frame of reference for the development of consciousness and of an ego, the central focus of consciousness. By virtue of this mode of development of ego consciousness, whatever has been actualized tends to become fixed and permanent, even rigid, as an essential part of and basis for ego development and ego stabilization.

The more threatened the ego has been by lack of a certain constancy in childhood, through lack of love and affirmation, the more the resulting instability is compensated by rigidity, by excessive psychic inertia. The original forms of actualization of archetypal energy into complexes, with their associated details—the first images of oneself in interrelation with the world —tend to remain rigidly fixed, even stereotyped, *a priori* frames of reference, by virtue of which consciousness orients itself. We regard and approach life in the light of our childhood values and conditioning, that is, in the light of our complexes. This would explain why our sense of being and of security are so tied to our familiar, personally-actualized frames of reference, stymying and destructive as they may be. Every challenge to our personal habit patterns and accustomed values is felt as nothing less than the threat of death and the extinction of our selves. Invariably such challenges evoke reactions of defensive anxiety, sometimes producing the neurotic and even psychotic fanatacism with which we are so familiar in individuals, groups and mobs. These defense reactions even carry a quasi-religious character, for they are concerned with our deepest relation to existence and to its mystery. Innovations, new or different "foreign" cultural influences, usually evoke rejection and religious fanaticism, regardless of their merits or demerits. We can also understand in this context the death and rebirth symbolism attached to any transformation process and the insistence on the need to "die" as a necessary complement to this fixity of existence in the ego alone. The practice of shock therapy shatters the distorted ego complex to the point of extinction; contact can then be reestablished with the hope of forming new patterns. Brainwashing causes the same kind of shattering or regression of the ego through deprivation, starvation, social ostracism by cell-mates, ruthless insistent attack upon basic outlooks and upon bodily awareness; this brings about a deathlike experience of ego-fragmentation which is then followed by a reconstruction in terms of the new and desired structural order.

As is to be expected, we experience psychic inertia most powerfully where parent archetypes are involved. Attempts to run counter to the established childhood patterns can strike the adult with terror because these patterns have been incorporated under the spell of what every child experiences as the parents' magical or god-like authority. The parents represent the fundamental elements of life and are the "great teachers" of mankind. They are in this sense the representatives of God on earth. Whatever has been evoked and trained into the child by them, especially the ways of experiencing natural life (mother) and order (father), cannot be challenged without fear and dread of paralysis, if indeed it can be challenged at all. The complexes conditioned by mother and father continue to function as if the pressing of a record from a master-record had taken place in the individual and as if the copy had then kept playing throughout his life.

An example may illustrate the subtlety of this process. An analysant told a story of going shopping for a dress, but when she found one she liked she could not quite make up her mind to buy it. It seemed to fit too well and she liked it too much; she felt it was too good or too fancy for her. A day or two later her rational judgment prevailed and she decided to buy it after all. But then she was beset by a quite irrational apprehension about going back to the store and facing the salesgirl. She feared the salesgirl would greet her with an angry "I told you so! You have no taste; you just waste my time!" As the patient associated to all this it turned out that these were her mother's reactions to her in the past. As a child she had been made to feel that only drab, sack-like, unimaginative clothes were appropriate for a decent girl. Her own inclination for more interesting or feminine clothes was condemned as poor taste. When after initial feeble protests she came around to mother's way of thinking she was invariably characterized in the above manner, which she now projected onto the salesgirl. Thus her "record was pressed" and even as a mature woman her ability to choose was stifled and she was prevented from finding her own standards.

Actualization in Childhood

It may help to clarify our view of the actualization process if we sum up the various forms it can take in respect to the archetypes constellated by the original family unit (primarily father and mother but also brother and sister). Actualization of the mother and father archetypes can be relatively favorable, along the lines of a harmonious relationship to men and women, authorities, one's own sense of responsibility, etc., in childhood and in later life. The tension of the relationship between archetypal and personal factors is then sufficient to supply motive power, but is not excessive or lacking as it is when actualization takes place under unfavorable circumstances in which the parental figures are destructive, oppressive or simply not present.

An unfavorable actualization will cause discordant relationships marked by defensiveness, withdrawal or inappropriate attraction in terms of the conditioned expectations. For example, if a man's mother functions as a saintly martyr, then his expectation of the life theme of support, love and motherliness has the motif of martyrdom. A martyred woman is attractive both without and within, as mate and as soul figure, even though the conscious view may be completely opposite. The unconscious refrain goes like this: A woman, to be proper, has to be a martyr or has to be made into one. And the anima, the man's inner woman, which is actualized through the way he experienced mother, makes him act like a martyr himself, unconsciously and even against his will.

An aspect of unfavorable actualization which is perhaps not sufficiently considered may come about because of an apparently exclusive and harmonious relationship to the parents or even because of an exclusively pleasant home atmosphere due to a deceptive lack of parental dissension. When the archetypal manifestations become too glorified through an unrealistically positive actualization, often the negative aspects cannot be accepted when they are met in later life. Also, in the face of so much "goodness" one's own negative aspects appear the more unworthy and wicked; they have to be ruthlessly repressed. The full human balance in which our lives operate and which is optimal for actualization weighs the black with the white. Needless to say, this ideal balance is rarely if ever to be met.

A special problem occurs when the personification of the archetype is hindered by the relative absence of the "key," the precipitating personal experiences: a missing or weak parent, for instance, or the absence of a typical situation. The absent or weak key fails to open the lock. The compelling urge toward incarnation of the image remains—indeed it is intensified through lack of energic discharge which normally takes place in the "recognition" of and interaction with that which is sought. Since conditioning through a human experience is lacking or frustrated, the image expectation has not become associated with and modified by human dimensions, human limitations and human frailties. It remains archaic, magical or starkly mythological, and out of touch with reality. The expectation becomes so exaggerated and unrealistic that no actual person or situation can satisfy it. Repeated frustrated attempts to incarnate the image condition the urge; it becomes a reflex-like shying away from further similar attempts. The energy which is withdrawn from the external world remains focussed exclusively upon the unconscious primitive image with its archaic numinosity. The absence of a warm, protective home atmosphere, let us say, may result in a quite unrealistic, regressive search, indeed demand, often widely exaggerated, for the missing key, which thereby becomes a lifelong obsession. Because of the unrealistic exaggeration of the demands which will not settle for realistic possibilities they cannot find even average or minimal satisfaction, thus they increase and a vicious circle is established. In seeking forever the love that our parents failed to give us we may make such unrealistic demands upon our partners that a relationship becomes impossible. Then we again feel deprived of the love which we yearn for and our demand increases with the same resulting impasse over and over again.

Another example of this phenomenon is found in the dream of a young man whose father was weak and timid and would never take any fighting risk. The patient dreamed that *he wanted to participate in a football game but noticed that the players were heavily armed with guns and pistols which they intended to use. Thereupon he decided to run away and hide in Copenhagen.*

The ball-playing symbolism is of the battle of life and of individuation. The ball, the focussing element of the libido, moves hither and thither in the conflict of opposites. Here the players appear in an archaic form—the ancient playing rites were in fact for life or death, with real arms; play and battle were synonymous.[25]

For our patient this frightening implication of the insufficiently actualized archaic images continues to scare him away from the contest of life. He takes refuge in Copenhagen, to which he associated Tivoli, namely amusement park, the only form to which his urge to play had become conditioned in the absence of the battling father. The result was inertia due to infantile regressive hedonism, punctuated at times with eruptions of frightening, uncontrolled aggressiveness.

Another patient, whose father seldom put in an appearance and actually had, through divorce, finally completely disappeared, dreamed that *after refusing to participate in a school football game, he found himself in a basement, confronted by a huge rat. The animal, full of hate, bared its teeth and threatened to jump at his throat and kill him.*

Here the phallic power of the biting tooth (the rat) appears in its most regressive, chthonic, infernal, inhuman form, in Hades, as it were, poised destructively, since its incarnation through the conditioning play of life did not occur. This patient had never found his manhood; hence, not trusting his strength he refused to play. The unassimilated aggressive energy turned against him, as it were, since it was not activated to be *with* him. This led to a suicidal depression. The above dream was dreamed when he came out of a coma, subsequent to an attempt at suicide.

To recapitulate: The first encounter, that between the child and parents or parental figures, not only actualizes but mediates—mediates between the compelling numinosity of the archetypal urgency and the capacity for human experiencing. Father and mother appear as all-powerful divine figures to the child; they are the first representations of the divine on earth; God is not only the projection of father, as Freud saw it exclusively, but father *and* mother carry the projections of the male and female archetypes of the divine.

Through experiencing the parents in their foibles and human limitations, in their fallibility and approachability and humor, the child experiences the fact that the "powers" within and without are not absolute (in which case only unconditioned obedient enactment or equally absolute resistance would be the only alternatives). They may be approached and related to, thereby their energic charge can be assimilated to the conscious personality instead of remaining fixed in interfering complexes. He learns that archetypal urges need not necessarily and always be taken at face value and be yielded to uncritically. He learns not to confuse symbolic urges and practical concrete reality. To act out a mythologem literally would be stark madness. It is always a question of how much may be realized in terms of what is humanly, practically and ethically possible. Hence the archetypes too may have to be resisted and bargained with—in order to assimilate them in forms of what is realistically possible, but never are they to be lightly disregarded.

It follows that parental inaccessibility through absence, remoteness, rigidity or brutality makes it harder for anyone to learn how to come to grips with his complexes, his inner powers, since he has not learned in their first actualizations as parents that they can be approached, related to, or dealt with.

Actualization in Adulthood

On the adult level archetypal actualization occurs principally in terms of the individual's attitudes to work, to his fellow human beings, friends, foes, competitors, beloved ones and to his social group. Only later does he become a problem to himself. The attitudes to work and fellow beings have by now been predetermined by his relationship to family, father and mother, conditioned in terms of social aggressive productivity and emotional interrelationship respectively. But the young adult usually regards them as expressions of his willed choice and individual thought and rationalizes them in terms of the convictions of ego ideals, *Weltanschauung,* through which he now attempts to establish his personal identity. Thereby he tends to overlook the archetypal basis of these very rational concepts, judgments and feelings. For they themselves rest upon his complexes or inasmuch as they are reformulated and acquired now tend to be conditioned by the dominant collective standards (or in opposition to them), by predominant philosophical, political, religious or simply collective, fashionable or Hollywood patterns, all of them variants of archetypal themes, coming and going according to their own autonomous rhythms.

Adult functioning then operates on two levels: that of the still continuing childhood-determined complexes and that of the conscious ideas, feelings and judgments which however are themselves partly complex-determined and also partly acquired under the influence of newly constellated personal factors, foremost among them being the urge to create an individual frame of reference, independent of or in opposition to what is felt as traditional and childhood-acquired. These two levels are more often than not in conflict or at least at variance with each other. And this conflict is projected to appear as difficult opposition or frustration from the "outside."

A person emotionally repressed as the result of his childhood conditioning may as an adult "believe" in emotional spontaneity and force himself to act as if he had it. This produces an unconvincing semblance that fails to bring about the hoped-for emotional response from others. For this he is likely to blame the lack of emotional spontaneity not in himself—this he believes he has overcome—but in the others.

The man who experienced the despotic father with the black mustache not only has a certain image of fathers and a certain expectation of the exterior manifestations of the world of law, order and discipline; he *himself* will act in a dictatorial, arbitrary fashion in situations requiring a fatherly or disciplined reaction. He will reject any situation which channels the archetype by means of the responsibility and stability which are not part of his actualized experience while at the same time seeking these attributes where they cannot be found. But it is in the external world and in other people that he sees and fights what in fact is his own "built-in" reaction pattern; the unrealized complexes are now projected as "shadow" (see Chapter 10), giving rise to endless conflicts and delusions.

If these are to be resolved it becomes necessary now to understand the formation of the complexes in the past and to accept responsibility for one's actions, as they result from the complexes in the present. Life and people are now to be approached by differentiating between the images which inform us (often mistakenly) about external objects and people and the meaning to be derived from them, when viewed as images of our own inner psychic structuring. Then we begin to realize external problems as reflections or projections of our own inner nature. Life as it unfolds for us informs us: "Thus art thou." [26] Our life-encounters give us a symbolic "as if" view of our unrecognized selves.

Psychic maturation requires that we become capable of recognizing the one-sidedness of our distorted complexes and the projections connected with them; it requires further that we develop the capacity to actualize and integrate at least some aspects of the as yet unrealized portions of the archetypes and that we suffer the conflicts which arise from the experience of the inherent ambivalences and mutual contradictions of the archetypes in terms of our complexes. This becomes possible through testing our reality in relationship encounters and being able to consider a symbolic approach to our affect-toned and problematic encounters and impasses as if they presented us with a mirror-view of our own unrealized natures. The need to incorporate what one's one-sided conditioning left out will endow with attraction—even fascination—those people who feature these qualities.

In a sense every projection may be viewed as an "intended" step to actualization. (In turn the process of actualization, if it is to lose its absolute, compelling character, must eventually be realized also as projection.) For instance, the tyrannical tendency which becomes part of our makeup through encounter with a tyrannical father may in later life repel us even when it is met as firmness and discipline in other people. It then becomes necessary to realize that the repellent element is the projection of the one-sided aspect of the archetype of the "fatherly" which has been actualized in us. By comparing and realizing the conflict tension between the tyrannical arbitrariness (which we project and now may recognize as part of our own makeup) and the other person's firmness and discipline (the projection "hook"), we can come to see and begin to experience that part of the archetype which we missed and might have continued to reject because we had no way of recognizing it.

Actualization in the Second Half of Life
Even in spite of our most heroic attempts we cannot reach perfection. The conflict remains between that which presses for realization and that which is possible between the partial childhood actualization and the unfulfilled, unexperienced portions.

Now the archetypal images impart to us what is potentially contained in the realization that our way of functioning is one-sided rather than the totality of a typical human mode of experiencing. To the person whose father complex has been actualized through a dictator experience, the world of the fatherly is solely in this actualized form. For him the world of order, discipline and initiative manifests itself in, and therefore *is*, despotic arbitrariness, for example. The possibility that he could experience this one-sided manifestation as merely the best possible expression of a transcendental encompassing archetype does not even occur to him when he is gripped by a pathological complex. The part which served for actualization represents the unknown whole for him and he is not aware that anything beyond this could be known. To him the images may speak now in terms of the "Old Wise Man," showing him thus what he missed and still has to strive to incorporate, in reaching out for wholeness.

In this phase of investigating our personal one-sidedness we can recognize the activity of the unconscious as concerned with unfoldment; it does not merely criticize and obstruct, it also shows us what the new elements are that seek expression. Dreams and fantasies point out the particular unlived, unrealized aspects before a symbolic actualization can become possible.

Mere interpretative understanding cannot replace living. In order to develop the ability to accept others we must first have experienced acceptance; in order to dare we must first experience the daring of a fellow being. Too much stress on understanding prior to experiencing, or premature interpretation, may even stifle a vital living experience. On the other hand lack of interpretation of our projections and failure to understand the symbolic character of our images, emotional urges and compelling drives may lead to irrational or destructive acts and force us into the same impasses ever and again.

In this actualization of the elements which have not been experienced before, two phases can be seen; we may call them concrete and symbolic actualization.

Concrete Actualization

As encountered first the new elements are relatively primitive and compulsive; we may sense that the fascination with a person who constellates entirely new feeling aspects is perhaps exaggerated but still we cannot free ourselves from its power. And indeed this may have to be lived through for the sake of a conscious experiencing in actual concreteness. It is frequently quite difficult to determine what has to be experienced symbolically and what has to be lived in concrete external reality, as it were. An unconventional love affair for example can be lived in the recognition that it may be the means for a mutual movement toward wholeness, an actualization of the growing potential in each person for as long as the compelling quality exists between the partners; or it may require eventually a full commitment in everyday terms. Or, in another kind of situation, our dictatorial superior may become more tolerable once we have seen our own dictatorial nature which was projected upon him—though we may also have to discover that the situation is still unviable in spite of our greater psychological maturity. It is important in any case to try to give the symbolic aspect its full due and to try to understand the meaning of what is happening in terms of the projections involved.

The personal encounter is indispensable for actualization and for the realization of our innate potential. Human fulfillment, maturing development and individual realization cannot take place through introverted analytical withdrawal alone; they require the encounter of an *I* with a *Thou*. But neither can the encounter lead to true relatedness unless it occurs simultaneously with an introspective inner search.

It helps our psychic growth if we can realize that the hero or monster, the selflessly loving protectress or devouring witch, are not necessarily the only qualities present in the people whom we encounter . . . not even our parents "are" just witches, tyrants or paragons of wisdom. Those relationships which arouse, beckon to us or repel us embody the archetypal "grand themes" which have been brought into actualization more or less adequately in our childhood by our parental encounters; now they confront us ever and again, making us renew old encounters or making us complete or compensate for that which is still incomplete. Thus our emotional encounters with others always constellate projections if they are meaningful.

Symbolic Actualization
Eventually we reach the limits of what in terms of change or accomplishment seems still possible, either subjectively, owing to our relative inability to enact all that which presses for expression, or objectively, when external limitations, standards or mores insurmountably happen to stand in our way, when direct incorporation would be simply absurd or destructive, or when we are faced with the double bind of equally valid conflicting necessities, virtues and fears. Then it is the meaning rather than the concrete expression of what the images and projections confront us with that asks to be made a part of our lives. What often is experienced as deadlock turns out to be an initiation into symbolic experience.

Many of our drives, particularly when unconscious, are animal-like, primitive, compulsive and potentially destructive to our human stature. Awareness and a feeling comprehension of their symbolic implications reduces compulsiveness and can lead to a transformation of the drives. Awareness of the projections and symbolic meanings involved enables us to *enact* rather than blindly *act out*, that is, to give conscious expression to compelling urges within the scope of the possible, the constructive or at least the mutually acceptable. The man described in Chapter 1[27] did not have to prostrate himself before every woman in order to be sexually potent once he understood and was able to experience the reverence for the world of the feminine.

Yet how are we to deal with the impasses which occur when we find ourselves faced with the terror of seemingly insoluble conflicts? What are we to do if we are following one valid approach which brings us into conflict with another, equally valid? When we become aware of what is happening do we continue in an old conditioned pattern which is inadequate or do we attempt to break it and find new paths? We might realize, for instance, that our old pattern involves being willfully domineering. If we try to fight it by telling ourselves that we have got to stop being domineering, we continue and emphasize the domineering attitude by applying it against ourselves—to no avail.

It is whenever we are up against such conflict situations to which no rational solution seems possible that a symbolic experience can lead us beyond the impasse. First, however, it is essential that the elements of the conflict or impasse are understood consciously and realized in the sense of being experienced as parts of one's own make-up and manner of reacting, and seen in that symbolic significance which points to our most fundamental inherent personality conflict. Then we discover that understanding and good will are not enough; compulsion and anxiety continue (perhaps even more painfully because of the awareness). We now find that the impasse must be endured, that our ego is powerless to bring about a solution. Psychological conflicts cannot be resolved by mere will, by consciously taking sides and deliberately trying to enforce new schemes. On the other hand that which we can consciously understand and which has real meaning for us can now be endured. Only suffering without meaning is unendurable. Whenever we attempt to take sides or to play one side against the other, we invariably increase the opposing force and thereby defeat our every effort. A psychological conflict can be dealt with only by holding on, with an extreme awareness of the meanings and implications, to both sides; by suffering the crucifixion, as it were, in the pain of the conflicting opposites *without identifying* with either one. This means that we must avoid trying to act out or change either side indiscriminately or inappropriately. We need not feel compelled to resolve the impasse or to do away with it.

This raises again the issue of the difference between discipline and repression. In the face of a seemingly insoluble conflict, awareness and discipline are called for. Repression is something else; it is the act of shutting our eyes in order to avoid the suffering of discipline. Repression will always call forth a compensatory counteractivity of the unconscious which will, through the back door, force upon us the very thing we are trying to repress. On the other hand, conscious discipline—deliberately planning, curbing or directing our acts in awareness of their effects, or renouncing action if that should be required—can be borne and is eminently human. Therefore we must first allow that which has been repressed to emerge so we can consciously experience it; but then we may have to restrain its destructive aspect and put it under our conscious discipline.

Conflict of opposing urges, feelings, duties, etc., thus suffered, eventually calls forth what Jung calls the reconciling symbol. This appears, not from the imagination or the fantasy of the analyst, nor from the inventiveness of the patient, but spontaneously from the unconscious itself, and the symbol is more often than not also an archetypal motif. It is an expression of the manner in which the objective psyche transcends the deadlock of unresolvable conflicts by the renewing, resolving or reconciling action of the archetypes.

A middle-aged executive, very successful in his professional life, found himself slipping into an ever increasing feeling of depression and a sense of meaninglessness resulting in inertia and isolation. He tried to cope with this state by willfully pushing himself more and more. But that merely aggravated the situation. Yet if he remained in a state of inertia nothing at all would happen. On the other hand when he continued in his accustomed way to push and force himself into activity, the depression only deepened. It was in the midst of this dilemma, for which his analyst did not have any ready answer, that he had the following dream:

"I was in bed with a young lady and had just finished intercourse. Then I heard a voice saying in Hungarian—my mother tongue—that I did not deserve the fa or fasz, I was not sure which, perhaps both."

In Hungarian *fa* means wood, *fasz* means penis. Hence he did not deserve the penis which is wood. He realized that in the dream he wanted it very much and that it was the girl who would not let him have it. This appears on the surface to be a castration dream. There was, however, no question of his potency or vigorous manhood, in terms of enterprising aggressiveness; indeed he was quite a go-getter and the dream made it abundantly clear that he had just performed quite satisfactorily.

The obscure language of this dream again alludes to an archetypal theme. The wooden phallus is a widespread cult object. In India at the spring festival the men dance with wooden phalli. In ancient Egypt the wooden phallus was carried as a processional cult object and represented the phallus of Osiris. Osiris was mutilated by Seth, his evil brother, who personifies animal desirousness. Osiris was dismembered and dispersed in thousands of pieces all over the earth. He was found by his sister Isis after a long and tedious search and made whole again. His phallus, however, was missing and Isis substituted for it a wooden one—not naturally grown but created —signifying a creativity that is not of the flesh but of the spirit, the phallus of immortality. With this phallus Osiris begot upon his sister the child Horus, the newly rising sun—consciousness.

To the young lady of his dream the man associated mere superficial success-hunting, impatient opportunism and materialism. Hence the phallus that this young girl—his extroverted opportunism—would deprive him of was the meaningfulness of spiritual depth, the creative power he lacked, which can be found only through patient search and renunciation of immediate material satisfactions. The dream then states: In your present relationship to your unconscious infatuation with success, you will never encounter the creativity which can only be found through suffering and patient search. It is not a question of doing or not doing, of pushing harder or giving up, but of finding a more fundamental meaning in both doing and not doing.

We are all, at times at least, inclined to feel that the reality of our lives falls short of our intuitive picture of some kind of completeness. But thereby we lose sight of the fact that the image of wholeness is itself meant to be a symbolic one, seemingly never literally or finally to be reached—a pole star that sets a direction for the traveler rather than a goal to be reached concretely. The way to reach closer to completeness then appears to lie in taking each step as it comes in terms of precisely what it *is* and at the same time *as if* related to an encompassing pattern. The symbol of wholeness helps as an assumption, but it can also become in another sense a real experience rather than a mere assumption. We can discover that, even while we feel fragmented, a sense of wholeness emerges through the attempt to see and accept *all* of the elements, both disruptive and dynamic, as they stand at any given moment, on no other scale of judgment than that of a meaning which ever and again must be discovered anew. One element not to be disregarded is, of course, the world of conventional standards— but that is only one and must be seen in its perspective with the neglected individual elements. Every human life unfolds around conflict. The conflict can be between individuality and circumstances; but it can also happen within the individuality itself as conflict of standards, virtues, urges and needs—as conflict of archetypal drives with other archetypal drives—and as conflict between fragmented or distorted initial actualizations of the archetypes and their innate urges toward wholeness and harmonization. The seeming inevitability of conflict among the archetypal "powers" can cause us to experience life as a hopeless, senseless impasse. But the conflict can also be discovered to be the expression of a symbolic pattern still to be intuited. It can be lived as if it were a drama, the play of life or of the gods, for the purpose of experiencing an ultimate meaning. Every drama proceeds from conflict through crisis to impasse or lysis and requires a villain— just as all music needs consonance and dissonance, uniting and conflicting voices. When one can feel with Goethe that "everything transient is but a symbol," then meaning can be found not only in creativity, joy and love but also in impasse, suffering and conflict. Then life can be lived as a work of art; one does not view it in terms of only one element—form or content or "being true to the materials"—but can come to see it in terms of the interaction of every element in it at any given time, all of them different facets of what we have called the myth of one's life. Conscious awareness in one's experiencing of as many of these facets as possible is obviously a fundamental task, a task which takes great courage and great capacity for imaginative experimentation with oneself—enduring and waiting, loving and suffering.

The Mythologem of the Symbolic Quest

The whole of life can be seen as a symbolic quest. This motif challenges us in the various facets and variations of what—to borrow Goethe's expression —one might call an *Urphenomenon* or *Urmythos*, an archetypal myth; namely a fundamental basic phenomenon, an aboriginal theme in which human experiencing tends to express itself. Particular mythologies, images and Gestalt patterns of feeling and acting can then be seen as individual variations on the basic theme.

This *Urmythos* can be postulated as consisting of certain elements:

A sense of the absolute or of the void, which is emptiness and fullness and nothingness and absoluteness of existence all in one.

Differentiation into separate elements; creation, which is separation or splitting of the all-one into the two and the many; the struggle which then arises out of the dualistic conflict; the need for redemption.

Search and suffering, love and desire as the urge for union.

Conquest, finding, fulfillment and union.

Loss and renunciation.

Redemption, the illusion of existence: redemption through realization of the "play" of life.

Return to or union with the all-one, either voluntarily or involuntarily.

The eternal return; rebirth and cycles of eternity.

These elements are expressed in a multitude of myths. The stories of creation all begin with the absolute void. The book of Genesis tells of the differentiation of the void into heaven and earth; the Greek chaos and the Chaldean Tiamat are similarly separated. The World Parents, Heaven and Earth, appear; creation means the coming of light—of the consciousness that separates or divides the aboriginal *One*. Then there is the threat or danger of falling back into nondifferentiation, as in the myths of the flood. Various myths express the battle of light against darkness, or good against evil; the hero slays the dragon of darkness and chaos, the hero wields his own power and embarks upon the quest for a conscious stand in the face of the Great Riddle or the enchanting power of regression. The light-bringer suffers, woos the princess, experiences danger, treason, betrayal, jealousy, happiness or renunciation. The hero passes through the ordeal or the torture or the threat of annihilation, finds wisdom and love, is crucified, dies and is reborn. These are the fundamental themes of which all myths are a part or a variation, sometimes emphasizing the feminine aspect of the experience but more frequently stating it from the masculine viewpoint. (In our Christian culture a familiar expression of this grand theme is the Credo of the Mass: the affirmation of belief in God, the creator, out of which was incarnated the Son who lived, suffered, died and rose again and will return.)

The hero or heroine's quest and his or her encounter with mythological antagonists can be summarized in psychological language as the ego's encounter with the ever-recurring typical form elements of the psyche. For everyone who works with the unconscious there arise the problems of initial adaptation to the outer and inner worlds (psychological types); the containing collective group (persona); the conflict with the repressed or unacceptable part of one's personality (shadow); the necessity to establish a relationship with the contrasexual background elements in the psyche—male (anima) or female (animus); and finally the encounter with the suprapersonal core of one's total personality and life-meaning (Self). In the sense that persona, shadow, anima, animus and Self are typical psychic configurations which express themselves as personalized complexes and have mythological cores, they may be regarded as archetypes. In actual dreams and fantasies they are represented in either personal or mythological images, depending upon the aspect stressed. Thus the anima may appear as Mary Jones or as a vegetation goddess, the shadow as a cruel king or the corner druggist. Always, however, their integration requires the assimilation of both the specifically personal and the general religious or mythological dimension.

8. Psychological Types

THE PRINCIPAL WAYS in which the ego meets the outer world as well as the inner world of the unconscious find their expression in what Jung classifies as his psychological types. The structure of the ego complex itself will be dealt with in a subsequent chapter.[1] Concerning the types Jung remarks:

> It is one's psychological type which from the outset determines and limits a person's judgment. My book [Psychological Types], therefore, was an effort to deal with the relationship of the individual to the world, to people, and things. It discussed the various aspects of consciousness, the various attitudes the conscious mind might take toward the world, and thus constitutes a psychology of consciousness regarded from what might be called a clinical angle.[2]

> In the course of many years I have had to treat innumerable married couples and have been faced with the task of making the standpoints of husband and wife mutually plausible. How many times, for example, have I not had to say: "Look here, your wife has a very active nature, and it cannot be expected that her whole existence should center round housekeeping." This is the beginning of a type-theory, a sort of statistical truth: there are active natures and passive ones. . . . There is a whole class of men who at the moment of reaction to a given situation at first draw back a little as if with an unvoiced "no," and only after that are able to react; and there is another class who, in the same situation, come forward with an immediate reaction, apparently confident that their behaviour is obviously right. The former class would therefore be characterized by a certain negative relation to the object, and the latter by a positive one.[3]

This constitutes a simple exposition of the type question as such, as well as of the attitudes of introversion and extraversion. Types are classes, groups of people with similar reaction patterns, typical attitudes that constitute

an essential bias which conditions the whole psychic process, establishes the habitual reactions, and thus determines not only the style of
behaviour, but also the nature of subjective experience. And not only
so, but it also denotes the kind of compensatory activity of the unconscious which we may expect to find.[4]

Jung calls such a habitual reaction a psychic *function*, which he defines
as

> a certain form of psychic activity that remains theoretically the same
> under varying circumstances . . . a phenomenal form of libido which
> theoretically remains constant. . . . I distinguish four basic functions
> in all, two rational and two irrational—viz. *thinking* and *feeling, sensa-
> tion* and *intuition.* I can give no a priori reason for selecting just these
> four as basic functions; I can only point to the fact that this concep-
> tion has shaped itself out of many years' experience. I differentiate
> these functions from one another, because they are neither mutually
> relatable nor mutually reducible.[5]

Extraversion and Introversion
Types are, in the first place, either extraverted or introverted. The extravert
is a person whose consciousness is predominantly directed toward external
objects—toward the outside world. The introvert is predominantly subject-
oriented—toward the inner world of the psyche; to him psychic reality is a
relatively concrete experience, sometimes even more concrete than external
reality.

Until Jung pointed out that these two types exist and are psychologically
of equal validity (and in fact need each other), introversion was used practically synonymously with autism or the schizophrenic tendency. In old
textbooks of psychiatry the schizoid person is frequently called an introverted or autistic person, both terms referring to the same psychological
state. In less obvious ways our culture still has a profound distrust of the
introvert and this attitude has serious implications for the introverted child,
who invariably finds himself at a disadvantage. The world of adolescence is
typically an extraverted world, depending largely upon reassuring adaptational cues from the environment; and in addition to having to swim
against this strong current the introvert finds he must struggle against an
educational system which suspects and discourages his kind of adaptation.
He is exhorted to be an individual, but he must beware if he tries. Many
adolescent depressions are due to this cultural attitude. The introverted
adolescent cannot easily find his place in this world if he is not "in" with
the crowd. There is, however, a certain justice, for in the second half of life

it is often the extravert who has the more difficult time, because as outer values recede he is more likely to find himself faced with meaninglessness. The introvert is likely to experience a sense of deliverance when he discovers the validity of his leading function; he has for the first time a feeling that he has come into his own and is able to breathe.

Both introversion and extraversion are present in every personality. To the extent that the conscious adaptation moves toward one, the other operates in a compensatory fashion, as part of and through the unconscious. This means that the introvert will suffer compensatory reactions from his primitive, unadapted, extraverted side and vice versa. The result of this is that each fears the realm in which the other is at home. The introvert instinctively pulls away from the external world; he has an object fear. People and objects have a peculiar way of tripping him up. He mistrusts them and expects the worst of them. The extravert has a subject fear; he mistrusts the inner world. He undervalues his inner self and projects this lack of self-valuation; the extravert's typical complaint is that nobody appreciates him or takes him seriously.

The Four Functions

Introvert and *extravert* describe the two basic types; these themes have their variations in the perceiving and judging functions. The perceiving functions are those of *sensation* and *intuition;* the judging functions are *thinking* and *feeling.* Jung has called the latter "rational" functions. This term, again, has given rise to some misunderstandings because in colloquial speech when we say "rational" we mean the logical form of conscious thinking. Feeling would not be termed rational in common usage. Therefore I prefer for clarity's sake to describe the functions of thinking and feeling as judging, apperceptual or interpretative functions.

Thinking and feeling, then, have to do with the order- or value-system to which we subject the findings or results of the perceiving functions. Thinking and feeling arrange the results of sensation and intuition into some sort of orderly system.

Thinking pertains to the objective interrelating of the elements which are perceived. When we say that four legs with a slab balanced on top will stand and will support the dishes we put on it, we perform an act of thinking. We have related the various elements to each other and have made a statement of which we are not a part. These are objective facts; this is so or this is not so, and it has nothing to do with us. It is, in other words, an objective judgment.

"Thinking," Jung says, "brings given presentations into conceptual connections." [6] It establishes connections of conceptual order between the representations which come to us as the result of perception, whether intuitive or through the senses. Thinking establishes a sequence of orderly connections among the observed facts, and is in this sense a manifestation of the archetypal drive toward order and meaning. It is one of the manifestations of the logos aspect of the Yang archetype (see Chapter 11); people have at times quite a compulsive need to establish orderly connections and to assume that these are also inherent in nature.

We discussed the two types of thinking at some length in Chapter 1.[7] Jung differentiates between active thinking which is will-determined, and passive thinking which is intuitive and associative.

Active thinking submits representations to a deliberate act of rational judgment and to a deliberate order or sequence whereby that which seems of necessity to follow a given event is regarded as being *caused by* the event. It is important to realize that the assumption of logical causation is imposed on given facts. This assumption gives us no end of difficulty when we are dealing with sequences of facts which are not readily amenable to this sort of approach, that is, those facts which Jung has called non-causal, acausal or synchronistic.

Passive thinking, as noted, has been called autistic thinking. It is fantasy thinking or intuitive thinking, of which Jung says:

Conceptual connections establish themselves, and judgments are formed which may even contradict my aim—they may lack all harmony with my conscious objective, hence also, for me, any feeling of direction, although by an act of active apperception I may subsequently come to a recognition of their directedness.[8]

In other words, I discover that representations follow each other in a fashion which I do not intend them to and which is not logical at all. I think of my fountain pen, then the aunt who gave me the fountain pen, her green hat, the bird that was as green as her hat, the cage in which the bird lived, the smell of the cage, the next door neighbor and so on. This is associative, passive thinking. It has, as practical dream interpretation shows, a definite and inexorable directedness and purposefulness of its own. In many situations it will lead more definitely to what we need to know than will directed logical thinking, although its goal will be very unexpected.

The two types of thinking cannot be engaged in simultaneously but the same person may be perfectly at home in both. The intuitive introverted thinking type usually can use both with ease.

Passive thinking is comparatively unconscious and is in a relatively loose connection with ego activity. Thus, a function which we usually consider to be the most consciously developed may actually operate in relative unconsciousness. Thinking is not necessarily something that the subject does himself, actively; it can also happen to him through the objective psyche. Thinking can be a conscious, willed activity, but it can also be autonomous in the sense that it takes the form of unconscious associational fantasies. It is, in other words, a prejudice to assume that it is necessarily our conscious selves who "do" either thinking or feeling. Feelings happen as moods; thoughts occur, regardless of our conscious will. Neither thinking nor feeling need be related to the conscious subject at all. Hence it is an error to assume that we can control our thoughts, not to mention our feelings, simply by resolving to do so. The popular slogans regarding positive and negative feelings and the power of positive thinking may all too readily induce us to turn our backs on those thoughts and feelings that do not meet our specifications. At times this may be necessary; but if used habitually as a way of avoiding conscious confrontation of undesired thoughts or emotions it is a way of repression. We may then no longer have these rejected feelings, but they will have us. We cannot choose to have thoughts or feelings that will not come, nor can we choose not to have those that do. We can at most fortify the energic charge of certain thoughts and feelings and direct others into more acceptable channels; but this is possible only through conscious confrontation, not by avoidance. If we try to disregard the main trend of the autonomous elements they will sooner or later exert their countereffect.

A fully realized thinking function would require the development of the capacity for direct thinking in logical channels as well as the capacity for consciously following the trends of fantasy activity.

Feeling has to do with the expression of the value which we give to that which we perceive. When we say that we do not like this table or that the table appeals to us, we have given a personal value to what we have perceived. Feeling, then, is a subjective value judgment. We cannot judge objectively and subjectively at the same time; we cannot simultaneously both exclude and include ourselves in the judgment. If for instance a judge decides subjectively, he will acquit or condemn the man whom he likes or dislikes; but to the extent that he is objective he will keep his feelings out of the matter. Thinking and feeling are mutually exclusive in simultaneity; to the extent that we lean toward the one we disregard the other. Feeling classifies the perceived contents in terms of their value to the observer. The system of order thus established is one of involvement rather than one of objective distance. It expresses our interaction with things and people in shades of rejection or acceptance.

There is a vaguer form of feeling which comes to us as moods. Moods are also value reactions, but they are not fully conscious. We unconsciously accept or reject a situation, are pleased or not, comfortable or uncomfortable. The less we are aware of specific feelings—the less we have consciously developed and used our capacity for feeling—the more we are subject to moods.

Sensation is concrete perception of objects and people by means of our five senses. It provides the basic framework of our lives and in its unalloyed state renders us the experience of what we commonly regard as reality in its most direct and simple form. Our senses tell us what *is*. *Intuition*, on the other hand, tells us what to all seemingly obvious appearances *is not*, at least so far as the senses are concerned. We may not be able to see, hear, smell, touch or taste something, but we perceive possibilities and probabilities as if they were presences. Intuition is a form of perception that comes to us directly from the unconscious. Yet this function, like undirected thinking, can be consciously developed and used although its mode of operation is not within conscious control.

A summary picture of the four functions might be given in terms of a judge at a hearing. The defendant is brought in and the judge notes that he is tall, well-built, blond and blue-eyed, is dressed in a dark pin-stripe suit and has certain specific nervous mannerisms. This judge is using his sensation function. Or he may see the defendant for the first time and have a sense that the man is innocent, in which case he may be using his intuition (or his bias—in which case his "hunch" will have a self-righteous emotional tone). Ask him afterwards what color the suit was and he probably will not know. Or he may hear the case and conclude that, from the evidence presented, it may reasonably be deduced that the man is probably guilty. Then he has been thinking and has possibly excluded some intangibles which may speak a quite different language. Or if the man reminds the judge too much of his detestable brother-in-law he may angrily say, "Six months in jail!" He would hardly be an impartial judge if his emotions intruded in this manner.

We have two pairs of opposites: sensation—intuition and thinking—feeling. (Any of these four functions may express itself in an introverted or an extraverted way.) A rough schematic view of their interrelationship in a given individual takes the form of a cross, with any given function at the top of the cross in the superior, that is, the most conscious position:

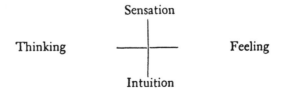

Usually, the opposite of the function favored by consciousness is the most undeveloped; Jung calls this the inferior function. It remains in an unconscious primitive state, is compulsive and therefore interferes with conscious functioning.

The most usual form of adaptation tends to be twofold; that is, one perceiving function and one judging function tend to be relatively highly developed. The "intuitive type" will usually be able to use either thinking or feeling almost as well as intuition. The functional cross can thus be represented as developed in a 1, 2, 3, 4 order, with 1 and 4, 2 and 3 as opposites:

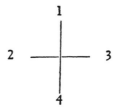

Thus in the case of a person with highly developed intuition, the sensation function may tend to be the most unconscious, with thinking and feeling balanced in the second and third positions of relative awareness. Whereas we would call number 4 the inferior function, the number 3, the opposite of the secondary auxiliary function, might be termed relatively undeveloped, that is, undifferentiated. The inferior function can be developed, but with great difficulty, and will always have to be taken into account as a possible blind spot. At times (especially when intuition is inferior) it can only be related to symbolically.

The polarity of extraversion and introversion is also related to the leading and inferior functions. If the leading and secondary functions are extraverted, the inferior and undeveloped ones will be introverted, and vice versa. If someone is an introverted intuitive-feeling type, he relies most heavily on introverted intuition and as the auxiliary function he will use introverted feeling. His thinking, as the opposite of number 2, will be less well developed and will be extraverted thinking; his use of sensation (extraverted) will be poor.

We must emphasize the fact that unconscious elements do not disappear. An inferior thinking function, for instance, does not represent an incapacity for thinking or even an absence of thinking. It means that thinking occurs without conscious participation, therefore on a primitive level. Moreover, the unconscious factors operate in a fashion which is compensatory to the conscious elements and when disregarded too much they may directly interfere with conscious functioning. Hence the inferior and undeveloped functions become the media for the expression of the unconscious, personal as well as collective. Our inadequate functions are the doorway through which our difficulties, problems, frustrations and sufferings reach or overtake us. When the ego is in a state of excessive identification with the leading function, the inadequate functions may exert a sabotaging effect on the conscious personality. The inadequate functions are the compellingly problematic stepchildren and most of analysis circulates around them in their various constellations and aspects.

The functional types are therefore also to be understood in terms of their compensatory structure; every functional type is balanced by its opposite in the unconscious. For example, the person whose thinking function is the most highly developed consciously may have to look for his capacity for feeling in his unconscious. He functions through both sides of the opposition, the one talking down, the other talking up—and often kicking up. Therefore an understanding of a functional type requires an understanding of the operation of the function opposed to the main adaptation, the inferior function,

> the function that remains in arrears in the process of differentiation. For experience shows that it is hardly possible—owing to the inclemency of general conditions—for anyone to bring all his psychological functions to simultaneous development. The very conditions of society enforce a man to apply himself first and foremost to the differentiation of that function with which he is either most gifted by nature, or which provides his most effective means for social success. Very frequently, indeed as a general rule, a man identifies himself more or less completely with the most favoured, hence the most developed, function. It is this circumstance which gives rise to psychological types. But, as a consequence of such a one-sided process of development, one or more functions necessarily remain backward in development. Such functions, therefore, may be fittingly termed 'inferior' in the psychological, though not in the psycho-pathological sense, since these retarded functions are in no way morbid but merely backward as compared with the more favoured function.[9]

Like complexes, inferior modes of functioning are not morbid in themselves; only when the tension between the undeveloped and the developed areas of the personality or between actual and potential development becomes disruptive can we describe the situation as pathological. We tend to make use of our preferred function, training and developing it into a habitual adaptation; the ego becomes more or less identical with the "superior function."

Just as the lion strikes down his enemy or his prey with his fore-paw, in which his strength resides, and not with his tail like the crocodile, so our habitual reactions are normally characterized by the application of our most trustworthy and efficient function; it is an expression of our strength. However, this does not prevent our reacting occasionally in a way that reveals our specific weakness. The predominance of a function leads us to construct or to seek out certain situations while we avoid others, and therefore to have experiences that are peculiar to us and different from those of other people. An intelligent man will make his adaptation to the world through his intelligence, and not in the manner of a sixth-rate pugilist, even though now and then, in a fit of rage, he may make use of his fists. In the struggle for existence and adaptation everyone instinctively uses his most developed function, which thus becomes the criterion of his habitual reactions.[10]

While consciousness identifies with the superior function, the inferior function becomes the medium through which the complexes express the opposing or complementary attitudes of the unconscious. A feeling type may be assailed by his complexes in the form of inferior, undifferentiated thinking (e.g., dogmatic opinions); a sensation type will be subject to negative or repressive intuitions (anxieties, intuitive fears, forebodings); a thinking type will be carried along or overwhelmed by unrealized, often negative moods; and an intuitive type will find himself in trouble because he overlooks the hard facts of everyday life.

Confrontation of the inferior function means that we come to face a neglected part of our wholeness. This function constellates the individuation problem; there is no individuation, no "becoming what we are" unless we recognize and relate to the inferior function.

We misuse our differentiated function in order to protect ourselves, very often in a wrong way; we use it to kill life when it threatens to become awkward. Up to a certain point this protection is quite valuable, but when you come to that place in your life where the development of your personality becomes an inevitable problem, then you are no longer allowed to kill life. Then you must accept life. . . . And as a rule people—particularly those who are in analysis—are simply forced through the logical development of analysis to take up their individual fates, their particular situation with all its advantages and shortcomings. You could call it "individuation."

Now in this great pursuit . . . you simply come to a dead end if you try to do it through your differentiated function. That has served you well in liberating you from the original unconsciousness—from the past—so that you can establish yourself as a separate social figure or unit. But when the question arises about the totality, the rounding out of your personality . . . then you must listen to other functions as well and particularly to the inferior function, because then you discover that there are situations in life with which one cannot possibly deal with one function only. Generally, in human life, a person with a differentiated thinking function will encounter a situation which he cannot solve by his mind alone, he will need feeling. An intuitive will come to an impasse where his intuition serves him not at all; he needs sensation, the function of reality, in order to be able to continue his life, because he has left too many situations unsolved, and finally he is overcome by them, nailed down by the unsolved problems behind, and only his reality function can be a help. And in sensation types, you can see how they get into a hole that is just nothing but reality and they need intuition very badly in order to crawl out of it, to have the feeling that life is really lived.[11]

When psychopathology develops in the first half of life it usually expresses the failure to establish a firm hold on external adaptation and to achieve a realistic ego development through making the most of one's superior functions. In the second half of life, from the forties on, danger arises when not enough attention is paid to the inadequate functions which now press for admittance, even though our lives may be satisfactorily adapted in terms of external reality. Now the task becomes one of discovering a deeper spiritual meaning in those realities and modes of experiencing which appear silly and irrational in terms of mere everyday practical adaptation and which are now presenting themselves for recognition, often in threatening ways.

This, however, is a simplified description of the type problem in individuation; sometimes we discover only at the end of a long road of suffering what our inferior and undeveloped functions are. When we "take up our individual fates" *all* of our functions appear problematic and our relationship to them is unconscious in varying degrees. Individuation necessitates a developing clarity in respect to the functional hierarchy most natural to us as unique individuals and this can only emerge slowly in conjunction with clarification of all the other factors involved in our psychic make-up.

We might also fall into the trap of assuming that the concept of wholeness means the complete achievement of a capacity to function consciously in all four ways both introvertedly and extravertedly, but this is neither possible nor commensurable with the basic reality of human structuring which includes both darkness and light. Our lives develop and expand by way of the conflicts between superior and inferior functions. Our failures come from the inferior functions but if we can learn to recognize the meaning of the accidents and sufferings they cause we can grow toward a wholeness which rests on the awareness of the existence and persistence of our dark sides. Whoever thinks that he is ever completely or even adequately conscious is like Socrates' fool who is not aware of his foolishness. Socrates adds: If the fool became aware of his foolishness he would be wise, at least to that extent.

It may be helpful to sketch the eight different types briefly, based on Jung's description of them in his *Psychological Types*.[12] For didactic purposes these descriptions will be exaggerated and one-sided. The personalities will be described as clear types with one developed function which means they tend toward pathology or caricature. Fortunately, we rarely meet such extreme cases in real life.

(1) *Extraverted thinking type*
The extraverted thinking type is related to external, i.e., collective, rationality. People of this type are concerned with understanding objective facts in terms of generally accepted ideas. They are unoriginal thinkers because they must follow established collective patterns. They are the well-known objective, materialistic, conventional and uninspired thinkers who often incorporate today's idea of the scientific method. They are usually men; they are exact, precise, dry, pedantic automatons who attempt to force everything into rational, intellectual formulations. They are the theoretical reformers and self-styled altruists; in their frame of reference everything can be figured out and planned rationally and they assume that everything can be carried out as planned. They cannot understand what is wrong with the world, why people have not done the right thing long ago—the right thing being that which is rational and logical and clear to them. They have an answer for everything. They seem like icebergs—and anyone dealing with them should beware of the possibility that there is an enormous block of introverted feeling below the surface. This inferior side has a negative character. They are utterly ruthless and inconsiderate in their relations with others. They have no way of recognizing the fact that their only emotional expressions reflect unconscious needs and urges. They are not aware that they have feelings. They have plenty of them, of course, and they are expressed as vague needs that are promptly rationalized and thus justified and given an almost absolute, divine character. These people are tyrants, inconsiderate of those nearest them—of spouses, children, other relatives and friends—and since they are motivated by unconscious emotions they are stubbornly aggressive-defensive, thus dogmatic, full of resentments and moods, and in a peculiar fashion lacking in integrity. Because of their unconscious emotionality their right hand will not know what their left hand

is doing. They may consider themselves completely upright but, without noticing it, will be quite evasive and dishonest when it comes to facing situations that require feeling.

Finally, their rationality becomes a creed and a religion for them. Nobody is so dogmatic and stubbornly dangerous as the man who "knows" what is "right." This creed-formation of their rationality is the expression of a threatened invasion by an irrational side which gives them no other choice but to prepare rigid defenses. (It bears repeating that the problem of an irrational side to which we are not consciously related is one of the main difficulties for most of us today.)

(2) Extraverted feeling type

The extraverted feeling type adapts in terms of external emotionality, of collective value scales. In the extreme form this type will be overconcerned with external relationships and feelings and therefore overly dependent upon the approval of others. As a result they have no concept of themselves except in terms of the approval, love and appreciation that others express toward them. They are preoccupied with social propriety; Jung goes so far as to say that their thinking has its back broken,[13] because it is ruthlessly subordinated to what is nice and proper. They are afraid that independent thoughts might run contrary to someone's feelings and that such thoughts might also be improper if they are contrary to what is generally accepted. People who function in this way are unduly concerned with maintaining a "congenial" atmosphere in which everyone agrees with everyone else.

Their inferior thinking function is characterized by a lack of subtlety: everything is "nothing but" black or white. The process and results of careful thinking are depreciated; instead of logical thoughts they have opinions, preferably about others. Hence this type is shallow, dogmatic and prejudiced. These people are obviously not reformers; they will never willingly step on anyone's toes. They are frequently found in sociable situations and are most often women. Their functional place in society is likely to be that of the good mixer who excels at getting people together and keeping parties going.

(3) Extraverted intuitive type

The extraverted intuitive perceives via the unconscious, we may almost say as if through extrasensory perception. He smells possibilities, ramifications and connections and is always after the new. He may observe an object or a situation and intuit a possible use for it that is quite unexpected. He may have a fine nose for the stock market, since he can anticipate developments. In its extreme form this type becomes acutely bored and distressed with anything old and familiar. He is always ahead of things, living in tomorrow.

"Don't fence me in." That which has been accomplished is already a bore or a cage, for he is ahead of others and of himself and in his constant infatuation with the new and different can become quite irresponsible. Extraverted intuitives are the promoters, the speculators, the initiators; they are the great beginners, rarely the finishers. They may be skillful politicians but they can also be irresponsible adventurers. Their nemesis lies in introverted sensation, which is their inferior function; they tend to misjudge and overlook concrete conditions and limitations, hence often misjudging their own position within the immediate situation. Therefore the speculators are often the ones who go broke. These people also overlook their own health —their own bodies—and consequently may maneuver themselves into impasses or work themselves to death.

(4) Extraverted sensation type
Individuals of the extraverted sensation type are the complete realists who are concerned only with objects and concrete facts. They tend to be extremely dry, matter-of-fact and down to earth—or they may be overly interested in sensual enjoyments and aesthetics. The gourmets or artists of this type will judge life in terms of how stimulating and exciting things are. Their sensuousness need not be particularly refined; they may approach a situation with the intention of deriving satisfaction through the senses only; that is, people and things are simply objects to be used; feelings and meanings are disregarded. Hence this type can be quite brutal and coarse in its extreme forms. One version is the man-about-town, the unscrupulous aesthetician, for whom events are merely beautiful spectacles, regardless of how much suffering may be involved. These men may be sexual exploiters— the opposite sex serving merely as objects from which they derive satisfaction.

Since introverted intuition is the inferior function, this type will be full of negative intuitions about himself and will usually project them onto others. He then experiences the projected intuitions in the form of vague jealousies, anxieties and fears, superstitions and forebodings. He suspects that "they" are scheming about him in secret, that "they" are cheating somehow, with harmful intent. At the same time, sensation-type extraverts are likely to be quite conventional and unimaginative, both in their thinking and in their system of morality (even the man-about-town has the conventional system just under the surface). In most cases they are the ordinary unimaginative citizens who see the immediate facts and nothing beyond, who do as they are told, just as everyone ought to do, but they are easy prey to rumors, suspicions and hysterias. Of course in the more refined forms they may be skilled observers or artists, since they have an excellent awareness of external reality. In such cases they will have a lively zest for living and a tremendous energy which they can use to recreate the world which they experience and contact through their senses.

(5) *Introverted thinking type*

Thinking types whose thinking is introverted are the theorists and philosophers who direct their thinking toward inner connections and conceptualizations. Outward facts to them merely exemplify and bear out their philosophical speculations. They are original thinkers but they may also become infatuated to the point of absurdity with their speculations. Then their "originality" is so extreme that others cannot follow them because their preoccupation with their own conceptual systems disregards reality. They hate to be bothered by concrete facts, for after all they have their beautiful theories. Existence to them is only an abstraction.

Extraverted feeling, their compensating inferior function, will plague extreme cases of this type with bizarre and inappropriate emotional reactions and with naive misjudgments of people. They can be sentimental egotists who callously disregard the feelings of those close to them, in the name of love for humanity or in the service of a great idea.

(6) *Introverted feeling type*

These still waters that run deep are usually women. Their feeling is contained within and tends to separate them from other people. The outside observer may think them unfeeling because their feeling is so intensely held within that it is directed toward an external object or person only with great difficulty. Their tensions are all inward; consequently they may outwardly appear to be banal, childish and often melancholic. They seem cold and remote and are difficult to approach, since they are primarily attentive to their own subjective reactions. Indeed, because of the intensity of their inner world and their sense of being overwhelmed by its power, they tend to shield themselves from outside contacts. They are likely to be shy and inarticulate, to find communication difficult. They hold others at arm's length because what is evoked is no small matter to them. Occasionally the accumulation of searing inner intensity may erupt in seemingly heroic, dramatic or drastic acts.

The thinking function of the introverted feeling type is primitive, concretistic and fact-bound. Individuals of this type are naive in evaluations which require thinking and are loath to engage in it. This inferior extraverted thinking is often projected in a negative form, causing the person to be over-susceptible to what others think, especially about him. This can make him almost paranoid at times; thus he is frequently subject to scheming, rivalries and hysterics. Like the extraverted feeling type, he tends to a "nothing but" kind of judging and to a rigid dogmatism.

(7) Introverted intuitive type

People of the introverted intuitive type experience and realize life in terms of the unconscious; to them the world of the archetypes is a concrete reality. They perceive ideas, images and inner possibilities; they are attuned to the psychic atmosphere. This type includes the medium and the mystic and the crackpot who are tuned in to the world of images and are out of touch with concrete practical reality. It also includes the founders of new creeds which offer the only salvation for mankind through the nth dimension of the nth brotherhood. Introverted intuitives are the ones who stumble over facts, the ones who cook the watch while looking at the egg to see what time it is; the external object is at war with them. They tend to misjudge concrete circumstances and overlook external limitations. They are impatient with those of slow understanding and easily become helpless and fearful in the face of external circumstances. They mistrust or reject concrete facts and tend to withdraw from them, preferring to leave the deed and the act to others while they take care of their great visions.

(8) Introverted sensation type

It is characteristic of the introverted sensation type to react so subjectively to projects and people that he tends to confuse external reality with the way he sees it. He perceives so thoroughly in terms of his inner interpretation of sense impressions that his responses may appear to be arbitrary and bizarre. As Jung says, these are the people who make us wonder why we exist at all, so far as they are concerned; they react to us in terms of their own detached response which often has little to do with us as we stand there. This subjectivity can lead to a compulsive neurotic dissociation from external reality to the point of paranoid suspiciousness.

Their subjective concern with their sensations makes people of this type devalue the object. Therefore, if they are artistic they will be abstractionists or at least will be able to work very creatively in terms of the material. Usually they are not artists; they just strike others as being remote and strange. They tend to shield themselves from external reality; while appearing to be composed and imperturbable they are actually just detached. They cannot be moved except on their own terms which may be quite out of tune with the facts.

The nemesis of the sensation-type introvert comes in the form of extraverted intuition. This type has a flair for everything gloomy, dangerous or ambiguous in his surroundings.

We may shudder at this recital of pure and unadulterated types, presented here in their extreme forms, unless we remember that no one is a single type. We use these functional classifications to indicate the "majority opinion," the preponderant trend of the conscious libido orientation. And lest we assume that the types or patterns of conscious adaptation be easily discernible, we might ponder Jung's facetious remark to the effect that at times a person's type can only be assessed with certainty some thirty years after his death.

It is helpful, however, to have this concept of the possible forms that adaptation can take in order to facilitate an understanding of the habitual orientation that is involved in conscious adaptation and of the relation and degree of balance that exists among the habitual and less-used modes of functioning. This observation again confronts us with the paradox that consciousness is not quite as conscious as it seems. We are seldom aware of our typological orientation, of the way our consciousness habitually adapts to inner and outer events. Moreover, and paradoxically, these adaptations of consciousness are anything but a matter of conscious, deliberate choice. Consciousness is not free to choose the way it wishes to adapt to life, because both consciousness and its adaptational modes are products of and determined by the unconscious. When we discover that our most fundamental conscious orientation is bound to an unconscious determinant we may be as shocked as Molière's Bourgeois Gentilhomme when he was informed one day that he had spoken prose all his life. He had not chosen to! When we discover our specific constitutional preformation we may be just as shocked, for we may even have been forced by childhood training or education into an adaptation that goes against the grain and this may be the cause of our difficulties and our dissatisfaction with ourselves. In such extreme cases we may find that the ego which is formed in opposition to constitutional predisposition is a pseudoego, and that the actual ego potential rests with the "alter ego," the shadow,[14] which is not in consciousness and which acts without conscious control. Then our "dark" aspects carry our best potentialities; we have a shadow personality that is actually superior to ego consciousness.

We speak of a person's most highly developed function as his functional *type.* (Whether he knows this and uses it fully is another matter.) The functions express our limitations as well as our capacities, regardless of our efforts to oppose them or of our lack of awareness of them. We cannot choose, for instance, whether we will approach situations predominantly with feeling or with thinking; at best we can realize what required response fails to come forth. Our responses appear to be prearranged for us by the interaction of constitutional predisposition and conditioning. Recognition of our functional type is of fundamental importance to us if we are to understand ourselves and others. Very often when two markedly different functional types get involved with each other—and more often than not they do get involved, particularly when they are of the opposite sex, because then they are likely to be attracted to one another—they will talk *past* each other. We might almost say that they are destined to meet in order to attempt the seemingly impossible: communication with one another. All too often each will feel misunderstood by the other and will feel that the other is reacting in an irresponsible, immature, irrational way, and this argument can be played back and forth *ad infinitum*.[15] It is as though a Chinese and a Frenchman met, each spoke to the other in his own language and then found the other utterly stupid and indecent for not responding as expected. It is important that we realize our own functional limitations, because this means that we will understand such difficulties in communication and will try some other approach—as the two strangers will have to realize that they must learn each other's language. But neither can we expect ourselves to produce spontaneously or immediately that which simply is not yet at the disposal of consciousness—again regardless of whether we think or feel we *ought* to react in a certain fashion. This does not mean, however, that we must forever resign ourselves to certain current functional limitations or that these limitations may be used as an alibi. Unconsciousness is merely an explanation, never an excuse. But it does mean that we confront in our functional limitations those aspects of our personalities that have the need, as well as the capacity, for growth.

We must remember that there are individual differences in capacity and potential regardless of the degree of function development; men are *not* created equal. A particular thinking type may have an undeveloped feeling function but compared to a particular feeling type the former may have a capacity for ten times more feeling. A person of greater capacity is likely to have a greater task ahead of him and thus perhaps a more difficult life; he may sooner or later be assailed by those forces within his own depths which seek realization. Here is the natural basis for the concept of *noblesse oblige*. One's crown is also one's cross.

What is to be expected as the effect of confrontation and awareness of the inferior functions? There is often a fear that the superior function might be damaged through a kind of displacement effect if an inferior function were to be brought closer to consciousness. Actually, this fear is unjustified; a better total balance is more likely to develop. As Jung stressed, in the previously quoted passage,[16] the superior function tends to be abused by being used in situations and in areas where it does not legitimately belong. A person with a superior thinking function may try to think his way through a situation that calls for feeling, to substitute thinking for feeling; thereby his thinking becomes unrealistic.

It cannot be stressed enough that the inferior function is inferior because of insufficient development rather than deficient capacity. A feeling type is perfectly capable of thinking; he just will not bother to do it. Consequently he habitually and automatically takes notice only of his feelings. The thinking type is capable of feeling but it happens in spite of him, more often than not (he does not do the feeling, it does *him*, in the form of unconscious emotion).

One's type begins to develop long before the capacity for understanding arises. It is not the result of understanding but is the premise of orientation; it is the glasses (often stained) through which we perceive the reality peculiar to ourselves. Typological orientation selects the materials of which *this* individual's understanding is composed. In our present time and culture, environmental influence is primarily exerted in the direction of extraversion and of thinking and sensation. We quite often find that a distorted typological adaptation has been pressed into these molds. The types most likely to be injured in this respect—victims of our current Western cultural bias —are those of introverted feeling and intuition. While still children they may find themselves misunderstood and may easily be deflected into an attempt at functional adaptation which is not genuinely their own.

9. The Persona

THE TERM *persona*, taken from the Latin, refers to the ancient actor's mask which was worn in the solemn ritual plays. Jung uses the term to characterize the expressions of the archetypal drive toward an adaptation to external reality and collectivity. Our personas represent the roles we play on the worldly stage; they are the masks we carry throughout this game of living in external reality. The persona, as representational image of the adaptation archetype, appears in dreams in the images of clothes, uniforms and masks.

In childhood our roles are set by parental expectations. The child tends to behave in such a way as to win approval from his elders, and this is the first pattern of ego formation. This first persona pattern is made up of collective cultural codes of behavior and value judgments as they are expressed and transmitted through the parents; at this point parental demands and the demands of the outside world in general seem identical. In the course of adequate psychological development it is necessary for a differentiation between ego and persona to occur. This means that we have to become aware of ourselves as individuals apart from the external demands made upon us, we have to acquire a sense of responsibility and a capacity for judgment which are not necessarily identical with external collective expectations and standards, though of course these standards must be given due regard. We have to discover that we use our representational clothes for protection and appearance but that we can also change into something more comfortable when it is appropriate and can be naked at other times. If our clothes stick to us or seem to replace our skin we are likely to become ill.

We must learn to adapt to cultural and collective demands in accordance with our role in society—our occupation or profession and social position —and still be ourselves. We need to develop both an adequate persona mask and an ego. If this differentiation fails, a pseudoego is formed; the personality pattern is based on stereotyped imitation or on a merely dutiful performance of one's collectively assigned part in life. The pseudoego is a stereotyped precipitate of collective standards; one "is" the professor or judge or society matron rather than an individual who gives the role its proper due at the necessary times. Such a pseudoego is not only rigid but also extremely fragile and brittle; the necessary supportive psychic energy from the unconscious is not forthcoming but rather is in opposition to consciousness, since such an ego is completely split off from the intentions of the Self. The pseudoego is subject to constant pressure from within and has no means of adjusting its precarious balance; it often straddles the boundary of psychosis. The threatening elements of the opposing objective psyche are likely to be experienced in projection upon the outside world to the degree that paranoid delusions arise, and the pseudoego deals with these by retreating further into the protective role-identification; the vicious circle again.

An extreme example of the psychic dissociation that accompanies the persona-identified pseudoego is given by Bennet in his description of a girl who was haunted by a double.[1] As a child she felt she had to be perfect to make up for her dead sister's absence, and by the time she had reached her teens she had fallen into a depressive state marked by repeated suicidal attempts to get away from "Kathleen," her pseudoego. She saw herself as "a tiny, undeveloped baby, still living in the first moment of existence, unable to conceive of love and hate as coming from the same source." She was entirely selfish and love-hungry. "The socially-adapted Kathleen, on the other hand, was a nineteen-year-old student, fond of music and painting, a good teacher, keen on literature and with a knowledge of French and German—a false and empty creature."[2] The persona identification which was the source of her failure to develop a genuine ego (the tiny, undeveloped baby) is clearly described in a dream of hers which is taken from Bennet's description: "*I am standing in a vast hall. It is very cold and I am . . . worried lest I had come to the wrong place . . . I became frightened and turn to run away, but I could not get away. Before me was a large mirror in which I could see myself in fancy dress. I was wearing black silk pajamas. . . . I wanted to take off the pajamas, not from myself, but from my reflection in the mirror. . . . I tore off one jacket after another and there seemed to be no end to it all, for on removing one another was revealed.*"[3]

The dream depicts the cold, depersonalized world (the cold hall) in which she becomes frightened through her dim sense of being in the "wrong place," as indeed she is. She cannot get away because she cannot get hold of herself; she is not in touch with herself but only with her reflected image, hence the persona identification cannot be "taken off," cannot be overcome. Under each jacket is another jacket; the naked selfhood cannot be reached in the cold atmosphere of a mere reflected reality.

A person in such a state needs the impact of individual feeling, which develops a sense of one's own individual identity. But he will protect himself, with a formidable array of "clothing," against having his real skin touched, against precisely this feeling impact.

When individuality is thus confused with the social role, when the reality adaptation is not sufficiently individual but is wholly collective, the result may also often be a state of inflation. Its victim feels great and powerful because he is a fine public figure, but he fails to be a human being or even to make the first steps toward becoming human. Such an inflated over-reliance upon the persona, or identity with it, results in rigidity and lack of genuine responsiveness. Such a person is nothing but the role, be it doctor, lawyer, administrator, mother, daughter or whatever part is so compulsively played. The example of Eichmann has shown how such a role-identified nonpersonality fails to develop a personal, moral responsibility; he has no ethical principles or personal feelings and values of his own but hides behind collective morality and prescribed manners. He has no conflicts of conscience because everything is settled beforehand in a stereotyped fashion.

It is hard for this kind of person, who usually thinks of himself as abiding by the highest principles, to realize that he is really immoral. It is rather shocking to discover that something deep within oneself may demand individual decision at the price of individual risk. There is such a universal human tendency to confuse one's clothing with one's skin that this differentiation becomes a crucial ethical problem.

At the opposite end of the spectrum, when persona formation is inadequate because of poor social training or rejection of the social forms as a result of feeling excluded in some way, one cannot play or refuses to play the assigned role successfully. Such a person will suffer from lack of poise, unnecessary defiance and overdefensiveness.

Personality development is thus interfered with at either extreme; an ill-formed persona is just as limiting as its opposite. An inadequate relationship to the persona archetype may range from a fixation in its purely collective aspect to a rebellious refusal or inability to accept any collective adaptation or demand. Examples of dreams that express the former condition are those of being unable to take off one's clothes, of being stuck in heavy armor, of being overdressed or of wearing heavy, overdecorated gaudy uniforms, of having an overly hard or tough skin. The opposite condition, the refusal of the collective, might be expressed in dreams of being at a party stark naked, of discovering suddenly while walking in the street that one has on a transparent gown, of appearing in filthy rags at a reception, of being an oyster without a shell or a flabby mass of jelly.

If the persona is too rigidly "stuck," if one lacks the necessary distinction between individual skin and collective clothes, one is in a precarious position; it is as if one's skin could not breathe. Actual skin diseases may even coincide with such difficulties. There was a young woman who had a severe skin eruption on her face, which resisted all attempts at treatment. She discovered in the course of analysis (which was undertaken for an entirely different reason) that she had a serious adaptational problem; she had always hidden the fact that she was Jewish when she applied for a job, in order to save face, as she expressed it. Psychologically speaking, it was as if she continually wore a mask on her face. The unconscious reaction to this failure to bare her face was expressed in the actual skin eruption, which ceased when she was able to risk exposure of her face psychologically.

Collectivity and individuality are a pair of polar opposites; hence there is an oppositional and compensatory relationship between persona and *shadow*. The brighter the persona, the darker the shadow. The more one is identified with one's glorified, wonderful social role, the less it is played and recognized as merely a role, the darker and more negative will be one's genuine individuality as a consequence of its being thus neglected. But on the other hand too much concern with the shadow, with one's "bad" side— overconcern with how one appears, with how unattractive and awkward one is—can make for a rather negative, defensive and miserable persona. This negative—that is, unadapted—persona will then express itself in stiffness, uncertainty or compulsive, primitive behavior.

Even though at first the ego finds itself in and through the persona, we have seen that the two are not meant to remain in a state of identity. We are performers in the social game, but we must also participate in another play. We are also meant to be our individual selves.

10. The Shadow

THE TERM *shadow* refers to that part of the personality which has been repressed for the sake of the ego ideal. Since everything unconscious is projected, we encounter the shadow in projection—in our view of "the other fellow." As a figure in dreams or fantasies the shadow represents the personal unconscious. It is like a composite of the personal shells of our complexes and is thus the doorway to all deeper transpersonal experiences.

Practically speaking, the shadow more often than not appears as an inferior personality. However, there can also be a positive shadow, which appears when we tend to identify with our negative qualities and repress the positive ones. We will return to this special instance later.[1]

The following example of the shadow is a classical one from a familiar situation. A middle-aged patient complains repeatedly and bitterly about her mother-in-law. Her description seems by and large to be correct and adequate, for her husband. independently of his wife, has provided a description which is practically identical. Mother is seen by both as utterly domineering, never able to admit another person's viewpoint, in the habit of asking for advice and at once deprecating it, always feeling at a disadvantage, abused, martyred and, as a result of all this, almost impossible to reach. Our analysant, the daughter-in-law, feels that her mother-in-law stands between her and her husband; the son must constantly serve his mother, and the wife consequently feels eclipsed. Her marital situation seems to be in a hopeless impasse. She has the following dream:

"I am in a dark hallway. I attempt to reach my husband, but my way is barred by my mother-in-law. What is most frightening, however, is that my mother-in-law cannot see me, even though a spotlight shines brightly upon me. It is as if I did not exist at all as far as she is concerned."

Let us remember again that a dream always points to an unconscious situation. It is complementary and reveals that which is not sufficiently within the field of our awareness. A dream will not restate a situation which the dreamer already sees adequately and correctly. Where there is doubt in the conscious mind a dream may help to resolve that doubt by reiteration, but whenever a dream repeats something of which we feel utterly convinced, a challenge is thereby raised by the unconscious; our projections are held up to us. On the surface this dream seems to confirm the daughter-in-law's conscious complaint. But what does it say when we look for an unconscious projection? It tells the dreamer one thing quite clearly: The spotlight is upon *you* and not on your mother-in-law. It shows her the unconscious qualities which she projects upon her mother-in-law and which stand between her husband and herself. The mother-in-law *in her* prevents her from reaching her husband. It is *her own* necessity always to be right, *her* tendency to create obstacles and deprecate everything, and *her* tendency to be the great martyr, which stand in her way. The spotlight is upon her but the mother-in-law does not see her; she is so gripped by and identical with the qualities ascribed to the mother-in-law that she is unable to see herself as she is, to see her own real individuality. As a result her own individuality is as good as nonexistent, and since she cannot see herself truly she also cannot in real life see her mother-in-law as a human being and therefore cannot deal adequately with the obstructionist tactics which she indeed does use. This is a perfect vicious circle which inevitably occurs whenever we are caught in a shadow projection (or in an animus or anima projection). A projection invariably blurs our own view of the other person. Even when the projected qualities happen to be real qualities of the other person —as in this case—the affect reaction which marks the projection points to the affect-toned complex in *us* which blurs our vision and interferes with our capacity to see objectively and relate humanly.

Imagine an automobile driver who, unknowingly, wears spectacles of red glass. He would find it difficult to tell the difference between red, yellow or green traffic lights and he would be in constant danger of an accident. It is of no help to him that some or for that matter even most of the lights he perceives as red really happen to be red. The danger to him comes from the inability to differentiate and separate which his "red projection" imposes on him. Where a shadow projection occurs we are not able to differentiate between the actuality of the other person and our own complexes. We cannot tell fact from fancy. We cannot see where we begin and he ends. We cannot see him; neither can we see ourselves.

Here is another dream example. This dreamer is very liberal, tolerant and broad-minded—at least he assumes that he is. He dreams: *"Coming home I find that my apartment is occupied by a fascist who, with his militia, has turned everything upside down. He has arrested everybody in the house and put them in chains. The place is a shambles."*

Our progressive, broad-minded dreamer is notified that there is a fascist, a totalitarian dictator in his house, that is, in his personality make-up. This collectivist quality which demands blind compliance has chained most of his lively faculties and created havoc. Our dreamer, of course, is a fascist-hater, in fact he will become very emotional and excited when the word is mentioned—just as the daughter-in-law becomes overemotional and angry at the thought of her mother-in-law. In each case the individual is confronted in his dreams with the very thing which he resents; it is presented as an integral part of his own personality and as one that may not be disregarded without danger. In each case that element is something which the dreamer is least willing to consider as part of his personality make-up.

This type of situation is so classical that one could almost play a parlor game with it—if one wished to court social ruin. Ask someone to give a description of the personality type which he finds most despicable, most unbearable and hateful, and most impossible to get along with, and he will produce a description of his own repressed characteristics—a self-description which is utterly unconscious and which therefore always and everywhere tortures him as he receives its effect from the *other* person. These very qualities are so unacceptable to him precisely because they represent his own repressed side; only that which we cannot accept within ourselves do we find impossible to live with in others. Negative qualities which do not bother us so excessively, which we find relatively easy to forgive—if we have to forgive them at all—are not likely to pertain to our shadow.

The shadow is the archetypal experience of the "other fellow," who in his strangeness is always suspect. It is the archetypal urge for a scapegoat, for someone to blame and attack in order to vindicate oneself and be justified; it is the archetypal experience of *the enemy*, the experience of blameworthiness which always adheres to the other fellow, since we are under the illusion of knowing ourselves and of having already dealt adequately with our own problems. In other words, to the extent that I have to be right and good, *he, she* or *they* become the carriers of all the evil which I fail to acknowledge within myself.

The reasons for this lie within the very nature of the ego itself; the development of the ego, as we shall describe more fully in a later chapter,[2] takes place as a result of the encounter between the Self—as a potential personality trend—and external reality, that is, between inner potential individuality and outer collectivity. On the first level of experience between right and wrong, which is the basis for self-acceptance, the beginnings of conscience are vested in and projected onto the outer collectivity. The child accepts himself in terms of fitting in. Harmony with the Self and thus with conscience appears at first to be dependent upon external acceptance—that is, upon collective and persona values; and those elements of the individuality which are too much at variance with accepted persona values cannot, seemingly, be consciously incorporated into the image which the ego has of itself. They therefore become subject to repression. They do not disappear however; they continue to function as an unseen alter ego which seems to be outside oneself—in other words, as the shadow. Ego development rests upon repressing the "wrong" or "evil" and furthering the "good." The ego cannot become strong unless we first learn collective taboos, accept super-ego and persona values and identify with collective moral standards.

It is most important to note that those qualities which at this point are repressed as incommensurable with persona ideals and general cultural values may be quite basic to our fundamental personality structures, but owing to the fact of their repression they will remain primitive and there-fore negative. Unfortunately repression does not eliminate the qualities or drives or keep them from functioning. It merely removes them from ego awareness; they continue as complexes. By being removed from view they are also removed from supervision and can thereby continue their existence unchecked and in a disruptive way. The shadow, then, consists of com-plexes, of personal qualities resting on drives and behavior patterns which are a definite "dark" part of the personality structure. In most instances they are readily observable by others. Only we ourselves cannot see them. The shadow qualities are usually in glaring contrast to the ego's ideals and wishful efforts. The sensitive altruist may have a brutal egotist somewhere in himself; the shadow of the courageous fighter may be a whining coward; the everloving sweetheart may harbor a bitter shrew.

The existence of or necessity for a shadow is a general human archetypal fact, since the process of ego formation—the clash between collectivity and individuality—is a general human pattern. The shadow is projected in two forms: individually, in the shape of the people to whom we ascribe all the evil; and collectively, in its most general form, as the Enemy, the personifi-cation of evil. Its mythological representations are the devil, archenemy, tempter, fiend or double; or the dark or evil one of a pair of brothers or sisters.

The shadow is a constituent of ego development. It is a product of the split which comes about through establishing a center of awareness. It is that which we have measured and found wanting. It approximately coin-cides with what has been regarded as *the* unconscious, first by Freud and now rather generally, namely elements repressed from consciousness. In un-conscious spontaneous representations the shadow is usually personified by a figure of the same sex as the dreamer.

Recognition of the shadow can bring about very marked effects on the conscious personality. The very notion that the other person's evil could be pointing at oneself carries shock effects of varying degrees, depending upon the strength of one's ethical and moral convictions. It takes nerve not to flinch from or be crushed by the sight of one's shadow, and it takes courage to accept responsibility for one's inferior self. When this shock seems al-most too much to bear, the unconscious usually exerts its compensatory function and comes to our aid with a constructive view of the situation, as in the following dream:

"*Somebody wanted to kill me with an apple. Then I saw that a neighbor of mine, whom I do not regard very highly, had managed to turn a rocky, arid plot of land, which I considered quite useless, into a beautiful garden.*"

This dream presents the shadow problem in two ways: first in archetypal terms and then in individual terms. To the apple the patient associated the notorious apple of the first chapter of Genesis—the devil's present. The unknown person threatening him with the devil's or snake's gift constellates an archetypal form of the shadow, the general human fact that *everybody* has to deal with a shadow problem. The actual neighbor whom he looked down upon represents the personal shadow. The dream says in effect: You are afraid that the shadow—that in you which offers the apple, the discrimination between good and evil, hence the awareness of the temptation of the evil in you—will kill you. And indeed by eating the apple man came to know death (Genesis 3:19); but the apple also signifies the implication: "Ye shall be as gods, knowing good and evil" (Genesis 3:5). The dream therefore points to the fact that this personal problem which is so shocking to him is a general, fundamental, human—hence archetypal— problem. The confrontation of one's own evil can be a mortifying death- like experience; but like death it points beyond the personal meaning of existence. It is important for the dreamer to realize this.

The second part of the dream says: It is your own shadow side—that in you which you find unacceptable, namely those qualities which you associate with the neighbor you despise—which takes an arid, unsatisfactory area and turns it into a paradise. The shadow, when it is realized, is the source of renewal; the new and productive impulse cannot come from established values of the ego. When there is an impasse, a sterile time in our lives—de- spite an adequate ego development—we must look to the dark, hitherto unacceptable side which has not been at our conscious disposal. Goethe in his *Faust* has the devil say of himself when asked, "Who are you then?" that he is:

> Part of that Power which would
> the Evil ever do, and ever does the Good.[3]

(The reverse of this statement is also true, that often enough the more we will the good, the more we create the evil—by overlooking our selfish in- tents or disregarding the evil, for instance, when we become professional do- gooders.)

This brings us to the fundamental fact that the shadow is the door to our individuality. In so far as the shadow renders us our first view of the uncon- scious part of our personality, it represents the first stage toward meeting the Self. There is, in fact, no access to the unconscious and to our own reality *but* through the shadow. Only when we realize that part of ourselves which we have not hitherto seen or preferred not to see can we proceed to question and find the sources from which it feeds and the basis on which it rests. Hence no progress or growth in analysis is possible until the shadow is adequately confronted—and confronting means more than merely knowing about it. It is not until we have truly been shocked into seeing ourselves as we really are, instead of as we wish or hopefully assume we are, that we can take the first step toward individual reality. It can be a discouraging experience to an analysant that in the beginning of analysis the dreams tend to be extremely critical and negative. It sometimes seems that they have almost nothing good to say—with one exception. It can happen that the ego formation has been based on one's inferior qualities. When one is unable to integrate one's positive potential and devalues oneself excessively, or if one is identical—for lack of moral stamina for instance—with one's negative side, then the positive potential becomes the characteristic of the shadow. In such a case the shadow is a positive shadow; it is then actually the lighter of the "two brothers." In such a case the dreams will also try to bring into consciousness that which has been unduly disregarded: the positive qualities. This, however, occurs less frequently than the too-hopeful, too-bright picture of oneself. We have this bright picture because we attempt to *will* ourselves into collectively acceptable patterns.

There are several kinds of possible reactions to the shadow. We can refuse to face it; or, once aware that it is part of us, we can try to eliminate it and set it straight immediately; we can refuse to accept responsibility for it and let it have its way; or we can "suffer" it in a constructive manner, as a part of our personality which can lead us to a salutary humility and humanness and eventually to new insights and expanded life horizons.

When we refuse to face the shadow or try to fight it with willpower alone, saying, "Get thee behind me, Satan," we merely relegate this energy to the unconscious, and from there it exerts its power in a negative, compulsive, projected form. Then our projections will transform our surrounding world into a setting which shows us our own faces, though we do not recognize them as our own. We become increasingly isolated; instead of a real relation to the surrounding world there is only an illusory one, for we relate not to the world as it is but to the "evil, wicked world" which our shadow projection shows us. The result is an inflated, autoerotic state of being, cut off from reality, which usually takes the well-known form of "If only so and so were such and such," or "When this will have happened," or "If I were properly understood" or "appreciated."

Such an impasse is seen by us, because of our projections, as the ill will of the environment, and thus a vicious circle is established, continuing *ad infinitum, ad nauseam.* These projections eventually so shape our own attitudes toward others that at last we literally bring about that which we project. We imagine ourselves so long pursued by ill will that ill will is eventually produced by others in response to our vitriolic defensiveness. Our fellow men see this as unprovoked hostility, this arouses their defensiveness and their shadow projections upon us, to which we in turn react with our defensiveness, thereby causing more ill will.

The following is a typical dream that occurred during such a state. "*I was in great fear of robbers and met a man who offered to protect me against them. But to my great dismay I discovered that this would-be protector was a robber himself!*" In another dream: "*The medicine which I very much wanted to have turned out to be the very poison which had caused my illness.*"

That realization and integration of the shadow leads to a break in our impasse and eventually toward psychic wholeness is expressed in the frequently occurring dreams previously mentioned,[4] in which a seemingly threatening person knocks at the door and wants to be let in; we are usually afraid to let him in, yet when he is admitted he turns out to be very helpful.

In order to protect its own control and sovereignty the ego instinctively puts up a great resistance to the confrontation with the shadow; when it catches a glimpse of the shadow the ego most often reacts with an attempt to eliminate it. Our will is mobilized and we decide, "I just won't be that way any more!" Then comes the final shattering shock, when we discover that, in part at least, this is impossible no matter how we try. For the shadow represents energically-charged autonomous patterns of feeling and behavior. Their energy cannot simply be stopped by an act of will. What is needed is rechanneling or transformation. However, this task requires both an awareness and an acceptance of the shadow as something which cannot simply be gotten rid of.

All of our long-trained moral senses revolt, not only against admitting but even more against having any dealings with the "fiend." We can see only moral blackness in it; indeed were this not so, it would not have been repressed in the first place and made into a shadow in the course of ego differentiation. This painful moral problem is evident in another dream of the man who had the fascist dream. He had complained bitterly about the sterility of his humdrum existence. He felt that he had artistic capacities yet had found no way to get in touch with them.

He dreamed: "*I was at last to meet my long-missing brother for whom I had always longed. From a distance he appeared as a fine, sensitive, artistic figure. But as he came closer I recoiled in terror and disgust, for I could then see that he was effeminate, weak, perhaps even homosexual. With pain and regret I withdrew and avoided meeting him.*"

This man could not bring himself to acknowledge his weak, sensitive side, which in the light of his accustomed convictions would appear to him as nothing but unmanly, sissyish, even degenerate. From a distance he confused his weakness with artistic sensitivity. But by cutting himself off from his "unmanliness"—or rather from that which did not agree with his one-sided ideal of manliness—he also cut himself off from the possibility of recognizing and channeling whatever real capacities might lie dormant within this weak, sensitive "other."

During the process of analysis dreams continue to call attention to the shadow in a critical fashion until it has been accepted in its many facets. Acceptance here involves the realization of qualities as data, as facts. It does not mean that they are to be acted upon or acted out indiscriminately. This would be identification rather than acceptance. It is important that the elements of the unconscious speak *to* us and not *through* us while we remain unaware of them. When they speak through us we are identical with them and in this sense are eliminated as ethical or moral subjects.

Somehow, almost everyone has the feeling that a quality once acknowledged will of necessity have to be acted out, for the one state which we find more painful than facing the shadow is that of resisting our own feeling urges, of bearing the pressure of a drive, suffering the frustration or pain of not satisfying an urge. Hence in order to avoid having to resist our own feeling urges when we recognize them, we prefer not to see them at all, to convince ourselves that they are not there. Repression appears less painful than discipline. But unfortunately it is also more dangerous, for it makes us act without consciousness of our motives, hence irresponsibly. Even though we are not responsible for the way we *are* and feel, we have to take responsibility for the way we *act*. Therefore we have to learn to discipline ourselves. And discipline rests on the ability to act in a manner that is contrary to our feelings when necessary. This is an eminently human prerogative as well as a necessity.

Repression, on the other hand, simply looks the other way. When persisted in, repression always leads to psychopathology, but it is also indispensable to the first ego formation. This means that we all carry the germs of psychopathology within us. In this sense potential psychopathology is an integral part of our human structure.

To restate what has already been touched upon in a previous chapter:[5] Repression is the opposite of discipline. Discipline implies the facing of an issue or of a negative quality and the decision to resist it under certain circumstances, knowing however that one cannot resist all drives at all times—just as one cannot fool all of the people all of the time. The drives have to be released to some extent, otherwise we could not experience them. But once let out they have to be disciplined. The shadow has to have its place of legitimate expression somehow, sometime, somewhere. By confronting it we have a choice of when, how and where we may allow expression to its tendencies in a constructive context. And when it is not possible to restrain the expression of its negative side we may cushion its effect by a conscious effort to add a mitigating element or at least an apology. Where we cannot or must not refrain from hurting we may at least try to do it kindly and be ready to bear the consequences. When we virtuously look the other way we have no such possibility; then the shadow, left to its own devices, is likely to run away with us in a destructive or dangerous manner. Then it just "happens" to us, and usually when it is most awkward; since we do not know what is happening we can do nothing to mitigate its effect and we blame it all on the other fellow.

There are also of course social and collective implications of the shadow problem. They are staggering, for here lie the roots of social, racial and national bias and discrimination. Every minority and every dissenting group carries the shadow projection of the majority, be it Negro, white, Gentile, Jew, Italian, Irish, Chinese or French. Moreover, since the shadow is the archetype of the enemy, its projection is likely to involve us in the bloodiest of wars precisely in times of the greatest complacency about peace and our own righteousness. The enemy and the conflict with the enemy are archetypal factors, projections of our own inner split, and cannot be legislated or wished away. They can be dealt with—if at all—only in terms of shadow confrontation and in the healing of our individual split. The most dangerous times, both collectively and individually, are those in which we assume that we have eliminated it.

The shadow cannot be eliminated. It is the ever-present dark brother or sister. Whenever we fail to see where it stands, there is likely to be trouble afoot. For then it is certain to be standing behind us. The adequate question therefore never is: Have I a shadow problem? Have I a negative side? But rather: Where does it happen to be right now? When we cannot see it, it is time to beware! And it is helpful to remember Jung's formulation that a complex is not pathological *per se*. It becomes pathological only when we assume that we do not have it; because then it has us.

Jung speaks in practical and symbolic terms about the most profound meanings of the shadow archetype:

> Recognition of the shadow . . . leads to the modesty we need in order to acknowledge imperfection. And it is just this conscious recognition and consideration that are needed wherever a human relationship is to be established. A human relationship is not based on differentiation and perfection, for these only emphasize the differences or call forth the exact opposite; it is based, rather, on imperfection, on

what is weak, helpless and in need of support—the very ground and motive for dependence. The perfect has no need of others, but weakness has, for it seeks support and does not confront its partner with anything that might force him into an inferior position and even humiliate him. This humiliation may happen only too easily when high idealism plays too prominent a role.[6]

Perhaps this sounds very simple, but simple things are always the most difficult. In actual life it requires the greatest art to be simple, and so acceptance of oneself is the essence of the moral problem and the acid test of one's whole outlook on life. That I feed the beggar, that I forgive an insult, that I love my enemy in the name of Christ —all these are undoubtedly great virtues. What I do unto the least of my brethren, that I do unto Christ. But what if I should discover that the least amongst them all, the poorest of all beggars, the most impudent of all offenders, yea the very fiend himself—that these are within me, and that I myself stand in need of the alms of my own kindness, that I myself am the enemy who must be loved—what then? Then, as a rule, the whole truth of Christianity is reversed: there is then no longer more talk of love and long-suffering; we say to the brother within us "Raca," and condemn and rage against ourselves. We hide him from the world, we deny ever having met this least among the lowly in ourselves, and had it been God himself who drew near to us in this despicable form, we should have denied him a thousand times before a single cock had crowed.[7]

11. Male and Female

ONE OF THE most basic forms in which we experience the universal conflict of opposites in ourselves and in our encounter with others is the male-female polarity. It therefore stands foremost among our psychological problems. There may be a dim, underlying sense of that oneness of which the mystics speak, but in terms of our daily reality we experience it in terms of duality and conflict: conscious-unconscious, light-dark, spirit-nature, positive-negative and, for consideration here, male-female.

Jung has initiated an approach to the understanding of the male-female polarity, in terms of broader archetypal implications, by introducing the Logos-Eros concept. He says: "The concept of Eros could be expressed in modern terms as psychic relatedness, and that of Logos as objective interest." [1] And further: "But I do not wish or intend to give these two intuitive concepts too specific a definition. I use Eros and Logos merely as conceptual aids to describe the fact that woman's consciousness is characterized more by the connective quality of Eros than by the discrimination and cognition associated with Logos." [2]

There has been a tendency in analytical psychology to use these initial and, probably as far as Jung was concerned, tentative conceptual aids as though they were complete or final characterizations of the male-female archetypes. I believe this has been confusing for, as I shall attempt to show, the Eros-Logos concept gives expression to only a part of the male-female archetypes. Moreover the mythological male figure of Eros is more likely to fit masculine than feminine dynamics. In my opinion, the mythologem of male-female can be approached more profitably in terms of the ancient Chinese concepts of Yang and Yin. Yang and Yin include "maleness" and "femaleness" as general principles or symbolic images; but this use of the symbols is not to be confused with masculinity or femininity as directly characterizing men or women. Everything in the world of concrete manifestation is held to partake of various proportions of Yang and Yin, including both men and women. These basic principles are purely symbolic representations of energies which are inclusive of what we commonly call maleness and femaleness.

170

In Chinese philosophy the Yang principle is represented as the encompassing archetype of the creative or generating element, the initiating energy; it symbolizes the experience of energy in its driving, moving aspects of strength, impulsation, aggressiveness and arousal. It presents the characteristics of heat, stimulation, light (sun, ray); it is divisive and phallic as sword, spear or penetrating power, and even shattering; it is in motion from a center outward; it is represented as heaven and spirit; it is manifested in discipline and separation, hence individualization. It arouses, fights, creates and destroys; it is positive and enthusiastic but also restrictive and ascetic (another separative tendency).

The Yin principle, on the other hand, is represented as receptive, yielding, withdrawing, cool, wet, dark, concrete, enclosing, containing (cave and hollow), form-giving and gestating, centripetal, in-going; it is not spirit but nature, the world of formation, the dark womb of nature that gives birth to drives, to urgings and instincts and sexuality; it is seen in the symbolism of earth and moon, darkness and space; it is negative, undifferentiated and collective.

It is important to note that the use of the terms negative and positive in this context does not imply value judgment, any more than do these terms when applied to electricity. *Positive* is used to describe an energy which is assertive, outgoing and initiating; *negative* an energy which is receptive or passive. Again we cannot overemphasize the fact that we are not defining but are describing or depicting the range of symbolic representations. We cannot define basic phenomena because we do not know what they "are." We deal here with entities or facts that are typically experienced and encountered in certain forms; we attempt to render such facts in terms of the "best possible description, or formula, of a relatively unknown fact; a fact, however, which is none the less recognized or postulated as existing." [3]

In his comments on the *I Ching*, the ancient Chinese classic, Richard Wilhelm characterizes the relationship between Yang and Yin: The "receptive primal power of yin . . . is the perfect complement of the Creative —the complement, not the opposite, for the Receptive does not combat the Creative but completes it." [4]

We are comparatively more familiar with expressions of the Yang principles of order, understanding, initiative, separation and consciousness which determine our conscious life. The Yang gives the manifest characterization to the conscious orientation of the man and, paradoxically enough, to the unconscious traits of the woman (her animus) which constitute a vector toward awareness and differentiation. The woman's manifest or conscious orientation—her Yin—is rather averse to conscious differentiation. The Yin is more puzzling to us than the Yang; it operates in the (often distorted) feminine orientation and in the man's anima. Also, in Jung's writings the Yin principle is not clearly distinguished from its Eros aspect and from relatedness. Here we may avail ourselves of the excellent characterization by Linda Fierz-David:

> As always when one interprets, one tends easily to idealize and, in this instance, to visualize *Yin the Receptive* as something akin to loving motherliness. We start with the mother image in order to actualize the feminine principle, but this is just what we must not do because the feminine is the opposite of the spiritual and the ideal. *Yin* is the mother-womb of the soul, conceiving and giving birth. Whatsoever falls therein is borne, ripens and is ejected, regardless. It is the ever-bearing, but also the inert. In conceiving, it remains indifferent, cold and unseeing. It stays immovably on the spot; only in giving birth does it shake and quake like the irrational volcano.
>
> It is in one sense really quite hazardous to realize this, for though the deeply feminine is the center from which all psychic life pours forth, just because of its vast inertia it is inimically opposed to all action, all consciousness and development. Just as outer nature, without man's intervention, ceaselessly creates and destroys in unconcerned and senseless continuation, allowing fruits to ripen and decay and animals to live and die, so the feminine without the active intervention of the conscious mind proceeds on an undisciplined and ever life-productive way.
>
> The feminine is not the primitive, for the primitive contains a relative amount of consciousness and development; it is rather the non-human and non-spiritual. The awesome point is that this non-spirituality, this non-humanity is yet a wellspring for human experience, similar to an ancient, sluggish beast which has watched man for thousands of years and now knows everything, long before it occurs. It is for us an almost insulting paradox that the non-spiritual should be wise, but thus it is. This wisdom is not friendly to man, for it never suits a particular time or person but relates solely to the stark, raw everlasting of the unconscious psychic life; and just as organic life never remains static, but goes on relentlessly—ever renewing even the organism in the single cell—so the feminine encompasses the whole vibrant ever-new rhythm of psychic activity, the inescapable change of every hardened form. Thus it contains and destroys all in one. It is unswerving stability and terrifying breakdown. It expresses itself in the sexual demand, in the adaptability of instincts, in shattering emotions, and, because of its wayward uncontrollability, in a truly devilish wisdom.
>
> In her inmost being every woman is moved by this feminine principle of *Yin*. Aside from all she says or does, aside from her most inti-

mate bond to people and spiritual values, it expresses itself in her as something strange and foreign, something "other" that unmistakably goes its own way.

Here she is pushed beyond any need of her own, or the needs of her nearest and dearest, by the compelling necessity of this rhythm. Here she does not recognize outer time and its demands but only the unmistakable signs of an inner ebb and flow. Quite unconsciously and involuntarily this deepest part of her is concerned only with the growth and maturing of life which demands its rights, must demand its rights, whether she wishes it or not.

This is what fundamentally makes women so mysterious to themselves as well as to others. The *Yin* in them demands the inexplicable and unknowable, pushes on to the next step in the unknown part of life, adds the yet unconscious part to the consciously known, and finds in every situation the germ of the new. It is therefore inexpressible, and all words and explanations can only give an artificial and untrue picture. This great darkness pregnant with life is the reality. To us that darkness seems suspect and morbid and we turn away from it whenever possible. Therefore the vibrant, living darkness of *Yin* is seldom recognized in its essential meaning by modern cultured women, in its natural expression of impulsive feelings and emotions which could contact the unknown depths of consciousness. Or if it is perceived at all, it is quickly thrust away under the cover of convictions, opinions, concepts and rationalizations that misconstrue and twist the mystery even as it emerges into being. That which could be understood by experiencing is cut off, crippled even in embryo. Then the deep substratum of the stream of psychic life is blocked, damned up, and it floods over in moments of unguarded unconsciousness, in overpowering affects that disturb and twist the meaning of everything around it. Or the *Yin* inserts itself slyly in the conscious and unconscious intrigues and suspicions of women with which they unwittingly poison themselves and those around them.[5]

It is obvious that what is described here is neither the connective quality ascribed to Eros nor—even less so—is it psychic relationship or relatedness. Indeed in some ways it can be seen that this aspect of Yin can be quite averse to, even destructive of, relatedness.

The scope of the Yang experience encompasses the world of discernment, spirit and order, but also of abstraction. It finds its representation in the symbolic images of masculine figures: father, wisdom, hero or companion, depending upon which particular aspect of the experience of the "moving spirit" is constellated. (We shall have more to say later about this typological division of the basic male archetype.)[6] The images, however, are not necessarily only human. The "powers" can also be represented in animal and plant symbolism, as the ancient representations of the divinities show. Zeus the Great Father, for example, appears also as the eagle, the swan, the oak and even the golden rain. In a similar fashion the feminine imagery of Yin encompasses the world of nature, life, matter, emotions, urges; it represents psychic, instinctual and concrete rather than spiritual experience, *existence* rather than *essence*, to use modern existential terminology. Its dynamism aims toward oneness, merging and involvement rather than separation and abstraction. "Man does, woman is." [7]

We can discern a polarity of outgoing or dynamic and inward-turning and in this sense static expressions within both Yang and Yin spheres. The dynamic aspect in the Yang sphere is like an action drive, an aggressive urge, phallic, moving, battling, challenging, striving for accomplishment, conflict and penetration; it is will and self assertion. We may call it the Martian pole. (Mars, the god of war personifies aggressiveness.) The static Yang pole manifests as reflection, consciousness, discernment, creative understanding, discrimination, cognition, meaning, reason and discipline, law, order, abstraction and nonpersonal objectivity. This pole corresponds to what Jung has called the spirit or Logos aspect. Both Mars and Logos aspects express the striving for an assertion of individual separateness.

Within the Yin scope the static pole is the one that Fierz-David described above as inert, indifferent, cold and unseeing, gestating and waiting; the mother womb of the soul and of natural life that ceaselessly creates and destroys, that is averse to consciousness and discipline. It is receptiveness and yielding, but also holding and containing; it is emotional experiencing and the endless dreaming flow of the world of images, of fantasy and intuition. It is impersonal, nonindividual and collective. This we may call the gestative motherly pole of the Yin, incorporated in the lifegiving and devouring, awesome Great Mother goddesses of mythology, such as the terrible Kali. It appears also in the representation of the goddess Natura (Physis) as the antithesis to spirit or Logos.

The outgoing, active pole of Yin corresponds to what Jung has alluded to as the Eros principle, without giving it "too specific a definition." [8] Eros, according to Jung's characterization, refers to the function of relationship. It is an urge to unite and unify, to get involved with concrete people rather than with ideas or things, but to get involved for the sake of the personal, subjective, emotional union rather than for the sake of any meaning or awareness of oneself or of one's partner. Hence this urge toward involvement, unity and relationship must not be confused with what we have come to call relatedness in the sense in which Buber, for instance, uses the term when he postulates a consciously empathic I-Thou *Begegnung*, that is, a meeting, confrontation or encounter. Such a *Begegnung* is a "recognition," a relationship of mutual creative involvement and understanding, of distance as well as of nearness. However the Eros aspect of Yin is not one of understanding but only of contact and merging, human contact and, indeed, human involvement, but still indifferent to understanding, to the basic "knowing" in its Biblical sense of loving understanding. Aphrodite, the oldest Moira who rules over "the whispering of maidens, laughter and hoaxes, sweet lust, love and loving kindness," [9] would seem an appropriate mythological figure. She leads to emotional involvement, hence is indispensable to relatedness. But true human relatedness requires more than erotic involvement, it requires confronting distance as much as connecting nearness, creative understanding as well as emotional involvement, aggressive challenge as much as patient inaction, waiting, caring and bearing.

> Give your hearts, but not into each other's keeping.
> For only the hand of Life can contain your hearts.
> And stand together yet not too near together:
> For the pillars of the temple stand apart.[10]

Full human I-Thou relatedness cannot simply be called an Eros function, as it has usually been presented in the writings of analytical psychology; it arises out of the interaction of Yang and Yin in their double polarity of love and challenging aggressiveness, of creative understanding and emotional gestation. It requires distance and separateness no less than involvement, the conscious integration of anger and hostility no less than that of love and friendliness. Hence it constellates and invokes the wholeness or totality of our human potential. Relatedness is the external interpersonal aspect of individuation. One cannot fully and truly relate to a "Thou" without encountering the deepest Self; in turn one cannot encounter the Self through introversion only. Our human fullness requires the actual meeting with a "Thou."

In thus characterizing the nature of the Yin and Eros drives and their relationship to psychological relatedness, I do not attempt to say what that which we call love is or is not. The experience of love seems to me an experience that defies psychological analysis—it is neither an art to be learned nor an instinct to be defined. Like God, love is a *mysterium tremendum*, capable at best of a symbolic characterization. One's psychological structure and functioning may make it possible or impossible for love to occur, but no analyzing or rectifying of psychological structuring can produce love; hence no definable drive could be said to *be* love. What Jung calls the Eros or involvement urge is indeed bound to play an important part where love occurs. Yet what a chasm exists between blind, passionate involvement and that love which is able and willing to give of itself, to understand and even to renounce its claims if this should be called for by the deepest needs of loving.

In their mythological representations the two Yin polarities have sometimes been combined in the Great Mother and Love Goddess figures. In Demeter-Persephone on the one side and Aphrodite on the other they are separately conceived, but Isis and Kali for instance contain both aspects. Evola's characterization of two main types of femininity is psychologically accurate. He speaks of the Demetric and the Aphroditic types,[11] the one functioning primarily as the mother who is oriented toward the collective, the other as the lover who is oriented toward the personal and individual. These types we shall meet later as corresponding to Wolff's Mother and Hetaira.

The two basic types of male (Yang) expression have found their mythological representation in the various divinities of war or strife and of wisdom. Mars or Ares is an example of a war god, and he, incidentally, is the lover of Aphrodite. (It has often been remarked that soldiers and harlots practice the world's two oldest occupations.) Divinities of wisdom include Zeus, who weighs the scales of destiny, Odin, who drinks from Mimir's well, and Brahman, who embodies absolute meaning.

Just as the mother's sustaining-devouringly destructive aspect tends to merge in varying degrees with the erotic, connecting aspect of Yin, as in Kali or the great moon goddesses, so also in Odin, Shiva or Zeus the wise and warlike characters are merged, bringing these figures closer to expressing the total Yang dynamism.

The principle of conscious I-Thou relatedness, of a loving relationship in mutual conscious acceptance and understanding which would include the other's shadow and aggressive aspects—hence not only attraction but also contradiction—seems to have hardly any representation in ancient mythology. A more elaborate mythologem appears for the first time in the symbolism of medieval alchemy, in the still relatively confused imagery of the *coniunctio*; there, out of the original chaos arises an *agens*, sulfur (Yang), and a *patiens*, sal (Yin), as well as an ambivalent Mercurius in the middle, having the tendency to unite the other two. This alchemical Mercurius is also Hermes Trismegistus, the "Three Times One," and the male-female Hermaphroditus. Mercurius not only unites like Eros but is also a trickster and confounder, and is aggressive and capable of anger; he is also capable of irrational, gestating wisdom, hence unlike Eros he represents a really comprehensive drive toward integration and relatedness.

One may conclude from the scarcity of true relatedness symbolism in mythology that the urge toward such a conscious personal I-Thou relatedness may have been constellated by the objective psyche as a pressing human problem only in relatively recent times, that it is truly a pioneering task of modern generations, without precedent in the historical past of mankind. In the past, personal interrelations were initiated by spontaneous emotions such as love and hate, and they were regulated by collective rather than personal standards. Today we find ourselves increasingly pressed to work out interpersonal connections, to come to terms with one another, on the basis of personal, individual—hence unpredictable—feelings not subject to normative regulation. We now feel for instance that marriage as a permanent relationship cannot merely be defined in terms of duties, but must be shaped into personal relatedness not only out of love and attraction but also out of mutual aversions and boredom; we have to deal with the partner individually on the basis of the acceptance of a whole person, by a whole person, rather than according to collective standards and codes. This is a relatively new and highly problematic challenge, to say the least. The need for primacy of personal relationship in marriage is just as new as the necessity for the various nations and faiths of the earth to live together in mutual acceptance, regardless of whether or not they approve of each other's social or religious beliefs, if they are not to risk extinction; as new as the urge for individuation, that is, for a self-acceptance that includes the negative, dark aspects of the personality as well as the light, conscious ones. Our traditional stories and fairy tales usually end when the hero "gets" the heroine in marriage; nothing is said or considered as to how they deal with the problems which arise out of their marriage and of their living together. This, however, is the point at which the real problems usually begin for modern people.

Thus in our actual lives the dualistic polarity between Yang and Yin is encountered not only on the level of general symbolic ideas but also in the very concrete polarity or interaction of the sexes in their relationship problems.

For men and women are not simply male and female; men cannot be understood as mere embodiments of Yang—as little as women are simply Yin creatures. We can understand this fact better if we remember that biology has shown us that the individual male has recessive feminine characteristics, rudimentary female sex organs and also female sex hormones in his blood stream; and the individual female has recessive male characteristics. Thus maleness and femaleness are determined not by an absolute but by a relative predominance of one set of characteristics over the other; the recessive set—femaleness in the man and maleness in the woman—merely operates out of sight, from a relative background position. Thus Jung's postulate of a recessive maleness in the woman (the animus) and of recessive femaleness in the man (the anima), which he arrived at through psychological observation quite independent of biology,[12] can be understood and accepted as analogous to the biological findings.

We may regard the psychology of the man as being determined by varying degrees of predominance of manifest Yang and of a recessiveness or background functioning of Yin. Correspondingly the woman is characterized by a relatively manifest predominance of Yin and by the recessive background functioning of Yang. But let it be noted that we speak of predominance to varying degrees; there are what we could call feminine- or Yin-motivated men and masculine- or Yang-motivated women. Moreover predominance is not to be confused with conscious awareness. The recessive background elements, anima and animus, are of necessity always unconscious, indeed they operate like separate, unknown personalities of the opposite sex—an unconscious woman in the man and an unconscious man in the woman—which have never yet entered the area of conscious adaptation and therefore tend to function in a relatively primitive and unadapted, inferior fashion until they become more differentiated through conscious effort. However, our manifest characteristics need not necessarily be fully conscious either. A man may be out of touch with his full masculinity and a woman with the full range of her femininity. Then the unconscious manifest personal characteristics may merge with, contaminate or modify animus or anima; the insufficiently masculine man is compensated by a masculinized amazon-like anima, the mannish woman by an effeminate or weak animus. The deficiency which this leaves in the personal adaptation is often made up for by pseudopersonal, imitated—rather than genuine—masculinity or femininity, such as bravado or intellectual rigidity in the man, feigned concern and sympathy or artificial mothering in the woman. The variations of Yang-Yin interplay in dominant and recessive personality determination thus can shape various types of male and female expression.

We shall now consider such a typological differentiation manifesting itself in the outward expressions of men and women as well as in the inner influence of animus and anima.

A tentative typological classification of "the Feminine" has been described by Toni Wolff.[13] It can be seen that the same ordering principle applies also to masculine adaptational structuring. This typology is archetypal, rests on fundamental instinctual traits and their response to, as well as influence upon, those traits shaped by environment and culture. Thus each kind of adaptation can again be described in terms of image, value system and pattern of behavior. A more detailed attention will be directed to the feminine typology since today's prevailing views of the feminine psyche are so sadly hackneyed and undifferentiated.

The feminine types, according to Wolff, take the form of a pair of opposites which function within the realm of the personal and a pair of opposites which function within the area of the nonpersonal. *Mother* is the collective and *Hetaira* (daughter, *puella aeterna*) the individual form of personal functioning, *Amazon* the collective and *Medium* the individual form of nonpersonal functioning. Mother and Medium also are forms of the static, Hetaira and Amazon of the dynamic, Yin manifestations. The static, gestating Yin appears in person-directed form in the Mother and as purely subjective experience in the Medium; the outgoing Eros aspect is depersonalized and object-directed in the Amazon (hence at its weakest) and person-directed in the Hetaira.

The *Mother* type represents a collective orientation to people, the protective, homemaking and sheltering attitude. When this form of functioning is unadapted, we encounter its negative aspect as possessiveness, overprotectiveness and unnecessary meddling which interferes with independence and the development of individual personality. The woman who functions primarily as Mother tends to see the man in terms of his social collective function as father and protector of the family rather than as an individual; she is concerned with the home as an institution and a containing warm shelter which needs a man—at times almost any man would seem to do—rather than as an opportunity for personal individual interaction. Similarly she expects her children to function in the way children ought to, that is, in proper adaptation to social demands and to her mothering of them, rather than as the individuals they happen to be; this also applies to anyone with whom she is concerned. This aspect of the feminine finds a representation in the various images of the Great Mother: as nourishing and protecting or destructively devouring, regardless of the individual.

The opposite type, the *Hetaira*, is instinctively oriented toward the individual and tends to be oblivious of sociological concerns. She is the eternal daughter or sister, the *puella aeterna*; she is concerned with and arouses the subjective individual aspect in men as well as in herself; hence she may tend to address herself to the shadow side of the individual to the same extent that the Mother will tend to disregard the shadow in favor of the social persona. This type of orientation represents Evola's Aphroditic aspect of the feminine archetype: the orientation to love and personal interaction as an ultimate aim rather than its subordination to and containment in social and family forms. Being given over to the concern with individual feeling, with its everchanging fluctuations, this type of woman may find it difficult to commit herself to any permanence in outer relationships. Indeed she may, like her male counterpart, the *puer aeternus*, shy away from any concrete commitment and forever lead a provisory life of emotional wandering. The mythological images which express this type are the love deities, hierodules and priestesses dedicated to the service of love; the seductresses, nymphs, beautiful witches and harlots also express its unadapted aspect.

A nonpersonal orientation, an objective attitude, which does not have to do with personal involvement but rather with objective cultural values and a woman's own external performance, indicates the *Amazon* type. This type is relatively self-contained and independent; she is a comrade or competitor rather than a wife or lover. This type finds its image in figures like Artemis the chaste huntress, Pallas Athene, the Valkyries and the Amazons. In its positive aspect this form of feminine expression appears in the tendencies toward independence and fulfillment of her own individual development. When unadapted it contains the danger of producing the efficiency fiend, the animus-ridden career woman who is insensitive to relationship needs and emotional values.

The *Medium* type mediates another nonpersonal realm, the deep abyss of the Yin; she is immersed in the subjective experience of the psychic atmosphere. This type lives in the expression of what is constellated by the unconscious; therein lies her potential and her danger—she is open to the intangible but often is oblivious of concrete reality, of the limitations and needs of people, relationships and things. All too readily she tends to remain in identity with the world of her subjective visions and then may tend to regard herself as the authoritative seeress or prophetess. Depending upon the presence or absence of ego firmness and conscious awareness of her own relation to and emotional involvement in the archetypal world that expresses itself through her, she may be a source of inspiration or of confusion. At her best this type of woman helps to mediate the powerful world of the objective psyche. At her worst she is in danger of inflation and of losing her own individuality and ability to discriminate, as some professional mediums and fortune tellers do; then they become the playthings of potentially destructive psychic influences and thereby become sources of psychic infection and decadence. The mythological prophetess, witch, seeress and wise woman, Sibyl and Norn, Sophia and Hecate represent this type.

It is important to discuss the differentiation of the feminine archetypes in some detail because of our culture's general view—despite many remarkable individual evidences to the contrary—that a woman can only be a woman if she finds at least one husband and breeds at least two or three children. The role of the mother is a manifestation of femininity in a perfectly valid, essential and vital form; it is a collective form, which has its place but is by no means the only channel through which the feminine may express and fulfill itself. The woman who operates foremost as Mother will encounter difficulties primarily with individual relationship—to herself as well as to others; this individual realm is that of her opposite, the Hetaira. To the Mother, the husband is primarily the *pater familias*, the head of the family; the children are the children—none is primarily a person. They matter in so far as they are elements of the family, and in this attitude lies the problem of too much mothering; the children may find it difficult to become independent individuals in their own right.

The woman who functions exclusively in terms of the Hetaira, that is, in terms of individual relationship above all, may be destructively heedless of the demands and needs of collectivity and of family life. For her the demands of an individual relationship or of her own individual growth may supersede social concerns, for instance the fact that she may happen to be married and may happen to be a mother. With this basic orientation she may have difficulty in being an appropriate mother. Realizing this weakness means that she may either have to give motherhood extra concern or renounce it altogether. On the other hand it is essential also for her to realize that mothering is not her main avenue of functioning. If she tries too hard to force herself to act her collectively assigned role she may neglect her genuine nature. If she identifies with her dominant type she may be oblivious of social and relationship necessities; for instance, she may be all too ready to walk out of a relationship, regardless of the needs of children, as soon as her personal feeling cools.

The woman who is constitutionally structured by the Amazon archetype is likely to be effective in a career but might find herself in difficulty, due to her insensitivity to the intangibles; she may try to compensate for this lack with a persona mask and try to play-act the sweet, helpless darling or inspirer of men. Owing to her unadapted receptivity (which is unavailable to consciousness), she is likely, under her assumed mask, to be a steam-rolling dragon, insensitive or oversuggestive.

Conversely, the woman who as Medium is extremely sensitive to the intangibles in the atmosphere will not succeed easily in pushing herself into external activity. She can bring to others those things which they do not sense themselves, she can be the *femme inspiratrice*, but she is not too likely to succeed in the business world. Her danger lies in her propensity for uncritical exploitation of her indefinable power.

I believe that the differentiation of the archetypal expression of the masculine follows a pattern quite analogous to Wolff's description of the feminine; there are corresponding predominant traits in the male psychology. We can delineate the *Father, Son* or *puer aeternus, Hero* and *Wise Man* as forms of expression.

The *Father* prototype, like the Mother, is the collective form of personal functioning. It expresses the Logos aspect of the Yang principle as structure and order. This is the archetypal leader, the voice of collective authority, the Lord, King or Tyrant, but also Protector, the figure concerned with hierarchical social order, whose word is law. He directs and protects, but knows only children or subjects, not individuals. This dispensator of the collective Logos and defender of the cultural structures is represented mythologically in the divine figures of rulers, lawgivers and kings, such as Kronos (who does not allow his children to grow up), Zeus, Odin, Our Father in Heaven and the King of Kings.

The opposite orientation of the Father is that of the *Son*, the *puer aeternus*, companion or brother. This is an entirely different form of maleness from the experience of the man as Father, and is in this sense opposed to it. Like the Hetaira, it is the expression of individual and personal concerns regardless of collective demands; it expresses the dynamic ever-active outward-directed Yang pole. Both Son and Hetaira types "love them and leave them," but with the Eros-motivated Hetaira the greater emphasis is on the former; the *puer* is better at leaving. The Son goes his own way, seeks individual relationships and his own individuality, his own inner treasure, in ever new settings, and he does not concern himself very much with authority or permanence. He is Adonis, Attis or Peter Pan. He is the eternal Friend, but also the challenging Enemy: either the light or dark brother. He is the Knight Errant, the eternal seeker.

The dynamic outgoing type of the masculine, oriented toward objective collective values, is the *Hero* or soldier or "go-getter" type. He fights, strives and accomplishes in the collective frame of reference. The various mythological fighter figures like Achilles and Siegfried do battle, but they show the capacity neither to preserve and rule nor to be receptive and wise—nor for that matter to be concerned with personal values. Nevertheless the hero archetype is a principal form of ego expression; it expresses the focussing of personal will or power effort. The first form of adult ego-structuring involves the establishment for oneself of a place in society. The finding of one's individuality comes later in the second part of life. (These phases of life development will be more closely considered in Chapter 17.)

The *Wise Man* or mana figure relates to the meaningful aspect of the Logos in a subjective way; he is idea- rather than person-oriented. The Wise Man does not fight but listens, receives, perceives; he is the scholar, teacher, sage, seer and philosopher: Tiresias, Mimir, Moses, Socrates, etc.

We must stress again the warning that these structural forms of feminine or masculine adaptation are to be regarded as archetypal; that is, they are inevitable and typical basic modes and variations through which the encompassing principles of Yang and Yin find expression in the individual human being. The Mother or Hetaira, the Wise Man or the Son are not actual persons; these designations stand for basic drives, for orientational patterns which tend to influence individual personalities in varying degrees, either through their main adaptation or through shadow, animus or anima.

Each man and woman has all four masculine or feminine structural forms
as more or less latent potentials, just as everyone has all four basic psychological functional traits (see Chapter 8). The structural form that is most
germane to the tendencies of the unfolding individuality will, in a way
analogous to the basic typological development, be first realized as a main
adaptational orientation. Gradually a second form offers itself, but again, as
in the typological development of the perception and judgment functions, it
will be a form that is not directly opposed to the leading adaptation; it will
be one of the other pair of opposing forms. That is, for the Hero this would
be the Father or *puer*, but not the Wise Man; for the Mother, the Amazon
or Medium, but not the Hetaira. The nonpersonal adaptation is thereby
added to the personal—or vice versa. The third adaptation—which would
be the opposite of the second—is likely to be more difficult to develop; and
the fourth, like the "inferior function," tends to remain a problematical
blind spot. Both third and fourth adaptations tend to operate more often
than not in a relatively primitive, compulsive and inferior fashion. They are
apt to express themselves mostly in their negative forms.

Suppose that a Mother-identified woman has the Amazon as her second
adaptation. She will have a good deal of push and energy in addition to
being motherly. She is likely to become president of her local club or chair-
man of the polio drive. But she might not be overly sensitive to intangibles
(the Medium being in third place and relatively undeveloped) and the
need for individually personal response is likely to find her unprepared both
in terms of her inner relationship to herself as an individual or her relationships to other people as individuals, since the Hetaira, the opposite of her
leading adaptational form, is quite undeveloped.

Should the Medium or mana figure be predominant, and the Mother the
second adaptation, we might find a woman who has a great deal of sensitivity as a mother, being quite susceptible to the vibrations of her environment; but she would not be a capable organizer. She may not be too adequate in terms of individual relationships but still likely to function better
in this area than in any businesslike activity, since the Amazon, as the opposite of the Medium, would be her most primitive adaptational form.

As with the perception and judgment types, it is unprofitable to disregard
the currents of our constitutional predispositions and inferior functions.
This means that we make best use of those particular force elements which
happen to be the most powerfully constellated; but also, for the sake of
growth as well as for our better functioning, we need to pay attention to
and try to potentiate the unadapted and inferior functions. A woman of the
Hetaira make-up may be able to operate fairly adequately in the realm of
the Amazon or the Medium, whichever happens to be her second quality,

but if she tries to play the Mother first she will be at best inadequate.

The dynamism of Yang and Yin types is analogous to that of the perception and evaluation types but there is no direct correlation between these two descriptive systems. In both areas the inferior functions constitute the framework for a lifelong challenge of an *Auseinandersetzung*, a need to come-to-terms-with. In both, the inferior functions come to expression through the shadow, animus and anima and thus constellate the individuation problem.

Wolff's was the first attempt at a typology of the feminine. She has been criticized for defining femininity predominantly in relationship terms, and subsequent formulations have used various archetypal patterns including the Greek Pantheon. The basic patterns were correctly discerned by Wolff, however, when her types are considered in relationship to a woman's self, rather than merely to the outer self.

12. The Anima

IN JUNG'S ORIGINAL FORMULATION, anima and animus are the archetypes of what for either sex is the *totally other*. Each represents a world that is at first quite incomprehensible to its opposite, a world that can never be directly known. Even though we carry within us elements of the opposite sex, their field of expression is precisely that area which is most obscure, strange, irrational and fear-inspiring to us; it can at best be intuited and "felt out" but never completely understood. These archetypes, then, are predominantly contrasexual, expressing the fact that there is nothing so totally "other" as the opposite sex (see also afterword, p. 316ff.).

By way of brief characterization, the anima represents the archetype of the man's Yin, the feminine within him, and the animus represents the woman's maleness, her Yang. Let us recall at this point that the shadow represents repressed unconscious *personal* characteristics—though it too has its transpersonal level—while anima and animus personify the *general* human *a priori* unconscious instinct patterns upon which many of these personal characteristics are based.

Anima and animus tend to operate like partial or separate personalities made up of different composite patterns. In man—as each is a different individual—each anima behaves like a different individual "other" personality with whom he is "stuck" or to whom he is "married." For the sake of individuation it is necessary for him to find out what this other personality is like, how it feels, thinks and tends to act. In a given situation one has to consider not only one's own reaction but also how the anima reacts, what she desires, likes or dislikes. Like a problematic partner, the anima has to be treated with attention and consideration but also with discipline and experimental interplay and challenge. This other personality can be disciplined only if we give her some means of expression and if we are also prepared to learn from her.

To clothe these concepts with some substance let us consider an actual case.

A young man who was desperate for love and union came for a consultation. He was looking for the woman who would fulfill him and live up to his ideals, would share his interests, be a home-maker, a comrade, wife and mother, who would also be artistic, inspiring, understanding and beautiful. He had not found such a woman. He had been infatuated with many different girls, but the closer he came to them the more his passion cooled. They annoyed him; he feared that he might drown or be overcome by their power or, as he put it, be sucked dry, or be fenced in by them; they were too demanding, too disappointing; thus his great love always vanished, only to be kindled by another one. He was restless and somewhat unreliable, although ambitious and with a brilliant mind. He had perhaps some writing talent—at any rate he had written some poetry—but for lack of discipline never produced anything substantial. He was snowed under by trifles and, restively impatient, always running after the next new project that beckoned around the corner.

Here are two of his dreams.

"*I come home to my current girl friend. We begin to enjoy a cozy evening together but gradually I begin to feel uneasy. I sense that the house is haunted. And indeed the house takes on quite a frightening aspect. I now find myself in an old, Victorian, ghost-ridden mansion; everything in it is dark and fearsome. Suddenly the ghost is before me: I see, as if suspended in the air, an old, old Puritan woman in 17th century dress. I am terrified.*"

Then abruptly the scene changes: "*A beautiful woman approaches me and draws me after her. I follow her into the water of a beautiful lake. Deep in the water she suddenly changes into a toad, produces a vile excrement and threatens to suck out my blood. I manage to struggle free and to catch and subdue her, but then she changes into a wild horse and gallops away.*"

Both of these dreams contain a number of feminine figures: the friend or possible bride, the Puritan woman, the siren or water sprite, also the toad and the horse. A psychological situation is presented here which could be formulated as follows: The factor which produces the projection that threatens to drown him has, at least partially, a nonpersonal quality; only one aspect takes the form of an actual contemporary woman. The historical or sociological part of her is incorporated in the Puritan woman of three hundred years ago; the other, the instinctual part, is on the animal level. It is this subhuman aspect which ensnares him, poisons him and threatens to suck his blood—his vitality—from him; all of this escapes his grasp.

For this dreamer the anima symbols are those of the frog, the vampire, the horse and the ghost; and there is also the historical part, represented by the Puritan woman, to whom he associated his mother. Later I shall give a further interpretation of this dream. At present we can merely conclude that underneath the Puritan garb there looms something animal-like, dangerous and seductive.

Now the question arises: What is the nature of this dreamer's projection?—for everything leads us to assume that a vast projection is at the root of his difficulty with women.

It will be helpful to quote Jung at some length here, in his description of the problem of the anima:

> What, then, is this projection-making factor? The East calls it the "Spinning Woman"—Maya, who creates illusion by her dancing. Had we not long since known it from the symbolism of dreams, this hint from the Orient would put us on the right track——the enveloping, embracing, and devouring element points unmistakably to the mother [and he adds in a footnote: "Here and in what follows, the word 'mother' is not meant in the literal sense but as a symbol of everything that functions as a mother."], that is, to the son's relation to the real mother, to her imago, and to the woman who is to become a mother for him. His Eros is passive like a child's; he hopes to be caught, sucked in, enveloped, and devoured. He seeks, as it were, the protecting, nourishing, charmed circle of the mother, the condition of the infant released from every care, in which the outside world bends over him and even forces happiness upon him. No wonder the real world vanishes from sight!
>
> If this situation is dramatized, as the unconscious usually dramatizes it, then there appears before you on the psychological stage a man living regressively, seeking his childhood and his mother, fleeing from a cold cruel world which denies him understanding. Often a mother appears beside him who apparently shows not the slightest concern that her little son should become a man, but who, with tireless and self-immolating effort, neglects nothing that might hinder him from growing up and marrying. You behold the secret conspiracy between mother and son, and how each helps the other to betray life.
>
> Where does the guilt lie? With the mother, or with the son? Probably with both. The unsatisfied longing of the son for life and the world ought to be taken seriously. There is in him a desire to touch reality, to embrace the earth and fructify the field of the world. But he makes no more than a series of fitful starts, for his initiative as well as his staying power are crippled by the secret memory that the world and happiness may be had as a gift—from the mother. . . . It makes demands on the masculinity of a man, on his ardour, above all on his courage and resolution when it comes to throwing his whole being into the scales. For this he would need a faithless Eros, one capable of forgetting his mother and undergoing the pain of relinquishing the first love of his life. The mother, foreseeing this danger, has carefully

inculcated into him the virtues of faithfulness, devotion, loyalty, so as to protect him from the moral disruption which is the risk of every life adventure. He has learnt these lessons only too well, and remains true to his mother. This naturally causes her the deepest anxiety (when, to her greater glory, he turns out to be a homosexual, for example) and at the same time affords her an unconscious satisfaction that is positively mythological. For, in the relationship now reigning between them, there is consummated the immemorial and most sacred archetype of the marriage of mother and son. . . .

This myth, better than any other, illustrates the nature of the collective unconscious. At this level the mother is both old and young, Demeter and Persephone, and the son is spouse and sleeping suckling rolled into one. The imperfections of real life, with its laborious adaptations and manifold disappointments, naturally cannot compete with such a state of indescribable fulfilment.

In the case of the son, the projection-making factor is identical with the mother-imago, and this is consequently taken to be the real mother. The projection can only be dissolved when the son sees that in the realm of his psyche there is an image not only of the mother but of the daughter, the sister, the beloved, the heavenly goddess, and the chthonic Baubo. Every mother and every beloved is forced to become the carrier and embodiment of this omnipresent and ageless image, which corresponds to the deepest reality in a man. It belongs to him, this perilous image of Woman; she stands for the loyalty which in the interests of life he must sometimes forgo; she is the much needed compensation for the risks, struggles, sacrifices that all end in disappointment; she is the solace for all the bitterness of life. And, at the same time, she is the great illusionist, the seductress, who draws him into life with her Maya—and not only into life's reasonable and useful aspects, but into its frightful paradoxes and ambivalences where good and evil, success and ruin, hope and despair, counterbalance one another. . . .

This image is "My Lady Soul," as Spitteler called her. I have suggested instead the term "anima," as indicating something specific, for which the expression "soul" is too general and too vague. The empirical reality summed up under the concept of the anima forms an extremely dramatic content of the unconscious. It is possible to describe this content in rational, scientific language, but in this way one entirely fails to express its living character. Therefore, in describing the living processes of the psyche, I deliberately and consciously give preference to a dramatic, mythological way of thinking and speaking, because this is not only more expressive but also more exact than an abstract scientific terminology, which is wont to toy with the notion that its theoretic formulations may one fine day be resolved into algebraic equations.[1]

The world of the anima represents the abysmal Yin element, the psychic aboriginal sourceground, the world of Goethe's "Mothers," which has existed in man prior to his experience of himself as an "I," an ego. Since it represents irrational psychic existence which is prior to consciousness, the anima consists of *a priori* urges and drives which are not created by consciousness, but which are the preconditions for consciousness, by which consciousness is secretly fed and from which it lives under the illusion of being able to free itself. We must particularly stress this *a priori* character in so far as it represents the archetypal image of the feminine in its most general form as it exists in the individual man and in men collectively.

As a numinous image, namely as an affective image spontaneously produced by the objective psyche, the anima represents the eternal feminine— in any and all of her four possible aspects and their variants and combinations as Mother, Hetaira, Amazon and Medium. She appears as the goddess of nature, *Dea Natura*, and the Great Goddess of Moon and Earth who is mother, sister, beloved, destroyer, beautiful enchantress, ugly witch, life and death, all in one person or in various aspects of the one; thus she appears in innumerable images of enchanting, frightening, friendly, helpful or dangerous feminine figures, or even in animal figures as we have seen— foremost as cat, snake, horse, cow, dove, owl—which mythology assigns to certain feminine deities. She appears as seductress, harlot, nymph, muse, saint, martyr, maiden in distress, gypsy, peasant woman, the lady next door, or as the Queen of Heaven, the Holy Virgin, to mention but a few examples. These are some of the many facets in which feminine nature, the Yin element, has ever been experienced by men.

As a pattern of behavior, the archetype of the anima represents those drive elements which are related to life as life, as an unpremeditated, spontaneous, natural phenomenon, to the life of the instincts, the life of the flesh, the life of concreteness, of earth, of emotionality, directed toward people and things. It is the drive toward involvement, the instinctual connectedness to other people and the containing community or group. Whereas separate individuality is personified as a male element, connectedness—the "containing" unconscious, the group and the community—is experienced and personified as a feminine entity.

As a pattern of emotion the anima consists of the man's unconscious urges, his moods, emotional aspirations, anxieties, fears, inflations and depressions, as well as his potential for emotion and relationship. Whenever a man acts in identity with his anima—unconscious of the moods that "pull" him—he acts like a second-rate woman. In this form the anima represents a man's relatively unadapted, hence inferior, world of nature and emotional involvement, loves and hates. Consequently the objective psyche presents itself to the man at first as a totally irrational, dangerously primitive, chaotic temptation, as an enchanting seduction.

Since what we are speaking of constitutes a level of operativeness which has not yet been in consciousness and to a great extent is not capable of ever being completely realized consciously, yet which at the same time demands awareness and confrontation, the process of gaining even partial awareness of the anima constitutes an indispensable means of approach to the nonpersonal dimension of the objective psyche.

The unconscious patterns of emotion and behavior function in a manner comparable to the intricate reflex patterns on the biological level. Such automatic patterns of behavior are evoked by typical situations to which they appear to be attuned, as key to lock. Such reflex-like reactions are automatic unless consciousness is able to step in and modify them. The reflex-like irruptions of the anima occur in situations which call for emotional and instinctual responses; more often than not this means that the responses come from the area of the inferior function, since the instinctual and intuitive-emotional response is what a person is usually least capable of providing consciously. When an emotion-charged situation arises and he attempts to react with reason, without *first* or at least *also* realizing his emotional response, he is likely to suffer an anima attack. When a situation evokes emotions and the emotional response is not channeled consciously, then inevitably the response will be forthcoming from the unconscious, regardless of his intentions and even in opposition to them. Then the man who fails to or cannot respond consciously with his feelings will get into a "state," and what is worse he will not even notice it. He will attempt to be rational, will point things out very logically to his *vis-à-vis*, most likely a woman, but his blood pressure will go up. And of course all because of her stupidity! As he is unable to channel his feelings consciously, he falls victim to a mood—the unadapted response of his inferior function. He is also apt to react poorly to a woman's tears since they aggravate his mood. Then he becomes fearful or angry without realizing why and can only fold up and surrender, run away or explode.

The dynamics of the anima can also produce serious depressive states. A young man in a state of depression that had totally paralyzed him and necessitated hospitalization had the following dream: *A woman had committed a crime, or was suspected of it, and the police gave her a choice between arrest and suicide. She tearfully chose the latter.* To this woman the dreamer associated a person with ruthless ambition. The police represented his view of conventional morality in terms of which he tended to judge himself. His reckless ambition (engendered, incidentally, by his mother) had indeed committed a crime; it had completely stymied his emotional development. His judgment of himself was punitive, so that he could not accept his shortcomings but only condemn them. Therefore, realization and acceptance of his anima, representing the full range of his emotional potential, was impossible. The only alternatives—almost equally destructive—were punitive self-condemnation and rigidity (arrest) or repression of the instinctual urges, which was tantamount to a psychological self-annihilation (suicide); thus the forced annihilation of the anima, his mood-personality, produced the threat of a depressive psychosis.

In order to clarify the actual manifestations of the anima pattern of emotion and behavior in the lives of individuals, we refer again to the concept of the complex as being made up of archetypal core and associational shell. Archetypal Femininity—the Yin element, the Eternal Woman—as it affects the male becomes actualized in a mythological core and in a personal shell, a network of associations which are formed during the process of childhood conditioning. Whoever incorporates the feminine image most decisively for the child provokes the pattern in terms of which the anima is actualized into the personal realm: mother, sister, aunt, nursemaid, grandmother, friend, or anyone who took mother's place in the event that she was absent.

By the laws of association, whatever experiences correspond to or are contiguous to the way the Feminine was first and most impressively met form a pattern of *a priori* expectations which continues to function throughout the individual's life. This will color not only his relationships with particular women but also his emotions, fantasies and imaginings, which express his complexes, giving shape to his particular bias in respect to love, artistry, ambition, encroachment, jealousy, resentment, etc. These are all precipitates of the personal experience with the Eternal Feminine as mediated or modified by his particular anima model. All of these elements present themselves as dream and fantasy images and as unconscious anticipations of external emotional encounters. They foster the search for the never-yet-seen in the form of anticipations and projections. These inner expectations, hopes and fears will automatically be projected onto people (who correspond to them in varying degrees). In other words, the complexes formed around the anima core direct the man's reactions to emotional situations and to particular women and also shape his unconscious expectations of the way they will behave.

Let us attempt to explain this as it applies to the patient who dreamed of the Puritan ghost. His mother happened indeed to be a Puritan ghost, quite unreal as a person, with outdated, rigid convictions that stifled her real feelings. She was domineering, possessive and demanding, yet sentimental. Without any sense or feeling for his individuality she was inherently rejective, while seeming to be solicitous. And of course she was also a strict and indomitable believer in puritanical principles of right and wrong.

The associations in which the archetype of Woman was incarnated for him were those which were typical of a self-righteous domestic tyrant. The anima took on the puritan aspects because this trait happened to exist in contiguity with the qualities of motherhood. If his mother had had blond hair, let us say, blondness would be another contiguity association, not essential to the meaning of femininity but coexistent in this case and eventually able to trigger an unconscious reaction against that pattern which mother incarnated for him. He was driven to rebel, and he yearned for its opposite. Thus mother, in terms of her own qualities as well as of the rebellious yearning she evoked, set the pattern for the way in which the world of the feminine exerted its attraction and/or repulsion upon him—from within as well as from without. For this man, attraction was to occur in the form of a poetic, imaginative, nature-connected "goddess," real or imagined, who concurrently inspired fear because of these very same unfamiliar qualities with which every woman was bound to threaten him. But he was always afraid to be caught by mother's likeness, by the tyrant he suspected in every woman no matter how fascinating and unlike mother she appeared to be.

Fear and attraction, in fact, always go together in the confrontation of the world of the absolutely other, the other sex. It is fear of the threateningly unknown and simultaneously a magnetic attraction of this same unknown. By her very nature the anima exerts this arousing and numbing fascination; the lovely siren and the dreadful witch are inseparable. One or the other of these qualities is likely to be accentuated, depending on the nature of the personal actualization; but its opposite is rarely absent, it merely operates in a more concealed fashion. Even in the case of a good relationship between mother and son, the pattern of expectation in regard to women has its element of secret fear. But a conditioning in terms of a trusting personal relationship with the original carrier of the anima image at least makes for a lessening of this fear and for a better chance to establish personal relationships. However, where the relationship to mother or the mother representative has been a negative one, as with an overpowering, rejecting or lovingly devouring mother, the fear and repulsion manifestly prevail. The women and situations which reflect the likeness of mother's destructive qualities and attitudes are feared and rejected. A man so conditioned will be drawn to women who on the surface appear to be mother's opposite. But only on the surface, for the anima invariably attracts in terms of its original imprinting. Below the deceiving surface, mother's likeness is always encountered eventually, either through the actual presence of the dreaded qualities or through their projection upon the woman. Eventually all women who first seem attractive turn out to be, or at any rate are felt to be, as dangerous as mother was. So also with our patient. At first friendship and cozy togetherness (as in the dream) seemed possible. But the greater the repulsion of the Puritan ghost, the more he was unconsciously paralyzed by reacting as to mother's tyranny. Women looked beautiful only from a distance; they could only be dreamed about, never concretely related to.

But there is a further factor. Since the anima represents the Eternal Feminine in its widest potentialities, its archetypal core contains much more than can ever be constellated by any actual mother. Our patient's mother was hardly a seductress; nor was she an inspiring Muse. In her the life of the nature demon was as good as extinct (thus she appeared in his dream as a ghost). Hence, in this man's actual experience of the archetype, the essential inspirational, spontaneous, natural part was entirely missing. He had never experienced this side in an actual human relationship, so that aspect now presented the urge and pull of what for him was the mystery of women. For even though it had never been encountered, it was an *a priori* part of his anima and the goal of his life's search. Not having been experienced in the "primary" encounter with mother, it now appeared in a nonhuman form in his unconscious, as the horse, the frog and the siren or water nymph. A fascinating attraction, forever beckoning, vanished at closer view and then beckoned again from another place, leaving him forever longing for that which had never been realized—and which could not be realized in this form, for no real situation can ever be as beautiful as this everchanging, colorful and terrifying being of his dreams. This very longing sucked his blood, drained his emotions and deprived him of his vitality, never allowing him to find peace within himself. He was seized by inexplicable moods, highly elated one moment, in the deepest depression the next, unaccountably and for no reason attracted to a "beautiful" woman, then unaccountably hating and fearing her for a vampire.[2] If he ever met a woman with a relative absence of the repulsive motherlike features it is unlikely that he would be able to make an initial relationship with her, for the actual concrete experience of interacting with such a "mother-unlike" person is lacking.

Moreover the Puritan and the sprite are now *in him* unconsciously. The domestic tyrant has become internalized, it is his power complex, fed by his own bossiness, his anima, and it is likely to make life unbearable for any woman who has to deal with him. She will have to be romantic, daring, stern, rigid and puritanical all in one and will have to minister to his needs according to his specifications. First he will lie with her, but the Puritan in him cannot forgive her for her loss of virtue or for any other failure to live up to the code of his demands. She will be expected to be spontaneous and natural, but woe to her if she dares to be herself!

It must be understood, of course, that not all aspects of the anima become constellated and activated during one man's lifetime. There are infinite individual differences and predispositions, not only in terms of initial experiences but also in what is prefigured. These differences can show up clearly in any given family. For example, two men have grown up with the same uninspiring, prosaic parents. One may have to undergo great suffering to find his poetic artistic side; the other may never even be bothered by such a need. The difference here need not lie in the environment but can be found in the different predispositions of the two men. To the extent that the one has the artistic predisposition but lacks encouragement from the parents, he may have to seek for he does not know what, until he discovers it. The other one may find even less encouragement, or for that matter more, and yet not be driven to search for an artistic side or use it. In other words, there is a realm of predetermined personality potentials (as postulated in Chapter 7) which are not merely products of the environment, though environmental factors may succeed or fail in evoking them.

As long as the anima remains in an unconscious state, like all unconscious elements, her means of expression are compulsively primitive—through complexes, identity, inflation and projection. These factors were considered when we discussed the complex in general terms.

Identity with the anima manifests itself in all sorts of *compulsive* moodiness, self-pity, sentimentality, depression, brooding withdrawal, fits of passion, morbid oversensitivity or effeminacy—namely in emotional and behavior patterns that cause the man to act like an inferior woman.

Inflation by the anima is a state in which ambitions, hopes and desires are confused with accomplished facts and realities. A minister who was fanatically impressed by the urgency of his particular mission had the following dream: "*I heard a voice as if from the depths of space. It said that if Suzy did not leave the parsonage I would have to.*" Of such a voice from afar, with such a strong sense of authority (analogous to the "hand of God" in Chapter 6), we might say that it was like the voice of the Self. His associations to "Suzy" were that she was no particular friend of his. Indeed he suspected that she did not care too much for him as a person. She admired him, even fancied herself in love with him, not because of himself but because he was a "man of God." His dream then says something like: There is an emotional personality aspect of you which is in love with the halo—with being the great "man of God." But unless that attitude leaves, unless you can gain some distance from it, you will fail as a minister (have to leave the parsonage yourself). For the inflation, the being in love with our own greatness, deprives us of our sense of human limitations. Then we become unrealistically exacting of ourselves and intolerant of others.

The inflationary aspect of the anima is most difficult to deal with because it tends to be so pleasantly convincing. Her illusion appears as obvious truth; one feels rather self-righteous and good about it. But, as we have seen by this time, just when we are most ardently convinced of an issue we are most likely to be in the grip of an unconscious power—hence most likely deceived.

The anima *in projection* is responsible for man's state of being in love or in hate. One has now met one's soul image, the ideal and only woman, or conversely an absolutely unbearable bitch. Both reactions are found to be fascinating and irresistable. In such situations there tends to be a compulsive involvement which we can neither deal with nor let alone. Were it simply the fact that the woman is so wonderful or so awful, we could either love her or leave her. But if we can do neither, then we are under the arresting spell of the archetype.

Relationships to the other sex are almost bound to be initiated by anima or animus projections. But true relatedness requires that we reach past the projections to the reality of the other person. For the actual reality of the other person is likely to be quite at variance with the projected expectations, hence while the projections continue to prevail one feels disappointed and let down by the partner when he or she fails to conform to the image. Actual relatedness between one person and another, namely a meeting of "I" with "Thou," is therefore impossible unless the most unrealistic anima or animus projections have been dissolved—no small matter to accomplish. As long as only the anima projection determines the relationship, it tends to produce rather a pseudo-relatedness—between illusion and illusion—in the form of mutual fascinations and/or explosive resentments and flight reactions when the negative projections appear (the Puritan ghost, vampire, etc.). But remember that projections and the relations or pseudo-relations which they engender are states in which we find ourselves; they occur of themselves and cannot be avoided by will or good intentions. Our only chance lies in developing an awareness of when they happen and of the projected qualities involved.

A frequent anima-animus relationship difficulty is engendered by the contradictoriness of multiple constellated aspects. Anima or animus may present their compelling qualities as polar opposites; that is, emotional attachments and expectations may be split and in contradictory opposition. One example is furnished by our first patient in this chapter; his responsiveness is split between the inspiring muse and the puritan housewife. The woman who would constellate the muse is enthusiastically worshipped, but alas she lacks the capacity for giving him a feeling of homeyness, the warmth of the hearth. The housewifely woman is appreciated for daily living but is felt to be a dull bore who suffocates the inspirational needs. Hence no actual woman can be related to quite satisfactorily, and often enough the image of the one type may appear and attract under the guise of the other, the *femme inspiratrice* who, when she is known more intimately, disappointingly turns out to be nothing but a "nice" homemaker—or worse still a harsh puritanical matriarch. Or she who is hopefully seen as a warm motherly type is discovered to be a cold fish, merely interested in artistic or intellectual problems or in her career, and impossible to get along with in daily life.

Another common form of such multiple anima aspects is the dichotomy of holy saint, pure virgin goddess versus seductive siren or harlot. The first is worshipped on a pedestal and even married, but she is too good for a real relationship. She is too pure to be soiled by the reality of her partner, especially by his sexual aspirations. Thus she may receive unconditional worship —at least while she manages to live up to the divine image projected upon her—and more often than not at the price of renouncing her actual human qualities; but she cannot catch the man's concrete, everyday love, and may even find him sexually impotent, for who can make love to and despoil a holy virgin? Thus the woman who is respected cannot be loved or physically desired, and the sexually arousing woman, with whom it is possible to have actual relations, cannot be respected.

The shadings and variations of possibilities in which such intrinsic contradictions can present themselves are endless, of course. The four basic types of configurations of the Feminine (Mother, Hetaira, Medium and Amazon) will generally set the patterns of combinations, variations and polarities in which anima conflicts manifest themselves, thus frequently bringing about relationships with more than one woman until the projections are realized. Contrary to the contention found in Jung's early writings that the anima is uniform, while the animus is represented by a multiplicity of figures,[3] it is my own impression that some form or degree of multiplicity is to be found in the unconscious of both men and women.

The man's anima projection always offers a great temptation to the woman. She will tend to identify with his expectation and hence play-act, pretend to incorporate the man's ideal or his real or imagined needs. As an "anima woman" she may become all things to all men, a flirt or even a wise wife or inspiring muse, anticipating all of her husband's or lover's needs and aspirations, thereby making him so dependent on her that he falls in with all her plans and does what is expected of him. The wise wife, for instance, skillfully manages her husband and the whole situation between them. But, in Harding's terms, such a woman always refers to *her* husband, *her* marriage . . . with emphasis on the possessive pronoun.[4] It is her instinctive power drive and possessiveness or her need to seek security in identifying with a conventional persona or inspiring angel ideal that may induce the woman to act out such a role—and may make her lose her own soul, her own real identity, in the process.

In order to become a full person—not merely a cipher in a social role, or a male animal—or indeed sometimes in order to hold onto his manhood, a man must confront his anima and try to establish a living, growing relationship with her. This is of course essential for his relationships with other people also. When consciousness is held in thrall by the power of the archetype, the complex, which is formed around the archetype's nuclear core, and its projection make it next to impossible to come near to the reality of the other person. Jung describes what can happen when there is no confrontation by the man's ego of the "other" within:

> Very often the ego experiences a vague feeling of moral defeat and then behaves all the more defensively, defiantly, and self-righteously, thus setting up a vicious circle which only increases its feeling of inferiority. The bottom is then knocked out of the human relationship, for, like megalomania, a feeling of inferiority makes mutual recognition impossible, and without this there is no relationship.[5]

Confrontation of the anima, or for that matter of any unconscious autonomous complex or drive, requires awareness of the nature of its autonomous expectations and personal response patterns. It requires the establishment of a relationship to the complex as an autonomous entity like an inner "Thou," allowing for and consciously adapting to its urges and needs, channeling its impulses whenever and wherever possible into expressions compatible with external reality and the ethical dictates of one's innermost conscience; thus not only taking into account one's own accustomed habits and the demands of one's family and community responsibilities but also serving the needs of that which wants to come to life.

The following dream gives an example of the dynamics of the confrontation. A man who has always avoided any emotional involvement dreams:

"While walking across the countryside I am suddenly attacked by a herd of blue geese. I call for help. The mistress of the geese appears. She is the woman I love, and with her magic wand she appeases the geese. I kneel down before her and offer her my troth. In return she graciously gives me a bouquet of flowers."

The dreamer's association to the geese was the Grimm Brothers' fairy tale called "The Goose Girl." This story tells of a princess who is despoiled and degraded by her power-hungry servant and is obliged to take care of the geese. These geese are the animal or instinctive aspects of the princess who has lost her real kingdom to the power drive, the servant maid. Geese are traditionally the companions of witches, the outlawed worshipers of the pagan divinities of nature. Another traditional interpretation of the goose motif is that of the universal aspect of the soul. The wild goose is able to move about everywhere, on firm land, in water and in the air. It is the bird of Hermes, who is the leader of souls. This fits in with the fact that the geese in this dream are blue, the color of the heavenly, the spiritual.

The dreamer is attacked, then, by unrealized life within himself, by an aspect of the anima, which has remained on the animal—i.e., drive—level. It has to do with the sacredness of the natural, the Yin or earth-soul experience which he has never realized. His one-sided male attitude, dominated by the power motive, has degraded the world of the feminine to the exclusively domestic level; he has thereby lost touch with his own feeling. The redeeming and transforming "magic" comes to him through the experience of and reverence for love in an actual relationship. He has to siphon some energy away from his ambitions toward worldly advancement into a personal relationship which offers him no gain in prestige. The woman who appeases the geese in the dream has the features of the girl he loves. As he gives his troth to the anima, commits himself and is loyal to a relationship and to his feelings as something to be respected and valued, the anima—his awakened feeling—gives him flowers; his life will henceforth bloom. This dream came at a point when the dreamer's life was deadlocked and at a standstill, dominated by conscious reasonableness and driving ambitions. He now began to discover unexpected depths of feeling in himself and became a human being.

The anima consciously confronted and related to may lead to the realm of "flowers"—fantasy and feeling will become consciously accessible rather than threatening. She leads to the source of creativity.

It is never a simple matter to meet the anima, however; she tends to appear with reflex-like speed, as an emotional reaction, before one has a chance to take heed, and by the time the ground has been surveyed she is gone, the feeling has vanished. An additional difficulty lies in the fact that the archetypes as such—the sources of all these reactions—cannot ever be integrated with any finality but continue to express themselves in ever new forms. Only their manifestations can be integrated, to the extent that one gets to know them, but the archetypes themselves are the

> foundation stones of the psychic structure, which in its totality exceeds the limits of consciousness and therefore can never become the object of direct cognition. Though the effects of anima and animus can be made conscious, they themselves are factors transcending consciousness and beyond the reach of perception and volition. Hence they remain autonomous despite the integration of their contents, and for this reason they should be borne constantly in mind.[6]

A fundamental fact we easily tend to lose sight of is that anima and animus are not subject to will and conscious control. We can never tame or eliminate them; we always have to be on the lookout for new tricks and surprises. Every intense affect indicates that anima or animus is at work. Unless we realize this we will always fall victim to the illusion that we have mastered it, and just when we feel self-righteous about this mastery we are already in the inflation which sets the next trap.

Experience of the archetype's autonomy is a jolt to our accustomed ways of thinking and feeling; it is therefore a turning point in the analysis. The discovery that archetypes and their induced complexes behave like separate personalities which are not subject to our conscious control leads to the first deadlock in every analysis. After shadow and anima or animus have been realized in all their implications every analysant attempts to deal with them through an effort of will and discipline. Only slowly and painfully does he come to the realization that he *cannot* deal with them in this fashion only. His reaction then tends to be one of sheer hopelessness, a "dark night of the soul." We all live under the illusion that we can control everything, or at least that we should be able to control everything, that wherever there is a will there is also a way and that nothing can ever happen to us unless we do it ourselves. The ego seemingly cannot renounce this illusion until we have suffered so long through conscious trials and failures that the weapons fall out of our hands. When we are thus at the point of giving up and finally feel that it is no use, that we cannot do it—then transformation begins. Then we become the object rather than the subject of an inner change. This point of utter despair is the turning point. The entrance to purgatory in *The Divine Comedy* is found at the lowest, deepest point of hell.

The acceptance of the anima as an independent other personality to which one is bound transforms her into an ally. (The same thing is likely to happen when a woman of flesh and blood is accepted in this way.) By paying attention to her unpredictable reactions one can discover what one's real emotions happen to be, regardless of will and intent. Such awareness transforms blind emotions into genuine feelings, opens the doors to the soul, to the integration of spontaneity, sensitivity, receptivity, adaptability and warmth, but also to the assimilation of aggressiveness and the inferior functions, hence of the ability to direct one's temper constructively.

Through actualizing the never-before-encountered inferior function, anima integration eases the pressure of affect-tensions, depressions, moods and "states," and opens the way to genuine relatedness by virtue of a better ability to see the other person as he or she really is. For to the extent that the anima qualities are consciously experienced they are no longer subject to that sort of projection which distorts our view of the other person's reality.

The anima constitutes a problem for the world at large no less than for the individual. Fear of the anima historically and collectively led to the degradation of women. Today this fear expresses itself in the masculinization of the world and the attending disparagement of femininity which is defined exclusively in terms of mothering and homemaking, hence the low ebb of woman's true self-regard as a woman, rather than as an imitator of male functioning. Failure to integrate the Yin world culturally has led to the widespread rigidity of abstract dogmatic mental attitudes, resulting in the sterile, instinct- and feeling-dissociated, overrationalistic society of our day. Also the objective psyche compensates collectively for this state of affairs. Compulsive anima invasions occur collectively in all expressions of mob psychology, mass psychoses and hate psychoses, which inexplicably erupt ever and again in our "enlightened" and "sensible" modern world.

13. The Animus

THE *animus* is the corollary to the man's anima and represents the woman's "recessive maleness" or Yang aspect, her urge for action, her capacity for judgment and discrimination. To the extent that these functions are not sufficiently conscious the woman judges people, things and circumstances—but especially men—by the authority of the unconscious image and the expected emotional pattern attached to that image rather than by their own qualities. Just as the man in an anima-dominated state is moody, undependable and withdrawn, the animus-ridden woman is ruled by preconceived notions, prejudices and expectations, is dogmatic, argumentative and overgeneralizing. An animus-possessed woman argues not to discover truth but in order to be "right," to win and to have the last word. She would rather be right in an argument than to take human relatedness into consideration. Life and men are judged and rejected if they do not fit the mold of her preconceived notions.

It is important to keep in mind that the animus represents evaluating systems which have never yet been confronted by consciousness. Their unconsciousness is not the result of repression. The animus, like the anima, signifies an *a priori* frame of reference. The concept of the animus describes those aspects of a woman that are the means by which judgments are formed—standards that she simply takes for granted, that she is not even aware of as standards; they seem to be facts, "obvious to everyone." "How can anyone doubt it?" "Since time immemorial (since father or mother told me) people have been and behaved thus." "This is the way things are!" Etc., etc.

The animus, then, is exceedingly difficult to contact because in searching for it one tends to look for errors in judgment—which may be there—while neglecting the judging process itself. The thinking or feeling functions may be perfectly adequate but the premises upon which this thinking and feeling are based may be totally unrealistic. These premises are not adequately investigated because they seem beyond question. Judgments and emotional convictions therefore have not been formed by consciousness but are rather the basis upon which consciousness has been founded and from which it has developed. Hence the unconscious world of the woman's animus contains a formidable array of undifferentiated convictions, stereotyped manners and inflexible morals (the animus is a great moralizer). We find here the source of feminine dogmatism, rigidity, self-righteousness, inflation, aggressiveness and possessiveness.

A practical example will illustrate how the animus functions. A woman who regarded herself as being full of loving concern for everybody was always doing *good* things, especially for her family. Unfortunately she was often ill and in need of care herself, and since she was so unselfish she naturally expected everyone else to be equally unselfish toward her, to anticipate and tend to her needs. It then developed that she was weak and ill most of the time and whenever there was no one at her service, doing her the good she had always done to others, she felt aggrieved, disappointed, bitter and resentful. But she forgave everyone and blamed herself for being an utter, dismal failure. As a result, her physical state was one of growing apathy and subtle resentfulness. It became increasingly difficult for her to maintain any relationships at all. She even discovered, to her terror, that she had homicidal urges and began to fear that she might harm her child. She had the following dream:

"*My father was trying to force his way into my bedroom while I was still in bed. I begged and pleaded with him to leave me alone, but he broke through the door and beat me mercilessly. I made no attempt to resist but lay prostrate before him. Then I went out into the street with a knife and viciously slashed at everybody in sight.*"

Her father was a kind gentleman of very strict high ideals who had taught her that one must always do good things for others, that one should never live for oneself and never take heed of anything but the need to sacrifice, and that self-concern and self-will should be ruthlessly repressed. As a child, whenever she had tried to be her natural naughty self she had been severely reprimanded and punished. Her parents would tell her that they did this for her own good, of course, that she was a very bad and egotistical child whenever she thought of herself and did not efface her own ways and impulses for the sake of others, always and unconditionally.

Her father, incidentally, had also been ill most of the time. No one ever diagnosed this illness; he was just "ill." He was a man of many projects which never came to fruition, ostensibly because of his goodness and high ideals; he was too busy protecting others and considering their needs. At home, in his own quiet way, he was a ruthless tyrant; everything had to conform to his expectations.

The patient's dream then pictured her as brutally beaten down before she had a chance to get on her own feet (out of bed), viciously invaded in her private, individual space. The intruder here is not so much the actual, "gentle" father as his unexpressed viciousness, the destructive effect on her of his world, his code of living. Honoring this code—which said: Always act for others and never allow your own needs to be expressed—had rendered her helpless and would continue to victimize her since she did not resist it.

The instinctual need for self-protection, the instinctual ego-drive of aggressiveness, could not consciously be channeled in terms of her father's code. Consequently it channeled itself unconsciously, in the form of resentment and bitterness and an utterly unconscious critical attitude toward others. She was unable to make direct demands, indeed she was quite unaware of the fact that she *had* any demands to make. Her ego needs for assertion as an independent "I" were not associated to her consciousness, but led a dissociated, separate existence of their own as unconscious and primitive—hence destructive—hostilities, aggressiveness and compulsive demands.

Underneath, and in compensation for, her sweet cover, her appearance of yielding goodness, lay hidden a vicious destructiveness, as the second part of the dream shows, but of this she was totally unaware. If we cannot give a reasonable place to *conscious egotism* we have no choice but to become *unconsciously egotistical*—it is the price we pay for too much virtue—and of the two, the unconscious egotism is incomparably more destructive because it is self-righteous and inconsiderately primitive. The unadmitted egotism found expression in this "good" woman in her domination of others through helplessness, illness and martyrdom.

She saw herself as unselfish, lovingly sweet, with never a bad thought; yet she exuded bitterness, dissatisfaction and resentment. Even as she gradually became aware that her "noble" attitude of being everyone's carpet bred inner resentment, she resisted every attempt at a change. "It is wrong to assert oneself." "Why?" "Because it is." "But how do you know it is wrong?" "Because it is, I *know* it is."

Note these answers. They are typical animus answers, i.e., answers given by an autonomous complex of stereotyped expectations through which the Yang archetype has been actualized. Other animus expressions come out as "ought," "should," "Why don't they?" "Why doesn't somebody?" or "Don't you think you ought?" Their pattern expresses prejudgment, that is, prejudice. A succinct example of this is expressed in another patient's dream: "*I saw my husband mowing the lawn up a steep mountainside. He pushed and pushed, against seemingly insuperable odds, until he finally collapsed.*" The husband here represents the inferior man in her, the animus; her association to her husband was that he was always extremely concerned with external appearance, with the "front lawn" that people can see. This inner man pushes the "ought," which has to do with appearances, to the point of collapse. And in fact, since all her energies had to be dedicated to maintaining external appearances, this lady did reach such a point. Why must these appearances be maintained? *Because!*

Another woman all but pushed herself to the point of collapse in her attempt to be the perfect housekeeper. Her standard reaction to her failure was self-reproach, since it "should" be possible to accomplish everything. Why? *Well, father expected it of mother and mother did it.* Upon closer questioning it turned out that in mother's day ample household help was available, whereas our patient had to do it all herself. The daughter had never consciously considered this fact, however; she merely operated under the unconscious compulsion that it "ought" to be possible.

We may recall also the case of the mother in Chapter 3 who, under the influence of the Eastern Potentate, judged what her daughter "ought" to be. The child was being pushed off her island, as the dream put it; the animus-driven mother rejected the reality of her daughter's being.

In an animus that has not yet been consciously confronted, the archetypal predisposition and capacity for relating to situations and people through individual evaluation is as yet inadequately actualized. It has remained on a relatively unconscious level of hackneyed, rigid and dogmatic collective convictions. The assortment of judgments have not come from individual experience and testing but from what "one" or "they" consider as the "oughts" and "shoulds" of life. These convictions, judgments and opinions arise directly from the unconscious, inasmuch as they are formulated and accepted without conscious individual evaluation of facts and circumstances. To the extent that such unconscious convictions are in command, the ego or conscious judgment is dissociated from what is to be the basis of its experience, from concrete reality of both things and the "other." It cannot really see or relate to the "Thou" that confronts it. The expected "ought," from the "other" and from the world, blinds the vision to what is actually there; it constitutes a denial and rejection of what the other is and hence precludes a genuine relationship. The woman becomes *involved* with people, buffeted by her own emotions and disappointments when they do not live up to her inner "prejudged" standards, but she is not related to the real needs or even the offerings of others. Not until she becomes aware of her own animus can she begin to strive for relatedness in an "I-Thou" fashion. Her situation is correspondingly opposite to that of man unaware of his anima. He will be *uninvolved* by conscious design, claiming not to "understand" matters of feeling, but he will be unconsciously and unrealistically involved by virtue of his irrational feeling expectations. His moods and her convictions both bar the way to relatedness.

Here is one of Jung's descriptions of the animus (which, however, emphasizes primarily the Logos-Eros aspects of the total Yang-Yin interplay):

Woman is compensated by a masculine element and therefore her unconscious has, so to speak, a masculine imprint. This results in a considerable psychological difference between men and women, and accordingly I have called the projection-making factor in women the animus, which means mind or spirit. The animus corresponds to the paternal Logos, just as the anima corresponds to the maternal Eros. But I do not wish or intend to give these two intuitive concepts too specific a definition. I use Eros and Logos merely as conceptual aids to describe the fact that woman's consciousness is characterized more by the connective quality of Eros than by the discrimination and cognition associated with Logos. In men, Eros, the function of relationship, is usually less developed than Logos. In women, on the other hand, Eros is an expression of their true nature, while their Logos is often only a regrettable accident. It gives rise to misunderstandings and annoying interpretations in the family circle and among friends. This is because it consists of *opinions* instead of reflections, and by opinions I mean *a priori* assumptions that lay claim to absolute truth. Such assumptions, as everyone knows, can be extremely irritating. As the animus is partial to argument, he can best be seen at work in disputes where both parties know they are right. Men can argue in a very womanish way, too, when they are anima-possessed and have thus been transformed into the animus of their own anima. With them the question becomes one of personal vanity and touchiness (as if they were females); with women it is a question of power, whether of truth or justice or some other "ism"—for the dressmaker and hairdresser have already taken care of their vanity. The "Father" (i.e., the sum of conventional opinions) always plays a great role in female argumentation. No matter how friendly and obliging a woman's Eros may be, no logic on earth can shake her if she is ridden by the animus. Often the man has the feeling—and he is not altogether wrong—that only seduction or a beating or rape would have the necessary power of persuasion. He is unaware that this highly dramatic situation would instantly come to a banal and unexciting end if he were to quit the field and let a second woman carry on the battle. . . . This sound idea seldom or never occurs to him, because no man can converse with an animus for five minutes without becoming the victim of his own anima. Anyone who still had enough sense of humour to listen objectively to the ensuing dialogue would be staggered by the vast number of commonplaces, misapplied truisms, clichés from newspapers and novels, shop-soiled platitudes of every description interspersed with vulgar abuse and brain-splitting lack of logic. It is a dialogue which, irrespective of its participants, is repeated millions and millions of times in all the languages of the world and always remains essentially the same.

This singular fact is due to the following circumstance: when animus and anima meet, the animus draws his sword of power and the anima ejects her poison of illusion and seduction. The outcome need not always be negative, since the two are equally likely to fall in love (a special instance of love at first sight). The language of love is of astonishing uniformity, using the well-worn formulas with the utmost devotion and fidelity, so that once again the two partners find themselves in a banal collective situation. Yet they live in the illusion that they are related to one another in a most individual way.

In both its positive and its negative aspects the anima/animus relationship is always full of "animosity," i.e., it is emotional, and hence collective. Affects lower the level of the relationship and bring it closer to the common instinctual basis, which no longer has anything individual about it. Very often the relationship runs its course heedless of its human performers, who afterwards do not know what happened to them.

Whereas the cloud of "animosity" surrounding the man is composed chiefly of sentimentality and resentment, in woman it expresses itself in the form of opinionated views, interpretations, insinuations, and misconstructions, which all have the purpose (sometimes attained) of severing the relation between two human beings. . . .

Like the anima, the animus too has a positive aspect. Through the figure of the father he expresses not only conventional opinion but—equally—what we call "spirit," philosophical or religious ideas in particular, or rather the attitude resulting from them. Thus the animus is a psychopomp, a mediator between the conscious and the unconscious and a personification of the latter. Just as the anima becomes, through integration, the Eros of consciousness, so the animus becomes a Logos; and in the same way that the anima gives relationship and relatedness to a man's consciousness, the animus gives to woman's consciousness a capacity for reflection, deliberation, and self-knowledge.

The effect of anima and animus on the ego is in principle the same. This effect is extremely difficult to eliminate because, in the first place, it is uncommonly strong and immediately fills the ego-personality with an unshakable feeling of rightness and righteousness. In the second place, the cause of the effect is projected and appears to lie in objects and objective situations. Both these characteristics can, I believe, be traced back to the peculiarities of the archetype. For the archetype, of course, exists *a priori*. This may possibly explain the often totally irrational yet undisputed and indisputable existence of certain moods and opinions. Perhaps these are so notoriously difficult to influence because of the powerfully suggestive effect emanating from the archetype. Consciousness is fascinated by it, held captive, as if hypnotized. Very often the ego experiences a vague feeling of moral defeat and then behaves all the more defensively, defiantly, and self-righteously, thus setting up a vicious circle which only increases its feeling of inferiority. The bottom is then knocked out of the human relationship, for, like megalomania, a feeling of inferiority makes mutual recognition impossible, and without this there is no relationship.[1]

Like the anima the animus appears in a great variety of images, in fantasies or dreams, or projected in "waking" fantasy upon a man. It takes the shape of any variation or combination of the four types of masculinity—Father, *puer* (Son), Hero or Wise Man—mentioned in Chapter 11. The Father variations are authority figures of all sorts, ranging from the actual personal father or grandfather to kings, presidents of the country or the local bank or country club, to holy fathers, ministers, bishops, etc., up to Zeus, Odin or God the Father, or just the "ideal husband" as *pater familias*. The Son or *puer aeternus* figure may appear as brother, son, friend, ideal lover and partner, the fellow next door, the unknown lover, gentleman, huntsman, seducer, or even a bum, or any mythological or fairy tale figure—Adonis, Prince Charming—which incorporates this image. The Hero may be a soldier, knight, or even a coachman, chauffeur or powerful boxer or wrestler, Achilles, Sir Lancelot or President Kennedy, a plain brute, rapist or destroyer, or simply the exciting or fascinating elevator man with the blue eyes. The Wise Man may appear as great teacher, guru, sage, magician, prophet, guardian of the treasure, or as one's highschool teacher, or simply Mr. X who claims to know, or as one's analyst is presumed to know, all the answers. It also includes the nature aspects: the faun and satyr, the eagle, bull, goat, dragon, dog or other male animal, and animals that have been associated with male deities, or simply phallic representations.

When not consciously confronted, this positive, potentially constructive animus tends to enter unconsciously and automatically into any situation that requires initiative, aggressiveness, action, discrimination, rationality and understanding. But it enters it in a reflex-like, autonomous fashion as blind hostility or steamroller-type dogmatism and instantly provokes anima reaction in the man, just as conversely the unintegrated anima provokes an animus reaction. Then we have the deadlock that Jung describes on page

206. The man makes strictly logical observations without even noticing their critical, or to the woman tactless, and hurtful implications. The woman responds with "righteous" indignation and all too frequently with irrelevant principles.

The animus forms the basis of complexes through the associational network in which father, brother, teacher and other authority figures become personalized and incarnated. Just as the man's relationship to mother or sister serves as the first model for his emotional patterns, so the relationship to father or brother shapes the woman's connection with the realm of meaning, rational order, initiative, aggressiveness, assertion and authority. A woman whose relationship to her father was favorable will have a pattern of expectation similar to the father's mode of expressing aggressiveness, order and authority. The woman whose relationship to her father was unfavorable will be equally bound by the father's pattern, but often in a negative fashion as the following example demonstrates.

A patient discovered that she always resented weak men, but paradoxically she had always been attracted to them. When first she met a man who attracted her, he struck her as powerfully masculine; only later would she become aware of his spinelessness, and then she would greatly resent him. When the question of her father was brought up in therapy she vigorously denied that he could have been a weak man. Her image of him was powerfully masculine; yet further questioning revealed him as a limp washcloth in his wife's vigorous hand. In total unawareness of his actual weakness the daughter had projected upon him the opposite picture, that of the hero archetype; for it was the hero archetype in *her* that strove, albeit unsuccessfully, to be actualized through father and animus. Through the associational network thus set up by her experience with her father, she continued to be attracted to weak men who by virtue of surface appearance were suitable for hero projection, namely as likenesses of her father. She would see in them the image of the archetypal mythologem that had never been adequately actualized for her, owing to her father's relative inadequacy as a man; but the actual attraction operated according to the form of maleness —the washrag variety—that she *did* experience as she was growing up.

Her father complex and her ego or self-assertion complex take the form of this search for the male hero, who is forever incorporated with varying degrees of resemblance to her father. The likeness of father appears not only in her expectation of men but also in her *own* standards of value and her behavioral propensities. Her own judgments, opinions, values and behavior reflect father's; when she comes to situations that require strength and persistence she automatically and habitually folds up and gives in as father would, in spite of her conscious intention to be strong and persevering. The autonomous instinct-response always fails her in respect to strength, for the animus has been actualized through channels of yielding weakness in the guise of professed strength. She will remain caught in her vicious circle and no change can be hoped for unless this basic discrepancy is consciously realized.

The woman whom we met at the beginning of the chapter further illustrates this kind of disruptive animus complex. Here is another of her dreams:

"I am lying in bed with two men. One of them resembles my husband but also has some of the features of my father and brother. The other man is unknown to me but he seems to be a sensitive, imaginative yet virile person. This man makes sexual advances. I refuse, yet I feel tempted. Now my husband attacks me with a knife; I am afraid he will kill me. In my terror I hear a voice which tells me that I should look at the other man's testicles but I am afraid that my husband will not let me."

The dreamer's brother had always ridiculed her and made her feel ugly, incapable and lacking in sex appeal. To her father, as we have seen, she associated pride, rigidity, self-effacement and weakness in the name of lofty ideals. The brother, driven into opposing father's ways, yet caught in father's morality himself, drove home the father's idea of self-effacement, at the same time demolishing any sense of her own value of herself that she had. She felt an obligation to live up to the high-minded ideals of her father, but like her brother she also opposed father's attitude without the inner stability to accomplish the act. Her brother's constant assurance that she was the failure which no one would admit father to be kept undermining her. Here we see that father furnished the broad, general viewpoint and brother the specific application and conflict.

Her husband in turn was as rigid as her father but with emphasis on pride and appearance. The merger of these three figures made a deadly combination indeed. The dream then says that the world of the father, brother and husband, namely the animus with whom she is in an intimate relationship (in bed), threatens to kill her. Her pride, self-effacement, rigid morality, dogmatic conventionality and sense of failure as a woman with which she is so intimately associated threaten to destroy her. However there is another aspect of masculinity which is as yet unknown to her: the sensitive, imaginative assertiveness which she has never acknowledged in herself or in others since it was outlawed in father's world. Now she is bidden to look at the testicles, at that which contains the seed or sperm, the creative potential. She should look for the creative possibilities, the strength and sensitiveness dormant in the assertiveness she had to reject. She feels that her husband, her rigid conventionality, her brother and his distrust of her capacities will not allow her. The animus in its actualized form of rigidity and weakness prevents her from discovering her own as yet unrecognized positive animus potential.

The other man who woos her, the not-yet-actualized animus aspect, represents that which has never yet been experienced in the self-effacing morality of the father, namely masculine assertiveness. This must now be investigated and aroused. But the jealousy of the inbred code (she still feels that nothing father did, said or believed can ever be questioned) frustrates her and becomes a source of her own hostility, even of homicidal urges. If she is to survive she must "look at the testicles"!

Here we have a typical example of Jung's symbolic approach to the dream. This seemingly obvious sexual dream is not concerned with sexuality *per se*, though it is concerned with sex as a symbol of relationship, of the drive toward relatedness and individuation; but it points further toward a threatening, destructive power and to the way it can be dealt with, in terms of creative and constructive potential.

In its most disruptive forms the animus operates as an unconscious power drive, as a devil of opinions under the guise of warm feeling and helpless femininity: the heart of gold with a keen eye on the pocketbook, the steel claw of collective judgment and ruthless egotism in the velvet glove of soft feminine behavior. Like every disruptive complex it expresses itself in identity, compulsiveness, primitiveness, projection and inflation, and in this form, as an unconscious, primitive, hence blindly destructive urge to separation, it interferes with the possibility for relatedness, love and understanding; just as the anima, the compulsive involvement urge, interferes with a man's rationality and his ability to comprehend, since he gets "all mixed up" with his undeveloped capacity to relate.

Since the actualization of the animus occurs predominately through the father-figure, the various father mythologems are also means of expression of the animus; the animus-ridden woman is the father's darling—if not actually, at least in her imagination. The myth speaks of the maiden who has been stung by Odin's sleep-thorn and put into a long sleep—unconsciousness—until the day when the hero shall awaken her, i.e., until the ego drive—self-awareness—is aroused. The same motif is found in the fairy tale of the Sleeping Beauty. Father's darling is also the Princess on the pea—she is too good for this world and too good for any man. This is true as well of the princess in the tale of King Thrushbeard: Afraid of men and resenting them, she is also utterly naive in reality situations; reality is too trivial, even despicable, because it can never measure up to the beautiful world of her imagination, nor can real men approach the Lord of her fantasy, to whom in her dreams she is married. The animus holds her in a slavery which to her appears like paradise.

This form of animus-possession is further expressed in the pattern of the woman who sits at the feet of some great master, as the only one who really understands him and is able to read his heart. Or she herself may go out and preach the ultimate, unalterable, final truth; at least she will be having the last word. As she withdraws from reality and from real relatedness she tends also to withdraw from her inner world of male qualities. For example, she will not credit her own reasoning power or capacity and thus will tend to parrot a great truth picked up elsewhere; or she may not credit herself with being able to accomplish anything of her own in an individual way. The result may be a *negative inflation*, which is a state of feeling too bad rather than too good. She feels that she is in no way good enough for this world, that she is always at fault, always wrong; hence she is oversensitive to criticism, both real and imagined. She is always on the defensive and constantly feels attacked. Any statement of fact is reacted to as criticism; any obstacle, any difficulty, any relationship problem proves that she is no good, a failure; all roads lead to depression, melancholy, tears, withdrawal, to the point even of suicidal moods. For the animus-judgment is projected outward; everyone attacks her, criticizes her, tears her down. She bitterly resents them all. Yet it is the power in herself that says to her, "You ought to," "You should," "You have failed," "You are no good," regardless of whether or not it is realistic.

It is difficult to conceive of such a psychological manifestation as a negative inflation. Yet it is a very common occurrence as the inflation of martyrdom, based on the sense that if one cannot be the best, one can at least be the worst—thus winning a halo and putting everyone subtly to shame. Needless to say, a negative inflation is much harder to deal with than a positive one, because in the latter case it is at least possible to challenge it directly. In the case of the negative type, however, such a challenge either meets no response at all or causes a reaction of devastation; moreover, every suggestion that anything may not be in an ideal state is reacted to as criticism and attack, which tends to reinforce the negative states and cannot be seen as an attempt to help.

When projected, the animus accounts for the woman's state of profound and unrealistic fascinations—she is either "in love" or caught in profound admiration for the "great" man—or, conversely, she violently hates and rejects the "wicked" man who somehow exerts a strange, inexplicable attraction. (The unrealized positive potential hidden in what to her feels only objectionable is the source of that unconscious attraction.) Nevertheless, animus projections are unavoidable; they are the first step and form the basis on which relatedness can be built, if the projections can eventually be seen and dealt with. However, to the extent that a projection persists, the unrealistic expectation is likely to prevent actual relatedness; when the reality of the other person does not fit the glorified image, a negative projection is likely to follow the positive one.

Since these assertion drives are closely related to the formation of the ego, their degree of conscious development will be closely correlated with the degree of a woman's ego strength. As women by and large tend to be less separated from their unconscious roots, the feminine ego characteristically takes a less definite and rational form than the masculine ego. Hence a portion of feminine ego potential tends to remain connected with the animus. To the extent that conscious contact with the animus is not maintained there will be a resultant loss of ego capacity and potential. Without conscious animus-contact, the feminine ego tends to take either an overly aggressive or a weak, insufficient stand or a combination of both extremes alternatively.

The less the ego drives are individualized in actual experience, the more compulsive and powerful they become in the animus; the more habitually and stereotypically passive and submissive the woman feels she has to be, the more compulsively hostile her animus is likely to be.

We have already referred to the animus that has been actualized in a situation where the father was weak. When male aggressiveness is not adequately actualized there is not enough of a challenge for the daughter to maintain her own ego stand. She has no opportunity to experience the sense of her own individual personality in relation to a strong masculinity, to discover that a woman need not unconditionally surrender to male demands, that she does not have to yield always to father's orders and judgments at the cost of her individuality, but may hold her own in a feminine way. Without this experience a woman tends to feel basically unsure of herself. She is likely to approach life through the collective subterfuges of "ought" and "should" rather than through her own feminine capacity for erotic—that is, person-oriented rather than abstract—instinctual adaptation.

We have also noted that typical human attributes and drives which have not been actualized in personal relationships nevertheless press for realization as potentials that want to take form. If a woman has not met the male power (and consequently her own power drive) in terms of an assertive father figure, this power will tend to lead a ghost existence. It is essential that she learn to contact this unconscious potential, through confronting her animus as it presents itself in her aggressive power and truth complexes, her own dream or fantasy images, value judgments and behavior patterns. Just as a man finds his access to the objective psyche through the anima, which has to do with the world of interpersonal connectedness and relationship, so the woman will find that there is no access to her unconscious, to a deep contact with her feminine self, unless she confronts the aggressive world which the animus represents. A woman cannot become a fulfilled human being without consciously integrating at least a minimum of aggressiveness, assertiveness and independent reasoning, and making it her own. To remain caught in the stereotype of the sweet, loving, motherly housewife who cannot think a thought for herself means death to the real personality. The animus when consciously confronted thus becomes her guide to self-development, to a capacity for clear, factual and causally-related thinking and an ability to arrive at conscious, considered choices instead of defensive opinions. The animus is the *psychopompos*, the guide to the spirit.

Integration of the animus—for the woman, the *opus major* which constitutes her individuation problem—requires conscious confrontation and *active* acceptance. The man's task of integrating the anima involves the conscious development of receptivity, experiencing and suffering his emotions and involvements, therefore a conscious awareness of and an openness toward finding himself involved with emotions and through emotions with people. The animus, as the woman's activity potential, requires in turn the developing of a consciously active initiative: learning to discriminate consciously, to clarify and separate, thereby to accept separateness, independence and responsibility, as well as rationality. To this end she has to learn to accept tensions as warning signals and to ask herself the magic word: Why? —rather than immediately identifying with and giving vent to her emotional reaction. Only by realizing that an autonomous unconscious power is at work can it be properly confronted. Here, questioning, reasoning, understanding and initiative in a highly conscious form are called for. The woman has to begin asking: What is it that I am now thinking? What is my judgment at this moment? What is my opinion and where does it come from? What do I really want and why? Where and how may there be a rigidity or righteousness of my own contributing to the impasse? Such questioning can lead to rational thought and understanding. The animus then will begin to relate a woman to her understanding potential, to her capacity for taking a stand and for self-assertion—but *as a woman;* that means in a feminine fashion, *not* as a man. In other words, she will not pull out the rapier of her incisive understanding and resentment in order to fence with her partner and prove herself right but will perhaps react with an attitude of acceptance, while understanding his train of thought. She might also point out some things—notably feelings—which he might have overlooked, or she might simply state her own needs. If she is not capable of this kind of consciousness her animus will tend to create difficult situations in which she is likely to act like an inferior or second-rate man, just as the anima-possessed man acts like an inferior woman.

For the man, conscious receptiveness to his feelings is relatively difficult; for the woman, conscious active questioning for the sake of rational discernment is the difficult task. But both will thereby relate themselves to that part of themselves, their inferior function, which has not as yet been brought into life. Essentially this means that the woman learns to say *"no"* not by compulsion or habit but by conscious, rational choice; the woman who can never say "no" to anyone or anything always says "no" in her heart. A woman has to learn to sense the urge to activity *within herself* in order to find her way to effective outer confrontations. The more skilled she has become at an active relationship with her inner man, the more effectively receptive she can be to an actual man when she so desires.

A particular trap of the animus which must be guarded against individually as well as collectively is exemplified in the feminist movement and the feminist attitude, which purport to claim equal rights for women by identifying with male values and thus underrating and destroying what woman really is and could be. One might speculate upon the possibility that there may be no archetypal pattern available in western Christian culture—that is to say, no archetypal pattern that has been accepted by this culture—that would enable certain types of women to find their true individuality in terms of their femininity. The basic rejection and denigration of feminine values as compared to masculine values is the heritage of our historically patriarchal culture. This has resulted in a situation in which the feminine individuation problem has become a pioneering task that perhaps is meant to usher in a new period of culture. The archetypal images arising during modern woman's individuation process frequently allude to pre-Judeo-Christian powers, such as the Dionysus-Ariadne, Demeter-Persephone or Eros-Psyche themes of Greece, or the Celtic or Chaldean priestess rites. Thus the problem of dealing with the animus contains an additional historical difficulty over and above that difficulty which is common to both sexes as they confront the archetypes of the objective psyche.

Lest the reader be misled by the plausibility or appeal of the descriptions offered in these pages, let it be stressed that the difficulty of the integration of animus and anima is a formidable one. Jung says about this:

> One can imagine how desirable it would be . . . to dissolve the projection. And there are always optimists who believe that the golden age can be ushered in simply by telling people the right way to go. But just let them try to explain to these people that they are acting like a dog chasing its own tail. To make a person see the shortcomings of his attitude considerably more than mere "telling" is needed, for more is involved than ordinary common sense can allow. What one is up against here is the kind of fateful misunderstanding which, under ordi-

nary conditions, remains forever inaccessible to insight. It is rather like expecting the average respectable citizen to recognize himself as a criminal. . . .

The autonomy of the collective unconscious expresses itself in the figures of anima and animus. They personify those of its contents which, when withdrawn from projection, can be integrated into consciousness. To this extent, both figures represent *functions* which filter the contents of the collective unconscious through to the conscious mind. They appear or behave as such, however, only so long as the tendencies of the conscious and unconscious do not diverge too greatly. Should any tension arise, these functions, harmless till then, confront the conscious mind in personified form and behave rather like systems split off from the personality, or like part souls. This comparison is inadequate in so far as nothing previously belonging to the ego-personality has split off from it; on the contrary, the two figures represent a disturbing accretion. The reason for their behaving in this way is that though the *contents* of anima and animus can be integrated they themselves cannot, since they are archetypes. As such they are the foundation stones of the psychic structure, which in its totality exceeds the limits of consciousness and therefore can never become the object of direct cognition. Though the effects of anima and animus can be made conscious, they themselves are factors transcending consciousness and beyond the reach of perception and volition. Hence they remain autonomous despite the integration of their contents, and for this reason they should be borne constantly in mind.[2]

Even though the shadow is strange and remote, it is still somehow within reach and can, at least to quite a considerable degree, be charted or sketched out, but the anima and animus are forever defiant of complete understanding or taming. After we think we have found out everything there is to be found out, they may appear in entirely new and unexpected forms, and there is never an end to this. They connect us with the limitlessness of the psyche itself. The shadow, one might say, is an unknown inland lake, animus and anima the ocean. This realization is extremely important from a practical standpoint, for it implies that only constant attention to the unconscious, an inner devoted tribute, is sufficient to enlist its cooperation. The unconscious realms cannot be analyzed away, cannot be defeated in battle, but, at best, by conscious confrontation, can be taken into account within the limits of one's individual capacity.

14. The Self

THE GOAL-DIRECTEDNESS of psychic energy which becomes apparent through the statements and "directives" of our dreams suggests a compensating and complementing entity which evidently operates not at random but in a patterning of development which appears to exist regardless of the dreamer's awareness and which is more often than not at variance with his wishes and ideas of his own state, sometimes quite disconcertingly so. For instance a woman who considered herself benign and sweet was not fulfilling a wish when she dreamed that her mouth was full of razor-blades! This image of sharp speech was hardly in keeping with her hopes or with her image of herself.

The compensating entity thus postulated has little regard for time and space as we experience them; it often seems to anticipate events that have not yet occurred, events we do not know will occur. For instance, when a patient dreamed of herself in a new job, being given roses by the boss, she had not at the time even fully realized her frustration in her current position. Of this she only subsequently became aware and with great hesitation and misgivings decided to change jobs. Eventually the new work and her relationship with her superiors gave her a sense of joy and fulfillment. Her dream-consciousness operated in anticipation of the events; this happens quite often and is entirely beyond conscious control. The patient in Chapter 2 who through reckless driving caused an accident did not have the accident immediately. The dream's message fitted his psychological situation accurately; he was causing injury to himself and others by his impetuous inconsiderateness, his "reckless driving" attitude. Later an actual accident did occur in exactly the manner of the dream. Something appeared to "know" the future event and to treat it as a past cause. It is as if something in the dreamer utilized a knowledge unavailable to the space-time-confined ego. At the same time its psychological implications were also true.

We have seen a marked "intentionality" throughout the dreams used as examples in preceding chapters. The question now arises: Who or what is that entity which appears to be in possession of this awareness, this knowledge and directive capacity, and with what is it concerned?

An answer to this critical question can be attempted only symbolically. This entity is experienced by consciousness *as if* it were a central planning system that is not part of, but includes and affects, the conscious system. This symbolic representation suggests a concept analogous to the ordering system postulated in nature by modern physicists and biologists. Since this concept represents a typical human way of experiencing existence we call it archetypal. However, unlike the laws of nature it presents itself as though it were *not* impersonal. It is not static, general or of unchanging validity, nor is it subject to increasing inertness—it does not run down as natural balancing systems do. We find it continually attuned, continually responding, reacting and spontaneously initiating new developments which appear *as if* particularly planned for a specific individual, even though arising and functioning regardless of, and at times contrary to, this person's conscious ideas, wishes and intentions.

If the total personality were to be considered as a city of which the ego regards itself as mayor, this city would contain not only inhabitants whom the mayor had never seen or heard of (the personal unconscious), but he would eventually find that there were other authorities which were not under his command, seeming to obey a central authority which he did not know existed and which resided elsewhere—in Central Asia, say, or on Mars. This central authority would give orders and the local militia would obey them, disregarding any conflicting orders the mayor may have given.

The question still remains: Who or what is this authority? What is the "other" directive unconscious center of the psyche? Jung called it the Self —the Self in contradistinction to the ego. He circumscribes it as follows:

> Inasmuch as the ego is only the centrum of my field of consciousness, it is not identical with the totality of my psyche, being merely a complex among other complexes. Hence I discriminate between the ego and the Self, since the ego is only the subject of my consciousness, while the Self is the subject of my totality; hence it also includes the unconscious psyche. In this sense the Self would be an (ideal) factor which embraces and includes the ego. In unconscious fantasy the Self often appears as a superordinated or ideal personality.[1]

The term "self" seemed to me a suitable one for this unconscious substrate, whose actual exponent in consciousness is the ego. The ego stands to the self as the moved to the mover, or as object to subject, because the determining factors which radiate out from the self surround the ego on all sides and are therefore supraordinate to it. The self, like the unconscious, is an *a priori* existent out of which the ego

evolves. It is, so to speak, an unconscious prefiguration of the ego. It is
not I who create myself, rather I happen to myself.[2]

Intellectually the self is no more than a psychological concept, a
construct that serves to express an unknowable essence which we cannot grasp as such, since by definition it transcends our powers of comprehension. It might equally well be called the "God within us." The
beginnings of our whole psychic life seem to be inextricably rooted in
this point, and all our highest and ultimate purposes seem to be striving towards it.[3]

Consciousness is phylogenetically and ontogenetically a secondary
phenomenon. It is time this obvious fact were grasped at last. Just as
the body has an anatomical prehistory of millions of years, so also does
the psychic system. . . . The psyche of the child in its preconscious
state is anything but a *tabula rasa*; it is already preformed in a recog-
nizably individual way, and is moreover equipped with all specifically
human instincts, as well as with the *a priori* foundations of the higher
functions. On this complicated base, the ego arises. Throughout life
the ego is sustained by this base. When the base does not function,
stasis ensues and then death. Its life and its reality are of vital importance. Compared to it, even the external world is secondary, for what
does the world matter if the endogenous impulse to grasp it and manipulate it is lacking? In the long run no conscious will can ever replace
the life instinct. This instinct comes to us from within, as a compulsion
or will or command, and if—as has more or less been done from time
immemorial—we give it the name of a personal daimon we are at least
aptly expressing the psychological situation. And if, by employing the
concept of the archetype, we attempt to define a little more closely the
point at which the daimon grips us, we have not abolished anything,
only approached closer to the source of life.[4]

Jung repeatedly stresses the fact that the concept of the Self constitutes
merely "the hypothetical summation of an indescribable totality." [5] His
terminology here as in other instances has given rise to innumerable misunderstandings because his use of the term *Self* does not coincide with
current psychological usage, where it is interchangeable with the term *ego*.
As we have seen, Jung's concept is entirely different. He sets up the hypothetical postulate of the Self as the center as well as the content of the total
personality; it is the root upon which the experience and consciousness of
individual being arises as a secondary phenomenon. The Self is experienced
or related to as to a postulated encompassing personality characterized by
individual wholeness and expressing a central guidance system directed toward conscious experience and fulfillment, a center which is not in con-

sciousness and therefore is not identical with the center of consciousness. This archetype expresses itself in the form of predestined wholeness, not however of general human wholeness but of the specific wholeness of an individual life, which seeks fulfillment. It may be viewed as an archetype of a central authority, a unitary field, which governs conscious as well as unconscious functioning, outer as well as inner reality; and it manifests itself in both realms in ways which appear to be governed by the laws of correspondence rather than by the laws of cause and effect. Jung refers to this phenomenon as *synchronicity* and frequently draws attention to its relationship to parapsychological phenomena. Outer events quite beyond our conscious control seem to correspond to and give form to various fundamental unconscious trends that are striving toward expression. A psychological problem that is taking shape within may concurrently find its enactment symbolically or directly through corresponding external events. These correspondences are not always exactly coincidental in time; as we have noted, a dream image of the inner state may precede an actual outer event which takes place in the form of that very image. Sometimes, if we are aware of such possible meaningful correspondences, we can be forewarned concerning our psychological state and what further difficulties or dangers may arise through it, as in the case of our reckless driver.

Frequently during the course of an analysis external events occur which bear out, illustrate or fall in line with a particular inner happening which has been initiated by the work with the unconscious. It would appear that the full reality of life is not within *or* without but is contained in an inclusive unitary field. The other side of this law is seen when our relationship to the unconscious and to life is sterile or repressive; nothing happens on the outside, or else whatever happens happens against us rather than for us.

This symbolic idea of the Self corresponds to the experience of a "border situation," man's relation to the unfathomable in the cosmos, as we described it in Chapter 5.[6] Hence it is understandable that the symbolism of the Self, expressing as it does an unknown, superordinated, directive and encompassing entity, tends to appear in the form of mythologems. In this form its symbolism is indistinguishable from the symbolism of the godhead. Such a description, however, refers only to the "how" of expression and experience, and we cannot stress this too emphatically. It is a symbolic description of the "how," not the "what," of either the Self or God. The question of the "what" is outside the realm of human speculation.

The *modus operandi* of the Self may be likened to the center of an energy field which aims toward fulfilling a life and personality pattern which as a potentiality is *a priori* given. We may liken it to an individually appointed wholeness, a goal of evolution. The ego then appears not as the "maker" of personality but as a relatively subordinate executor of an unconsciously prespecified plan, a plan which goes beyond conscious ego goals and values and may even contradict them. As we shall see later, in greater detail, the efforts of the ego strive to preserve the *status quo* of the personality and its value systems; the Self is often intent on change and reevaluation, a seeming threat or challenge to the established ego order.

The first stirring of the Self seems to require the establishment of an executor, a firm ego capable of adequate social adaptation and having ethical values in accordance with the morality of the containing social group. The Self archetype actualizes through the ego complex in terms of parental and cultural patterns.

Maturity and development demand a confrontation of the ego and the Self. The necessary adaptation of the ego is challenged by the Self's urge for the ego's transformation. When this occurs in the form of an abrupt invasion of the ego by inimical drives and images, it can mean the dissociation of personality.

Even when the confrontation can be faced by the ego without a shattering of structural order, it often presents serious moral and ethical problems. The demands and expectations of the Self are frequently at variance with the established ego values. "For my thoughts are not your thoughts, neither are your ways my ways, saith the Lord." [7]

The confrontation with the shadow challenges our view of what we are and shows us elements within ourselves which are at variance with our adopted code of ethics. Anima or animus confront us also with drives and urges contrary to those standards.

Confrontation with the Self, however, can result in a direct challenge to the intrinsic validity of our standards. They must pass the acid test of what is really important, what is good or bad in the face of the fact that we will eventually die, that in our own individuality we must find meaningfulness in or beyond group and family mores with which to face ourselves.

Our collective morality is challenged by what presents itself as individual conscience and as the meaning of a uniquely appointed life. In this phase those elements formerly held under strict control, our amoral or immoral natural appetites, longings and urges, may need to find active expression in the newly developing wholeness pattern. The former "evil" is brought to serve a new "good."

Jung has conclusively demonstrated that this process of transforming the "vile," "primitive," "base" facets of our personality into new life energy underlies the symbolism of alchemy in its endeavor to transform base substance into gold—a gold other than ordinary gold: "*Aurum nostrum non est aurum vulgi.*"

This far from simple undertaking is not a license to dabble in vice and corruption but an excruciating task confronted at every turn with moral conflicts and painful ethical decisions. Yet in the process the unique, individual, spiritual essence, the inherent core of human existence is distilled. Jung says about this:

> Natural man is not a "self"—he is the mass and the particle in the mass, collective to such a degree that he is not even sure of his own ego. That is why since time immemorial he has needed the transformation mysteries to turn him into something, and to rescue him from the animal collective psyche, which is nothing but a hodgepodge.
>
> But if we reject this insignificant assortment of man "as he is," it is impossible for him to attain integration, to become a self. (*Note:* This does not mean that the self is created, so to speak, only during the course of life; it is rather a question of its becoming conscious. The self exists from the very beginning, but is latent, that is, unconscious.) And that amounts to spiritual death. Life that just happens in and for itself is not real life; it is only real when it is known. Only a unified personality can experience life, not that personality which is split up into partial aspects, that bundle of odds and ends which also calls itself "man." [8]

Or again:

> The achievement of personality means nothing less than the optimum development of the whole individual human being. . . . The development of personality from the germ-state to full consciousness is at once a charisma and a curse, because its first fruit is the conscious and unavoidable separation of the single individual from the undifferentiated and unconscious herd. This means isolation, and there is no more comforting word for it. . . . [But] it also means fidelity to the law of one's own being. . . . [and] in so far as every individual has the law of his life inborn in him it is theoretically possible for any man to follow this law and so become a personality, that is, to achieve wholeness. But since life only exists in the form of living units, i.e., individuals, the law of life always tends towards a life individually lived. [9]

That state or life dynamism in which consciousness realizes itself as a split and separated personality that yearns and strives toward union with its unknown and unknowable partner, the Self, Jung has called the *individuation process*. It is a conscious striving for becoming what one "is" or rather "is meant to be." However, since the goal of this process, the Self, is like an "*a priori* existent," "the God within us," individuation is always a road, a way, a process, travel or travail, a dynamism; it is never, at least not while one lives in time and space, a static or accomplished state. It is "becoming," not "being." The Self as the "goal" of the individuation process may be likened to the pole star: one may plot one's course by it, but one does not expect to reach it.

The many symbolic representations of the Self, of which we can give only a few examples, are images that point to totality or wholeness—of either a psychological or a transcendental (infinite or eternal) character—as well as to a central entity of order and direction. The former, or encompassing, images have circular, square, cubic or global shapes or have some other infinite or eternal character: the uroboros (the mythological snake or dragon that eats its own tail and thus devours itself), the phoenix (which consumes itself in the fire that maturates the egg out of which the new bird arises), the treasure beyond value, the indestructable diamond, the water of life, the elixir of immortality which requires the pilgrimage or dangerous quest, or the alchemical "philosopher's stone" which turns base substance into gold. The latter, centered images are the cross, wheel or radiant sphere, the world clock[10] or the directing star (pole star, star of Bethlehem). All of these images point to a total personality which has the character of wholeness (this of course does not have anything to do with "perfection" as we shall see later) and which has a central directive focus. This wholeness is also expressed in another characteristic way. Since the "I"-experience is conditioned by the way the body experiences itself first as a child, the Self archetype frequently is symbolically represented in adult dreams as the child—a unique new individuality reacting to and transcending life as it happens to be now—the potential for future growth.

We will consider two examples that demonstrate the manner in which the images and the moral revaluation demands of the Self tend to become constellated.

One is the dream of a young man who was in a general state of confusion of values, trying hard, failing, becoming discouraged, reaching the point of losing courage. He had a strange fascination with sexual promiscuity. He participated in some of the organized orgies taking place in the city and he had also come under the influence of drugs. He was frightened and felt guilty about this but was not able to resist the fascination. He was very perceptive and used his keen insights to antagonize people, always letting them know precisely what was wrong with them.

He had the following dream:

"I am embracing a girl at an orgy. My face is toward her sexual parts and I am rather repelled by the odor, but then I notice a beautiful diamond in her clitoris. Now everything feels right and beautiful."

His association to the girl was that she reminded him of his own worst problem. Like himself she was perceptive and intuitive, yet tended to lose touch with reality, owing to her preoccupation and fascination with bizarre drug and fantasy experiences and by virtue of her lack of self-discipline. In connection with the diamond he remembered a picture he had at home of a rose with a jewel in the center. This association points to an archetypal motif. The young man had never heard of the "Jewel in the Lotus," which is a phallic sexual cult image (representing the union of opposites: lingam and yoni, Yang and Yin) and is also the Buddha in meditation.

In pre-Christian mythological tradition we quite frequently find that sexual customs and images serve to express central religious mysteries. Even our patient had vague feelings of this sort and was greatly relieved when he was told that they were not "crazy" but had mythological precedents. He had met the girl of the dream at one of the orgies in which he had participated and which he characterized as group "celebrations" enacting mostly oral sexuality. Her behavior he described quite spontaneously with the words, "just like a priestess performing a temple dance." Historically the term *orgia* meant secret worship or worship conducted in the precinct of the mystery. It does indeed derive from a religious use of sexuality that became secularized and subsequently forgotten, yet is "remembered" by the objective psyche. (Orality will be discussed in the following chapter[11] as an early bodily form of instinctual expression that pertains to taking in or depending upon.) Even though it is less explicit, sexual symbolism appears in the language of many Christian and Sufi mysteries, even in the language of the church, as in the union of *sponsus* and *sponsa*, Christ the heavenly bridegroom uniting with the Church as his bride, or in Jewish mysticism, the union of God with his bride the *Schechina*. In "The Psychology of the Transference"[12] Jung elucidated the symbolism of the *coniunctio oppositorum* by the use of a series of alchemical pictures of male-female encounter and cohabitation.

Kerényi, in fact, describes the universal goal of initiation within all the ancient matriarchal mysteries as that of copulation (*"Ho telos ho gamos"*), the sexually enacted union.[13] Fierz-David says about this:

> The experience of the mysteries touches in a decisive fashion the depth of sexuality in which the divine and the animal, the holy and obscene, are inseparably united . . . there it is balanced as on a razor's edge whether the most sublime may be reduced to the most base. . . . In the higher initiation of the mature person the goal is the mysterious union of the human soul with the divine spirit—a "holy marriage" which is meant to make him the "twice-born" one and to lead him toward immortality.[14]

Our young man was totally unaware of this symbolism. He merely remembered, or rather was inexplicably touched by, the picture of the jewel in the rose. (Interestingly enough, the rose as the "perfect" flower is quite frequently the equivalent of the Eastern lotus in the religious symbolism of the West.) But we are justified in concluding that his dream uses sexual imagery to point to a mysterious, religiously meaningful state of the union of opposites—of consciousness and the unconscious, man and nature, personal and transpersonal—which reaches beyond the dualistic experience of the ego. It is probably for this reason that sexual symbolism so frequently appears charged with a sense of awe, even of terror, of a *mysterium tremendum*, even though it may be masked by and reduced to the level of the pin-up picture. Not only may religiousness appear as sublimated sexuality, as Freud postulated, more often nowadays sexuality expresses unrealized religious seeking, a yearning for union with and oneness in the Self.

The following dream series (consolidated for simplification), parts of which have already served as illustration of the shadow problem in Chapter 10, contains additional examples of images of the Self and may give further insight on how a renewal of life may come from seeming evil.

The dreamer was a middle-aged executive. Professionally successful, he found himself in an increasing state of tension and suicidal depression. He dreamed:

"*A dark demon, a kind of nature or water devil attacks me. He tries to kill me with an apple. I attempt to subdue him but he always eludes me. Finally we wrestle and he maneuvers me onto a narrow, slippery ledge bordering an abyss. Now he slips away, leaving me in this dangerous position, unable to move in any direction. But then he suddenly throws me a rope and pulls me to safety. He also gives me a pick or drill and I understand that I am to dig my way to the center of the earth with it. As I attempt to do this I reach the garden plot of my neighbor whom I detest and find that he has carved out a beautiful garden from barren and useless rock.*

"*Then the picture changes. I find myself strapped to a dentist's chair. The dentist shakes his head and tells me that this is going to be a very awkward and dangerous operation, for it is necessary that he drill straight through me to the center of my abdomen. I submit to this.*

"*Now two figures lead me into a secret chamber where a solemn meeting is in progress around a square table. Presiding over this meeting are a knight or soldier in splendid armor and a Lord Mayor with a chain of office around his neck. However, I am led to this table by a delinquent boy whom I knew in my youth and a tattered, dirty, tramp-like fellow who has the appearance of a mendicant friar of the Middle Ages. These two also seat themselves at the table. I am given only a small stool at the corner of the table. I am offered some food which is quite repulsive, but I accept it. I eat and push my drill deep into the ground. Flowers grow in profusion around the drill; it is transformed into a blossoming tree."*

This dream is an example of what American Indian and African cultures call a "big dream." Such dreams usually confront us with aspects of our fundamental life myth and often anticipate a development independent of our accustomed space and time categories.

The antagonist here is not merely the personal shadow, the personal vices; it is a demonic, mythological figure corresponding rather to the archetype of the opposing protagonist of man in the traditional image of the dark angel or Satanic demon. It corresponds to what Jung has called the dark aspect of the Self, namely the obscure, dangerous, obstructive, apparently evil element that is part of life in general, of everybody's life and of human nature, that irrational aspect of natural existence that always slips away and evades our grasp and has not become civilized or moral; it is untouched nature, for better or for worse—and it is for worse while it remains unconscious.

This adversary threatens the dreamer with an apple, that apple with which the first tempter, the serpent of Paradise, threatened Adam and led him toward the "knowledge of good and evil." The dreamer is threatened by a confrontation with his unrealized demon which will necessitate his taking a stand in respect to the good and the evil in himself. It demands his awareness of the destructiveness dormant in his unrealized urges. He is threatened by the demand to become more conscious through recognition of the conflict between his urges and drives and his ethical ego-conscious convictions. The attempt to dismiss the problem by repression (to subdue the demon) drags him to the edge of disaster, to the danger of a breakdown, from the pressure of his unacknowledged urges. He is immobilized in a dangerous situation where he cannot move in any consciously known way. His effort to do the "right" thing results in sterility. Only the demon who is also the daimon, namely the possible creative potential, is the helper who throws him the life line which can pull him out of his struggle and who also gives him the tool with which to seek the center. The pressure of the unrealized Self does not permit him or us to remain in a state of spiritual sterility; it pulls us out in spite of ourselves and may lead us to our true centeredness, if we are able to move with it consciously.

The next motif is that of the enclosed garden, which may also appear as a central square or sheltered place of any sort, such as the inner court of a castle, a church, a place of peace or refuge—all symbols of the centering aspect of the Self from which comes strength and protection. This garden has been hewn out of barren rock by a personal shadow figure, the neighbor whom the dreamer detests for his unruly restlessness. The garden has been made out of that very material which he considered contemptible, sterile and useless; in other words, his despised and repressed side is capable of producing growth. This image repeats the message above, that it is the negative side of his personality, his inferior function, that is to be the source of redemption (just as the supreme value for the young artist was to be found within his destructive impulses). Here, the dream also adds that to penetrate to the center of himself constitutes an extremely painful and risky operation but will also transform his grasp of reality (symbolized in the motif of the teeth).

Finally there is the image of the square table where the dissociated elements of the psyche are united in partaking of integration (the communion meal). Here the dreamer meets the presiding warrior and authority (Hero and Father) aspects of himself which, as a business administrator, he has perfected into the leading qualities in his life through his extraverted sensation and thinking functions. Again, it is his inferior, unrealized sides, this time more clearly presented as the delinquent boy of his childhood and the tramp or beggar (these figures correspond to the Son and the Wise Man, equivalents of the demon of the previous section), who guide him to the centering platform (the square table), the wholeness of his life. The three men and the boy take the four seats at this table; the dreamer's place is on a small stool at the side—a place which indicates the approximate position taken by the ego in the drama of life: a little corner seat, by sufferance, in the presence of the powers that be.

The food which the dreamer is offered at this meal, the stuff of life, is not of his choosing; it is handed to him by the Self, composed of the central directive figures at the table. But his acceptance of it will make his own growth possible, for as he eats, the lifeless drill, which was merely an abstract tool for probing into the dark depths, serves to support the growth of flowers, life's renewal and beauty. (This is also the theme of the Tannhäuser story.)

The dreams of both the artist and the executive thus stress the fact that new values—diamond, wholeness, life-food, flowers—are to be found through accepting and even being led into what appears to be evil to the traditional conscious view. Renewal comes about through the assistance of the opponent and through the acceptance of what one doesn't really care for, of what has heretofore been rejected, hence not assimilated. We regard it as evil, but it may be so only while it is allowed to remain unexperienced.

The artist had been raised by a puritanical grandmother who stressed that sex out of wedlock could only be lewd and sinful. Even though he was drawn to experiencing the orgiastic quality of sex, he was bound by her viewpoint and tried to repress it as evil. The attempt led him into alcoholism and drugs: Dionysus' revenge!

The businessman regarded his personal feelings and religious inclinations as soft, escapist and absurd; they would destroy his manhood and his contribution to society, and in his frame of reference this seemed immoral. These neglected functions appear in his dream as the delinquent boy and the ragged monk, expressing the level onto which his consciousness had forced them; yet they were part of his "leading" daimon. Only after the "repulsive" meal—the communion—with them was the lifeless drill capable of blossoming.

Jung has been seriously misunderstood and misquoted on this point. When he says that we have to experiment with evil [15]—Martin Buber attacks him for this[16]—he means that we must experiment with what may appear to be evil to our ego-identified attitude and to our collectivized value system, because it is still the primitive daimon. But we must struggle with, accept, follow it, not identify with it. This means paying attention to our own deepest conscience and guarding against falling in with that which this deepest conscience reveals to us as destructive. In this sense the young man who dreamed of the diamond in the clitoris was not being urged to become a sex pervert or a drug addict; the implication, rather, in the context of age-old spiritual meanings, is that the indestructible value is to be found through consciously experiencing those urges which his anima presses upon him; that is to say, he must experience the power and intentionality of his drive toward wholeness in terms of his emotional and sexual problems. Put another way, his dream implies that he can affirm a religious experience of the transcendental—of that which is of ultimate concern—by encountering it not in ascetic, repressive or suppressive virtuousness but in the majesty of ecstasy and joy, as expressed in sexuality. His narrow, puritanical upbringing had made all joy, especially sexual joy, suspect, indeed evil. Thus deprived of any religious significance, the world of Venus-Aphrodite and Dionysus exerted a fascination from the unconscious which brought him to promiscuity and threatened drug addiction. He was drawn by a power, a god, which he did not realize or understand and which he consciously denied. Therefore it "had" him by unconscious fascination. One might assume that most drug addicts and alcoholics are misguided "seekers for the spirit" (alcohol has been called *spiritus vini*). They are impelled to seek a form of the spirit to be found in the world of Dionysus, the god of renewal through the light from below, from the earth rather than from the heavens, and who signifies the necessity to find life and meaning in the ecstasies and terrors, in the beauties and agonies of this concrete world, not merely in the remote, abstract spirit realm as it is commonly understood.

Both patients' dreams react to a serious dilemma between the demands of reality adaptation and the seemingly irresistible pull of the dreamers' inferior sides—expressed in one through his drug addiction and wayward sexual urges, in the other through his depressive, introverted moods that would have him withdraw from his external life's task. In both instances, simply satisfying, indulging or repressing either of the two conflicting sides offers no solution. One cannot simply resolve that the danger does not exist, that it can be held under control or disregarded. This attitude could lead the one into deeper drug addiction, the other to possible suicide. On the other hand if they merely give in to their primitive urges, the one might become a deliberate sexual pervert and drug addict, the other regress into infantile emotionality and a bizarre fantasy world. It is indeed a deadlock, for to uphold only reality, suppressing wayward urges, can mean sterility, a psychological impasse and indeed psychopathology; to give way to the repressed urges can mean dissipation and depravity.

In a really serious moral impasse it is our heretofore accepted virtues, not our vices, that crucify us. At the root of every profound ethical conflict we find that every "right" also occasions a "wrong." In order to benefit one side or person we hurt another; yet to achieve our individual wholeness, the reality of our innermost "good," we are required to risk the experience of our own evil, in the form in which we find it. This recognition of the primitive side which demands life space in our own terms of evil puts us in a double bind; whichever way we move seems wrong.

Yet it appears that only through suffering the deadlock, living through the opposition of ethical demands, can the experience of meaning be born. Aniela Jaffé says in *Der Mythus vom Sinn:*

> . . . there is a law that an unknown or unconscious content can only be grasped by consciousness by recognizing its manifold aspects or by differentiating it from its opposite. . . . "a being without opposites is completely unthinkable, as it would be impossible to establish its existence." [17]

The path out of the dilemma can only be found by waiting and consciously holding on to both sides of the conflict, by making the utmost effort to keep both sides in fullest possible awareness without repressing them or falling into a state of identification. This means nothing less than that the conflict with all its excruciating implications must be endured consciously; we cannot seek to terminate it forcibly by taking sides, by enforcing a premature decision. Symbolically this amounts to a crucifixion; by our consent, our acceptance of this suffering we are nailed to the cross of the opposing drives. We keep the apparent evil in full sight and continue to wait for a way that allows us to express its energy in constructive rather than destructive ways, though this may seem impossible at the moment, both in terms of morality and of existing reality.

Thus there are two kinds of effort which can and must be made in order to redeem the adversary: the effort to keep from repressing the "evil" or looking the other way, and the effort to avoid acting it out uncritically in naive identification. Both efforts imply the ability and willingness to confront, accept and yet discipline ourselves. Confrontation here means that we not only know about our drives and problems but that we also experience them. We experience the shadow side, recognizing how it holds us under its sway, trying to recognize it and to recognize when it operates through us. Similarly it is not only a matter of knowing *about* the anima and animus but of suffering their impact consciously while it occurs. In this way the archetype is confronted as it speaks *to* us rather than *through* us to others; it speaks to us at the precise moment when we realize what we actually feel and express or what character it is that now expresses itself through us and our urges; it also speaks when, in an awareness of the driving force, we try to find a constructive or creative expression for it. This painful confrontation cannot occur without discipline and an active attitude of responsibility—of moral responsibility.

Acceptance means that we are aware of the inevitability of some form of this autonomous power which we can neither avoid nor control, that we realize our lifelong responsibility for being this particular type of person. We then accept the fact that we can only apologize or pick up the pieces when we cannot avoid falling prey to this power, and we admit that we have to pay for it. Acceptance means taking the responsibility not for being subject to certain drives (for we do not make ourselves) but for placing and expressing them appropriately and constructively or inappropriately and destructively. It is responsibility not for what we *are* but for what we are *doing* with what we are. And it is here that we may choose and must choose. Christ's admonition that "ye resist not evil" [18] may be taken psychologically to refer to the acceptance of the drive itself; God's injunction to Cain, "Sin lieth at the door . . . and thou shalt rule over him," [19] refers to the responsibility for controlling the act in full awareness.

Only when we accept and confront the autonomous powers in us can we exercise choice and responsibility for the manner and timing of our expression of their energies in a constructive way; then the evil may serve the good. Our life's task thus becomes like the task of taming a wild, potentially dangerous animal. Most often the unconscious insists that the "animal" must not be killed but restrained if it is to be re-trained. But neither may it be restrained at all times and everywhere; it needs also a chance to roam and to express its vital urges where they may not harm but may do some good even though the transition from the wild to the tamed way of action is fraught with danger. The "animal" needs feeding and tender, understanding care and respect for its intrinsic "otherness." As the drives themselves become changed in the process of transformation, the formerly dangerous intrusions can become helpful capacities leading to the fulfillment of our individual wholeness.

Inevitably the "dark" and neglected left-behind parts of the Self sooner or later press for recognition; it seems as if the devil, in the shape of our own personal evil, applies the sting to make us find new ways out of our inertia. Thus in the beginning of *Faust* Goethe has God say:

> "Mankind's activity can languish all too easily,
> A man soon loves unhampered rest;
> Hence, gladly I give him a comrade such as you,
> Who stirs and works and must, as devil, do." [20]

Eventually, at the point where the irresolvable conflict is brought to its most excruciating tension, where the ego has come to the end of its wits, when we realize that all attempts notwithstanding we cannot bring about a change by our own effort, then what Jung called the reconciling symbol, the *new directive* from the unconscious, may present itself. This new directive is part of the myth of one's life. It expresses the law of our being, which does not arise from our own planning but comes to us as the result of our efforts and struggles, from a source or center unknown to us.

To the extent that the struggle with one's own antagonist is avoided a conscious relationship to the Self is lacking. Then its demands and urges will be projected; we yearn to experience through others what we fail to bring to realization within ourselves. We expect fulfillment of our ambitions through our children, we want to be filled with love by someone else when we have been unable to tap the sources of the ability to love within ourselves. When an inner readiness is lacking we may not recognize love even if it is offered.

It is only in the lowly and unfinished areas of our lives that we can find the prospect of renewal. This great truth is expressed in the mythologem of the Savior's birth in a manger. There can be no greater psychological tension than that existing between the opposites of finite, stabilized ego and infinite, unfinished, unexpected Self. In their repeated encounter lies continuous renewal; the conscious experiencing of their conflict can be most painful, but when a relationship has been established through the symbolic approach, life becomes increasingly full and meaningful . . . and unexpected.

15. The Complex of Identity:
The Ego

AT THE BEGINNING of our century Freud's charting of unconscious dynamics revealed the startling fact that we are more than the ego, more than the "I" we know ourselves to be. The idea of an unconscious has now become more or less accepted. We have become used to the division of our psyches into an area of ego consciousness which we assume to be rational and knowable and an area of unconsciousness which we concede to be unknown and even in part unknowable.

However, as we begin to investigate the ego we are startled to find that even the area of consciousness is not as rational or explicable as we had thought. The crux of the difficulty, as Kant made clear, lies in the fact that the "I" is trying to observe itself. We are touching here upon the most critical impasse of all psychology, namely the fact that the psyche is both object and subject of the search. When consciousness studies the unconscious there is at least a semblance of subject-object separation but when consciousness attempts to make a statement about itself it is like the eye trying to see itself, and we are confronted with the height of a logical impasse. How does consciousness or the ego (are they different?) come into being? Where does this entity merge with the unconscious? At every step the mystery deepens. If we do not even understand the ego, what is left then for us to understand?

One feasible approach to this impasse is in the method we have been pursuing in regard to elements of the unconscious. We renounce the attempt to say just what the ego *is* and limit ourselves to describing what it is *like* and how it manifests itself. But even with this limitation we shall have to discover that we know very little about this area of which we have assumed that we know most if not all there is to be known.

We may remember that as children we pondered such questions as: Why am I my "I" and not his "I"? How does his "I" feel different from

231

mine? And what is "I"? Now we might add: Who or what thinks about "I" and asks the question?

If we try to define the ego as the center of personal identity and consciousness, we find we are reasoning in a circular fashion. What is consciousness if not connected with the ego and what is identity if not referred to the same recurring "I"? As Kant says, at the basis of our knowledge of ourselves there lies only "the simple and utterly empty idea: I; of which we cannot even say we have a notion." [1]

Jung admits: "The nature of consciousness is a riddle whose solution I do not know." [2] We will find, in fact, that we can only define it in terms of the unconscious, of which we know nothing! Jung continues: "The ego, ostensibly the thing we know most about, is in fact a highly complex affair full of unfathomable obscurities. Indeed, one could even define it as a *relatively constant personification of the unconscious itself*, or as the Schopenhauerian mirror in which the unconscious becomes aware of its own face." [3]

Various schools of thought seem to agree that the ego involves a sense of continuity of body and mind in relation to space, time and causality, and that it gives rise to the individual's sense of unity and to his tendency to reduce multiplicity to oneness by means of memory and rationality. Based on the functions of memory and of logic, the ego is a unit which resists the flow of change, as opposed to the unconscious which is always changing.

We may start with a threefold operational definition of the ego. (1) It functions as the center, subject and object of personal identity and consciousness, that is, consciousness of personal identity which extends and continues through time, space, and cause-and-effect sequence and which is capable of reflecting about itself, as in Descartes' "*Cogito ergo sum.*" (2) It is the center and originator, seemingly at least, of personal choices and decisions and plans of action, and the point of reference for value judgments. (3) It is the originator of the personal impulses, the will which translates decisions into actions toward specific goals.

However, after we have explored the difficulties of defining the accustomed everyday ego, we find that there are many evidences of multiple egos, and our difficulties increase. The "I" is apparently capable of being fragmented, changed and re-formed. *The Three Faces of Eve*[4] reported the phenomenon of multiple egos or personalities, with one "person" operating at varying times in terms of two different identities which eventually were replaced by a third. In cases of complete amnesia a new and different ego identity will arise. In situations of shock, mystical experience or brainwashing, the ego is apparently fragmented; the old ego even dies and a new "I" is born, though there is at the same time a certain continuity of the observing self.

Arthur Koestler describes the experience of a fragmented ego.

> On the day when Sir Peter (Chalmers) and I were arrested, there had been three occasions when I believed my execution was imminent. . . . On all three occasions I had benefited from the well-known phenomenon of a split consciousness, a dream-like, dazed self-estrangement, which separated the conscious self from the acting self—the former being a detached observer, the latter an automaton, while the air hums in one's ears as in the hollow of a seashell. . . .
> The experiences responsible for this change were fear, pity, and a third one, more difficult to describe. Fear, not of death, but of torture and humiliation, and the more unpleasant forms of dying . . . and finally, a condition of mind usually referred to in terms borrowed from the vocabulary of mysticism, which would present itself at unexpected moments and induce a state of inner peace which I have known neither before nor since.[5]

Similar dissociations of one's sense of identity or ego into an observing consciousness that experiences a mystical peaceful bliss and an acting consciousness which is encased, as it were, in the shell of an anxiety- or pain-ridden robot-like physical body have been observed in psychotic states, in near-death states caused by accidental shock or severe illness, and under the influence of drugs such as LSD or under anaesthetics. In such states people have described the sense of floating above ground while observing their body-selves lying on the bed below them, or of seeing themselves enacting past or present life activities.

In the deepest and most lasting forms of ego dissociation and re-formation the willing and judging egos become separated from the sense of personal identity and are so changed as to produce a sense of being "reborn." This transformation can occur within the religious frame of reference and in the individuation process of depth psychology. It can also be forced, as in "brainwashing." In all of these forms there have been profound emotional or moral experiences which disintegrate the former ego structure.

According to Robert J. Lifton's study of brainwashing in Communist China, the goal of "rebirth" is consciously sought:

> Both Dr. Vincent and Father Luca took part in an agonizing drama of death and rebirth. In each case, it was made clear that the "reactionary spy" who entered the prison must perish, and that in his place must arise a "new man," resurrected in the Communist mold. Indeed Dr. Vincent still used the phrase, "To die and be reborn,"—words which he had heard more than once during his imprisonment.[6]

For more familiar examples of the changeable ego, we have only to look at our dreams. The dream "I" often has faculties which the dreamer does not have, such as being able to fly, to decipher unknown languages, and so on. It sometimes appears to be separate from still another ego which is represented in the dream as the "real I." As St. Augustine asked in his *Confessions* about his state during sleep: "*Numquid tunc ego non sum, Domine Deus meus?*" ("Oh God, am I not myself then?")[7]

In any normal person's dream the "I" as identity-carrier may appear altered and dissociated. It may seem to have lost the conscious ego's values and action capacities and to have taken on strange new ones; the dream ego frequently feels and acts in a way which is uncharacteristic of the waking ego, or it cannot act at all, as in the dream of wanting to run away but instead standing paralyzed on the spot.

A dream of the Communist poet W. Herzfelde is quoted by Sonja Marjasch in her study "*The 'I' in Dreams*"[8] as an example of the fragmented ego. Herzfelde reports the continuing powerful influence in his life of a recurrent dream about a man he feels he must find and liberate:

> All I knew was this (I knew it because I saw it plainly before my eyes, and quite near-by): he was chained to a raft and, together with others whom I did not see, had to row without relief, day and night. And he would have to row through all eternity if I did not succeed in finding him. The chains that bound him, the oarlocks in which the long oars scraped, were red and scaly with rust. At each stroke they screeched. Their rhythmic screech expressed the whole torment of his galley-slave existence.
>
> To free him was my great hope. But not his. For he knew nothing of my task; he did not even know that I existed. But I knew about him; I could not forget him and his terrible lot. His liberation was the meaning of my existence, for this creature devoid of knowledge and devoid of hope, this man on the raft, held by rust-red chains; he was I, myself. He did not know it, but I knew it, knew that finding him meant freeing me.[9]

Can we find some psychodynamic characterization of all these evidences of various egos? Jung's concept of an ego complex has room for this fluctuating composition and also distinguishes between ego and consciousness. (Consciousness and ego depend on each other to the extent that Jung uses the phrase "ego-consciousness.") He describes the ego complex as a composite of mental elements resting on the five senses: "a synthesis of the various 'sense-consciousnesses' in which the independence of each separate consciousness is submerged in the unity of the overruling ego."[10] He thus uses the term "ego-consciousness" to signify the partiality of our experience of this complex: we cannot be conscious of all the things we have ever known or of everything our senses register at any given moment. The ego is not the exclusive representative of the total human being. We may perhaps propose an *identity* or *unity* complex which is assumed to function like all complexes—father, mother, power and other complexes—in that it attempts to exert its own energic influence, quite often regardless of the total psychic equilibrium, and which tends to behave at times as if it were the only central, or at least the most essential, psychic structure. What we experience as personal identity or ego would constitute the personal shell of this complex.

The concept of an ego complex makes sense of the evidence of fragmentation and changeability which we have noted. Since the shell of a complex is made up of material stemming from personal history and conditioning, it would understandably be subject to change and reconditioning.

But what is the transpersonal archetypal core which manifests as the ego complex? Jung says of this:

> Inasmuch as the ego is only the centrum of my field of consciousness, it is not identical with the totality of my psyche, being merely a complex among other complexes. Hence I discriminate between the ego and the Self, the ego is only the subject of my consciousness, while the Self is the subject of my totality: hence it also includes the unconscious psyche. In this sense the Self would be an (ideal) factor which embraces and includes the ego. In unconscious phantasy the Self often appears as a super-ordinated or ideal personality.[11]
>
> The ego is the only content of the self that we do know. The individuated ego senses itself as the object of an unknown and superordinate subject.[12]

What Jung points to, and frequently expressed privately, is that those elements of the Self whose qualities defy the time and space dimension become visible in the manifest personality. It is as though the efforts of the Self to manifest in concrete existence result in man.

Jung's position here in regard to an organizing superordinated center, an archetypal urge toward psychic totality and wholeness, of which the ego is a limited and partial actualization, grew out of his researches into the objective psyche. He was able to demonstrate that the ego's sense of being in this central and dominating position is illusory; and here is a crucial point of difference between Jung's psychology and other psychologies which are based on the central ego. Even Freud's "id" is a concept which assumes the ego to be in a position to judge these purely chaotic and irrational urges by its exclusively rational standards. Jung's concept of the Self in contradistinction to the ego is, as we have seen, that of an archetypal factor of an *a priori* totality-pattern, a personality potential which seems to operate as an organizing center for the psychological development of the empirical individuality. The archetype of the Self, the nuclear core of the identity complex, comes into actualization as an ego in the personal shell of this identity complex, namely through that network of associational images which are drawn to the archetypal predisposition by correspondence and contiguity. Our empirical, unique personal identity which we call "I" could be seen as the personally conditioned form of a transpersonal identity. The personal shell of the identity complex can indeed be subject to fragmentation or can take more than one form, as multiple personalities and as waking and dream egos.

In terms of the basic dynamics of archetypal manifestation discussed in Chapter 7,[13] the Self as a predisposition which is "empty" in itself actualizes as representational images and as patterns of emotion and behavior. The Self is represented in dreams, fantasies and myths in archetypal images of oneness, centeredness, wholeness and eternalness. In the ego these appear as ideas and images about one's relation to oneself and the world: one's self- or body-image, what one is like or should be like in terms of permanence and body identity. The emotional value system of the Self seeks manifestation in the ego as the standard of one's choices and values. The goal-directedness of the Self—what might be called its pattern of behavior—seeks expression in the ego's search for satisfaction and fulfillment through exercising one's will in the pursuit of the goals of one's choice. And lastly, the nonactualized aspect of the archetypal totality exerts its compensating or opposing influence. This results in the Self-ego tension or estrangement.

We shall now attempt to describe how the pre-existing individuality, symbolized in the archetype of the Self, actualizes itself as ego or as the empirical personality which knows itself as "I," and how this resulting ego finds itself in a state of conflict with the Self.

1. THE ACTUALIZATION OF THE SELF ARCHETYPE
THROUGH THE BODY EXPERIENCE

The actualization of the archetype of identity or unity occurs through those associational images and concepts in which this identity is originally experienced, that is, in the form of the body scheme of oneness in the multiplicity of the parts of the body and of our physical urges. The first self-image is identical with the body-image; then there arises consciousness of oneself as being a body which has a name and which comes to be experienced as *my* body. The infant speaks of himself first as "Jimmy" who does this or that; only later is that body which everyone calls "Jimmy" addressed as "I". This basic fact of self-experience is expressed in our language through such terms as "somebody," "nobody" or "anybody," all pointing to personal identity by virtue of being a body. We also use the legal term *habeas corpus*: the judge or court is to "have the body."

Ego consciousness is thus founded on the physical senses, in terms of sensory record images, as Jung has called them.[14] The transcendent "total" consciousness of the Self becomes constrained into the limitations of the sense-perceptional frame of reference of the physical body. The psyche manifests and experiences itself through a soma. In consequence of this somatization or incarnation, certain body-determined forms of ego conditioning arise. They are:

(a) The union-separation dilemma.
(b) The feeling of inferiority with its competing power drive (Adler's inferiority complex, traced by him to a sense of bodily inferiority).
(c) The psychodynamics of the body openings (Freud's infantile sexuality).
(d) The ego's anxiety in respect to change.

(a) The union-separation dilemma
Probably the most elementary experience as a body is that of separation at birth; the loss of the paradisical all-identity produces individual separateness but also existential anxiety, as the original unitary reality encompassing a total field experience is split into the dualistic subject-object relation, which serves as basis for the developing consciousness. The universal expression of this initial pain of separation, both psychic and physical, is the infant's first cry. The experience of independent bodily existence evokes a reaction which we commonly associate with pain, misery and suffering.

The next milestone on the road to ego formation is the experience of encounter. At about three months the baby smiles for the first time at a human face in motion near it. This does not mean recognition of a particular person, for any moving model having two eyes, a mouth, nose and forehead will serve the purpose.[15] According to Spitz, "the infant has acquired the capacity to rediscover in reality the object which corresponds to what is present in his imagination." [16] This is an instance of what we have referred to in Chapter 7 [17] as the recognition of that which has never yet been seen, the recognition of the "outer" object that corresponds to the inwardly prefigured archetypal pattern. It is analogous to the recognition by the butterfly of its mate and of its proper hatching environment. "It indicates that conscious and unconscious have been separated from each other. The recognition, the act of smiling, is manifestly a conscious, directed, volitional act." [18] It is a first individual expression of pleasure and joy. The joy of encounter now balances and complements the pain of separation. Both are indispensable conditions for adequate functioning of the individual. Thus, human ego development is basically conditioned by, and continues to unfold between, the divisive Yang pole of separateness and the connecting Yin pole of union. Between these polarities of separation and encounter —the loss of oneness and the reestablishment of oneness through meeting —the sense of identity continues to grow throughout the life of the individual. Hence the sensations and emotions through which the infant body initially experiences its identity and which thereby shape the emerging self-image are largely determined by the relationship to the parents, particularly the mother. Mother incorporates union; indeed she is the original union, the all-oneness from which a gradual separateness occurs—one might say under protest. After the physical separation of birth there remains a psychological identity between mother and child which dissolves only slowly and gradually. Thus the mother's attitude toward the child is much more crucial in ego formation than is the father's. Indeed, as Spitz[19] has shown, the body's very survival and growth depend upon the loving acceptance of the infant by the mother or by a maternal person. A deprivation of emotional warmth and bodily contact in early infancy may produce malnutrition, developmental arrest and even death. In a somewhat simplified way it can be said that the child's sense of existing as a unified being, hence its self-image and identity, is conditioned by the particular emotions of its parents (especially the mother) and its consequent relation to them as the archetypal Yin and Yang experiences of containment and separation become personalized for him through the mother and father. Under optimum circumstances, the "I" is first experienced as contained, loved, protected and sustained, nourished and enclosed by the mother, and later challenged, driven, directed toward ideals of one sort or another by the father. Healthy ego structure is based on a containment-separation balance, namely a parental attitude to the child as one who is loved and yet accepted as an individual separate from the parental self-image and who can be trusted to form his own responses and strive for his own goals. Needless to say, an ideal balance is rarely to be found. The scales are always tipped to one side or the other since the parental reactions are determined by their own complexes and projections. Parents are themselves children of parents and would need a practically mystical enlightenment if they were always able to strike just the "right" middle balance. Thus the emerging self-image will be modified by either too little separateness or too little loving acceptance. The first tends to result in insufficient ego strength, insufficient self-reliance and independence; the second leads to exaggerated ego reliance, self-rejection (the ego cannot accept the shadow reality), guilt, difficulty in trusting and relating, and possibly an overemphasis on selfishness and egotism.

A child-parent relationship which is marked by too little separateness fosters in the child a persisting identity with the all-powerful parental world. Life and its mastery are taken for granted; there is no need for individual striving. The ego fails to develop fully because of dreaminess, inertia, inflation, lack of reality-adaptation; the child is not fully born into life and responsibility. Life is a Peter Pan world which is to supply endless enjoyment and everything is to happen by itself. Love and relationship tend to be symbiotic rather than real encounters. This attitude and its compensation through the unconscious are typified by a young girl who dreamed that *unless she bestirred herself and got out of bed she would lose everything;* or in the dream of a young man *who was playfully gathering driftwood when his help was needed and was struck down by an electric shock from a high tension wire.* An insufficient experience of separateness in the early years fails to prepare the ego for life's high tension potential.

A relationship in which the child has too little loving acceptance leads to a sharpening of the inferiority-power tension, to feelings of inadequacy, guilt and badness; other people seem better, more capable, more desirable, and this child therefore becomes resentful, envious, overaggressive, hateful and lacking in self-confidence. His self-rejection will seek compensation in rebelliousness, over-independence, over-ambitiousness and aggressiveness.

(b) The inferiority feeling

The child's relation to the parents has other universal consequences. The growing ego, experienced through the child's little body self-image over against the all-powerful adult world, is bound always to experience itself as relatively inadequate and inferior. Here is a basic element of the ego or identity complex; it is the "poor little me" who is deprived of my "rightful" place under the sun—Alfred Adler's "inferiority complex," with the ensuing power drive which tries to compensate for this inferiority. The inferiority-power balance may be regarded as inevitable in ego formation. Indeed it is one of the three basic forms of experiencing one's body identity, as we shall see. The various modifications and intricacies of the inferiority-power drive with which Adler's Individual Psychology concerns itself hence are basic variations of ego psychology; from this viewpoint one can understand and appreciate Adler's relative disregard of the unconscious.

(c) Orificial dynamics

Initially the child's sense of identity in its interaction with the world of things and people is actualized by virtue of the awareness of the body's interaction with the world through its openings of ingestion and excretion, in terms of what Freud was first to describe as infantile sexuality, with its pleasure-anxiety polarity, and in terms of the child's and his parents' reaction to the body experience.

While we accept Freud's basic observation, there is evidence that these body activities are not merely pleasure gratifications *per se* but are part of an ego development which, owing to the subject-object split, encounters itself as the body-self and the world as "other" through the body. These activities represent the first archetypal centering of libido by focusing consciousness upon the directly accessible bodily expressions of those instinct functions which involve the world of matter and other people in relation to the ego. The attitude which the parents and later the "parental" cultural group have toward the body and its functions help to determine the quality and degree of self- and instinct-acceptance ranging from over-restrictiveness to over-indulgence. Self-image and the emotional quality of identity experience are based upon and modified by the conditions of being a "good" or accepted child so as to become acceptable to oneself. Thus they are conditioned by external factors of acceptance.

The body activities through which the ego develops are principally oral, anal and urethral, and only lastly genital. Each comes to have a distinct significance which persists throughout life in some form, depending on how consciously these meanings can be incorporated into the self-awareness of the ego. Orally, we grasp into ourselves. Anally, we hold and force out substance, formed matter; we prevail, we establish our own impulse expressions where automatic life manifestations are concerned. Urethrally, we pour forth, give and create, or we restrain and control ourselves. Genitally, we arouse ourselves and enter into union with the "other."

Orality, as in sucking, drinking and kissing, represents a stage of dependence which expresses receptiveness and yielding, but also demandingness. The use of the teeth as in biting and eating expresses clinging, grasping, even greediness. Orality expresses the basic need for sustenance, support and protection, the aboriginal source of which is actualized through the mother's breasts. The mouth is the first organ of perception as well as acquisition; orality thus expresses the drive toward taking into oneself, absorbing, contacting, grasping (in the sense of understanding)—as well as grabbing into one's possession.

Consequently orality is the channel for the infant's dependency reaction to the separation from the bliss of the aboriginal oneness, now experienced as separation from identity with the mother's body. This separation creates a demand that one's needs (particularly those for food and maternal nearness) be continually satisfied by the environment. The environment's failure to do this creates a sense of frustration. This frustration actualizes the pleasure-pain (anxiety) polarity which Freud described as the basis of ego identity and which expresses the ego's sense of separateness when faced with the fact that one's needs can be fulfilled, one's existence protected, only with the help of others. Anxiety about dependence upon others, about ourselves as separate entities, as lone individuals, remains an integral part of individuality and evokes the need to acknowledge and compensate for or to repress this sense of dependence. We form various kinds and degrees of contact, attachment and relatedness with others or we deal with our dependency needs by submerging our individuality in the crowd.

In orality both aspects of the Yin function are expressed: on the one hand, the devouring, drawing-in, absorbing, containing and destroying tendencies; on the other, the erotic contacting and involving tendencies which are organically expressed in the polarity of the greedy sucking and the loving kiss.

The anal phase of identity experience—Freud called it the sadistic anal phase "because satisfaction is then sought in aggression and in the excretory function" [20] is one of establishing aggressive self-assertion. Identity is now experienced in the effort of a deliberate pushing and pressing, thereby turning the automatic intestinal activity into one's own accomplishment. An impulse is experienced from within, as it were; this impulse can be emphasized or deemphasized and disciplined according to one's own choice. Its active "expression" produces concretely visible substance of one's own "making." Through anality the infant experiences himself as a maker, an independent subject who can express his own impulses and exert his own power. The infant can carry out the act of defecation only by himself; he withdraws from others in concentrating upon his powerful pressing efforts which produce visible and tangible results. "Defecation thus provides the pattern for experiencing oneself as subject of the power to gratify physical needs on one's own." [21] The anal experience is one of power over substance and objects, assertion and control over matter, objects or people. It primarily actualizes, in terms of bodily experience, the "Martian" aspect of the Yang archetype. It represents the first experience of self-will, defiance and an egotistic power attitude. It establishes the first point of reference of a self-consciousness in the flowing earth and "swamp-intestinal" existence— the endless cycle of natural life and exchange of matter. The original primitive fecal magic is expressed in its more developed form in the mythologem of killing the swamp monster (as in *Beowulf*). Anality represents self-assertion, assertion of existence, power, possession, control over mother, objects and people as well as over oneself. It expresses the holding and wielding of might and power; it is egotism, but it is also the necessity to strive for an ego; it includes aggression and, in its extreme form, sadism—in the mythologem, the dragon-killing power deed, the ego separation from the maternal unconscious. It is the very attitude of will- and power-expression *par excellence*.

The strange game of "mooning," which has led to innumerable scandalous incidents in the U.S., offers an example of the irrational emergence of archetypal anal symbolism. The more bizarre, the more it is repressed and not understood. In this game, "three or four boys will crouch down in a car, lower their trousers and, at a signal, push their bare bottoms out of every available window. This pastime originated . . . in Southern California and has crossed the country." [22] There have been various incidents, such as a male exposing his buttocks in the rear window of a car to a mother and daughter driving in the car behind him on a highway; another young man in a car exposing his buttocks with a cigar in the cleft to a group of girls in a drive-in restaurant; a group of students exposing their buttocks from a train passing through a city; a group of male students exposing their buttocks from a dormitory balcony to a group of girls in a passing bus.

Exposing the buttocks is also an apotropaic gesture against the evil eye.[23] What we see in this bizarre "mooning" is the spontaneous eruption of a primitive compulsion to an ego assertion in the face of or against what is felt as a threat from the feminine, the Great Mother, the unconscious, which arises in a generation that feels itself increasingly threatened by depersonalization in a society abounding in mass education, conformism, herd psychology and "momism."

However, the aggressive use of individual power also means competition, combat, rejection and destructiveness. Hence it arouses anxiety—either about others stronger than oneself and capable of retaliation, or about one's own destructive effect upon others whom one looks to for support, approval and love. This fear becomes unified in the deep fear of all concrete, earthly energy expression and especially of power expression.

Anality actualizes the Yang principle, not only in its combative Martian aspect but also in its necessary compensation of discipline.

To comprehend the significance of the next phase of body-identity experience, the urinary or phallic experience, we have to take into consideration the symbolic level of experiencing which has been associated with urination. Havelock Ellis, in his chapter on "Urethral Eroticism," [24] elaborates quite extensively upon the emotional, sacral and magical significance of urine. Not only does it appear as "water *par excellence*," it is even sacred water, which confers purity, regeneration and benediction, and drives away evil demons. In some rites when actual water is used it has salt and yellow coloring added to confer upon it the property of urine. Rain is conceived of as urination of a divine being and, like rain, water and semen, urine is associated with fertility. Urination would seem to represent an outpouring of creative, fertilizing energy of mana character, of life-and-love-bestowing quality, stirring, stimulating, exciting, as well as conferring health and salvation. In accordance with this, the kidneys are regarded as "springs of feeling." The apocryphal Wisdom of Solomon (Chapter 1) calls God "a witness of the reins [kidneys] and a beholder of the heart." The Psalmist

(139:13) sings, "Thou hast possessed my reins,"—instead of, as we would say, "my heart." The bladder has been called the chief seat of the soul.

In the outpouring of the water, the primitive energy expression turns from the relatively egotistical or introverted attitude of orality and anality, centered in the subject, toward an outgoing phase of involvement which eventually culminates in relatedness and the union of the opposites of sexuality. Havelock Ellis observes that sometimes young children like to show their love by urinating on a beloved person. Thus the urinary experience represents a yielding to or controlling of an outgoing libido stream. The ego learns to choose between allowing the outpouring to pass or withholding it. The choice between controlling or yielding to emotion and affect is thus invested in the ego. The control of the urinary function (the goal of toilet training) incorporates the necessity for restraining one's urges, needs and desires in deference to an ideal which the ego experiences as superordinated to itself. This emphasis on restraint is more pronounced than in anality where the major effort is toward pressing and forcing. The collective ideal, supplied to the child by parental and cultural ideals, may later be modified by the ego's own propensities and finally may be sought and perhaps found in the transpersonal patterning of the Self. The urge and its restraint form the instinctual basis for an identity which one experiences in giving, in becoming master of oneself, a morally disciplined "pure" person. Abenheimer[25] refers to Plotinus' description of the ego as a subject which can control passions and physical needs through its contact with the Logos. This ascetic phase (*askesis* means "practice") has always been regarded as of the highest value for man; it idealizes maleness in its logos aspect and has often been the object of highest pride, for instance among the American Indians. However, in its extreme forms, as in mortification of the body and its desires and urges and as in its contemporary form of emotion and drive repression in the service of merely rational and traditional ideals, it can result in a weakening of the ego's connection with its psychic base and in emotional and erotic impoverishment.

Under the influence of this disciplined phase the anal expressions become tabooed as "dirty" and are repressed. The taboo of dirt and dirty—namely, "selfish" bodily expression and gratification—is both literal and figurative. Dirt is not merely earthly matter; is is also egotistical pleasure, it is satisfaction, especially of the body, it is egotistical strife (dirty fighting), and what is deemed brutal gratification of one's individual needs (dirty behavior).

Close to the urinary phase is a genital preoccupation in the form of masturbatory activities. This could be regarded as the first appearance of true sexuality *sensu strictiori*, hence of relationship which, like sexuality, presupposes two separate complementary entities.

In masturbation the initial body-instinct identity experiences self-arousal, thus actively confronting itself as an object toward which it, as subject, takes the initiative—the first step toward the mystery of "I" versus myself and "I" versus "Thou."

The masturbatory symbolic experience of bestirring and deliberate self-arousal, rather than merely choosing to go along with or holding back the reflex-like urge toward assertion or letting go, adds thus a new dimension—the mystery of creating. The "I" confronting the "not-I." For an urge but dimly felt is responded to in calling it forth to full expression, in giving it a dimension of experience not existent before, rather than merely expressing, restraining or yielding to what is already felt as existing. As I arouse myself the original all-identity is for the first time effectively split into a dualistic experience.

Masturbation is still a self-centered narcissistic activity, but in experiencing one's own body in this way the body substitutes for a "Thou." At this point "I" and the world are still partly merged but their final separation has begun. "Atum, who indulged himself in Heliopolis, took his phallus in his hand in order to arouse pleasure. A brother and sister were produced, Shu and Tefnut." [26] Out of the encompassing one there arise the two in the masturbatory symbolism. When that fully dualistic experience of "I" and "Thou," myself and world, subject and object is reached, original primitive magical all-identity is overcome. Thus sexual symbolism is relatedness symbolism. Masturbation expresses that final point of transition from narcissistic nondualistic participation to the relative freedom of dualistic consciousness.

Abenheimer[27] points out that each of the three modes of experiencing oneself as a subject (dependent, aggressive and impulse-controlling) is basically in conflict with the other two. The orally demanding subject wants help and dependence, the other two want independence. The subject of the power (anal) urge is concerned with concrete accomplishment preferably at the expense of others; the moral and ascetic (phallic) urge with far-away, lofty ideals of unselfishness. The dependent one fears loss of contact with and support from others in consequence of hurting or insulting them, that is, he fears separation and hence his own destructive tendencies; the power subject fears the power of others and being subjected to them; and the ascetic subject fears himself, fears the loss of control over himself and thus fears still another kind of dependence on others. The dependent subject yearns for the all-loving mother; but when ego power or egoism are repressed in favor of unselfishness, then as a compensation the forcefield of the chthonic devouring mother arises from the unconscious in a fear-inspiring form. Mother and matter, emotions and objects are feared and rejected as dirt and dirty.

Different cultures tend to emphasize different aspects of these conflicts within the ego structure. As Abenheimer says:

> Christian emphasis on love vilifies the chthonian powers, Nazi emphasis on chthonian powers ridiculed love. Puritan ethics distrust human love, reject the chthonian powers and try to live by rational control only.
> These conflicts within the ego as subject are, of course, most important in psychopathology. The paranoic, for instance, is obsessed by his longing to be loved. He has rejected the dirty chthonian power in himself as well as outside and tries to be perfect and deserving of love. Yet he has lost hope of finding reliable love. Therefore his demanding dependent side has to be suppressed too and he lives by the controlling pure will only. In most neuroses the chthonian subject of physical power is feared and repressed. In hysteria the person frequently alternates between being a childish demanding ego and a "male," controlling, superior being. In phobias people do not fear any specific danger in the world but they fear either their sense of being powerless because they have lost access to their chthonian power or they fear the intrusion of these chthonian powers into their pure ego.[28]

In "normal" ego development an attempt is made to balance the three conflicting modes of being a subject by shifting from one to the other according to situational requirements. Actually, however, in most instances one or even two modes are repressed and in their repressed form operate through the shadow, the alter ego. Hence the shadow contains modes of functioning in the world which would be of value to the one-sidedly oriented ego if integrated, whether this be the acceptance of dependent needs, of power, of emotional expression or of self-discipline.

(d) Anxiety about change

The actualization of identity through the body has another very significant result. Since the sense of personal identity is experienced as body identity it feels threatened by anything which threatens the body, indeed is inseparably tied to the survival of the body. Body indispositions change the level of ego acuity and of self-awareness. This is amply borne out by the sense of ego dissociation and alteration which occurs during the body changes caused by drugs, hunger, thirst and illness. The universal fear of cessation of personal existence through the death of the body is based upon ego actualization through and as a body.

Finally the self-image takes form through a store of experienced images, through memory-based ideas of sameness; the continuity of the self-image is built up through the preservation of sameness. The expression of this process is the *psychic inertia* referred to in Chapter 7;[29] any basic change of psychic structuring is naturally reacted to as a deathlike, namely ego-threatening, menace. There are two main facets of this inertia. Our sense of personal identity forever feels the same as the identity we experienced as a child; we all still feel young and the loss of youth seems a threat to our primal identity. We continue to think of ourselves as boys and girls: "Bring one of the boys," or "Let's go, girls!" we say even at the age of seventy-five.

Psychic inertia is also evident in our resistance to any form of change in conditioned patterns, no matter how promising or favorable it may be. Any psychoanalyst knows from dealing with "resistance" that every basic psychological change entails a deathlike experience for the ego. New possibilities produce so much anxiety that the most destructive past adaptations seem safer and inspire more confidence. We can thus readily understand the death and rebirth symbolism of transformation, religious as well as psychological, and we can comprehend the techniques used in brainwashing to break down the ego structure.

So pronounced is the inertia principle as a basic structuring element in ego formation that it can be formulated in an expression similar to the law of inertia in physics: Every pattern of adaptation, outer and inner, is maintained in essentially the same unaltered form and anxiously defended against change until an equally strong or stronger impulse is able to displace it. Moreover, every such displacement or alteration is reacted to as a deathlike threat to the ego. Apparently the formation of fixed behavior and reaction patterns, as has been experimentally observed in animals, is basic to the formation of the human ego.

Lastly, of course, the fear of death which terminates the body-based experience is felt as the threat of "nothingness" and the annihilation of what to the limited ego experience appears as the total personality.

2. THE ACTUALIZATION OF THE SELF ARCHETYPE
THROUGH VALUE JUDGMENT AND WILL

In addition to finding expression in primordial images, the archetype takes form also as predetermined emotional expectations and value judgments of good-bad, right-wrong, pleasant-unpleasant, etc. The ego complex as the actualization of the Self becomes the carrier and arbiter of purposeful and practical—but also moral and ethical—choices; it becomes the arbiter of action according to a conscience which is first conditioned—and thus appears as though structured—by the demands of family and cultural groups. Ego strength is proportional to the capacity to make decisions, and the necessity to decide for oneself increases ego strength and self reliance. "Man was created for the sake of choice," is an old Hebrew saying. Yet Jung observes that "the more one sees of human fate and the more one examines its secret springs of action, the more one is impressed by the strength of unconscious motives and by the limitations of free choice." [30] Motives and standards of choice are not invented by the ego but are structured by the actualization of archetypal predispositions through personally acquired value standards. In other words, the developing ego's value system is parental and cultural, positively or negatively; the child either identifies with or opposes the parental and cultural value systems.

Acceptance is essential for the growing ego. Since acceptance is based on being a "good" child, parental standards are incorporated by the ego. Invariably in the earliest stages, parental approval is largely based upon the child's toilet training accomplishments and "proper" behavior; thus our "individual" value standard, our first form of conscience, is largely structured upon control and repression of instinctual urges and upon approval-getting external adaptations, that is, upon persona and ideal values. The "I" grows through learning self-denial, through resisting instinctual gratifications and through establishing a "proper" adaptation to the external collective demands of group, society and work-performance needs. Whatever individual *a priori* Self-qualities or dispositions do not fit into this idealized pattern or external standard of behavior are split off from the ego's conscious image of itself and of its behavior pattern and form the shadow. Under the cultural and parental value system, ego, persona and shadow thus grow in step with each other.

The development of the ego's first value system results in varying degrees of deluded Self-estrangement. When someone says, "I know myself perfectly well, I know all my problems," and is asked for a description of himself, he will invariably describe a persona ideal in which he was raised, and will name as his "problems" or faults those attitudes which he considers improper deviations from it. He gives a picture which may have precious little to do with his own fundamental reality. In extreme cases this can go so far that the ego is really nothing but a pseudo-ego, that is, nothing but persona. The typological adaptation, for instance, may be attempted in a fashion that is quite foreign to one's own inherent potential. It is very often the case today that we attempt to adapt with extroverted thinking, which is collectively idealized, even though it may be our weakest attribute. In these times we all have the need to consider ourselves as thinking people, thereby disregarding and neglecting our feeling and intuition which may potentially be our strongest functions.

While parental and culture-conditioned values thus determine the developing ego's value standard, nevertheless its strength depends upon an *illusion* of freedom to choose and decide for itself, which it cannot yet have without conscious awareness of the Self and its delimiting and enabling aspects. The ego's strength depends upon using its "own" available power, its will for compensating, its feeling of inferiority in the face of the overwhelming power of the godlike adults. What we may call the initial illusion of conscious will and freedom of choice is essential: growth therefore depends upon at least a minimal disobedience of and revolt against parental values. Ego development means utilization of the power drive, an intrinsic ego instinct. A child is tempted to do precisely what he should not do, and that is necessary, otherwise he has no feeling of his own existence. In short, disobedience bears a crucial relationship to ego consciousness; the ego is shaped through the experience of willful separation.

Thus the archetypal energy of the Self finally takes shape as goal-directed, purposeful patterns of behavior. As actualized in the developing ego, this tendency forms the capacity to achieve what one intends to do; this is will power. A basic test of ego development and ego strength is the ability to assert one's own will in the face of opposition and resistance, and to exert one's drive for power. Jung says here:

> It is of the greatest importance for the young person, who is still unadapted and has as yet achieved nothing, to shape his conscious ego as effectively as possible, that is, to educate his will. Unless he is a positive genius he cannot, indeed he should not, believe in anything active within him that is not identical with his will. He must feel himself a man of will, and may safely depreciate everything else in him and deem it subject to his will, for without this illusion he could not succeed in adapting himself socially.[31]

This necessary ego function called willing is also the ability to say "no." It is a separative act. It is the ability to say "no" to our drives, to ourselves and to others. Hence the ability to will rests not only upon the "anal" capacity for self-expression and push but also upon establishing and observing taboos on the "urethral" ability of self-restriction. Without taboos there is no means for training the will or achieving discipline. The child's experience of being surrounded by taboos cannot be set down to an arbitrary highhandedness of parents or culture but is an indispensable necessity arising from a need of the psyche to develop adequate ego functioning.

The manner in which the parents exercised their own power drives and restrictions will, again, affect the child's ego pattern. These are the personal experiences which determine the form of actualization of the Self's tendency toward goal-directedness. There are many variations on this theme. The ego patterning is shaped by the parent with whom the child has the closer tie but the influence of the parent of the same sex, when not dominant, will continue as a shadow quality. For example, a weak father can paralyze the will power of his son even though the son may consciously rebel against this weakness and be a go-getter (thus shaping his ego according to the pattern of the overdriving mother who most likely completes the picture). However, the father's weakness will probably appear in the son's unconscious tendency to fall prey to feeling attacks and to driving women.

There is no ego development without power drive, no power drive without ego development. This means, too, that anger and hostility are indispensable qualities of ego development, since these are instinctive reactions when ego assertion is thwarted. These reactions cannot be by-passed; they are the price we pay for becoming conscious personalities. The less positive result of the power drive development is that the more we succeed in controlling, the more we assume we can control everything; hence ego development, when unchecked, leads to inflation—the inflation of modern man who assumes himself to be the master of nature and recognizes no master above himself.

The negative form of this ego inflation is the unwillingness to "play ball" when life does not meet us on our own terms. Negative inflation comes as depression and refusal to live, that is, refusal to play the game which we did not invent and in which we cannot dictate the terms. This is difficult to recognize as inflation, but this too is based on the ego's notion that it should be in control of life.

We must remember, however, that all of civilization rests on this ability to control oneself, life and nature and upon training this ability by instituting taboos.

16. The Ego-Self Estrangement

THE ACTUALIZATION of the Self as an ego means constriction or even distortion of the Self, since the available social, as well as parentally sanctioned, elements which structure one's ego-image, value systems and goals will always be limited and therefore limiting. Personal characteristics which are developed but which fail to fit the ego ideal are split off as the shadow. Potential characteristics which do not fit into the predominant typological adaptation remain totally unconscious as anima or animus. In this sense the development of the ego complex means both a differentiation and a fragmentation of the original undifferentiated Self. Not only may one's value systems and goals be at variance with the "intentions" of the Self, but specifically one's self-image or, more correctly, one's ego-image—the idea that one has of one's identity—may be quite at variance with one's true reality. It is of great importance to become aware of this ego-image which paradoxically is usually unconscious and thus subtly colors our conscious outlook. This sense of identity is based on conditioned value standards, on corresponding self valuations and, more often than not, devaluations such as: "I have no right" (that is, no right to assert myself or to have what I want or be what I really would like to be), "I am or ought to be responsible for everything," "I am a fake," "I am weak and helpless" or "I should find it all very easy." These ideas may have little if any foundation in the actual reality of the personality structure and may indeed more often than not be quite at variance with it. Based upon such an unrealistic evaluation, the ego's adaptation to life will be characterized by varying shades of unreality, by inferiority feelings and compensatory defensiveness, until and unless the faulty image is realized and corrected.

Fordham's concept of "deintegration" [1] may clarify our description of the actualization of the Self. He regards the Self as an encompassing, total and undifferentiated potential which spontaneously divides itself. He says that in the "primary integrate" or "original state" of the Self,

> there is no relevant distinction between mind and body. In order to derive psychic structure from the integrate I assumed that it deintegrates; when the first deintegration occurs was left an open question.

. . . The flood of stimuli provided by birth itself and the release of breathing, crying activities producing anxiety must certainly be an early deintegrative state. . . .

The primary integrate is, subjectively, a phenomenonless state. I have applied this idea to some schizophrenic children by assuming that basically they are so integrated as to be inaccessible. Their inability to express themselves is primary and so is conceived to depend upon a hard core of the personality which cannot be reached, there being no means with which to express what is there; i.e., it has not deintegrated.[2]

A patient of Fordham's who nearly died of a severe illness many years before she started analysis told him that she felt "the emptiness at the time of her illness was full of a power without form, so she could not express anything." Fordham refers to Kant's empty "I" in a new way here:

Long ago Kant postulated a transcendental ego . . . "the simple and utterly empty idea: 'I'; of which we cannot even say we have a notion". . . . Substituting self for "I" reaches what I have in mind: an original self integrates without phenomena. It is first manifest in infancy and persists to be represented in philosophy and religion, for instance in the oriental doctrine of maya [namely, that the phenomenal world is a sort of creative illusion that can ultimately be dispensed with].[3]

The deintegration of the original phenomenonless Self-totality is followed by the separation of the still undifferentiated persona-ego-shadow group, as a first area of consciousness, from the animus-anima-Self unit. The "I," which at this point is still largely identical with the persona, then separates from the shadow, which becomes the personal unconscious. To the extent that a further deintegration between ego and persona occurs, a basic sense of "I" as an independent entity can arise, as the first basis from which a reintegration of persona, shadow, animus or anima and Self-totality toward a more encompassing conscious personality can be attempted, through the ego's conscious confrontation of these "others."

The deintegration which Fordham describes is merely an apparent separation; we experience the development of the ego *as if* the "not-I" elements were excluded. The illusion of freedom of the ego—the illusion that the actions of the total personality and the motivations of the ego are independent of the entities from which it has separated itself—is based upon the sense that our thoughts, our feelings and our willing are our own creations; but in fact they are autonomous entities arising from the unconscious, and dynamically all of these elements are in a constant mutual interplay.

The conscious, wishful self-image of myself as a "good" person who always behaves properly, that is, "is good," continues to be determined by the persona ideals and sabotaged by the repressed "badness" (shadow); or if I see myself as a rebel against parental standards, I still inadvertently acknowledge and adhere to these unconscious standards, in that I *must* react against them.

The "I" identity thus is "a synthesis of the various 'sense consciousnesses'," the images, values and intentions arrived at by the deintegration and conditioning of an original, phenomenonless, yet potentially preformed personality. An individually unique response-capacity reacts to, identifies with and adapts to the way one is seen and desires to be seen by the most important others, to how these others behave, to what values they believe in and what goals they strive for; and this process is the one we have described as the actualization process.[4]

The equivalence between Self-actualization and Self-fragmentation means that the ego pattern is of necessity and *always* more or less at variance with the actual reality of the total personality. The ego image, with its value system and intentions, is selectively determined by the response of an inherent potential to particular environmental conditions, hence can be at best only a partial actualization under "normal" childhood conditions, in fact is often a distorted actualization when adverse circumstances prevail in childhood. Moreover, the ego structure must have a basic static quality if a sense of identity is to develop; it is therefore always at variance with the steady motion, flow and change of the objective psyche, the archetypal world.

We see many examples of Self-alienation through the distorting effect of ego-actualization. One patient always felt as a child that her mother and brother thought she was stupid and ugly, and she came to believe it herself. In adopting this view of herself and expecting always to be regarded in this way by others ("for I really *am* ugly and stupid"), she became timid and sullenly resentful. She felt that everyone cares only for himself, never for anyone else, and she fell into a state of inertia; she lacked motivation and nothing seemed worthwhile. Yet her analysis, as it progressed, brought out the fact that there were intensely active, interested and aggressive qualities in her which had remained on the shadow and animus level and from there influenced her negatively.

As another example: An emotionally sensitive child may, under the influence of a hostile and rejecting environment, develop into a very glib, arrogant, aggressive and seemingly insensitive personality and may regard himself so as well. The sensitive "other" does not enter into actualization but remains in abeyance as an unpaid debt to life and to his wholeness, as it were.

In summary, the ego can be said to be a static, fragmented or distorted actualization of the Self, a structure of *Self-estrangement.* In this sense the notion that we have of our "I" as our familiar, continuing sameness is an illusion, as Eastern philosophy claims; the experiment of incarnation of the Self is always partial, distorted and rigid, somehow at variance with the "real" or "total" identity.

It is one of the most fundamental paradoxes of psychic life that the psychic totality requires and demands this partial actualization in an initial distortion as an ego, then reacts to it, usually in the second half of life, by a compensatory, complementary opposition aimed at consciously reaching toward the original unconscious potential wholeness in an actual experience which is now to include consciousness. We then have to liberate the "other" one who was "chained to a raft and had to row, together with others whom I did not see"—as Herzfelde's dream expressed it.[5]

The drama of life seems to develop like a dialectical play between the initial one-sided starting position of ego-orientation—that which we find we "are" when we have come to the first awareness of ourselves—and the later opposing claims of the Self which pull in a new direction with the demand that we become what we are "meant to be." The pull of the Self toward rearrangement of the established pattern of the ego reaching out of a frame of reference which is quite at variance with it, is bound to be disturbing; it may even appear to be an inimical intrusion or a temptation and betrayal (". . . and lead us not into temptation"). Jung's description is a vivid one:

> As a totality, the self is by definition always a *complexio oppositorum,* and the more consciousness insists on its own luminous nature and lays claim to moral authority, the more the self will appear as something dark and menacing.[6]

Moreover, even when there is a more balanced attitude on the part of the ego, the Self can be an enemy as much as a friend, since it is as if blind to space and time conditions. The ego must sometimes take a stand against the pressing demands of the Self. If the Self is to be manifested in the phenomenal world through the ego, if it is to have feet, so to speak, these feet must have a firm standpoint in a daily life which is hedged about with legal requirements to fulfill, reputations to maintain, and responsibilities to carry out at home and in the community, and of such matters the Self knows nothing. Sometimes the Self's urges can keep the ego from becoming strong enough to oppose it. The ego which listens too early to the voices of the deep (before it has established an adequate adaptation to outer reality) may fail to develop fully; then neither will the Self be adequately manifested.

We can now better understand the sense of menace arising from intruding aspects of the unrealized Self as expressed in such dreams as that of the Eastern potentate who threatened the life of the dreamer's daughter unless he was admitted.[7]

The great difficulties involved in the turn toward wholeness, toward admitting that which has not yet been experienced, are also colored by an ambiguous and pervasive sense of guilt. We feel that we are disobeying and betraying something. The fact that the ego structure has developed through estrangement from an original totality of the Self carries with it a sense of guilt and is expressed in many myths as the loss of paradise or the separation of man and God. The dualistic split of the unitary world is a problem never to be fully overcome, a never-healing wound—at least for the ordinary ego consciousness which is felt as forever separated from the natural flow of innocent oneness which was known in the mythic Golden Age. The split carries with it a ubiquitous feeling of guilt; to *sin* originally meant "to miss the mark," namely to miss the integral intent of the Self. The anxiety caused by the sense of not having appropriately expressed an archetype—an unmanifested, hence unknown, potential—can be excruciating.

Guilt feeling also arises from another source. The ego's accustomed childhood-conditioned standards of right and wrong must be violated if the new possibilities are to enter. (One of these standards today is self-reliance; we feel we are abdicating responsibility for ourselves if we admit that we need help from others in solving our problems.) Thus we are crucified by the opposing needs of Self and ego. One guilt helps us toward finding the lost wholeness, the other holds us back.

A typical paralysis—the result of being caught between conflicting standards of Self and ego—is illustrated in the case of a young man who was raised with strictly Calvinistic goals and values which extolled the virtues of work and duty as the only means of salvation and progress in life and regarded pleasure as wrong or even sinful. He eventually found himself at a complete impasse; all initiative and interest in living disappeared. He resented having to work but felt guilty if he did not work or even if he considered a change to some kind of work which he might enjoy more. He felt chained to the workbench of duty and family care, yet he could not break the iron chain in order to find some playfulness or enjoyment with which to fill his so-called egotistical needs. His sense of morality and his "conscience" rejected this.

He dreamed: "*I found a rather luxurious bag which belonged to a rich playboy. I knew that this bag contained everything I needed to get through the day, but since it was not mine I felt I had no right even to touch it. Even so, I took hold of the bag, then felt guilty, as if I had stolen it, so I put it down and walked away. Then suddenly a terrible storm arose which threw me back. It was as if I were nailed to the spot and could not move.*"

This dream carries an alarming message. The storm, which in traditional symbolism stands for the spirit, the *Ruach Elohim*, the breath of God, the force of life and of nature, arises against the dreamer when he refuses to "steal," to take to himself what in terms of his accustomed value system he believes does not belong to him but to a "playboy," who is immoral in his frame of reference. The dreamer refuses to take the play attitude which does not belong to the world of his own limited ego morality and ego structure, though the dream says that this is what would help him through life (through the day) and that to follow his accustomed code of morality would be to go against the spirit of life and would lead to paralysis. This conscience is a false conscience; it is at variance with the spirit of life.

This dream is a modern expression of a truth concealed in the traditional rendering of the second chapter of Genesis: to obey the command not to eat from the tree of knowledge would have meant persistence in primitive, infantile, nature-identified unconsciousness (hence the Gnostic idea that the serpent is no other than the Saviour himself who initiates the world of salvation through urging men to consciousness).

But the process of coming to consciousness, tied as it is at first to separation from unconscious instinctual life and to a distortion of the wholeness of the Self and then to a need to oppose psychic inertia of the ego, is an *opus contra naturam*[8]—against the natural resistance of both ego and Self, even though paradoxically it is also required by the Self and striven for by the ego. There is a feeling of risk, of anxiety and guilt, as the increasing pressure of the opposing poles is registered and reacted to unconsciously. For example, a person whose original ego-structuring has developed in rebelliousness against over-mothering and who has become stubbornly independent and over-rational—thus too much cast off from the unconscious matrix—may find himself unconsciously driven by the compensating urge to yearn and search for a warm, loving motherly figure who can be trusted and submitted to emotionally. He will find himself caught in a conflict of anxieties, in respect to both his habitual mistrustful independence and his equally strong unconscious counterurge to trust and to submit. Conscious understanding has to enter here and sort out this natural chaos.

Just as the person who fears and mistrusts emotional dependency may be impelled, contrary to his fears, to yearn and search for these very dreaded emotional ties, he who shuns independence and aloneness may be driven to seek them. Thus there unfolds in endless combinations and countercombinations the vast dramatic play of move and countermove which is personality development—and life. This play demands readaptation, yet something basic in our nature also opposes this readaptation.

Eventually when we resolve to try to go along with the new urges and attempt to use our will power to make ourselves change, we discover that we cannot will what we want, that we cannot make ourselves different through direct effort, that we are called upon to serve two masters, as it were, the accustomed built-in past and the opposing demand of the future, and that every attempt to serve the one arouses the opposition of the other. Then we suffer the "crucifixion of our virtues" described in Chapter 14. For the only way we can become different is to attempt the seemingly impossible task of bearing the conflicting anxieties and serving each of the opposing demands according to our limited capacity.

A dream typical of this situation: "*I was led into a tower room from which there was a vast sweeping view over an immense, wide, hitherto unseen, beautiful horizon, a new vista of liberty, a new possibility. But I could not bear to look. I was seized by an attack of unbearable dizziness and anxiety at this view from the heights and I felt like pulling away in fear; I wanted to crawl down the stairs, away from that grand view.*"

To the static, habit-based ego the demand for change and transformation can indeed be a dizzying, even a death-like threat, and this may be a basis for the psychological phenomenon which Freud classified as the death drive, namely the urge to dissolve and transform that which has previously been established.

> Tell it no one but to sages
> For the crowd spurns the desire
> I exult what through the ages
> Has aspired to death by fire.[9]

Conflict with oneself appears to be a basic, constant and inevitable element of life functioning, perhaps *the* most basic. Our whole developmental pattern is structured in such a way that conflict with and dissolution of what once has been established are unavoidable; our original ego development makes us fear and oppose that which life puts in our way as the goal of our search when the secondary, compensating, unactualized aspect of the Self enters the stage.

In view of the necessary transformation-in-conflict, we may regard distorting or traumatizing childhood experiences—the results of which we have to labor to overcome in our later lives—not only as pathological and thus perhaps avoidable incidents but also as the inevitable ways in which a personality becomes initially structured, the first act of a dramatic play which is life. In the dramatic conflict or impasse here initiated we find a pattern—the ego-Self estrangement—without which no play could unfold. Furthermore, and regrettably, we may say that the sharper and the more painful the impasse, the more tragic but also more gripping and interesting the play.

This play theme is often found in dreams. For instance: "*I was on stage*

*facing playwright, stage manager and audience, all waiting for me to play
my part. I realized that I alone was totally ignorant of the role and the lines
expected of me. Apparently I had to find them by improvising. Just as I was
about to give up in despair, I heard a woman* [the anima] *whispering to me
from the prompter's box in order to help me."* While we are expected to
find and express our creative freedom in the prearranged play through improvising—and only through improvising can we find freedom—the unconscious nevertheless helps by "prompting" us—if we can hear and understand its "whispering."

Or another dream motif: *"I am challenged to play the best possible game
with the cards dealt me by an opponent who deals ever-changing hands."*
Again, our ego freedom lies not in the choice of the cards but in discovering
or developing the best possible tactics, in terms of the cards we happen to
hold, against our formidable antagonist, the Self, our real hidden and basic
being, of which our "I" seems but a temporary and passing structure but is
nevertheless a structure which is required and impelled to make the most of
itself, to play for keeps, indeed for its very life. Playing for keeps is, interestingly enough, a motif found in primitive rites, for instance in Aztec games,
in which the team losing the game was sacrificed, or in the rites of the
contest and the sacrificial death of the Year Kings.

The conflict between ego and Self, the basic anxiety-charged life conflict,
can then be seen and experienced as the agony of crucifixion, of unbearable
suffering unto death; or it can be the expression of the pain of the Greek
agon, the play contest in honor of the god. Hence life and the ego-Self
conflict may also be experienced as a play for the purpose of nonpersonal
realization, a challenge to artistic creative improvisation in the face of the
conflicting demands with which we find ourselves confronted; then life becomes "formation, transformation, Eternal Mind's eternal re-creation." [10]
Here is a typical dream expressing this view: *"I came into a gloomy
church. I had to replace the sombre pictures of the stations of the cross by
painting pictures of dancers, players and athletes in bright lively colors."*
The ego drama of life is to be experienced not only as unavoidable suffering
but also as challenging contest, play and dance.

Ideally then, in its proper function, the ego is the center of consciousness which adapts its functioning to outer as well as to inner reality as
distinct from itself. This means that the ego, when in its proper place, has
the function of an arbiter which attempts to reconcile warring parties—but
it is also one of the parties. This function of reconciliation requires, first of
all, that the ego get to know the various entities that are to be reconciled.
But it is a kind of knowing which cannot keep itself aloof; it has to be a
knowing in the original sense (in Biblical phraseology, for instance) in
which knowing is the same as entering, experiencing and loving.

If this is to be accomplished, the ego has both to exert and to restrain its power drive, not only in respect to inner and outer entities but in respect also to its own position and needs as conscious center. This means that the function of the ego is not only one of controlling but of balancing and directing. It has the function of personality development and personality organization: development in terms of itself as an identity, organization in terms of external adaptation. Furthermore, it has the task of emotional integration of experience, that is, of adaptation to the inner world by realizing itself in relation to the Self, to the total functioning authority.

The ego has to recognize its position as separate from the external world, thus dissolving *participation mystique*; it is called upon to set itself apart from and in relation to the internal world of emotions and drives, thus dissolving projections and unconscious identity. The optimal stance that the ego can strive for—without necessarily hoping that it can ever be accomplished fully—could be described as a continual awareness of the conflicting polarities likely to appear in ever-new forms as old ones are resolved: of waiting and seeing, of living things out, weighing various aspects and bringing them into balance, ever ready to work with the materials at hand. In this way, as it confronts its relative position to the Self as a transcendental symbolic postulate, it stands a chance of reducing the threat of that inflation which comes from losing sight of the limitations of its position and power in relation to the unconscious "personalities," and thus it may be able to integrate the meaningfulness of the drama of life through experiencing it symbolically.

The Self, on the other hand, presents itself psychodynamically as a complementing, organizing, determining entity, an urge toward a union of opposites that includes the conflict with the "adversary" or the "evil," a union that includes the resolution of this conflict into the law of one's being and future development. It constitutes a psychic entity characterized by the symbolism not only of an individual wholeness and a potential center but also of a common ground of all human experience: a paradox like that to which Nicolaus of Cusa referred when he spoke of God as a circle, the center of which is everywhere, the circumference of which is nowhere. Certain definite elements demand to enter a certain person's life and not the life of another. The Self dynamism reconstellates the "unitary reality" that we lose sight of during ego development.

The Self is the entity, then, that "plots" the way for an individual life, that directs and demands in an individual fashion. But the Self also insists that the ego take responsibility within the limits that are set for it. The wisdom of life lies in discovering where individual will and choice can operate, where limitations and responsibility begin and end.

Two dreams already mentioned[11] will illustrate this point. A young woman of highly irresponsible nature dreamed that *she was sitting in a car with a pleasure-loving and irresponsible friend. She did not know who was driving the car but she found herself being pursued by a truck driven by a murderer who was determined to run them down. The only way she could save herself was to push the driver of her car aside and take the wheel into her own hands; then she would be able to escape.* This dream says in effect: Unless you take full responsibility yourself, you will be run down. On the other hand, the dream about the "hand of God" as well as the dreams of this chapter show how drastically our ego decisions may be delimited or cancelled by the Self. The Self's directive will always depend on the particular action needed to redress a psychic imbalance.

The Self as an *a priori* pattern of unfoldment thus encompasses a totality which is partly conscious and partly unconscious, hence is of unknowable extension. It contains and includes the ego with its capacity for understanding, awareness and choice; the relationship between ego and Self, when it is dynamic, appears to function as if the Self had chosen a partner and given him full responsibility within his particular functioning (awareness, understanding and choice). Buber expresses this in a very beautiful and psychologically sound formulation:

> It is senseless to ask how far my action reaches and where God's grace begins; there is no common borderline; what concerns me alone, before I bring something about, is my action, and what concerns me alone, when the action is successfully done, is God's grace. The one is no less real than the other, and neither is a part-cause. God and man do not divide the government of the world between them; man's action is enclosed in God's action, but it is still real action.[12]

The ego, in other words, is the medium we are given for functioning in and choosing life, while knowing that there is no choice without awareness and that this awareness includes also the limitation of our choice: we may choose to eat or not to eat only that food life offers us.

Again and again we find ourselves in impasses which demand choice; indeed without choice there is no consciousness. Choice is based upon a value system of right and wrong, good and evil; the principle of evil, then, is an indispensable element in ego development and choice, and the *mysterium iniquitatis*, the mystery of evil, is evidently inherent in existence, hence in creation. Though its implications have often been suppressed the mythologem has made this clear; even in the highly expurgated traditional King James version of the Bible, Isaiah (45:7) quotes God as saying: "I form the light, and create darkness: I make peace, and create evil: I the Lord do all these things."

There appear to be two opposite pitfalls in the ego position taken in individual lives. If ego responsibility is not taken or if the Self is disregarded, destructive forces will threaten from the unconscious. In reference to the first pitfall Jung says:

> It must be reckoned a psychic catastrophe when the *ego is assimilated by the self*. The image of wholeness then remains in the unconscious, so that on the one hand it shares the archaic nature of the unconscious and on the other finds itself in the psychically relative space-time continuum that is characteristic of the unconscious as such. Both these qualities are numinous and hence have an unlimited determining effect on ego-consciousness, which is differentiated, i.e., separated, from the unconscious and moreover exists in an absolute space and an absolute time. It is a vital necessity that this should be so. If, therefore, the ego falls for any length of time under the control of an unconscious factor, its adaptation is disturbed and the way opened for all sorts of possible accidents.
>
> Hence it is of the greatest importance that the ego should be anchored in the world of consciousness and that consciousness should be reinforced by a very precise adaptation. For this, certain virtues like attention, conscientiousness, patience, etc., are of great value on the moral side, just as accurate observation of the symptomatology of the unconscious and objective self-criticism are valuable on the intellectual side.[13]

In respect to the danger to an ego that is insufficiently rooted in reality, there is an old Talmudic story:

> Four there were who entered into Pardes [Paradise]: Ben Azzay, Ben Zoma, Akhar and Reb Akiba. Ben Azzay looked and lost his life. Ben Zoma looked and lost his reason. Akhar cut down all that grew; he lost his very faith. Reb Akiba alone entered in peace and departed in peace.[14]

The experience then may be a shattering, destructive one, it may lead to complete disruption, it may lead to inflation or it may be integrated. Only when the ego can preserve its own identity and separateness from the Self and not be burned in the fire of cosmic dissolution—only then can individuation take place. We must be aware of the danger. There is merely a thin borderline between individuation as a conscious process and the disruption and dissolution of the personality—breakdown or even psychosis—which takes place when the unconscious gains the upper hand. (Hence also the closeness of genius and insanity and the danger of "short cut" methods of entering the unconscious, such as drugs.) The outcome of the confrontation with the numinous powers depends upon the attitude of the ego. The fundamental determining factor lies in the ego's ability to avoid the inflation and merging and to maintain its separateness in and after the union. Jung continues:

> However, accentuation of the ego personality and the world of consciousness may easily assume such proportions that the figures of the unconscious are psychologized and the *self consequently becomes assimilated to the ego.* Although this is the exact opposite of the process we have just described it is followed by the same result: inflation. The world of consciousness must now be levelled down in favour of the reality of the unconscious. In the first case, reality had to be protected against an archaic, "eternal" and "ubiquitous" dream state; in the second, room must be made for the dream at the expense of the world of consciousness. In the first case, mobilization of all the virtues is indicated; in the second, the presumption of the ego can only be damped down by moral defeat. This is necessary, because otherwise one will never attain that median degree of modesty which is essential for the maintenance of a balanced state. It is not a question, as one might think, of relaxing morality itself but of making a moral effort in a different direction. For instance, a man who is not conscientious enough has to make a moral effort in order to come up to the mark; while for one who is sufficiently rooted in the world through his own efforts it is no small moral achievement to inflict defeat on his virtues by loosening his ties with the world and reducing his adaptive performance. (One thinks in this connection of Brother Klaus, now canonized, who for the salvation of his soul left his wife to her own devices, along with numerous progeny.)
>
> Since real moral problems all begin where the penal code leaves off, their solution can seldom or never depend on precedent, much less on precepts and commandments. The real moral problems spring from *conflicts of duty.* Anyone who is sufficiently humble, or easy-going, can always reach a decision with the help of some outside authority. But one who trusts others as little as himself can never reach a decision at all, unless it is brought about in the manner which Common Law calls an "Act of God." The Oxford Dictionary defines this concept as the "action of uncontrollable natural forces." In all such cases there is an unconscious authority which puts an end to doubt by creating a *fait accompli.* (In the last analysis this is true also of those who get their decisions from a higher authority, only in more veiled form.) One can

describe this authority either as the "will of God" or as an "action of uncontrollable natural forces," though psychologically it makes a good deal of difference how one thinks of it. The rationalistic interpretation of this inner authority as "natural forces" or the instincts satisfies the modern intellect but has the great disadvantage that the apparent victory of instinct offends our moral self-esteem; hence we like to persuade ourselves that the matter has been decided solely by the rational motions of the will. Civilized man has such a fear of the *"crimen laesae maiestatis humanae"* that whenever possible he indulges in a retrospective coloration of the facts in order to cover up the feeling of having suffered a moral defeat. He prides himself on what he believes to be his self-control and the omnipotence of his will, and despises the man who lets himself be outwitted by mere nature.

If, on the other hand, the inner authority is conceived as the "will of God" (which implies that "natural forces" are divine forces), our self-esteem is benefitted because the decision then appears to be an act of obedience and the result a divine intention. This way of looking at it can, with some show of justice, be accused not only of being very convenient but of cloaking moral laxity in the mantle of virtue. The accusation, however, is justified only when one is in fact knowingly hiding one's own egoistic opinion behind a hypocritical facade of words. But this is by no means the rule, for in most cases instinctive tendencies assert themselves for or against one's subjective interests no matter whether an outside authority approves or not. The inner authority does not need to be consulted first, as it is present at the outset in the intensity of the tendencies struggling for decision. In this struggle the individual is never a spectator only; he takes part in it more or less "voluntarily" and tries to throw the weight of his feeling of moral freedom into the scales of decision. Nevertheless, it remains a matter of doubt how much his seemingly free decision has a causal, and possibly unconscious, motivation. This may be quite as much an "act of God" as any natural cataclysm. The problem seems to me unanswerable, because we do not know where the roots of the feeling of moral freedom lie; and yet they exist no less surely than the instincts, which are felt as compelling forces.[15]

The assimilation of the Self into the ego constitutes a state of megalomania in which one loses sight of one's concrete, personal and human limitations. One feels called upon to do great things, one would play God, nothing seems impossible—a general tendency in our time in which conscious reasoning and willing have even assumed a position of ultimate authority.

In his later writing Jung speaks of the adequately established conscious relation between the ego and the Self as

> the union of the whole man . . . with the world—not with the world of multiplicity as we see it but with a potential world, the eternal Ground of all empirical being, just as the self is the ground and origin of the individual personality, past, present, and future. . . . it is the relation or identity of the personal with the suprapersonal atman, and of the individual tao with the universal tao. To the Westerner this view appears not at all realistic and all too mystic; above all he cannot see why a self should become a reality when it enters into relationship with the world of the first day of creation. He has no knowledge of any world other than the empirical one. . . . Such thoughts are unpopular and distressingly nebulous. He does not know where they belong or on what they could be based. They might be true or again they might not—in short, his experience stops here and with it as a rule his understanding, and, unfortunately, only too often his willingness to learn more. I would therefore counsel the critical reader to put aside his prejudices and for once try to experience on himself the effects of the process [of individuation] I have described, or else to suspend judgment and admit that he understands nothing. For thirty years I have studied these psychic processes under all possible conditions and have assured myself that the alchemists as well as the great philosophies of the East are referring to just such experiences, and that it is chiefly our ignorance of the psyche if these experiences appear "mystic."
>
> We should at all events be able to understand that the visualization of the self is a "window" into eternity, which gave the medieval man, like the Oriental, an opportunity to escape from the stifling grip of a one-sided view of the world or to hold out against it.[16]

Finally there arises the crucial and practical question: How do we know when the relation between ego and Self is "wrong"? How do we know when we are taking too much responsibility or when we are taking too little? How do we know when the position we take is keeping the Self from helping us, challenging it to stand in our way? The very fact that this feels like it is happening, that we feel deadlocked, may be the answer to that question. We are given notice that we are not on our assigned road by the very fact that we are meeting the "adversary," by the very fact that we are deadlocked or threatened. This is depicted in the mythical story of Balaam.[17] Balaam was called by the King of Moab to curse Israel. He was warned by an angel of the Lord not to go to Moab but he did not listen. On his way he came to a narrow path and there the ass on which he rode would not budge, for the angel barred the way. The prophet did not notice the angel but the ass did. A fine point: Our instinctual animal side is more sensitive and astute in critical situations, when the path becomes "narrow," than is our nicely developed brain.

Thus when we find ourselves facing only obstacles and hindrances and sterility, we may consider whether or not we may be in an uncooperative position in respect to the Self. In turn, often enough our calling, the direction of our road, is shown by that which incites both fascination and fear, which beckons and terrorizes at the same time. The Self's aid rather than its obstruction may be summoned by an attitude which asks: What does this situation ask of me or intend to teach me? How may I serve this problem for the sake of life and the transpersonal value? rather than: What can I get out of this in terms of personal gain? Where the issue of ultimate meaning is constellated, transformation will eventually occur, even though only by way of a great deal of suffering. As the ego offers itself up to combat with the Self, as it were, and risks its existence in being equal to the demand, saying, like Jacob, "I will not let thee go except thou bless me," something happens to the world of drives. The adversary becomes the helper. That which hitherto has been a threatening or destructive entity can become cooperative and reveal its constructive potential when we risk finding a place for it and when we seek its inmost core of meaning.

But if we understand anything of the unconscious, we know that it cannot be swallowed. We also know that it is dangerous to suppress it, because the unconscious is life and this life turns against us if suppressed, as happens in neurosis.

Conscious and unconscious do not make a whole when one of them is suppressed and injured by the other. If they must contend, let it at least be a fair fight with equal rights on both sides. Both are aspects of life. Consciousness should defend its reason and protect itself, and the chaotic life of the unconscious should be given the chance of having its way too—as much of it as we can stand. This means open conflict and open collaboration at once. That, evidently, is the way human life should be. It is the old game of hammer and anvil: between them the patient iron is forged into an indestructible whole, an "individual."

This, roughly, is what I mean by the individuation process.[18]

17. Ego Development and
the Phases of Life

THE EVOLUTION OF the ego is the evolution of that aspect of the Self which is manifested in time and space; a continuous evolution thus goes on as interaction between an actualized personality centered in the ego and a potential wholeness centered in the Self. The characteristic forms of this interaction vary in the different phases of life. Jung says about this:

> Life is (the) story of the self-realization of the unconscious. Everything in the unconscious seeks outward manifestation, and the personality too desires to evolve out of its unconscious conditions to experience itself as a whole.[1]
> The term "self" seemed to me a suitable one for this unconscious substrate, whose actual exponent in consciousness is the ego. The ego stands to the self as the moved to the mover, or as object to subject, because the determining factors which radiate out from the self surround the ego on all sides and are therefore supraordinate to it. The self, like the unconscious, is an *a priori* existent out of which the ego evolves. It is . . . an unconscious prefiguration of the ego. It is not I who create myself, rather I happen to myself.[2]

These two statements are a summation of what differentiates Jung's attitude toward the psyche from other approaches. This shift from the notion of a personality centered around the ego to the concept of a personality that is determined by and rotates around the unconscious center, the Self, seems to be as difficult for most people to reconcile with observable facts as was the Copernican theory at the time of its introduction. It once seemed obvious that the sun rotated around the earth; it seems just as obvious to most of us today that our life is centered in or around our egos.

Jung's approach to psychology provides us with a way of deciphering the manifestations of that hypostatized center in our individual lives. This way

265

is the symbolic mode. By means of it, the ego can find an appropriate position of partnership with the Self which will make mutual cooperation possible.

Ego evolution can be divided into three phases. Childhood is the phase of actualization during which an undifferentiated all-identity begins to "deintegrate," the original ego-Self identity gradually separates and elements from the environment interact with archetypal potentials to produce a first actual personality. Generally in this phase people and things are experienced as overwhelming or threatening "powers"; the ego perceives them as if they were magical and later mythological entities. The second stage establishes the separation of ego and Self. In this phase of middle or adult life, that of ego-Self estrangement, people and things are just people and things. The only power that is acknowledged is that of the ego—and this is expressed in the familiar "where there's a will there's a way." The third stage is that of the "return," the rounding out and fulfilling of the personality potential. The movement in this stage is toward individual wholeness. The nonrational elements press for integration; the ego is drawn toward the reestablishment of a relationship to the Self, not in unconscious identity as in infancy but in the form of a conscious encounter. Consequently this phase cannot be explored until there is an ego strong enough to stand up to the Self. This phase comes to an end when life terminates; the images in which the unconscious speaks of death would seem to suggest that the ego then returns to its original identity with the Self. This final merging is to be prepared for by the conscious encounter, by a conscious ego-Self relationship. Existence is experienced symbolically as a mystery beyond oneself, beyond the ego's capacity for rational understanding, beyond people and objects, as a transpersonal being which can be grasped only symbolically.

The evolution of the ego away from and back to the Self can be expressed in a parabolic curve; Jung compares it to the curve of a projectile. Its phases as enumerated above are to be taken only as approximations of evolutional trends, not as absolutely separated stages of development. There is a good deal of overlapping; for example, there are often aspects of the ego that cannot be developed until the symbolic attitude of the "return" becomes available.

1. INFANCY AND CHILDHOOD

(a) Unitary Reality
In the first phase, in infancy, life operates in a magical dimension, in what Neumann calls a "unitary reality" of the archetypal field.[3] The psyche of the child seems to operate like a relatively undifferentiated wholeness, a

pattern of integrated, instinctual responses in an encompassing field, where subject-object separation in the adult's sense has as yet no validity. This manner of operating can be compared with the way a plant or animal functions in a total field. Ego development gradually splits this instinctual "unitary reality" into an inner subjectivity and an outer objectivity. Üxküll describes this containment of the animal in its *Umwelt* as follows:

> Subject and object are dovetailed into one another, to constitute a systematic whole. If we further consider that a subject is related to the same or to different objects by several functional cycles, we shall gain insight into the first principles of the "Umwelt" theory: all animals, from the simplest to the most complex, are fitted into their unique worlds with equal completeness. A simple world corresponds to a simple animal, a well-articulated world to a complex one.[4]

There is as yet no rationally experienced difference between within and without, between subject and object, between psyche and soma; for the ego which rests upon the division of these categories is not yet present. Neumann quotes E. W. Sinnott's example of organic life-functioning in order to demonstrate the actual functional oneness of "inner" and "outer" life, as well as the reality of this pre-psychological (pre-ego) "absolute knowledge" of the encompassing field:

> In one group of slime moulds the individuals are single cells, each a very tiny and quite independent bit of protoplasm resembling a minute amoeba .These feed on certain types of bacteria found in decaying vegetable matter and can readily be grown in the laboratory. They multiply by simple fission and in great numbers. When this has gone on for some time a curious change comes over the members of this individualistic society. They cease to feed, divide, and grow, but now begin to mobilize from all directions toward a number of centers, streaming in to each, as one observer describes it, like people running to a fire. Each center exerts its attractive influence over a certain limited region, and to it come some thousands of cells which form a small elongated mass a millimeter or two in length. These simple cells do not fuse, but each keeps its individuality and freedom of movement. The whole mass now begins to creep over the surface with a kind of undulating motion, almost like a chubby worm, until it comes to a situation relatively dry and exposed and thus favorable for spore formation, where it settles down and pulls itself together into a roundish body. Now begins a most curious bit of activity. Certain cells fasten themselves securely to the surface and there form collectively a firm disc.

Others in the central axis of the mass become thick-walled and form the base of a vertical stalk. Still others, clambering upward over their comrades, dedicate themselves to the continued growth of the stalk. Up this stalk swarms the main mass of cells until they have risen several millimeters from the surface. These . . . now mobilize themselves into a spherical mass terminating the tenuous stalk, which itself remains anchored to the surface by the basal disc. In this terminal mass every cell becomes converted into a rounded, thick-walled spore which, drying out and blown away by the wind, may start a new colony of separate amoeba-like cells. In other species the structure is even more complex, for the ascending mass of cells leaves behind it groups of individuals which in turn form rosettes of branches, each branch terminating in a spore mass. In this process of aggregation, a group of originally identical individuals is organized into a system wherein each has its particular function and undergoes a particular modification, some cells to form the disc, others the stalk, and others serving as reproductive bodies.[5]

Neumann comments that this example demonstrates the directive power of a transcendent unitary reality.[6] An infinite number of mutually independent unicellular individuals obey an apparent plan which results in the formation of a differentiated shape through an ordered sequential development. A development usually ascribed to instinct, thus to a quasi-psychic entity, appears here not in an organism but in a group of unicellular "individuals"; and the directive center appears, at least to our state of consciousness and awareness, to be outside these individuals.

The child's state of unitary reality is also characterized by the relative absence of any differentiation between subject and environment, comparable to what Lévy-Bruhl has called *participation mystique* in the psychology of the primitive; the infant or child acts in a state of unity with everything that is going on around it. The child is not so much influenced by what this environment does or says as by what it *is*. Even the reactions of the mother during pregnancy may tend to affect the child's reactions and fate and may tend to incorporate themselves into its emotional pattern, as the evidence of hypnotic regression has suggested. As everyone who has had children knows, the infant reacts instantaneously to every emotional change or vibration of the mother and the environment; in fact, not only instantaneously but simultaneously, and regardless of whether or not the mother is aware of her own state. The psychic atmosphere is so much a part of the infant that, as Spitz has described it, a dearth of sheltering love in the earliest weeks and months has immediate serious physical results. When infants have been raised with attention to perfect hygiene and careful diet but have been denied human contact, they have withered and died in spite of their excellent surroundings.

(b) Deintegration

Separation from this unitary reality begins in the first phase of life development, with the purpose of establishing a center of consciousness, an ego. We have studied this process in some detail and have described Fordham's term "deintegration" in reference to it.[7] In his words:

> This term is used for the *spontaneous* division of the self into parts—a manifest necessity if consciousness is ever to arise.
>
> In choosing this word I have in mind a distinction from disintegration, a condition which is associated in experience with destruction or splitting of the ego into a number of fragments. It [disintegration] presupposes an ego which is already formed, and consequently the experience is a danger to its whole integrity. Deintegration on the contrary is conceived as a spontaneous property of the self behind ego formation. Expressing it anthropomorphically one could say that it springs from a desire of the self to become conscious, to form an ego by dividing itself up.[8]

Out of the aboriginal wholeness and unity there now develop the various emotional and perceptual reactions and archetypal trends, and last but not least the ego capacity for identity, consciousness and willing. It is important to note again that this ego development is seemingly initiated and brought about by the Self. We can observe the first indication of this when the child begins to say "I," at around the eighteenth month, for at the same time he will begin to draw circles. Here, in the spontaneous scribbling of the child, is the first appearance of what we have come to know as a symbolic representation of the Self. Also quite often when the child tries to assert himself or to defend himself against the environment, he will do so by drawing a square or circle.[9] The Self manifests for the first time as ego in this way.

Deintegration means not only ego formation but also subject-object division. The presence of an ego postulates a dimension of non-ego, the world of objects "outside" and the world of archetypes, emotions and urges "within." It means the beginning differentiation of the archetypes out of the unitary field and the development of perception, emotion and action potential. Fordham says:

> We can describe a deintegrate by saying it is a readiness for experience, a readiness to perceive and act, but there is as yet no perception or

action. Both come into consciousness together without distinction between subject or object. It will, however, appear from outside as if the
infant were object-seeking and as if the infant were trying to express
itself in specific ways and selecting its object with the utmost care. Indeed we assume that only when the object exactly fits the deintegrate
can a perception occur, for only then can we conceive a state of affairs
when there is no distinction between subject and object so far as the
infant is concerned.

By way of amplification we may consider what happens if the correspondence between object and deintegrate is not exact. In the first
place it will not be perceived at all and nothing will happen, but later
on there develops a tolerance of the object failing to fit exactly on to
the deintegrate. From this springs a dawning consciousness of a distinction between subject and object.[10]

We have previously described this process as the early actualization of
archetypes, as the gathering of perceptual, emotional and behavioral material around "the archetype as such" by correspondence association.[11]

The first beginnings of speech now appear—speech in the sense of differentiating words, in contradistinction to the previous words of general "cosmic" meaning, when "mama," for instance, meant everything from "milk"
to "go away" to "come" to "I want to sleep." The differentiation of speech
begins concurrently with the first saying of "I" and the drawing of circles
and squares and is preceded by the "no" motion which in our culture is the
shaking of the head. Ego appearance, no-saying, choice and differentiation
coincide, at about the eighteenth month, according to Spitz.[12] The capacity
to reject and to choose between right and wrong are the intrinsic qualities
necessary for ego development and these capacities are produced by the
intention of the Self.

In this stage, it is as if the ego fragment or infant ego, which begins for
the first time to perceive itself as a focus of permanence, sees itself surrounded by a vastness of existence on which it is utterly dependent, from
which it is only insufficiently separated and which appears as completely
overpowering. This phase in the evolution of consciousness, both of the
individual as well as of the species, has been symbolically represented in the
images of the divine infant (infant consciousness) held by the Great
Mother, namely the World-Mother, the aboriginal unconscious, the Self
which is felt as nothing less than an overwhelming cosmic power. For the
infant, the real mother actualizes this containing Self. She is experienced as
an overwhelming, awesome, cosmic, lifegiving power. Her behavior, emotions and appearance mediate the ways in which life and the Self are antici-
pated. Or, to express this concept in another way, the stage of containment

by the mother follows that of complete psychological identity of infant ego and mother, who in this phase is truly the Great Mother, world and Self in one inseparable unit. When the infant's ego begins to emerge, this archetypal experience of the Great Mother is projected upon the woman who happens to be this infant's actual mother or fills the role of mother.

(c) *The Magical Dimension*
The above description is of course a symbolic one. If we used a more modern image, a modern mythologem, we could speak of the mother-infant energy field. But the infant has as yet no such capacity to distinguish between symbolic and literal experience. Neither has the schizophrenic. For them, objects and people "are" the very powers which we regard as symbolically represented or projected. This fact can be seen in the small child's lack of differentiation between an image and the object it represents. A little girl will feed her doll with real milk or hold an apple for the picture-book horse. The beginning deintegration of this unitary presymbolic oneness, of what could also be called *Umwelt* or field-identity, engenders a state that I have called the *magical* phase of development.[13] The laws under which beginning consciousness engages in its encounter with the still encompassing unitary reality are not what we call rational. The operation of this magical dimension of the unconscious can be observed also in some aspects of primitive psychology. As the development of consciousness proceeds through the mythological and rational stages this magical dimension will recede but will continue to function as a dimension of the unconscious, always ready to compensate for, complement or disturb the conscious outlook. The dynamics of this dimension strike the rational consciousness as weird and inexplicable. The term *magical*, as I use it here, is not meant to refer to "the art which claims or is believed to produce effects by the assistance of supernatural forces or by mastery of secret forces of nature."[14] It does not describe such a deliberate manipulation of forces; rather I use it to refer to certain specific energy phenomena—physical and psychological—which correspond to a dimension of functioning that has been recognized in one form or another (and called magical) in every past culture. This dimension of functioning makes itself felt directly and overwhelmingly without differentiation among or separation of image, emotion and action pattern. Any part of an event evokes the whole (*pars pro toto*) and any part can substitute for any other. Images "are" affects and compel action. This constitutes what we are accustomed to calling suggestibility. To an extreme degree it characterizes the psychology of the child and the primitive. All of this is a direct expression of archetypal energy which can occur even after the differentiation of the ego is under way.

For the infant, every object and experience may be assumed to be a total experience characterized by image, affect and action equivalence. The infant is surrounded by and dependent upon the all-powerful world, focussed in the mother. The beginning ego consciousness establishes a vigorous resistance to this "otherness" that threatens to absorb and overwhelm it from outside, just as the inner "otherness" dissolves it in unconsciousness and sleep. An enormous exertion, the first power struggle, is required to resist the unconscious within and without. In the aboriginal primitive presymbolic situation, the power effort is consequently directed against the Mother, namely against the force, within as well as without, which would tempt and draw consciousness back into its dark chasm, back into mother's womb. There is a recognition in primitive rituals that the germ of the ego must be guarded against being devoured by the mother, the nature-world and the forces of the unknown. These apotropaic rites are themselves archetypally determined, not rationally invented. They are spontaneous productions of the deintegrating unconscious directed against its own regressive urge. Such ritual elements may therefore spontaneously arise from the unconscious in the form of weird compulsions, such as the "mooning" described in Chapter 15.[15]

In the world of the infant (between birth and approximately the second year), as well as in that of the primitive (which offers us the nearest observable instance of a magical frame of reference), we find that manifestations of psychic energy are predominantly instinctual, emotional and affective. Just as the primitive magician, by means of his ecstatic frenzy, "forces" natural events to his will, so the infant, by virtue of the mutual instinctual identity, seems to coerce the mother into satisfying its demands by its screaming insistence and by the compelling emotional appeal of its helplessness. For the mother, the child's necessities are the same as her own instinctive love-urges, and to these the infant responds instantaneously as in a telepathic identity.

In such an infantile and primitive state of identity there is a total immersion in mother, family, clan, group, tribe and nature. The "maker" is still one with the "made," the doer one with what is done, the fighter one with the opponent. (In order to exorcise an animal, man becomes the animal himself; he disguises himself as the animal or draws the animal, as the many discoveries of cave magic show us.) So it is not merely the mother but also the containing group, the social collective, which is endowed with numinosity and suggestive power in the magical frame of reference. This fact is important for the understanding of the compelling authority of group mores, group convictions and collective moralities which persists when the magical frame of reference has been consciously outgrown by ego rationality but continues to operate as a dimension of what is then designated as the unconscious. In the realm of the inferior functions there continues, then, an irrational sense of identity with group attitudes, mores, emotions and judgments, an extraordinary sensitivity toward their suggestive influences and a fear of affronting group taboos, so that they carry a magical threat when disregarded. We know that susceptibility to suggestion, a typical feature of the magical dimension, is maximal in the primitive, during childhood and when we are tired, sleepy or under the influence of a group. Under hypnosis an insensitivity to pain may be suggested which is sufficient for painless childbirth or surgery; and in this state suggestibility has even produced a change in the body tissue. A person in a hypnotic trance can sustain second degree burns from a pencil which the hypnotist describes to him as a burning match. In all of these states, individual self-awareness is weakened in respect to the energy of the unconscious, and it is the magical dimension which is touched.

When magical functioning is predominant, as in the early phase of development under discussion, consciousness is incapable of differentiating between image or quality and the object itself; there is no abstractive ability. This is a presymbolic mode of functioning, thoroughly unreflective and emotionally toned. In the magical phase something which to us would be a symbol "is" that to which it merely alludes. Primitives worship animals, stones and other objects; children clutch a talisman—a doll or blanket, or a pet. The image "is" the archetypal power; it activates behavior and events, even biological states, in a manner analogous to the instinctual evocation and response, the *Umwelt*-field identity observable in animals.

Magical functioning is also characterized by a marked predominance of ESP or telepathic phenomena which lead to the unconscious participation and psychological identity with affect-evoking people and events; hence the infant's extreme sensitivity to and dependence upon the emotional quality of its surroundings. Time and space dimensions are only relatively valid or are even as though suspended.

An important effect of the all-identity quality in magical functioning is the lack of differentiation between causation, willing, responsibility and guilt. Since no objective causes are distinguished, everything is experienced as if it were subjectively motivated and had to be dealt with by means of taboo and ritual. Whatever happens—whatever is said, felt, done or experienced—has been willed by a "power," by "them," but the subject feels compelled to make some sacrifice to the power in order to placate it; magical functioning is characterized by intense fear, guilt and fatalism. We see this operating in children and in primitive mentalities, in the habit of invariably blaming oneself or others for every mishap without regard to natural, impersonal causation. We also see it breaking through in mob and scapegoat psychology and in the general irrational mistrust of the stranger or foreigner. The black, for instance, carries the projection of the white man's fear of the dark, spontaneous, instinctual side of himself which must be exorcised when he is met only on this level; this is an area which Laurens van der Post has explored in his perceptive books about Africa.[16]

In this state of identity with the all-embracing, magically overpowering environment, the infant's psychological and even physical survival are utterly dependent upon the parents (foremost the mother) who are the principal archetypal power figures; they are gods to the young child. The infant is dependent not only upon what the parents do or say but upon what they *are*, regardless of whether or not they realize this and, in fact, the more so the less they realize it. The infant's psyche is not yet separated from the parents' unconscious. Birth has been merely physical up to this point; a real psychological separation does not occur until much later, perhaps not until the sixth or seventh year. This close psychological identity is further revealed by the fact that little children quite often dream about the problems of their parents. And since they are themselves still immersed in their magical dream world, they could be said to live these problems. This can be particularly fateful when the parental atmosphere is marked by outward, conscious goodness and concern but sustains underneath a current of unrealized resentment, hostility and tension. Such an atmosphere of unconscious hostility is poison for the infant. The presence of unrealized conflicts and general tension within or between parents always adds to, if it does not originate, guilt feelings in children; the experience of conflict and the experience of guilt are almost identical; we all react to conflict tension with guilt. The parents' conflicts are experienced by the child as if they were his own. The parents' repressive attitude or rejection of each other is experienced by the child as a repression or rejection of his own individuality; we saw this in the case of the asthmatic little girl who dreamed of being pushed off the island by the goat people.[17]

Ego development occurs during the magical phase in terms of the body, as described in detail in Chapter 15,[18] and this development provides the first frame of reference for the actualization of archetypal faculties. Conscious experience of the world, the subject-object relation, comes first in terms of the interaction between "I"-body and "they"-bodies. The images which represent larger concepts when the adult's experience becomes highly differentiated and symbolic are formed in the body frame of reference.

The child's dimly felt powers are *bodies*. Bodies and objects constellate or mediate the otherwise unfathomable. This is the way primitive animism and totemism function. Even the highly civilized adult retains the body imagery; much of his unconscious material expresses itself in terms of body symbolism. The body has been described in psychoanalytical literature as the source or origin of symbolic experience, but it seems more appropriate to say that the body provides the *basic frame of reference* for symbolic experience.

The child's sense of self-acceptance, conscience and guilt are basically shaped by the reaction of the most important other bodies to his own body and its functions. Therefore, to the extent that bodily expressions—bodily play; oral, urethral, anal and genital expressions—are too rigidly repressed or emotionally rejected, to that extent may ego development be interfered with. The arrested aspect of the ego which first manifests as bodily experience retains a maximum—because unreleased—charge of affect intensity; the arrested aspect is manifested also in its fixation on this original concretistic level, in compulsive masturbation or anal preoccupation. Such repressed primitive "enclosures" may continue as sources of psychic disturbance, with neurotic or even psychotic potential.

(d) Mythological Experiencing

Gradually the preoccupation shifts from the body level to fantasy in more general images and then in concepts, and there develops an awareness that the images or concepts are not necessarily quite identical with the objects they purportedly represent. This development can be regarded as the beginning of the mythological mode of experiencing,[19] which gradually replaces the purely magical one. The developing ego emancipates itself from the magical threats of the devouring, dissolving all-oneness by means of fantasy activity (*non-directive thinking*, in Jung's terminology). The archetypal elements, affects and drives that would tend to dissolve the nascent ego appear as threatening powers—witches, goblins, demons, dragons, monsters, wild beasts—to be slain or propitiated by heroic or wise and beneficent figures. The early state of unconsciousness tends to be represented in images of the mother and of the Feminine. The development of consciousness and rationality—as it asserts itself against the hitherto overwhelming "containing powers" within and without—is usually depicted as a male figure who embarks upon the heroic quest. It is in this mythological phase, approximately during the years from 6-7 to 12-14, that the father takes on increasing importance; the father archetype—the drive toward independent, self-reliant assertion, discipline and order—presses for actualization through a male guide.

Thus the early magical body symbolism is amplified and partly replaced in the mythological phase with a symbolism of imaginary "others." The archetypal elements make themselves known—are actualized—as numinous fantasy images carrying certain typical emotional and behavioral implications. For instance, a sense of inadequacy would express itself in compulsive oral or masturbatory activity on the body-magical level; on the mythological level it would manifest itself in fantasies of threats of destruction by monsters, beasts or witches, or in redemption by the good fairy. Only rational consciousness (after age 14) would be able to comprehend and verbalize the experience in psychological, abstract, symbolic terms, namely to call the feeling a "sense of inadequacy" and thereby gain further distance from the affect.

(e) Fear

In the magical and mythological phases, that sense of inadequacy based upon the disproportion between the small ego and the overwhelming power of the magical world which surrounds it causes a reaction of fear— fear, because the nascent ego, in which all sensation, emotion and experience are vested, is under the steady threat of being dissolved by the surrounding "maternal" entity and because the attempt to use one's own power may bring about retribution. The practical importance of this fact is that fear is a normal experience for the infant and need not be fought, except when pathologically excessive. Certainly it cannot be rationalized away completely. This existential fear is never to leave us for as long as we live; it operates as a transpersonal stimulus for the development of consciousness, with which to oppose what is feared. In other words, without this fear, there would be no psychological development. Of course when ego development is seriously interfered with, this fear may take on excessive dimensions. Even so, it may still be most effective not to attempt merely to rationalize it away but to concretize and propitiate it on the mythological level, when that level has become activated.

For example, a child had been having frightful nightmares about a fox which just stood there and stared at him and would not leave. I proposed that he attempt to establish contact with this fox and see what it wanted of him. He said, "The fox is a very sneaky fellow." I suggested, "Maybe the fox wants you too to be a little smarter; see if you can go with the fox and learn from him." He thought that he could try that; whereupon the fox was satisfied. The little boy made a step forward in his psychological development; he learned to rely upon his own innate foxiness, his capacity to reason. (And the fear could move on to the next point of development.) In dealing with magical fear it is helpful therefore to make use of the mythological framework where the developing mind is a mind of images. All fairy tales describe how the hero is threatened by magical powers or beings and how these powers can be dealt with. Another point about childhood fear is that it includes the fear of darkness, since it is the fear of being swallowed again by the aboriginal unconscious—consciousness is light and unconsciousness is darkness—and this fear, again, is a normal occurrence in children.

(f) Conscience

The increasing separation from the unconscious and from the unconscious automatism is felt as though it were a break in the natural order, entailing as it does individual choice—choice between right and wrong. Choosing means "killing," sacrificing the many possibilities for the sake of the one which is chosen. And it involves the risk of being wrong—hence it entails guilt. Also, as we have noted, causation, guilt and responsibility are not separated in the magical phase, therefore a sense of individual responsibility, as opposed to general guilt-anxiety, develops on the basis of individualized, personal guilt feelings. Fear and guilt, being natural occurrences in childhood, should not be fought as such but directed into the mythological patterns which offer psychologically workable ways of propitiation and personalization in this prerational stage. Also it is important that parental authority express standards of right and wrong in a sufficiently permissive or flexible way so as not to stifle the ego's capacity to learn by making its own mistakes. Whenever one feels that it is a catastrophic event to have been wrong, one is led to avoid choice and decision. The development of an individual personality is thereby stifled. Needless to say, the opposite extreme of a moral relativism which fails to provide any right and wrong standards can be equally disastrous through failing to offer the first indispensable orientational guidance.

The most important archetypal trend for the developing ego is the drive toward establishing an inner standard of right and wrong, instead of the merely propitiatory obedience patterns of the magical level. Conscience at first develops in the form of what Freud called the *superego*. It is first experienced through the authority of those outer beings who claim the knowledge of right and wrong, namely the parents. Conscience becomes crystallized in those terms in which it happens to be experienced during the childhood stage and these will be predominantly persona values, since it is the external adaptation to parental values and demands and to the cultural standards of what is considered appropriate behavior that establishes the first sense of right and wrong. (Sometimes this outer standard can take rather grotesque forms in relation to the inner predisposition of the individual.) Conscience seems at first to be identical with persona and superego; a more individual conscience can be developed when the sense of one's identity becomes identical with the rational judgments of the ego as we reach middle life and can question the validity of the superego standards; and only in later life can our truest, really individual conscience be found, at the price of conflict and suffering through the confrontation between ego and Self.

It is characteristic of early childhood that dreams are more often than not archetypal in nature. They are therefore dreams that deal with the total life in its most fundamental dimensions and are often nightmarish and frightening, since they are charged with the numinosity of a stratum from which the ego strives to be free. These nightmares are not to be taken too tragically nor need we be unduly disturbed about their occasional frightful character, since they are archetypal and introduce motifs that belong to an entirely different and symbolic phase. An example of this is the dream of a child who saw himself lying in a bathtub filled with blood into which blood flowed from all sides. The imagery in this dream is found in Mithraism. In the Mithraic mysteries the initiant was put into a hole, a bull was slaughtered and its blood was poured over him. This was the baptism by blood, namely the initiation into the world of the mature adult who has slain the bull, has overcome the compulsive power of instinctuality and emotionality. The dream implies that this child will at some time also be initiated, perhaps drastically, into the necessity or capacity to "slay his bull" of instinct compulsion.

As they approach adolescence, boys and girls tend to go somewhat different ways, as Neumann showed,[20] for out of the original ego-Self identity the male psychology develops by opposing it, that is, by opposing mother and Self and finally fighting it directly (the symbolism of the dragon fight); whereas the young woman finds herself by maintaining the original identity. Consequently the woman's ego tends, by and large, never to be as separated from instinct and the unconscious as the man's does. For a woman the identity and concern with "belonging" to people and things is natural. This is not so for the man; he often has a hard time discovering the world of belonging. Thus for the woman, relationship problems tend to arise from her difficulty in accepting separateness; for the man "belonging to" and dependence tend to be the major obstacles.

2. ADULTHOOD

In the middle period of life, the period of ego-Self estrangement, things and people are no longer experienced as powers but seem to be just people and things. The sense of the "numinous" tends to be lost. The ego with its rationality and conscious will-control is dominant, and the only source of power seems to be my "I" and somebody else's "I"—the area of competitive combat is delineated. The connection with the aboriginal Self seems lost and, one could almost say, should be lost. The normal adult believes that he is master of his own fate. Jung has the following to say, as noted in Chapter 15:

It is of the greatest importance for the young person, who is still unadapted and has yet achieved nothing, to shape his conscious ego as effectively as possible, that is, to educate his will. . . . . He must feel himself a man of will, and may safely depreciate everything else in him and deem it subject to his will, for without this illusion he could not succeed in adapting himself socially.

It is otherwise with a person in the second half of life who no longer needs to educate his conscious will, but who, to understand the meaning of his individual life, needs to experience his own inner being.[21]

In middle life the ego has supreme command; the adult phase is ruled by the ego's concern for adaptation to external reality, to people and things, mainly by virtue of the power drive which strives to satisfy its needs for survival and competitive control and to avoid displeasure. This is the time of the monarchical rule of the ego, a rule which rests on a sense of permanence, independence and rationality, and is structured and held together through self-discipline. The task of the ego now is to adapt to the external "real" world through the development and use of the superior functions; this development involves also the repression of the inferior functions. This repression is now unavoidable for the sake of social and work adaptations which require the use of our most developed functions. Rationality and conscious will and purpose now rule supreme.

Since adaptation is primarily to the external world, the introvert has a rather hard time of it. The natural introvert may very often feel himself a failure in this phase of life, because demands all go in the other direction. The extravert who joins clubs and organizations has such an easy time of it, while the introvert cannot seem to make the grade. There is no help for this but to tell him that there will come the day when he will have the better of it and the extraverts will be faced with difficulties, when the tables will be turned and the need for conscious introversion will arise in the second half of life. Of course the introvert's way is not made any easier by the fact that the world at large still depreciates the introverted attitude and puts a high premium on extraverted adaptation.

In middle life the only psychic reality seems to be the ego's subjective experience of itself; we can barely take notice yet of any other, inner world. This means that in this stage further actualization and confrontation of archetypal energy must occur through one's interpersonal relationship problems. The ego's concern is with the external world; the unconscious compensates for this by confronting it with inner psychic reality in terms of outer personalizations or projections. Archetypal actualization now presents itself in terms of personal concrete imagery—that is, in terms of personal symbolism of familiar people and objects. Bill and Susan tend to incorporate Yang and Yin or evil and good in their problematic aspects; we no longer deal with saviors or witches. Now the ego may also experience itself as a concrete psychological person in the present moment; only when the shadow, the badness, is actualized in the other fellow rather than in a remote mythological image can I become fully "I" and measure my will and efforts against a concrete reality. As long as the shadow was a vague terror in the night or a tree demon there was no possibility of finding the central archetype in one's own personality. The step to archetypal realization through interpersonal relations needs to be taken away from the vagueness of the *participation mystique* and must be consciously experienced at simple face value before it can be recognized as an outer expression of an inner fact.

We operate now in terms of ourselves versus the world which is *there,* outside us, for we have discovered that we are not just our bodies; we have not yet discovered, however, that we are not just our egos either. Therefore all the "not-I" that is not *here* is *there,* outside. The only place we can meet shadow, animus or anima—that part or those parts of ourselves which we have not realized—is through the other person. The corrective influences in our lives therefore occur through projection, through meeting our competitors, our enemies and our beloved. As far as we are concerned they are all obviously whatever we see in them. (How could it be otherwise, since we see it so clearly!) Yet this illusion is still essential, for it is through it that we get to know ourselves as "I" and to test our strength against the "not-I" which we meet in the external world.

On the other hand the very fact that the personality is vested exclusively in rational consciousness and in the ego means that there is also an increasingly complete personality dissociation, as whatever is unacceptable to this ego is split off in the form of the opposing and projected shadow. The compensating function of the unconscious really begins only in this stage of full psychic deintegration or dissociation. To the child the unconscious is a rather vaguely marked-off extension of its hazy consciousness, but in the second phase it begins to be at variance with conscious functioning. Personality develops through meeting opposition and having to learn to transform it into compensation and cooperation, on the external stage. In the latter part of life this has to be accomplished in respect to the inner "Thou" and the transpersonal infinite "Thou" or Other, the Self.

As the shadow differentiates, it functions as a separate split-off personality consisting of those personal traits that are unacceptable to the ego ideals. Similarly, animus or anima—the not yet assimilated spiritual, separative, assertive tendencies, and instinctive, emotional and connective urges—make their influences felt in projections. Attractions and aversions then present us with the first external partnership problems. For the first time we meet the challenge of the need for relatedness, in which a developed

"I," no longer identical with the "not-I," consciously confronts a "not-I" and is confronted with the necessity to come in terms with it. Needless to say, in this early phase of attraction and repulsion by virtue of projection, such real relatedness is still rather out of reach. In this phase of life, relationships are primarily seen in terms of their extraverted elements—we form friendships, fall in love, experience incompatibility, and all of this is generally ascribed to or blamed upon the other person.

The confrontation of the outer world—the need to establish ourselves successfully in respect to society, work, family and interpersonal relationships—is now Life. But true relatedness requires the awareness of shadow, animus or anima in order that they may not distort our view of the "other" through their projection; hence the possibility of relatedness belongs essentially to the second half of life.

Interpretation and therapeutic work, when they occur during this phase, proceed primarily in terms of interpretation and direction on the object level, through uncovering faulty adaptations to external reality. Of particular concern are the effects upon external adaptation of insufficient separation from the parental world and of the disruptive complexes which were conditioned through parental influences. This is the phase, therefore, in which the usual reductive psychoanalytic interpretation—which interprets personality problems in terms of childhood difficulties—is viable. On this level of experience it is helpful to say: I react to so-and-so because this and that happened between myself and my mother and father, etc. The adult has to understand how he became what he is in terms of interaction with other people. (We may add further that the infantile elements encountered here can also be described in straightforward terms such as "castration fears," because on the infantile level there is no difference between symbolic and actual castration.)

Guilt feelings, when they occur on the adult level, have to be dealt with by converting them into rational responsibility, by promoting the realization that a law of cause and effect is operating. When someone feels he is wrong or something is amiss, he *does* have something to do with it and it is his own personal responsibility to act and to control himself—even to change himself. He has to learn what to do and how to do it, unlike the child or primitive to whom everything is willed by powers which he cannot control and of which he feels himself to be the victim.

The danger of this phase is the assimilation of the ego by the Self; an insufficient separation, in which the ego is fascinated by the collective unconscious, gives itself up to day dreams, lives in fantasies and confuses fantasy with reality. Or one's aspirations are so great and uncompromising that in actual reality nothing or only very little can be achieved. For realization in the here and now requires a renunciation of the infiniteness of the many

possibilities of the intuitive Great Vision for the sake of its finite and few
limited aspects which, through concentration and work, can be made concrete. This problem was posed to a young patient in the following dream:
*"I wanted to board a bus but had no money to pay the 15¢ fare because I
was not willing to break a five dollar bill. Consequently, I was thrown off the
bus."* If the ego fails to give its energies to the seemingly small and limited
tasks at hand because it wants to deal only with big ideas, then it cannot
move on, it misses the bus and the personality is not ready for the next
phase, that of ego-Self reintegration.

3. AGEING

Jung's own remarks can best introduce our consideration of the final phase
of life.

> Statistics show a rise in the frequency of mental depressions in men
> about forty. In women the neurotic difficulties generally begin some-
> what earlier. We see that in this phase of life—between thirty-five and
> forty—an important change in the human psyche is in preparation. At
> first it is not a conscious and striking change; it is rather a matter of
> indirect signs of a change which seems to take its rise in the uncon-
> scious. . . .
>   The very frequent neurotic disturbances of adult years all have one
> thing in common; they want to carry the psychology of the youthful
> phase over the threshold of the so-called years of discretion. . . .
>   As formerly the neurotic could not escape from childhood, so now
> he cannot part with his youth. He shrinks from the grey thoughts of
> approaching age, and, feeling the prospect before him unbearable, is
> always straining to look behind him. Just as the childish person shrinks
> back from the unknown in the world and in human existence, so the
> grown man shrinks back from the second half of life. It is as if un-
> known and dangerous tasks awaited him, or as if he were threatened
> with sacrifices and losses which he does not wish to accept. . . .
>   Ageing people should know that their lives are not mounting and
> expanding, but that an inexorable inner process enforces the contrac-
> tion of life. For a young person it is almost a sin, or at least a danger, to
> be too preoccupied with himself; but for the ageing person it is a duty
> and a necessity to devote serious attention to himself. . . .
>   A human being would certainly not grow to be seventy or eighty
> years old if this longevity had no meaning for the species. The after-
> noon of human life must also have a significance of its own and cannot
> be merely a pitiful appendage to life's morning. . . . Whoever carries
> over into the afternoon the law of the morning . . . must pay for it

with damage to his soul, just as surely as a growing youth who tries to carry over his childish egoism into adult life must pay for his mistake with social failure. . . .

It is particularly fatal for such people to look back. For them a prospect and a goal in the future are absolutely necessary. This is why all great religions hold out the promise of a life beyond . . . which makes it possible for mortal man to live the second half of life with as much purpose and aim as the first.[22]

The repressions of the first half of life which served ego development can now no longer be maintained. The bill will now be presented for what was by-passed in the earlier years. Whatever was left behind, indeed had to be left behind because it was not suitable for external adaptation, for success and practical use, demands now to be heard and realized. The questions present themselves: Who am I? What am I here for? What is the meaning of my existence? What am I moving toward? What is my own story—that is, what is the meaning or myth behind what appears as the conflict or (all too often) the seeming chaos of my existence?

The demands of the unconscious no longer press toward external adaptation—unless of course the needs of the preceding phase have not been adequately fulfilled. If we have been lagging on the journey we will still have to make up for tasks undone. But when ego development and external adaptation have been adequate, the developmental needs will change at this point. We will feel the demand for adaptation to the relatively disregarded world within, the world of the psychic *Urgrund*, the aboriginal ground of being that is "not of this world," is not identical with the "real" external world and its needs. The objective psyche, the transpersonal, the infinite, as it manifests in the here and now as an urge toward an individual realization in terms of the myth of one's being, must now be faced consciously. The adaptational demand is toward the Self as a symbolic transpersonal reality and mystery. This means that the symbolic approach to existence—that approach in which the phenomena of life point beyond themselves toward the experience of the ineffable—wants to be accepted.

Shadow, anima and animus can no longer be dealt with solely through their projections onto other people. They must be confronted within. The Self demands to be faced as the "wholeness" law of one's individual life; collective morality will no longer suffice. We become especially aware of the intrinsic conflicts of existence: conflicts of leanings, duties, loves, responsibilities and commitments, of external demands versus inner needs. Existence seems to confront us in the form of apparently irreconcilable opposites which crucify us; the inner split opens wide before us. This state can lead to the realization that these opposites are not to be solved by rational or will-determined efforts of the ego, that they are to be borne and eventually to be recognized in their symbolic meaning as expressions of the play of life itself.

Drives and urges that formerly had to be repressed for the sake of unification of the personality under the rule of the ego, tendencies or qualities that were useless or even a hindrance to external adaptation, demand now to be realized for the sake of an integral wholeness of one's total being. The ego finds itself delimited by the Self. Formerly the personality was endangered by insufficient assertion of the ego; now the psychological danger comes from the ego's attempt to maintain its dictatorial attitude and self-sufficiency. Yet paradoxically the ego cannot and must not even attempt to renounce control. Rather it has to experience consciously its limitations and its relative powerlessness in the face of the reality of the objective psyche— the mystery of the transpersonal "Thou." As the Jewish legend has it:

> When the time arrives for her to emerge from the womb into the open world, the . . . angel addresses the soul, "The time has come for thee to go abroad into the open world." The soul demurs, "Why dost thou want to make me go forth into the open world?" The angel replies: "Know that as thou wert formed against thy will, so now thou wilt be born against thy will, and against thy will thou shalt die, and against thy will thou shalt give account of thyself before the King of Kings, the Holy One, blessed be He." But the soul is reluctant to leave her place. Then the angel fillips the babe on the nose, extinguishes the light at his head, and brings him forth into the world against his will. Immediately the child forgets all his soul has seen and learnt, and he comes into the world crying, for he loses a place of shelter and security and rest.
>
> When the time arrives for man to quit this world, the same angel appears and asks him, "Dost thou recognize me?" And man replies, "Yes; but why dost thou come to me today, and thou didst come on no other day?" The angel says, "To take thee away from the world, for the time of thy departure has arrived." Then man falls to weeping, and his voice penetrates to all ends of the world, yet no creature hears his voice, except the cock alone. Man remonstrates with the angel, "From two worlds thou didst take me, and into this world thou didst bring me." But the angel reminds him: "Did I not tell thee that thou wert formed against thy will, and thou wouldst be born against thy will, and against thy will thou wouldst die? And against thy will thou wilt have to give account and reckoning of thyself before the Holy One, blessed be He." [23]

The open conflict between ego and non-ego and the experience of the ego's limitations prepares consciousness for its ultimate limitation: physical death. About middle life the first dreams of death usually appear, in rather masked and veiled form, as a rule, simply as a reminder that it now has to be faced. This is like the downward trend of the trajectory of a shell that has risen, has met its height and is now beginning to descend. It is not possible to maintain the height; the progress of life is now downward but no less goal-directed than it was on the ascent. The Self, which created the ego and then withdrew, now reappears to be faced and engaged in dialogue. I now experience myself as "not-I," as opposed by psychic entities for which I cannot account, which have wills, intentions and meanings that are quite different from what I will and intend.

If the ego cannot consciously reorient itself to this "change of life," which occurs for both sexes, and become conscious of its limits in this phase, psychopathology may result. We all know of instances of "unexplainable" depressions in successful people; it seems impossible to everyone that the executive becomes an alcoholic at the height of his success or decides to jump out of the twentieth story window on the day of the testimonial dinner.

The compensatory function of the unconscious and of the Self now increasingly produces symbols and images of a transcendental, unitary reality. The moving power of existence is no longer vested in ourselves or in other people but in something beyond us and behind the world of objects. Now is the time to come to the realization that "everything transient is but a symbol." [24] Freedom and creative initiative become possible through conscious experimentation with the possibilities of realizing our hitherto inaccessible natures, which all too often turn out to be other than what we expected or hoped for—or even feared.

It was in respect to this phase that Jung originally formulated his concept of the individuation process—a becoming of ourselves and a fulfillment of our roles as we move from an unknown and unknowable source of being to separate existence through the illusion of ego permanence and supremacy of ego-will and then turn back to the aboriginal source, carrying with us the fruits of conscious awareness that we have gained while we traveled the trajectory of the curve. It becomes particularly important during the downward trend to look upon our problems and our delimitations and difficulties in symbolic rather than causalistic, reductive terms; no longer to say we are thus and such because mother and father did this and that to us, but to ask: "What can I make out of it?" "What does it mean in terms of my potential wholeness that I had to become thus in order to develop how and where?" "What is the meaning of my problems and what have I to fulfill in this life?" Freedom and creative initiative are to be found in using the abilities of the conscious ego to bring to realization the intents of shadow, animus, anima, and Self within the confines of what is humanly possible. Thereby we play a game of experimental improvisation and the game we play is life.

Let us recall a dream of the young woman we described in Chapter 6.[25] Her personality pattern was warped by the constant disruptive invasion of hate and resentment which repeatedly maneuvered her into attitudes and situations that seemed to ask for punishment, to which she then reacted with paranoid martyrdom and with further resentment. Her analysis revealed both the childhood conditioning and its effect upon her psychological reactions. But what was she to do with merely these insights? The dream gives a hint: *"I was sitting in a classroom. The teacher asked a riddle in a foreign tongue to which the answer was, 'It is the crucifixion because the cross is the tree of life.'"* This was the answer the unconscious gave to the riddle of the life-meaning of her injury through her childhood. The destructiveness was to be experienced *as if* inflicted upon her so that she might grow through suffering it in conscious confrontation. The myth of her life was shown her as that of furthering life through consciously suffering the evil—not only the other person's but foremost her own—rather than acting it out. In this way the mystery of ultimate selfhood was to be found by her—perhaps a deeper and truer martyrdom in the original, literal sense of the term, meaning "witness" to the mystery.

Another example of the symbolic presentation of the mystery of one's life is that of a man who started analysis late in life. As a result of his strictly fundamentalist upbringing he knew all the rules of right and wrong, but his feelings were stifled; his life was at a standstill. (He is the same man who had the dream of a ship that was running against the wind but standing dead still.) [26] He was faced with the need to find meaning in his stagnation. In the course of his analysis he learned to understand the nature of his problem; he realized that he was unable to make contact with his feelings, but beyond this realization he could go no further. He then had the following two dreams, only a week apart:

"I was in a buggy, an old-fashioned buggy of the eighteen hundreds. With me was a very attractive woman, all dressed in black, with a high stiff collar and a very serious expression on an utterly pale face. She was silent and I felt myself deeply drawn to her; I had the feeling that she held the precious meanings of my life. The carriage began to move, and while the woman seemingly held the reins in her hand, the carriage gradually began to leave the ground and go up into the air."

"I was in bed with my brother, head to foot. A puppy tried to jump into

the bed but my brother threw it out. Then I heard from far away the voice of my grandmother calling to me: 'It is five minutes to four!' "

To his brother he associated a stiff, traditional and rigid pride-conditioned outlook on life, to the puppy instinctual and emotional life. The grandmother had been long dead. Four o'clock was the time he had had a heart attack the preceding day. (He had lived with a chronic heart ailment for the previous twenty years.) Four o'clock to him was also the time for a coffee-break when, as he said, you drop what you are doing, go out for a bit of food or drink and return to your work refreshed.

In the first dream this man is in the carriage with an aspect of his anima that seems to belong to another world, to a bygone past. Something that antedates his present life drives him away from the earth, heavenward, that is, toward death. She seems to hold the fulfillment that he is yearning for, as the buggy moves away from the ground. The grandmother in the second dream is the ancestral mother, the "sourceground," the "origin" who calls to him that it is five minutes before the break, the temporary interruption of work, which is to come in the form of a heart attack. He died on the day of this dream. He told me the dream in the morning and that evening collapsed and died instantly of a heart attack.

These dreams carry a remarkable message. Death is presented as being like a coffee break, a transient interruption of one's workday for the sake of resting. The dreams say: You are confronted with your brother; you are interlocked with your shadow problem, which makes you incapable of accepting the new impulse, the puppy that wants to jump in. Never mind. It is time for a break, for a pause, before returning to the job. Your soul-structuring is still attuned to a past period and cannot adapt itself to new demands; hence it leads you away from the earth. Death appears here not as a threat but as a fulfillment, a temporary next phase, in view of the limitations inherent in this man's conscious structuring within this life.

Jung underscores the importance of such an attitude toward death in his essay "The Soul and Death."

Many young people have at bottom a panic fear of life (though at the same time they intensely desire it), and an even greater number of the ageing have the same fear of death. Indeed, I have known those people who most feared life when they were young to suffer later just as much from the fear of death. When they are young one says they have infantile resistances against the normal demands of life; one should really say the same thing when they are old, for they are likewise afraid of one of life's normal demands. We are so convinced that death is simply the end of a process that it does not ordinarily occur to us to conceive of death as a goal and a fulfillment, as we do without hesitation the aims and purposes of youthful life in its ascendence.

. . . Life is teleology *par excellence*; it is the intrinsic striving towards a goal, and the living organism is a system of directed aims which seek to fulfill themselves. The end of every process is its goal. All energy-flow is like a runner who strives with the greatest effort and the utmost expenditure of strength to reach his goal. Youthful longing for the world and for life, for the attainment of high hopes and distant goals, is life's obvious teleological urge which at once changes into fear of life, neurotic resistances, depressions, and phobias if at some point it remains caught in the past, or shrinks from risks without which the unseen goal cannot be attained. With the attainment of maturity, and at the zenith of biological existence, life's drive towards a goal in no wise halts. With the same intensity and irresistibility with which it strove upward before middle age, life now descends; for the goal no longer lies on the summit, but in the valley where the ascent began. The curve of life is like the parabola of a projectile which, disturbed from its initial state of rest, rises and then returns to a state of repose.

The psychological curve of life, however, refuses to conform to this law of nature. Sometimes the lack of accord begins early in the ascent. The projectile ascends biologically, but psychologically it lags behind. We straggle behind our years, hugging our childhood as if we could not tear ourselves away. We stop the hands of the clock and imagine that time will stand still. When after some delay we finally reach the summit, there again, psychologically, we settle down to rest, and although we can see ourselves sliding down the other side, we cling, if only with longing backward glances, to the peak once attained. Just as, earlier, fear was a deterrent to life, so now it stands in the way of death. We may even admit that fear of life held us back on the upward slope, but just because of this delay we claim all the more right to hold fast to the summit we have now reached. Though it may be obvious that in spite of all our resistances (now so deeply regretted) life has reasserted itself, yet we pay no attention and keep on trying to make it stand still. Our psychology then loses its natural basis. Consciousness stays up in the air, while the curve of the parabola sinks downward with ever-increasing speed.

Natural life is the nourishing soil of the soul. Anyone who fails to go along with life remains suspended, stiff and rigid in midair. That is why so many people get wooden in old age; they look back and cling to the past with a secret fear of death in their hearts. They withdraw from the life-process, at least psychologically, and consequently remain fixed like nostalgic pillars of salt, with vivid recollections of youth but no living relation to the present. From the middle of life onward, only he remains vitally alive who is ready to *die with life*. For in the secret hour of life's midday the parabola is reversed, death is born. The second half of life does not signify ascent, unfolding, increase, exuberance, but death, since the end is its goal. The negation of life's fulfillment is synonymous with the refusal to accept its ending. Both mean not wanting to live, and not wanting to live is identical with not wanting to die. Waxing and waning make one curve.[27]

It is vital to face the fact that we must live our lives in the light—and under the shadow—of the realization that on the one side permanence is an illusion and yet on the other side, as far as the objective psyche is concerned, there is a continuity of development and psychic existence. We do not fully live unless we can live as if every next moment were to be our last and at the same time as if our life span were to be infinite; as if the time at our disposal were both unlimited and limited, irreplaceable and expendable.

The decisive question for man is: Is he related to something infinite or not? That is the telling question of his life. Only if we know that the thing which truly matters is the infinite can we avoid fixing our interest upon futilities, and upon all kinds of goals which are not of real importance. Thus we demand that the world grant us recognition for qualities which we regard as personal possessions: our talent or our beauty. The more a man lays stress on false possessions, and the less sensitivity he has for what is essential, the less satisfying is his life. He feels limited because he has limited aims, and the result is envy and jealousy. If we understand and feel that here in this life we already have a link with the infinite, desires and attitudes change. In the final analysis, we count for something only because of the essential we embody, and if we do not embody that, life is wasted. In our relationships to other men, too, the crucial question is whether an element of boundlessness is expressed in the relationship.

The feeling for the infinite, however, can be attained only if we are bounded to the utmost. The greatest limitation for man is the "self"; it is manifested in the experience: "I am *only* that!" Only conciousness of our narrow confinement in the self forms the link to the limitlessness of the unconscious. In such awareness we experience ourselves concurrently as limited and eternal, as both the one and the other. In knowing ourselves to be unique in our personal combination—that is, ultimately limited—we possess also the capacity for becoming conscious of the infinite. But only then! [28]

Life has always seemed to me like a plant that lives on its rhizome.

Its true life is invisible, hidden in the rhizome. The part that appears above ground lasts only a single summer. Then it withers away—an ephemeral apparition. When we think of the unending growth and decay of life and civilizations, we cannot escape the impression of absolute nullity. Yet I have never lost a sense of something that lives and endures underneath the eternal flux. What we see is the blossom which passes. The rhizome remains.[29]

18. Therapy

AN EXHAUSTIVE OR even adequate consideration of the process of therapy, the interpretation of dreams, the analytic encounter, transference and countertransference is impossible for us here. These topics are so fundamental and complex that we can attempt no more than a glimpse of their outlines. Each would require a volume in itself. Moreover, neither the interpretation of dreams nor the conduct of the therapeutic encounter can be learned or even adequately understood from a theoretical presentation only. It must also be remembered that the systematic presentation in the preceding chapters is a symbolic description—no more and no less. It is the "best possible description or formula of a relatively unknown fact—a fact, however, which is none the less recognized or postulated as existing"—a fact, or facts, rather, that operate in a fashion far from the neat and systematic way in which they appear in a merely theoretical presentation.

As a basis for a general understanding of the therapeutic process we must recall that a fundamental law of interaction between conscious and unconscious has been postulated; namely that the unconscious relates to the conscious personality in a manner which corresponds to the way this conscious standpoint itself approaches or fails to relate to the unconscious. To the extent that we disregard or are unaware of the urges, demands and requirements of the unconscious we will find that it is not in a position to compensate constructively or to complement within a dynamic range but is forced to disturb and to sabotage, to compensate disruptively. On the other hand if we can take into consideration the elements and requirements of the Self—considering this in its widest sense as expressed in the objective psyche—if we can attempt to channel the inner necessities into expressions which are compatible with the needs and limitations of our developmental phases, as well as of external, rational requirements, then the unconscious will tend to cooperate. Even though we may not be in a position to fulfill the inner demands, the fact that we pay attention to them enlists a cooperative rather than a disturbing response. To the extent that we try our hardest and still stumble, at least we will receive pointers as to how and why we stumble. To the extent, however, that we prefer to say, "I understand all

my problems and need not look further," we may encounter correspondingly annoying or shattering obstacles and obstructions. But also when we
fail to use our conscious judgment and sense of responsibility to the limits
of our capacity, relying rather on fantasies, signs or oracles to the exclusion
of personal judgment or decision, we are likely to fail to elicit the cooperation of the unconscious. The ego has to take a first decisive stand in order
to elicit a compensatory countermove. There is a legend that when Moses
commanded the Red Sea to part nothing happened until the first man
stepped into the waters—only then did they recede. A truly dialectic partnership between ego and unconscious seems to be required.

It is common for the person who is at odds with the unconscious to
attribute the resulting phobias, anxieties and neurotic tensions to various
external problems, usually insoluble ones. As we have seen, these disrup-
tions really come from the pressure of unrecognized but essential personality aspects—in our time, most frequently repressed feeling and religious or
spiritual values. A great many people who think they live in fear of the
threat of the atom bomb are in reality afraid of a psychic atom bomb—the
compressed power of unknown inner needs which are vaguely sensed as a
threat that might shatter the seeming peace which the conscious adaptation
has established.

The approach to life's difficulties which sees them as indicative of lost
meaning may, of course, lead us to overemphasize the element of meaning,
to see any disturbance as a punishment for not living as we "should" within
the full range of human functioning. Suffering does indeed result from unrealized meaning but it is *also* an existential threat to the meaning. Such
suffering and illness must be lived through, they cannot be interpreted
away. Neither can the experience of the absolutely irrational and absurd be
ignored. These are part and parcel of the paradox of human existence,
hence of the reality of the human position. Only when we are able to accept this reality will it be possible for us to find, in our individual lives, the
transpersonal, irrational, ultimate kind of meaning which cannot be
"made" but which rises from the depths of the unconscious as spontaneous
symbol or mythologem, unmistakably one's own and yet "given."

While suffering thus remains suffering, a legitimate part of experience, it
may become more bearable if it is seen as a road that can lead not only to
pain and annihilation but also to a widening and deepening of one's sense
of being. Illness attains a higher dignity once it is recognized not only as
senseless wastefulness but also as meaningful experience.

On the other hand neurotic suffering can also indicate an inability to
integrate new adaptational needs, new meanings which press toward integration. Neurosis, however, does not necessarily point to character weakness, although it may indeed do so. A breakdown in the capacity to inte-

grate the stream of our experiences may be caused by the magnitude of the new life within, of the unrealized potentials and talents. Hence it may constitute a patent of nobility, so to say, a challenge too portentious to have thus far found a way of fulfillment.

Suffering can play a creative role if the conscious standpoint is effectively related to it. We have learned that the ideally adapted and contented person, free of problems, can be a rather dull, uninteresting and uncreative type. It does not follow, of course, that neurotic or psychotic traits are in themselves prerequisites of creativity, as is sometimes believed. Creativity is not the result of neurotic or psychotic tendencies, but of an individual's ability *to transcend them*, to direct the tendencies toward chaos into consciously accessible channels by shaping them into some sort of concrete expression of their intrinsic meaning. It is the firmness, the effort and the skillfulness of the conscious ego's position that finally decide whether the onrush from the deep will bring about chaos and meaningless suffering or whether the suffering can instead provide the dark background from which the light of a new order may arise. Needless to say, this effort may at times be a Herculean one. Conscious standards will have to be changed and widened, conscious values, patterns, outlooks and living habits fundamentally altered. This is nothing less than the birth of a new man, if the new meaning is to come to life in us rather than to lead to destruction. Yet this seems to be the way in which life forever renews and transforms itself.

Therapy is, in essence, the effort to effect an adequate relationship between the ego and the unconscious needs, to bring into awareness their relative positions in respect to each other and to discover the requirements for a continuing cooperative partnership. Therapeutic progress depends upon awareness; in fact the attempt to become more conscious *is* the therapy. Once we are really aware of habitual compulsive behavior or of the motivation of obsessional traits—not merely abstractly or theoretically but in experiencing what is happening and the significance of what is happening while it happens—we cannot act out the impulse any longer in the same naive and self-righteous fashion. We are no longer identical with the urge. As identity lessens so do compulsiveness and primitivity. What we say or do in anger, for instance, is likely to be more destructive while we still assume that we act in a justified defense of morality or rationality or whatever the rationalization may be. Deprived of such justification and recognized for what it is—nothing but anger—the impulse is deprived of some of its power of conviction; it comes out more hesitantly, perhaps even with a touch of humor, hence it can be more easily handled, controlled and redirected. We can then try to overcome the personal anger if needs be and express it as aggressiveness elsewhere rather than being compelled by it to overcome that awful other person or situation. Moreover, this awareness of the limitations which our emotions impose upon the moral righteousness of the ego's position reduces the inflation of the ego. As the ego is more humble and prepared to listen and to learn, the unconscious is likely to complement rather than obstruct.

In therapy it is first necessary to become aware of the gaps and contradictions in our conscious position, to clarify and understand the implications of our professed convictions and value systems; because more often than not our unexamined conscious position is that we would like to have our cake and eat it too. In a more positive form we could describe the conscious position as a collection of requirements, duties and necessities that are often in mutual conflict; often we are crucified by our virtues. Responsibility and duty may pull us one way, love and affection may demand the opposite course. Indeed love may conflict with love, duty with duty. We are sometimes aware of such a conflict but more often we force at least part of it into the personal unconscious because it seems pleasanter to pretend that it does not exist—until we find out how destructive a repressed conflict can be. At this preliminary stage awareness brings about a clarification of the inherent conflicts that have been repressed, sometimes quite needlessly, into the personal unconscious. After the clarification of the conscious position therapy then concerns itself with establishing the range of tension and conflict between conscious and unconscious positions. There is first the conflict between ego and shadow, that is, between what we hopefully believe we are and the reality of our personality which has been repressed. This leads to the exploration of the position and demands of the objective psyche, of those elements which never have been nor could have been in consciousness: animus or anima and Self. Eventually the unconscious will begin to provide not only descriptions of the existing impasse but also positive suggestions for possibilities of development which could reconcile the opposing positions, showing us what avenues of development are available to us, what paths are required of us or closed to us, according to the inherent plan of the Self.

Essentially, then, the course of therapy that follows Jung's approach is based on a continuous dialogue between the conscious ego and the unconscious. Thus the direction of therapy is not determined by the analyst's ideas of what is or should be normal nor by the analysant's hopes and expectations but by what might be called an autonomous process: the unfolding of the inherent plan or pattern of the unconscious, the "replies" to the ego as the dialogue unfolds. This direction comes through the understanding of dreams, fantasies or artistic expressions which show what attitudes or impulses are to be brought into concrete realization. The center of gravity of the Jungian approach thus could be said to rest upon the purposes and guidance of the unconscious. In dealing with any problem there is a certain amount of rational common sense that we can use and must use first, whether we are in analysis or not. But when we come to seemingly insoluble conflicts, it can make a great deal of difference whether or not we are able to avail ourselves of the counsel of the unconscious or must rely only on our rational faculties, our conscious ideas of right and wrong. Where the non-Jungian may tell the analysant what is right or normal and should be done, the Jungian would be more inclined to admit that he has no way of knowing, that it is necessary to see what new standards of normalcy or possibilities of solution for this particular individual the unconscious may reveal.

This means that Jung credits the psyche with a potentiality toward self-healing. The idea that the unconscious contains also the healing potential and not only the disturbing elements was one of Jung's unique and revolutionary discoveries.

This healing potential operates through the tendency toward compensation seemingly inherent in the psyche, namely a tendency to bring forth the "other side" of every conscious view, emotion or impulse. This "antithetical" reaction will be the more pronounced the more one-sided the original "thesis" (to use the terminology of Hegelian dialectics). The tension between "thesis" and "antithesis" not only generates a dynamic life tension toward motion and flux; it also presses toward the creation of an encompassing third, a "synthesis" which modifies, transforms and eventually supercedes the original opposing two. As the newly won position becomes rigidified, it is met in turn by an antithesis, a newly compensatory reaction. Thus constant flux and transformation are, seemingly, demanded by life.

The aim of Jungian analysis is to aid the transition from the initial mere opposition which tends to be prolonged, indeed often seemingly stalemated, and in which the conscious view attempts to hold on rigidly to its own side and to repress its opposite. For instance, identification with an ever-loving attitude at the price of repressing one's hostile reactions and feelings engenders a resentment in the depth of the unconscious which may stalemate, even paralyze, our capacity for spontaneous personal affection, leaving us instead with the rather gray artificiality of a forced "good will" toward everyone but toward no one in particular.

Acceptance and realization of our hostile and aggressive impulses, painful and risky as it seems, may in turn bring forth a capacity for spontaneous affection in the face of and in spite of openly expressed anger and hostility, eventually transforming them as well as the merely willed affection into genuine tolerance and warmth.

Transformation, therefore, rather than sublimation is the goal of Jungian analysis. Traditional psychoanalysis aims toward a compromise between the urges of the unconscious id, the reality adaptation of the ego and the morality demands of the superego, through sublimation, which is a disciplined substitute expression of otherwise unacceptable drives.

Transformation, however, postulates a change of the drives themselves so that there is no longer any need for sublimation. As a result of transformation the drives would cease to be threatening and destructive and would become converted into helpful elements. This goal is to be brought about by a widening of the ego's awareness of its scope and a subsequent shift in the ego's position and approach to the drives which opens new channels of expression. The unconscious opposes an extreme and uncooperative ego position but proves potentially helpful to an ego which is ready to take a more accepting and experimentally cooperative position.

The urge toward transformation is inherent in the configuration of the unconscious itself and is identical with the drive toward "individuation." Individuation occurs through "realization," genuine experiencing in actual encounters or situations; it is not sufficient to depend on theoretical understanding. Coming to terms with the objective psyche rests upon the analysant's efforts to understand and test in real life experience the hints and messages from the unconscious. This constitutes a symbolic quest into unknown territory. That it is unknown to the analysant is no more than one would expect; but in terms of its ever newly and differently unfolding uniqueness, it is also unknown and unpredictable to the therapist.

The therapist consequently finds himself in a new role which is quite at variance with the traditional image of the knowledgable psychiatrist who diagnoses and treats a clinical case with sage counsel. He can no longer regard himself as a detached observer who recognizes what is right or normal and advises his patient accordingly. As one who is to aid in the birth of new meaning as unknown, and indeed unknowable, to him as it is to his patient, the therapist plays a role more nearly that of a midwife or of an experienced senior partner in a common undertaking, a common search. The patient can no longer be only an object of therapy, a case to be placed on a couch where he is to produce his subjective material for the purpose of diagnostic evaluation by a relatively uninvolved objective therapist. The patient is not an "it," an object of therapeutic manipulation, but is an individual, an unknown and unknowable "Thou" to be faced and respected by the "I" of the therapist. (Martin Buber's terminology is very apt here.) The therapeutic relationship becomes an existential encounter, and indeed Jung felt that if any change is to occur at all it must touch and affect both participants.

We can therefore understand why Jung was the first to do away with the couch and with the detached note-taking therapist behind it. He chose to sit face to face with his patients; this fact is more significant than may appear at first sight. Freud's explanation for the use of the couch was that it enabled the patient to relax and to spin out free associations in something like a soliloquy, and that it enabled the therapist to be uninvolved and therefore to deal objectively with his patient. However, he is reported to have remarked privately—and this is equally significant—that he himself could not stand being stared at by various people for a whole day.

The idea of an uninvolved therapist studying his patient like a clinical case or a laboratory animal was something Jung regarded as impossible and —even if it were possible—undesirable. He considered a direct, personal encounter to be absolutely unavoidable and essential. The absence of the couch is one expression of an unpremeditated and unprejudiced affirmation of the unfolding reality of the other, in whatever fashion he happens to present himself. Above all, the analysant is not something to be fitted into a pre-existing theory or category. Jung expressed himself on this point repeatedly and advised the beginning therapist to "learn the best, know the best —and then forget everything when you face the patient."[1] He warned therapists never to believe that they can understand what is going on inside the patient. They must always be open to be taught, to be shown differently and to adapt their preconceptions to *that which meets them*. This emphasis means that no attempt is to be made, or indeed can be made, to categorize the data which is presented. It cannot be fitted into preconceived categories, whether of sexuality or power or resistance or censorship or whatever. Any and all categories may apply at one time or another, may have to be tried or may never fit at all. That which is expressed is to be taken on its own merits; we must find its own meaning, without assuming that we know it already. This readiness to accept any hypothesis, any angle, any means of explanation, if it somehow will clarify a given problem, is fundamental to Jung's approach. The clarification can come from a volume of Freud or from the symbolism of a book of gypsy wisdom or an alchemist's codex or the saying of an ancient sage.

If the analyst can never know what is happening on the other side, how can he know whether or not his formulations and interpretations do justice to the material and whether or not they are adequate?

Since neither he nor the analysant can "know" with any degree of certainty, they both have no choice but to rely upon what we may call the self-balancing equilibrium of the psyche. The pressure for meaning that arises from the depths of the objective psyche is not allayed by inadequate or inappropriate formulations, but repeats its disturbing demands, symptoms or images until its "intents" are realized. Robert Frost describes how this principle is revealed in everyday life:

> One of the lies would make it out that nothing
> Ever presents itself before us twice.
> Where would we be at last if that were so?

Our very life depends on everything's
Recurring till we answer from within.
The thousandth time may prove the charm.[2]

In the analytic encounter, where there is hope that the necessary number of recurrences will be reduced, a symbolic bridge can be established with the objective psyche, and the analyst "who has ears to hear" will suspect when he has made false assumptions. The subject matter—that is, the objective psyche itself—will correct him by failing to respond, by "objecting" through dreams or through emotional or physical symptoms. Thus again we hypostatize and reality-test an autonomous authority in the objective psyche that reacts and by reacting can assist and guide us.

Furthermore the analysant's resistances, his feelings of unease will not be allayed by false or inadequate interpretations. Jung says about this: "There is no single theory in the whole field of practical psychology that cannot on occasion prove basically wrong. In particular, the view that the patient's resistances are in no circumstances justified is completely fallacious. The resistance might very well prove that the treatment rests on false assumptions." [3]

The objective psyche tends to react favorably or unfavorably depending upon the appropriateness of our approach to it. The basic guidance does not come from the analyst any more than it does from the patient; the verdict about which approach is right or wrong comes from the unconscious in the form of further dreams. The analyst neither accepts nor rejects the patient's interpretation of his dreams; he offers his own interpretations but does not impose them; he lets the reactions to the various interpretations speak for themselves, taking his direction from subsequent developments. Both analyst and patient have to follow the lead of the unconscious—the patient because of his ignorance and the analyst because of his ignorance, both of which are premises of the work.

One may, of course, ask a question at this point. Why should there be any need for an analyst at all? If therapy occurs through the encounter and the lead of the unconscious and if the analyst cannot know the way to recovery, could not the patient do it himself? Why may not an encounter with any person do? Indeed, any encounter in which the emotional implications and reactions as they point to our sensitive areas and blind spots are experienced consciously will have a transforming effect. However, the value of the usual encounter is limited by the fact that it is our blind spots that lead to conflict and impasse in these encounters, through mutual projections and illusions, and such an encounter all too often then brings about or gets "stuck" upon the very impasse we hope to resolve. The analyst is presumed to be experienced in searching out the meaning and the nature of such impasses so that more of the unconscious aspects of the personality may be realized in the encounter. One of the two people involved must be able to read the nonrational language of unconscious expressions and images and must be able to direct his attention upon the other's unconscious problems with a degree of detachment, without being personally remote. Then through this focusing encounter an autonomous process is set into motion by virtue of the evocation of unconscious forces, as a flame leaps into being through the contact of spark and tinder.

While this process is evoked by the meeting of two personalities and involves both of them, it occurs for the sake of the patient or analysant and the searching attention is focused upon him. The therapist functions as an involved experienced participant and mentor who accompanies the patient through the labyrinth of the unfolding psychic dynamics. He is the participant observer rather than the detached observer, for he is himself instrumental in evoking and modifying through his own personality structure that which is to be observed.

This novel way of viewing the process of psychic transformation can perhaps be made more intelligible through an analogy taken from modern physics—the indeterminacy principle. It has been found that a totally objective observation is impossible because the presence of the observer always affects and modifies what he is about to observe. What presents itself is consequently always the product of both or all elements present and acts in a unitary fashion. Some form of energy is liberated and set into motion by the encounter and this energy is perceptible to the experienced observer only through the patterning of elements susceptible to its influence. We have already considered the example of the magnetic or electric field, invisible *per se*, in which iron filings arrange themselves in a specific pattern which makes the field effect visible.[4] However, when we deal with an encounter between two different field patterns, then the result is a third configuration different from either of the original two but resulting from and inclusive of them. Positive and negative magnetic poles each arrange iron filings in a circular pattern but out of their mutual encounter an elliptic pattern results that includes both of them.

This analogy gives us a comprehensible image of what happens when two people meet. Their psychic field patterns interact. Something happens, something clicks one way or another and their unconscious patterns "arrange" themselves relative to each other in a typical fashion whether they know it or not, or care to or not; the less they are aware of it the more compulsive the effect of the occurrence will be. In this field, this energic configuration, they both share.

We can see therefore that true relatedness between two people depends vitally upon an awareness of the quality of the field effects involved. If we do not know what moves us we are in no position to understand what we are doing, nor are we in any position to choose what we wish to do. We may think we decide what we want to do but what actually happens may be quite another matter. Without an awareness of the psychic fields in which we operate, any idea of freedom of will, decision or of relationship is an illusion.

The quality or kind of psychic-field complex, the archetypes that will arise in a personal encounter between therapist and patient, the way the analysant will experience himself and his reactions in the therapeutic relationship will depend largely upon the living response of, and in fact upon the very person of, the therapist himself. What he believes or knows or does not know is important for the interpretations he will give, but therapeutically his knowledge is secondary compared to the sort of person he is, the nature of his interactions or noninteractions with his analysants, and what fields, what archetypes, spirits, demons or ghosts are called forth in his encounters with patients.

Jung's conception of the analyst's function is not that of leading or directing and certainly not of forcing his theories on the patient. As Heyer formulated it, the analyst's task is to create an "enabling space." [5] The analytical situation may be compared to a living space into which we enter. Very different thoughts, feelings, memories and moods arise in accordance with the particular space in which we find ourselves. Those awakened in us when we step into a church are fundamentally different from those a hotel calls forth; the seashore evokes something different from the mountains, spring constellates one atmosphere, fall another, etc. In just this way a space, an atmosphere is created between analyst and analysant. This space is co-determined to a decisive extent by the therapist himself—not by his opinions, intentions or good will but by his own actuality, his own inner wealth or poverty. Knowledge, theory and background are necessary and desirable but they do not, cannot take the place of a vitality, a capacity to tune in, to respond to the manifold and differing qualities of individual experiencing of the depth and expanse of one's own living space. The more varied the palette of the analyst, the greater are the nuances of color, character and style which he is able to grasp and with which he can harmonize; the more encompassing his range of understanding and the greater his ability to "see through" in a guiding sense, the greater the "enabling space" for the patient. The therapist creates an atmosphere in which a mutual encounter is to take place, an encounter which enables development and growth. He will of course have to step in and offer his experience and his awareness of unconscious dynamics and help with explanations and interpretations but he will not necessarily lead the process.

The most important element in therapy is the personal encounter, commonly referred to as *transference* and *countertransference*. Jung's view of the transference and his manner of utilizing it again went beyond Freud's relatively limited approach. Freud regarded the intense, not infrequently exaggerated emotional reaction to and involvement with the therapist, the intense interaction of the psychic fields in the setting of the therapeutic encounter, as a neurosis. He spoke of the *transference neurosis* which he defined as a transferring of the patient's original neurotic, distorted relationship to parental figures onto the therapist. This view is valid, but too narrow. In the Jungian frame of reference the transference is seen as the emergence not only of personal conditionings and personal complexes but also of their archetypal cores, by virtue of projection. They arise "as if" they referred to the partner of the meeting, the therapist. Hence it is not only a process of re-experiencing personal distortions but also of actualizing new, archetypally constellated possibilities. Since the encounter with the parents mediates the first experiencing of Yang and Yin, the two main channels of life experience, their re-emergence in the analytic encounter will be of the most decisive importance. Thus the transference calls forth a spontaneous emergence of the most critical complexes and unresolved archetypal problems—especially those centered around anima, animus and Self—which in their striving for consciousness are experienced through projection upon the therapist (or in any encounter for that matter with any person who can be reacted to as a spiritual model or authoritative guide).

The way in which the constellation of an archetype or energetic field takes place is exemplified by a new candidate for therapy who told me after the first five minutes that he would like very much to work with me because he felt very close to me. His reason was that I reminded him of his grandfather. Such things are mutual, however, and I had felt a similar closeness to him. When I asked myself about my own feeling I realized that I felt toward him as I would toward a son. Neither of us had even considered this situation a few seconds before, but we were both caught in the field of the father-son relationship; as we met, "father-son" came down and enveloped us. And as father to son the feeling developed, regardless of whether we chose so or wished so or liked it or did not like it. In terms of this father-son interplay, the relationship unfolded, in the "field" of the "fatherly." It was to be predicted that sooner or later he would have to gain his independence by some show of "disobedience" or revolt against the "father" and that the "father" would have to accept the fact that his "son" needed the freedom to operate without, or contrary to, the "father's" counsel.

What happened here was the unitary event of a configurating force. It would be quite artificial to split it into the traditional concepts of transference and countertransference, which imply that the analyst first has something transferred to him and then transfers something back. Nothing abnormal or neurotic had happened here. Rather it was something inevitable which in one form or another occurs in all relationships and makes its appearance whenever two people meet. The individuals involved will of necessity win or lose under its sign and it is best that they find out—the sooner the better—under what auspices the relationship operates regardless of their personal conscious wishes or preferences.

We have recognized the archetypal cores of the complexes as the elementary form patterns of psychological experiencing by means of which the human psyche responds to every important or critical life situation, both inner and outer. Their first emergence occurs in response to our parents and becomes modified through our actual experience with them and, while further modified by later life experiences, they tend to retain the typical character and libidinal content of their original conditioning throughout life. The archetypes of the Great Father, the Great Mother, the Wise Man, the seductress, the devouring witch, the spiritual guide, the redeeming Messiah, etc., are then projected along with shadow, animus and anima in their personalized forms into every encounter that even remotely allows for their emergence.

When they emerge in relation to the analyst, the situation provides the possibility for a concrete realization of these unconscious *a priori* human drives, which include sexual and emotional but also spiritual elements. Now archetypal reactions occur in response to and within the framework of a consciously accessible human encounter and can be confronted and analyzed there; thus the analysis of the transference serves not only to clarify and correct the interpersonal relationship in the analyst-analysant encounter but also provides an opportunity for *experiencing* many otherwise inaccessible emotions or drive elements that strive for actualization and consciousness through "I-Thou" encounters. It is not enough to approach them theoretically through the merely intellectual understanding provided by the interpretation of dreams and other expressions of the unconscious. They also need the concreteness of the "Thou." Our basic unconscious constellations are thus potentially realizable in the personal encounter with the therapist. The therapist's readiness to accept the transference and his ability to understand it, as well as his own emotional reactions (countertransference) provide the "enabling space" which brings to light not only the neurotic elements but even more so the critical, developmental and resolutional elements. The transference contains not only the projection of distorted archetypes but also the projection and hence the first possibility of actualization of those aspects of the archetypes which had existed only as potential. Thus the transference is not a neurotic reaction which could be avoided but an inescapable normal element of every therapeutic encounter, a part of a constellated "I-Thou" field of the search for consciousness. Through it the analysant is enabled to experience and to begin to incorporate elements that were not consciously accessible to him in his previous relationships.

The importance of this kind of experience can hardly be overestimated, for another aspect of this way of approaching the therapeutic encounter is the implication that it is a part of a two-way process; inescapably, the countertransference—from the therapist toward the analysant—corresponds to the transference. The therapist, too, has complexes and as yet unrealized archetypal predispositions which result in projections and various forms of emotional involvement; but if the therapeutic encounter is to become a realistic possibility the therapist must be able to become aware of the nature and meaning of his projections upon the analysant, he must be neither completely involved nor uninvolved. He has to have one foot in but also one foot out. The countertransference must not have the same totally involved and unconscious character as the transference; if the therapist too were swept away by the same current of irrationality from which he is to help his patient emerge, he could not provide the necessary foothold. The interaction between analysant and analyst is not a one-way street but may be compared to the "lines of force" of an energy field, made up of mutual conscious and unconscious feelings and attitudes. Thus the relationship cannot be one in which a doctor merely treats a clinical object while he himself remains safely out of the fire. The difficulties that arise in the therapist-patient relationship cannot be simply dealt with on the basis of a resistance which the patient ought to overcome. They may point also to areas in which the therapist himself needs ever greater awareness. Jung observes:

> The analyst must go on learning endlessly, and never forget that each new case brings new problems to light and thus gives rise to unconscious assumptions that have never before been constellated. We could say, without too much exaggeration, that a good half of every treatment that probes at all deeply consists in the doctor's examining himself, for only what he can put right in himself can he hope to put right in the patient.
>
> It is no loss, either, if he feels that the patient is hitting him, or even scoring off him: it is his own hurt that gives the measure of his power to heal. This, and nothing else, is the meaning of the Greek myth of the wounded physician.[6]

Thus the therapeutic encounter can be thought of as a sort of laboratory or workshop situation, as a kind of psychodramatic stage upon which the

analysant enacts his problematic events and experiences the analyst's concrete as well as theoretical reaction. The analysant thus discovers how he
feels, what responses he elicits, in regard to his potentialities and his ability
to react in new ways. But his opposite, the other member of the workshop,
finds that the shoe fits the other foot as well; the development within the
analysis is bound to be colored and determined by the unconscious biases,
attitudes and backgrounds of both, as well as by their ability to accept these
and bring them to conscious realization. But the analyst must be able to
orient himself and to explain the stations along the way. This is the main
reason for Jung's original insistence that the analyst be analyzed first.
Teaching occurs not by precepts merely but by example. It would be
against common sense to hire a guide to take us up to a remote area that he
has never seen himself; nobody can lead us through a darkness with which
he is unfamiliar. Hence a thorough analysis of the analyst—indeed, in my
personal belief, the continued maintenance of the analyst's analysis—is absolutely necessary.

The personality and attitudes of the analyst are crucial in determining
what will come to the fore and even the manner in which it will present
itself in the analytic situation. It has been repeatedly observed that encounters with different analysts not only produce different events, they even
produce different kinds of dreams, since the analysant's unconscious reacts
to the therapist's unconscious. The analyst's unconscious premises, his relationship to his own unconscious, and his ability to integrate what happens
consciously are the keys to the kind of "enabling space" that is created; the
sort of person the analyst *is*, not what he believes in, determines the character of the space in which the problems and the unconscious tendencies and
archetypal potentials of both partners may unfold and interact and come
into actual experience. By virtue of this interaction, a process is initiated,
the process of transformation, which leads by a tortuous—indeed a labyrinthine—path toward eventual clarification and resolution. Like everything
that functions on the archetypal level, what is constellated by this "I-Thou"
encounter operates as a unitary reality field. Hence if anything of transforming importance is to happen it is bound to involve, affect and even
change both partners in the encounter, not just one. Jung remarks that

> often the doctor is in much the same position as the alchemist who no
> longer knew whether he was melting the mysterious amalgam in the
> crucible or whether he was the salamander glowing in the fire. Psycho-
> logical induction inevitably causes the two parties to get involved in
> the transformation of the third [the constellating healer archetype of
> the Self] and to be themselves transformed in the process, and all the

time the doctor's knowledge, like a flickering lamp, is the one dim light in the darkness.[7]

The doctor knows—or at least he should know—that he did not choose his career by chance; and the psychotherapist in particular should clearly understand that psychic infections [that means getting involved and affected by the other person's affect problem] however superfluous they seem to him, are in fact the predestined concomitants of his work, and thus fully in accord with the instinctive disposition of his own life.[8]

The individuation problem may be constellated with like meaning for analyst as well as patient, even though on different levels of psychological awareness. The analyst must work on his own problems simultaneously in order to help the patient to change. The constellating activity of the unconscious which raises new problems never comes to a stop as long as life lasts, not even for analysts who—one might be tempted to assume—"ought to know better."

Furthermore, no analyst can be everybody's analyst. It is extremely important that a proper matching occur for the sake of an appropriate "enabling" encounter; or, shall we say, that at least a minimum of rapport should exist between the two. If this is not the case it is quite irrelevant whether the analyst is good or bad—he will be bad for this person.

Once the analytic process has begun to come alive, the progress of therapy follows a tortuous path, because it cannot depend on neat rationalizations about what is wrong and *should* be improved. Indeed, the word *should* has no place in therapy, for who is to know what should or should not be? What may be one man's meat is quite possibly another man's poison and what we have found to be valid yesterday may not be valid for today's particular life situation at all. We follow those leads that the unconscious gives us; it is the unconscious that describes for us the elements to be considered and this is never rationally predictable.

Ordinarily the first phase of an analysis has to do with the uncovering of hitherto unrealized feelings; also facts about what usually are our less commendable aspects are brought to our attention. The most brilliant insights normally occur within the first few weeks or months, but alas they do not lead us very far. We recognize what is fundamentally wrong but unfortunately we know very little of what we can do about it. We have seen an aspect of the personal unconscious, namely that which already has been or at least is readily capable of being conscious, but we have yet to experience the roots which feed it from the objective psyche: anima, animus and Self.

There now comes what we may call the long, long pull, the most trying part of the process; and the most frustrating discovery is the fact that its direction is not direct but seems to lead us in circles. When we survey the order in which the dreams raise various aspects of our problems we even get the impression of a seemingly irrelevant back and forth and circular movement. A problem is raised, then another connected with it, a third, a fourth; we assume we understand them, and behold the dreams return to the first—but in a slightly different fashion, from a slightly different vantage point. When, by hindsight as it were, we later survey the course of development through several years we cannot escape the impression of an autonomous process of evolution, a definite path which the dream patterns of the unconscious seem to follow, as if they "knew" where they wanted to go and how to get there. But this path is not direct nor even circular or spiral. It is a movement toward a center that is more adequately depicted in the ancient and medieval (spiral) labyrinth patterns which are found in many places of worship and burial. The labyrinth is one of the oldest of symbols; it depicts the way to the unknown center, the mystery of death and rebirth, the risk of the search, the danger of losing the way, the quest, the finding and the ability to return. If we follow the path of the labyrinth from the floor of Chartres Cathedral we can observe that in the course of

its tortuous evolution it not only connects the periphery with the center (the Self) but actually fills out and covers the total plane surface of the circle; in striving for the center the path integrates the total circle, the total field. We may muse on this symbolism. . . . Perhaps what matters in our life's development is not that we reach a goal of perfection but that we expand our field of awareness as much as possible as we follow the path of our problems. Perhaps what matters is not so much the reaching of a goal but the conscious journey on the labyrinthine path.

Of course there is also a valid rational reason for this labyrinthine progression. We deal here with a total field; every part of this field is related to another part and it is impossible to right one thing without righting it in all its ramifications and interrelationships.

Eventually, as we become more fully aware of our problems, another critical point is reached, when insights really have occurred and we try to act upon them. We then discover to our dismay that our attempts to solve them by an effort of will avails us nothing, that our good intentions, as the saying goes, merely pave the way to hell. Good intentions all too readily can foster the illusion that we have settled an issue, when actually it is far from settled and seems to have not the slightest intention of ever being settled. This leads to a deadlock in which we see we need to change but cannot, try as we may. We know we need to renounce our egoistic controlling attempts but we cannot even make ourselves do that. We are up against the paradox that discipline and conscious effort are indispensable but do not get us far enough in our really critical areas. We reach the point where we are tempted to give up in despair because after all, what's the use? We begin to feel that analysis is like deliberate, organized torture; the most problematic things are rubbed in again and again and no matter how we exert ourselves there is no way to change them.

This state has its meaning too. As Dante puts it, the entrance to purgatory is at the deepest point of hell. A resolution of this seemingly hopeless impasse eventually occurs by virtue of the awareness that the ego's claim of a capacity to control rests on an illusion. Without the actual experience of this sort of impasse the ego cannot renounce its claim to the central position. It is only when we have come to our wits' end, and this in the face of our most sincere and extreme efforts, only when we realize that we are hopelessly incapable of changing ourselves, can we begin to accept our real existential position in the life drama. When we are able to say, "This is I, this is my being, and nothing can save me from or free me from being this sort of person," then we have come to a point of acceptance that initiates a fundamental transformation of which we are the object, not the subject. Transformation of our personality occurs *in* us, *upon* us but not *by* us. The unconscious changes itself and us in response to our awareness and acceptance of our station, of our cross. Up to this point the unconscious may have been highly critical and often almost abusive; now it begins to become helpful, and positive elements begin to emerge. This aid may occur at any phase of the analysis to the extent that we do see and are "touched" and are aware of our limitations, not merely intellectually but in the depths of our bowels, in our feelings and in our despair. Whenever we put ourselves too low, the unconscious will lift us, and whenever we put ourselves too high, the unconscious will put us down.

The point of hopelessness, the point of no return, then, is the turning point. Here—where the psychological situation seems to be deadlocked, where we find no rational resolution for the conflicting impulses—is where sooner or later dreams or fantasies will appear which not only show but initiate possibilities of development. Then the reconciling symbols arise. But as we have said these symbols and these ways of resolution are usually those which conscious reason could never have discovered. It is these images from the unconscious which will indicate a direction that will bear fruit for the particular individual in this particular situation.

> Here we must follow nature as a guide, and what the doctor then does is less a question of treatment than of developing the creative possibilities latent in the patient himself.[9]

> The psychotherapist who takes his work seriously . . . must decide in every single case whether or not he is willing to stand by a human being with counsel and help upon what may be a daring misadventure. He must have no fixed ideas of what is right, . . . what not—otherwise he takes something from the richness of the experience. He must keep in view what actually happens—for only that which acts is actual.[10]

Thus the patient is not so much told about himself as *put in touch with himself*. He must pay close attention, must make constant conscious efforts to grasp the mediating forms that may aid in the transformation of the destructive complexes.

A peculiar phenomenon that characterizes the transformative stage is that the changes which now occur at first escape one's notice. Those around us are aware of them before we are; they may notice that we are much easier to live with. For when the changes finally take place they seem to do so in spite of our efforts, not because of them. The transformation is accomplished, not by a deliberate act, but by an action of the unconscious upon and through the unconscious. This is the change in the unconscious itself, which we do not effect, but in which we participate. It does not occur mechanically but, as we have seen, is the result of our efforts to find the most extreme boundaries of awareness and to accept the limits within which we operate.

From this point of view, we see that what we call therapy is nothing less than an adjustment to the basic demands and needs of one's life, in inner terms as well as outer, and that this process is the one we have described as individuation: the discovery and maintenance of an appropriate relationship between ego and Self.

The circular or spiral, indeed labyrinthine, aspect of the process could also be called a constant oscillation, a back and forth pendulum-swing in differing directions and dimensions of ever newly constellated pairs of opposites. Everything operates in pairs of opposites—everything is a dialectical process. The relationship between ego and Self is also dialectical; it can be an "I-Thou" relationship, just as between analyst and analysant. This means that neither ego nor Self takes control; if one or the other does, something is wrong, because every dictatorship is bound to produce a revolutionary trend. The true dialectical relationship involves a mutual recognition of limitations and boundaries which, at the same time, are points of encounter, where the partners touch. Since the only permanent thing in life is lack of permanence, no established boundary line ever remains. The process is an ever-changing one, ever renewed and ever renewable. Every problem "solved" constellates a new problem. The conversation between unconscious and consciousness, between Self and ego, between God—infinite life—and finite man, never ceases.

Hence the transformation process is a continuously evolving one; the concept of being "analyzed through," if it still exists, is absurd. Jung called it an attempt to dry out the ocean; if it could be done it would be a catastrophe. It would dry up the source of life. To the extent that we penetrate beyond the personal, we touch aspects of the Self. But this is not a one-time affair; we are not then able to rest contentedly upon the picnic grounds of accomplishment. The dialogue continues and develops; we touch the Self in varying degrees and times and in varying positions and aspects, and in developmental stages that will vary, for the simple reason that while we do know in practical terms, within the analytic situation, where the unconscious begins and where our consciousness ends, we do not know such a thing as an end of the unconscious. The objective psyche never ceases to produce and to compensate, to throw new problems in our way. The moment we have had a glimpse of something central and whole and greet it joyfully, ready to relax in the assurance of having "solved" our problem, we are likely to be hit from another direction.

Therefore the process which is called therapy, the healing of something

310 The Symbolic Quest

supposedly ill, consists of introducing or furthering the normal psychological process of personality development. There is no fundamental difference, then, between so-called sickness and health, psychologically speaking, except for a difference in approach at times. Basically, the Jungian approach to personality development contains just as great a benefit for the so-called well person as for the one who is psychologically disturbed. Both may experience the unfolding of their deepest and fullest possibilities. "Sick" and "well" are relative terms; many neurotic or even psychotic disturbances are caused by hindering a natural and needed creative unfoldment; then the unconscious potentialities that have not been recognized will disturb conscious life. In this sense also the neurotic or disturbed person will meet his most profound possibilities through therapy rather than merely accomplishing a return to "normalcy." He may, in other words, be sick because he has been confined to being nothing but "normal" and "average" and has more than this to offer.

By uncovering the guiding aspect of psychological symbolism analytical psychology holds a key to far more than the relief of overt neuroses and psychoses. Through deciphering the messages of the objective psyche it is possible for us to come face to face with the creative sources of our existence and to unfold the deepest meanings of our lives. The fullest utilization of the creative elements constellated by the archetypes requires, as we have tried to emphasize, an existential experience of their reality; we must actually be touched emotionally by the reality of their autonomous power. It is through this kind of experience that we are "moved" and thus changed.

When the dissociation between conscious and unconscious personalities is healed and redirected, individuation takes place; we become truly ourselves. This is the aim of therapy, and, it would seem, of Life.

Afterword

EMOTIONAL EXPERIENCING

BY EMPHASIZING the reality of the psyche Jung meant to stress that what formerly was seen as "nothing but" subjective notions or thought forms expresses objective dynamics. Once we accept that assumption we are forced to realize that this "objective" reality needs to be encountered experientially and emotionally, not merely verbally and abstractly.

To facilitate such encounters of the "objective" reality of the spirit we often need to widen our therapeutic approaches as well as our conceptualizations.

In the earlier days of psychoanalysis and analytical psychology emphasis was placed relatively one-sidedly on verbal communication and understanding without also sufficiently stressing the equal need for nonverbal emotional experience.

The model of psychotherapy we inherited from the fathers of psychoanalysis was talking therapy. Verbal interpretations and introspective understanding were the classical methods. Body awareness, gestalt therapy and the contributions of the object relations schools were disregarded, and group therapy was held to be anathema during the classical days of Jungian practice. For the duration of one's analysis, personal relationships, to the extent that they were problematic, were even to be suspended in the early days of psychoanalysis. The experience of the relationship itself was not considered an essential part of the process. One's relationship to collectivity and community was given little or no importance. Interpersonal relationships were assumed to take care of themselves once the inner life was in order.

This limited approach is sometimes sufficient to bring about a reorientation and a personality change. But quite frequently it is not.

A chief reason for the failure of the purely introverted and verbally interpretative method is that such a purely reflective approach often fails to "touch" the biological level of the autonomous nervous system and of hormonal activity, both of which are intimately associated with the deeper layers of our affects. This fact was not sufficiently realized during the ear-

311

lier part of this century when the groundwork for psychoanalysis and analytical psychology was laid out.

Therapy is no longer only verbal and cognitive. Jung himself stressed
the importance of artistic expressions, the role of imagination and meditation which he called "active imagination," in the individuation process.
Therapy now includes dealing with affect and body awareness through
body work, therapeutic touch, movement, psychodramatic enactment and
group process. We know now that unless feelings reactions or affects can
be felt as embodied, they cannot be said to be fully in consciousness,
hence are not yet subject to transformation. Unless one's shadow problems
can be talked about with one's peers in a group setting rather than only
with one's therapist, they often have not yet been really accepted.

Role playing and enactment, adaptations of Gestalt and psychodrama
techniques, can readily find integration with the Jungian methodology.
They serve as auxiliary techniques for deepening, intensifying and working
through whatever unconscious material—personal, archetypal or both—
happens to be constellated in the course of the accustomed analytical process.

Enactment

Enactment is not to be confused with "acting out." Acting out is an attempt to relieve tension by a release of pent-up impulses. It is an automatic and often quite unconscious compulsive behavior. Because of its
psychological destructiveness, acting out is frowned upon in psychotherapy. Enactment, on the other hand, involves conscious and deliberate
psychodrama. It is "performed" within responsible limitations and with
respectful regard for the other person. Initially, it does not relieve but
rather increases tension and anxiety. It is constructive in its effects by virtue of facilitating an experiential realization of one's emotions.

In enactment, analysands are invited to imagine themselves as a particular figure, object, complex, partner in a relationship problem, or archetypal figure that happens to be relevant to the conflict or problem at hand.
The material may come from dream, fantasy, or imagination, or from past
or present relationship problems. The analysands are asked to express their
experience as that figure or person using the "I" form. They also may
engage in a conversation or argument as that figure with a partner, or as
themselves with that figure, and listen to "its" as well as to their own
responses. The following example may illustrate the process as well as the
insights that it may mediate which the more traditional methods would
not necessarily do.

An analysand, who was referred to me for a consultation by a therapist-
in-training, had had a dream of a landscape dominated by a centrally lo-
cated, brilliant square-shaped quartz crystal. A voice was heard saying: "It

is the four in red." Then the patient was at breakfast and worried whether or not to eat.

The therapist in training was impressed by the archetypal symbolism of the square, the four, the crystal that would seem to be pointing to the *lapis* of alchemy; all these images refer to the theme of wholeness, centrality and individuation. The redness was taken as passionate intensity. The dream was assumed to express a vision of the transcendental center, the Self. However, it was not clear to the therapist what practical significance to ascribe to that dream.

As I listened to the dream and pondered its symbolism I felt a bit uneasy. To take it simply as an archetypal display seemed somehow a bit too pat and did not quite fit. I felt that something was missing. Since no associations were forthcoming, I asked the patient to "act" or "be" the crystal, first nonverbally, without saying anything; then to tell me in the first person what she felt as the crystal; and then to talk to the crystal.

In being the crystal, she stood rigidly and tensely in the middle of the room and just stared. Then, speaking as the crystal, she said: "I feel hard, immobile, straight and tense. I cannot move, and I resent being pushed around by other people." When she asked the crystal what it wanted, it answered: "I want to be released and taken out of the box. I feel confined and scared."

Next, I asked the analysand to "stay" with all those reactions and feel and see what they evoked. This released a flood of feelings and memories, quite at variance with the beautiful vision; but it did point to the psychological problems that were at the center of her individuation problem.

What she had expressed while "being" the crystal reminded the dreamer of her father's mineral collection. Over this relatively small and insignificant collection, her father used to make a good deal of fuss. He repeatedly and painstakingly arranged, rearranged, labeled, classified, reclassified, pigeonholed and cleaned it. From here the associations led to her father's general perfectionism, his small-minded, pedantic and rigid orderliness and overcritical attitudes, by which she had felt suffocated and inhibited from giving expression to her own sensitivities and artistic interests. In connection with these memories she associated to the four in the dream the dreaded failing grade it represented in the European high school system. In the face of her father's perfectionism she always felt like a failure and so often dreaded going to school that she did not want to eat breakfast.

Enacting opened up a whole area of affect which mere verbal associating and amplifying had not touched. The "inner landscape" was revealed as dominated by a rigid and pedantic animus that induced a sense of failure and fear of living in the dreamer. Only after these elements had been realized, that is, made real on the level of actual here-and-now experiencing, could the individuation implications presented by the crystal, the "central, indestructible core," be brought closer to realization.

Group therapy

Analysis in a group setting adds a wider experiential dimension to the usual dyadic form of therapy. Instead of being a shortcut it offers an intensification of therapy by providing a "lab" experience. Neither mass analysis, nor a means to adapt to collectivity, it offers a chance of coming to terms with collectivity by consciously confronting it. It offers the possibility of reality-testing of one's self-validations and insights, and of one's behavior in relationships. The experience of the group archetype and one's transference projections onto groups and collectivity, as well as the resulting effects upon one's suggestibility and one's tendency to conform, become possible to a degree that does not occur in the usual dyadic setting.

The group also provides a place in which to work experientially through one's sibling and family problems and rivalries; competition and power complexes; sense of not being accepted, supported, protected or sheltered; and problems with trust and openness. All these issues are concretely encountered through the mutual interactions of the group members. The themes are played out, enacted and reality-tested rather than merely talked about. In dyadic therapy only some of these issues are experienced in the transference-countertransference to the individual therapist.

In individual therapy the transference and countertransference to the individual analyst stages, even ritualizes, the basic themes of the life drama. The interaction may start out initially as a neurotic acting out on both sides. Eventually, it is hoped and expected that the therapist catch on to the role of his or her own complexes as well as to the psychic induction from the client in making him or her play and modify his or her enactment of the "assigned" archetypal role. In thereby being able to introduce a corrective experience, the transference drama mediates archetypal healing power. Yet in the dyadic setting, this dramatic interaction is limited by the unavoidable limitations of the therapist's personality. He or she cannot possibly be expected to fit into all the roles that the various dramatis personae of the various analysands constellate and require as partners for the enactment of their various life plays. Also the professional stance and the relative authority that, inevitably, the therapist carries may sometimes prevent or at least reduce, at other times overly infantilize, the analysand's enactment of his or her life-play role.

This deficiency can be met and compensated for by the multitude of constellations among the more numerous group members and by the fact that in the group one also interacts with one's peers. One analysand once exclaimed: "But these are human beings!", thus involuntarily admitting that to her the analyst was not quite a human being.

The group also helps to translate insights into actual life situations. Too often it happens that a problem has been "understood" but that understanding cannot really be applied. Typical life situations do not necessarily occur in the consulting room. Too often analysands carefully avoid confronting raw reality even with the one person they supposedly trust. They would rather talk about yesterday's happenings, as they perceive them through the eyes of their bias and distorted self-image. Frequently, the therapist, too, prefers a certain professional distance and shies away from an emotional involvement of too personal a nature or of one that touches his or her own more sensitive complexes. Hence many issues are talked about but actually remain outside the analytic encounter. Dreams, it is true, may point up these difficulties. But this in itself does not necessarily solve the problem of where and how to connect their messages with the actuality of emotions and behavior.

In the group, on the other hand, complexes are not merely discussed. They occur right there for everyone to see. They can be worked through in a setting that is questioning, confrontative but also offering peer support and peer sympathy. One's peers can and do provoke complexes and manage to catch a greater variety of affect reactions than the single person of the analyst. In a group, one is more likely to be caught *in flagrante*, creating one's own difficulty. It is harder to get away with rationalizations. But there may be also a greater experience of acceptance in the group, owing to the fact that one's peers are under no professional obligation to accept one but do it because they have or are in the process of discovering that they are in the same boat. It is often an astounding and profoundly moving experience to discover that one's nonprofessional peers not only fail to react with disgust and condemnation at terrible and shameful secrets but confess similar difficulties. In groups the therapist's shadow is often more apparent, and that can be a great relief. For in groups, it is not only possible but inevitable and desirable for the therapist's shadow to show itself.

The possible shock effects of a therapist's shadow expressions, which might prove shattering to oversensitive analysands in the single dyadic session, can be diluted by the group's reaction which may confront the therapist directly, something that the "single" analysand may not have dared. They can also be witnessed as they are directed to other group members who are able to handle them and/or are being supported in this by the group. Some of the most stubborn transference and countertransference illusions can thereby be alleviated.

The most unexpected and paradoxical potential of analysis in a group, which, to my knowledge has not been mentioned heretofore, is its peculiar individualizing capacity. Through conscious confrontation, no less than with other potentially compulsive dynamics, the group archetype can be freed from its overwhelming power over the individual. To the extent that this happens, one finds it easier to establish a more truly individual relationship to collectivity.

THE GENDER ARCHETYPES

The concepts of anima and animus as they apply to consciousness and gender are in need of revision. A good deal of rethinking has been stimulated by clinical experience as well as by the impact of feminist criticism. In the following I shall propose a reformulation that is at variance with classical Jungian theory.

Jung's original formulation limited animus and anima to a contrasexual dynamic only: animus pertaining to women, anima to men, as "projection-making factors" (see pp. 187 and 205) which give to the unconscious of men and women a contrasexual imprint. On the strength of accumulated clinical experience this limitation does not seem to be justified. The man's unconscious contains unassimilated archetypal and personal male components just as the woman's contains unassimilated archetypal and personal female components.

According to Jung's definition, "woman's consciousness is characterized more by the connective quality of Eros than by the discrimination and cognition associated with Logos," and "in women . . . Eros is the expression of their true nature, while their Logos is often only a regrettable accident" (p. 205). This formulation ties the animus concept to an a priori assumption of women's natural inferiority of discrimination. At best this is patronizing, at worst outrightly insulting to women. Moreover, this formulation is not borne out by facts. While, by and large, women may be more averse to purely abstract argumentation, this does not permit us to infer an inborn natural deficiency in their ability to think clearly. This formulation confuses an archetypal dynamic with its culturally conditioned contents.

Jung defined animus and anima as archetypes of maleness and femaleness, namely primordial principles of structure and form. We must be careful, therefore, to distinguish between the archetypes themselves and their cultural, familial and personal contents, which are the complexes or shadow aspects which they engender. In fact, Jung expressly stated that

> Though the *contents* of anima and animus can be integrated they themselves cannot, since they are archetypes. As such they are the foundation stones of the psychic structure, which in its totality ex-

ceeds the limits of consciousness and therefore can never become the object of direct cognition. Though the effects of anima and animus can be made conscious, they themselves are factors transcending consciousness and beyond the reach of perception and volition. (*Aion, CW* 9 ii: par. 40)

Anatomical and hormonal dynamics are expressions of archetypal structuring. Anatomically and hormonally, both sexes partake of both female and male dynamics. It is therefore justified to postulate that, by analogy to rather than "because" of this fact, both genders are likely to be also psychologically under the influence of both male and female archetypal structuring. We describe maleness as an analogue of Yang, representing Lingam, heaven, linearity, externalization, ordering law, assertive doing and separative partialness. Femaleness is analogous to Yin, Yoni, earth, being and wholeness, circularity and internalness, instinct, affect and idealization. This indeed was Jung's viewpoint. We have, however, no reason to assume that every man has managed to assimilate all contents of the male archetype or every woman the contents of her potential femaleness. Hence both sexes will be in need of compensation and complementation by all those gender qualities of either kind that happen to have been but inadequately developed. Specifically, since the animus is a potential psychopomp, it must be presumed to compensate for an inadequate discrimination and cognition of logos, whenever this should be the case, in men no less than in women, just as the anima may also compensate, as psychopomp, for an inadequate awareness of connecting needs in women or men.

In other words, as archetypal drive potentials, namely vectors to qualities that have never yet been in consciousness, animus and anima must pertain also to unrealized potentialities of one's own gender, to still missing aspects of masculinity in a man and of femininity in a woman. Not all the masculine potential of a man or the feminine potential of a woman is of necessity consciously developed and integrated. Some animus Yang elements are always likely to be undeveloped or inadequately or perversely conditioned in a particular man and likewise anima Yin elements in a woman.

Men can be as stubbornly dogmatic, unreasonably belligerent, cranky and power-driven as "animus-possessed" women; they can also be quite deficient in discrimination and will then compensate for that deficiency with that very primitive dogmatism and hunger for power which have been ascribed to the animus in women.

In turn, women can be quite unrelated and hysterically overemotional and moody, as seductively unrelated and depressed as men, when their primitive anima takes over.

It is not necessary to explain this by resorting to such needlessly complicating terminology as the animus of the anima or the anima of the animus. Doing so serves only to maintain a systematization that is not even borne out by clinical facts.

Men are not necessarily more spiritual than women, nor do women have a monopoly on soul and instinct. The notion of spirituality as a predominantly male characteristic and of soul as a female property are heirlooms of nineteenth-century romanticism. They are timebound within culturally conditioned actualizations of the Yang/Yin archetypes. These culturally determined expectations and complexes are no longer valid in our time. A predominantly logos-oriented man may, in addition to his perhaps seductive anima, also be obsessed by the need to integrate a heroic animus that, while unconsciously obsessive, makes him overly combative and quarrelsome rather than objectively assertive; a philosophically inclined woman may have a compensating anima trend that induces unconsciously seductive behavior. There are many clear-thinking women who are more logos-related than many feeling- or intuition-type men who have inferior thinking functions.

In all these instances animus and anima function as archetypal trends that attempt to call forth missing aspects of a still-to-be-reached wholeness within one's own, and not only within the contrasexual, gender.

Hence, by analogy to what was described in Chapter 16 with respect to ego and Self, the ego can be assimilated to, or overwhelmed by, the equisexual as well as the heterosexual archetype. Ordinarily, however, except perhaps in cases of homosexuality or transvestism, the mature ego tends to identify with the equisexual archetype. In this case one's self-image is determined by being a "man" or a "woman," usually stereotyped in terms of one's cultural, familial or other bias.

A weak or damaged ego may be overwhelmed or assimilated by both the contrasexual and the equisexual archetype. Then we have the familiar states of possession. A woman's ego may be driven to act out the Great Mother Goddess or may be filled with Jehovah or Ares power. A man may be a cantankerous warrior underneath his purportedly peace-loving and conciliatory ego adaptation or act out a Great Mother or Aphroditic playboy stance.

The characterizations of anima and animus given in Chapters 12 and 13 continue to be valid. But they apply to both sexes and not only to the opposite sex. Whenever an adapted instinctual or emotional response to involvement with people or things is called for but fails to occur, the anima fills the vacuum. Inadequate discrimination or failure of called-for assertiveness calls forth an animus reaction.

It follows then, that shadow figures and qualities may also appear in contrasexual and in not only in equisexual form. They may represent unconscious, repressed qualities, which are projected upon and optimally depicted by a person of the opposite sex. By means of gender we cannot distinguish shadow from animus or anima quality. When a quality represented by a particular figure is psychologically clearly definable, that fact points to the personal rather than the collective unconscious and differentiates the shadow from animus or anima.

Archetypes are a priori patterns of behavior, emotive and perceptive potentials. When they appear in dreams or fantasies they are characterized by a special magical, mythological and numinous quality. They appear as Powers, Gods, demons, devils, anonymous and strange sinister or fascinating persons or personality types such as "the lover," "the stranger," "the child," or animals or animal-like figures that cannot be well defined in personal or rational terms. In this category we have to classify also the so-called archetypal shadow, represented by devil or angel or any other anonymous, inferior or superior numinous figure, indistinguishable from animus or anima.

These are all collective, archetypal elements rather than personal shadow figures. Their significance cannot be approached by rational definition but only symbolically as "best possible expressions" of an unknown or unknowable content.

According to Jung, the Self, in particular, is a wholly unknowable, indescribable, undefinable entity that cannot be distinguished from the God image. Hence it is usually represented by totally impersonal numinous forms, such as mandala, light, stone, globe. These representations can be grasped, if at all, only symbolically. They bear no relationship to gender at all. They represent a wholeness pattern superseding the opposites including gender.

Since consciousness-determining figures, spiritual guides, psychopompic animus figures appear equally in the conscious as well as unconscious material of both sexes, we can no longer maintain that consciousness is a masculine Yang quality and unconsciousness a feminine Yin quality.

During the patriarchal cultures, consciousness was, indeed, shaped predominantly by masculine Yang values, while the Yin dynamics tended to be devalued, repressed and relegated to unconsciousness. During that cultural phase masculinity therefore represented forms of collectively valued consciousness. However, in our time feminine Yin values are reentering and restructuring the conscious collective value system. They are becoming cultural determinants and co-shapers of a new consciousness for both sexes.

In turn, archetypal actualizations that are represented as person-, group- and time-conditioned complexes of the personal unconscious or shadow are specific, rationally describable behaviors, feelings and viewpoints. Emotionality, power drives, objectivity or dogmatism are examples of such concrete rationally definable psychological qualities which we have tended to ascribe to animus or anima. In fact, they are archetypally engendered elements of personal complexes. I would see them as positive or negative shadow dynamics. They result in definite projections and expectations both upon the other and upon one's own sex.

As shadow they are capable of being made fully conscious. Their qualities are psychologically definable and understandable by analogy and metaphor, rather than as the best possible description of an unknown or unknowable transpersonal content.

The stingy grocer around the corner may represent a definable shadow quality, stinginess for a woman, the uncanny mysterious dark stranger a black magician animus for a man. An anonymous child may represent a growth potential and pertain to the animus/anima realm or when it is felt as a divine child, to the Self. If it is a particular child, little George or Linda, it may need to be seen as a shadow element, representing a regressive or neglected quality that still needs loving care, attentive nursing or disciplined containment.

Needless to say, what, for the sake of theoretical understanding, was described here in a neat system of classification does not necessarily present itself in such a simple fashion in reality. In actual clinical experience, shadow, animus, anima, ego and Self representations may be rather fluent, with many overlappings that necessitate a fine sense of discrimination for what happens to be personal or transpersonal and numinous.

PROJECTION AND SYMBOLIC EXPERIENCE

An important need for our time is being able to find the presence of the Spirit as an "objectively given" in our relations to others and to matter and the restoration of the sense of the sacred in the external dimension of the world. In the absence of this, individuation would amount to a solipsistic withdrawal from external reality. This tendency has, unfortunately, been encouraged by Jung's at times ambivalent formulations, particularly by his too general use of the concept of projection and the ensuing failure to discriminate between projection and symbolic experience. The result was a not entirely undeserved imputation of psychologism onto analytical psychology.

Projection refers to an erroneous perception of subjective "inner," psychological dynamic perceived as a quality of an external object. It is the actualization of a psychic content as if it belonged to another person or object. When we project we tend to ascribe our own unconscious qualities and complexes to others instead of realizing them as our own definable psychological characteristics. This is a distortion of reality, as has been pointed out previously (see p. 60).

But when it comes to archetypal dynamics the projection factor can apply only to their personal psychological contents, not to the archetypes themselves. As referred to before in connection with animus and anima, Jung is at pains to stress that the archetypes can never become objects of direct cognition and that only their effects or contents can be made conscious. Since they are beyond perception and volition, archetypal dynamics cannot be equated with "inner" or subjective contents either. They are neither "inner" nor "outer"; they belong neither to the subject nor to the object but are transcendental dynamic principles. Consequently, in experiencing archetypal dynamics one does not erroneously ascribe to the object what in reality pertains to the subject. The projection concept simply does not apply. It is irrelevant to the situation. Whenever we confront archetypal dynamics we experience symbolically. The perception is not erroneous but occurs "through a glass darkly." It is "the best description, or formula, of a relatively unknown fact; a fact, however, which is none the less recognized or postulated as existing"; it is an "admittedly anthropomorphic—hence limited and only partly valid—expression for something suprahuman and only partly conceivable. It may be the best expression possible, yet it ranks below the level of the mystery it seeks to describe." The experience accords with Jung's definitions of the symbol (see p. 18).

When, therefore, Jung for instance speaks of "the projection of a highly fascinating unconscious content which, like all such contents, exhibits a numinous—'divine' or 'sacred'—quality (CW 12: par. 448), or when he states that "Christ . . . signifies the self; that is, he represents the projection of this most important and most central of archetypes," he contradicts his own definition of the symbolic. For the sacred, the divine or Christ are never known or definable personal, or for that matter personal psychological entities. (At most they might correspond to what he later called psychoid, i.e., psyche-like.) They are unknown and unknowable transcendental factors, recognized as existing. They come under the heading of symbols and of the experience and perception of symbolic reality.

Admittedly, the situation is complicated by the fact that the archetypal experiences are usually filled or contaminated with projections of unconscious personal complex material. Hence it is all too easy to confuse archetypal core with personal complex shell and dismiss the reality of the numinous core as projection. The numinous impact of experiencing the power of the fatherly or motherly, of the heroic, or of the sacred as such, in a person, an object or place is likely to be colored by personal expectations or conditionings, hence by projections.

When I am moved and perhaps transformed by the indefinable power that touches me through a woman's personality, she transmits to me the experience of the anima or of the goddess. When I feel or am convinced, however, that this particular woman, because of certain characteristics which happen to attract me, is the woman of all women, is like a goddess, I project my own expectations or images of the goddess. These expectations and images are, after all, results of conditioning; they are my personal complex contents of the anima archetype. They attract because of their similarity to character qualities which, in terms of my relationship to my mother or to mother-like figures, who were the first embodiments of the anima archetype, have become attractive to me.

Likewise, the power of the father may be felt, indeed mediated, in a particular person or in the image of the divine as strength or sternness. These qualities are projected; they pertain to one's unconscious personal psyche. But the numinous sense of a mysterious power, of support, strength or order, the sense of transcendental logos and ultimate meaningfulness that might pervade the way a particular person or object is experienced, the undefinable sense of power and numinosity adhering to nature, trees, stones, flowers, particular places cannot be dealt with or "taken back" as projections. They belong to the mysterious realities surrounding our lives, which are important to acknowledge reverentially. But while they are accessible to us only symbolically, they are no less real for that matter. It is precisely the disavowal of the symbolic level of experience that accounts for our loss of connection to the sacred in our relationships to others as well as to nature, to the critical impasses in our social lives as well as in our ecological crisis.

True individuation occurs through living the fullness of one's life, its joys, pains and defects as symbolic actualizations of a Self reality which is "suprahuman and only partly conceivable" but nonetheless "recognized as existing."

Notes

CHAPTER 1
1. Bitter, *Meditation in Religion und Psychotherapie*, p. 13.
2. *Another Country*, p. 128.
3. *Psychological Types*, p. 601.
4. *Psychology and Religion*, par. 307.
5. *Psychological Types*, p. 601.
6. *Ibid.*, p. 602.
7. *Seelenkunde im Umbrich der Zeit*, pages 123*f.*
8. *Ibid.*, p. 122.
9. Chapter 5.
10. *Op. cit.*
11. Pages 43*f.*
12. *Morphologie*, p. 77.
13. *Language and Thought of the Child*, p. 237.
14. *An Essay on Man*, p. 32.
15. *Science and Humanism*, pages 25*f.*
16. *Ibid.*, p. 22.
17. *On Modern Physics*, p. 56.
18. *Images and Symbols*, © in the English translation Harvill Press, London, and Sheed & Ward Inc., New York 1965, p. 34.
19. *The Development of Personality*, p. 7.

CHAPTER 2
1. Freud: "The dream is a pathological product, the first member of the class which includes hysterical symptoms, obsessions and delusions." *New Introductory Lectures on Psycho-analysis*, pages 15*f.*
2. *Modern Man in Search of a Soul*, p. 6.
3. Freud: "Thus its content was the fulfillment of a wish and its motive was a wish. . . . When the work of interpretation has been completed, we perceive that a dream is the fulfillment of a wish." *The Interpretation of Dreams*, First Part, p. 121.
4. The *animus*, to be discussed in Chapter 13.
5. See also Chapter 4 and Chapter 11.

CHAPTER 3

1. See pages 29*ff.*
2. See Chapter 7.
3. Heyer, *Vom Kraftfeld der Seele.*
4. *Columbia Encyclopedia,* p. 68.
5. *Psychology and Religion,* par. 746.
6. *Archetypes and the Collective Unconscious,* pars. 489–626.
7. *Psychology and Religion,* par. 935.
8. *Archetypes and the Collective Unconscious,* par. 502.
9. *Ibid.,* par. 508.
10. Pages 818*f.*

CHAPTER 4

1. Since this book was prepared it has become apparent to me that it is important to distinguish more clearly between *projection* and *symbolic realization.* The former should refer to qualities that are capable of being integrated into one's personal structuring, while the latter involves a relation to the transpersonal symbol. Further investigation of this distinction holds great promise as a way of clearing up confusions which now exist between psychology and theology.
2. *Psychology and Religion,* par. 21.
3. See *Studies in Word Association.*
4. *Psychology and Religion,* pars. 21–22.
5. In Foreword to Jacobi, *Complex/Archetype/Symbol,* pages ix–x.
6. *The Psychogenesis of Mental Disease,* par. 80, fn. 4.
7. *Ibid.,* par. 82, fn. 5.
8. *Numinous* is a term taken from the Latin *numen*—the awe, terror, energic and oracular impact of divine manifestation. In Latin *numen* and *deus* are similar terms, but *numen* always implies the appearance of the deity in its most powerful and deeply moving form. Jung coined from this a noun which he called *numinosity,* denoting awesomeness, the quality that touches us and shakes us to the core, regardless of whether or not we understand it.
9. In Foreword to Jacobi, p. x.
10. *The History of an Infantile Neurosis,* p. 97.
11. *Modern Man,* p. 91.
12. *The Practice of Psychotherapy,* par. 179.
13. *Op. cit.,* p. 22.
14. *The Structure and Dynamics of the Psyche,* par. 594.
15. References to the "collective unconscious" as they occur throughout the further text refer to what has been defined as the "objective psyche" in Chapter 3.
16. *Op. cit.,* pages 25–27.

CHAPTER 5

1. *Two Essays on Analytical Psychology,* pars. 202–406.

2. *Symbols of Transformation*, par. 150.
3. Page 6.
4. *Images and Symbols*, p. 34 and p. 57.
5. "Pharao und Jesus als Söhne Gottes," pages 268f.
6. *Psychology and Religion*, par. 307.
7. *Structure and Dynamics*, par. 414.
8. *Images and Symbols*, p. 19.
9. *Civilization in Transition*, pars. 371–399.
10. *Poetic Edda*.
11. *Myths, Dreams and Mysteries*, pages 25–26.
12. *Structure and Dynamics*, par. 108.
13. *Psychology and Religion*, par. 497.
14. *Ibid.*, par. 6.
15. *Ibid.*, par. 8.

CHAPTER 6
1. *Memories, Dreams, Reflections*, p. 3.
2. *Ibid.*
3. *Psychology and Religion*, par. 138.
4. *Ibid.*, par. 534.
5. Luke 3:3.
6. *Zu Rainer Maria Rilkes Deutung des Daseins*, p. 29; translation by E.C.W. The more recent publication (*Rainer Maria Rilkes Deutung des Daseins: Eine Interpretation der Duineser Elegien*, Munich, Kösel-Verlag, 1961) is a slightly different version.
7. Quoted from Adler, *Studies in Analytical Psychology*, pages 120–121.
8. Isaiah 55:8.
9. *Aion*, p. 449 (German edition).
10. Acts 2:13.
11. Eliade, *Images and Symbols*, p. 19.
12. "M. M. Remembered," in *Playboy*, January 1964, p. 102.
13. *Life*, Vol. 57, No. 6, p. 77.
14. *Ibid.*, p. 70.
15. John 1:14.
16. *Life*, Vol. 52, No. 21, p. 8.

CHAPTER 7
1. *Complex/Archetype/Symbol*, p. 34.
2. *Ibid.*, p. 37.
3. Jung, Introduction to *Woman's Mysteries*, pages ixf.
4. Jacobi, *op. cit.*, p. 35.
5. Schrödinger, *Science and Humanism*, pages 18ff.
6. "The Significance of the Genetic Aspect for Analytical Psychology," p. 42.
7. Jung, *Psychological Types*, p. 603.
8. See Chapter 11.

9. Again, we will deal here with dreams because they are nutshell evidences of the way the unconscious operates. This does not imply that all analytic work has to be based on nothing but dreams; it merely is the most practical means for work and also the most practical means for demonstration.
10. See Harding, *Woman's Mysteries*, pages 169*ff*.
11. See Kerényi, *Gods of the Greeks*, pages 22*ff*.
12. *American Psychologist*, Vol. 16, No. 11, pages 681–684.
13. *Ibid.*, p. 683.
14. *Ibid.*, p. 684.
15. Üxküll, "A Stroll through the Worlds of Animals and Men," p. 11.
16. Neumann, *Der Schöpferische Mensch*, p. 62.
17. *Biologie und Geist*, pages 175 *ff*.
18. *Ibid.*, p. 177.
19. *Ibid.*, p. 123.
20. *Psychological Types*, p. 557.
21. *Op. cit.*, pages 74–75; italics added to "or in a complex or symptom."
22. Schrödinger.
23. "Reflections on the Psychiatric Consequences of Persecution," pages 201–202.
24. *On Aggression*, pages 68*ff*.
25. II Samuel 2:14, 16: "Let the young men now arise, and play before us. . . . Then there arose and went over by number twelve of Benjamin . . . and twelve of the servants of David. And they caught every one his fellow by the head, and thrust his sword in his fellow's side; so they fell down together."

CHAPTER 8
1. See pages 231–249.
2. *Memories*, p. 207.
3. *Modern Man*, pages 96–97, 98.
4. *Ibid.*, p. 99.
5. *Psychological Types*, p. 547.
6. *Ibid.*, p. 611.
7. See pages 24*ff*.
8. *Psychological Types*, p. 611.
9. *Ibid.*, pages 563*f*.
10. *Modern Man*, p. 101.
11. Jung, "The Interpretation of Visions," pages 147–148.
12. Pages 412–517.
13. *Ibid.*, p. 451.
14. See page 160.
15. "Interpretation of Visions."

CHAPTER 9
1. "The Double," pages 384–396.
2. *Ibid.*, p. 393.

3. *Ibid.*, p. 389.

CHAPTER 10
1. Page 165.
2. Chapter 17.
3. Page 40.
4. See page 48.
5. See page 133.
6. *Civilization in Transition*, par. 579.
7. *Psychology and Religion*, par. 520.

CHAPTER 11
1. *Civilization in Transition*, par. 255.
2. *Aion*, par. 29.
3. *Psychological Types*, p. 601.
4. Page 9.
5. "Frauen als Weckerinnen seelischen Lebens," p. 490.
6. See pages 181–182.
7. Graves, *Man Does, Woman Is.*
8. *Aion*, par. 29.
9. Kerényi, *The Gods of the Greeks*, p. 69.
10. Gibran, *The Prophet*, p. 20.
11. *Metaphysik des Sexus*, p. 211.
12. See *Aion*, especially "The Syzygy: Anima and Animus," pars. 20–42.
13. "Structural Forms of the Feminine Psyche."

CHAPTER 12
1. *Aion*, pars. 20–25.
2. The analogy to the "witch-hunt" of the Puritan epoch is obvious.
3. *Two Essays*, pars. 296–340.
4. *The Way of All Women*, p.12.
5. *Aion*, par. 34.
6. *Ibid.*, par. 40.

CHAPTER 13
1. *Aion*, pars. 29–34.
2. *Ibid.*, pars. 38, 40.

CHAPTER 14
1. *Psychological Types*, p. 540. In the first English translations of Jung's work, the word *Self* was capitalized where it denoted the archetype as opposed to the commonly used term referring to a separate individual identity. In the Collected Works, published by the Bollingen Foundation in the U.S. and by Routledge & Kegan Paul in England, the archetype is represented by a lower-case initial *s*. The original usage has been adopted throughout this volume (except for quoted extracts from the Collected

Works) in order to differentiate the archetype from the dictionary definition.
2. *Psychology and Religion*, par. 391.
3. *Two Essays*, par. 399.
4. *Memories*, pages 348–349.
5. *Mysterium Coniunctionis*, par. 129, fn. 66.
6. See page 77.
7. Isaiah 55:8.
8. *Psychology and Alchemy*, pars. 104–105.
9. *The Development of Personality*, pars. 289, 294, 295, 307.
10. *Psychology and Alchemy*, p. 194.
11. Pages 240*ff*.
12. *Practice of Psychotherapy*, pars. 353–539.
13. The Greek cannot be successfully translated, but literally it means "The
goal, the union." The implication here is that the goal (of the initiation)
is a union that involves both instinct and spirit.
14. *Psychologische Betrachtungen zu der Freskenfolge der Villa Dei Misteri
in Pompeji*, p. 118.
15. *Civilization in Transition.* pars. 858–886.
16. "Religion und modernes Denken." See Jung, "Reply to Buber."
17. Page 29. Jaffé quotes from Jung, *Structure and Dynamics*, par. 414.
18. Matthew 5:39.
19. Genesis 4:7.
20. "The Prologue in Heaven," lines 100–103.

CHAPTER 15
1. *Critique of Pure Reason*, The Paralogisms.
2. *Structure and Dynamics*, par. 610.
3. *Mysterium Coniunctionis*, par. 129.
4. Thigpen and Cleckley.
5. *The Invisible Writing*, p. 350; *The God that Failed*, pages 67–68.
6. *Thought Reform and the Psychology of Totalism*, © 1961 by Robert J.
Lifton, p. 66.
7. *Confessions* (X, 30).
8. *Spring* 1966, pages 68–70.
9. *Ibid.*, pages 68–69.
10. *Structure and Dynamics*, par. 614.
11. *Psychological Types*, p. 540.
12. *Two Essays*, par. 405.
13. See pages 103–137.
14. *Structure and Dynamics*, pars. 614*ff*.
15. *A Genetic Field Theory of Ego Formation*, p. 16.
16. *Ibid.*, p. 20.
17. See pages 117, 122.
18. Spitz, *ibid.*, p. 20.
19. "Hospitalism," pages 53–74.

20. An *Outline of Psycho-analysis*, p. 154.
21. Abenheimer, "The Ego as Subject," p. 66.
22. Grafton, "The Tense Generation," p. 17.
23. Elworthy, *The Evil Eye.*
24. *Studies in the Psychology of Sex*, Vol. 2, Part 2, pages 376ff.
25. *Op. cit.*, p. 66.
26. Pyramid Texts, spell 1248, in Sethe, *Pyramidentexte.*
27. *Op. cit.*, p. 67.
28. *Ibid.*, p. 68.
29. See pages 123–125.
30. *Practice of Psychotherapy*, par. 365.
31. *Ibid.*, par. 109.

CHAPTER 16
1. "The Relation of the Ego to the Self," p. 97.
2. *Ibid.*
3. *Ibid.*, p. 98.
4. See pages 106ff.
5. See page 234.
6. *Psychology and Religion*, par. 716.
7. See pages 43ff.
8. The term used by the alchemists for the task of transforming base metals into gold.
9. "Selige Sehnsucht," *West-Ostlicher Divan*; author's translation.
10. *Faust* II, p. 182.
11. See pages 90 and 88.
12. In Collancz, *Man and God*, p. 140. Originally from Buber's *Hasidism* which is out of print and virtually inaccessible.
13. *Aion*, pars. 45–46.
14. From *The Dybbuk and Other Great Yiddish Plays*, translated and edited by Joseph C. Landis, Copyright © 1966 by Bantam Books, Inc., p. 31.
15. *Aion*, pars. 47–49.
16. *Mysterium Coniunctionis*, pars. 760, 762.
17. Numbers 22.
18. *Archetypes and the Collective Unconscious*, pars. 521–523.

CHAPTER 17
1. *Memories*, p. 3.
2. *Psychology and Religion*, par. 391.
3. "Narcissism, Normal Self-Formation, and the Primary Relation to the Mother," pages 83f.
4. "A Stroll Through the Worlds of Animals and Men," p. 11.
5. *Cell and Psyche*, pages 26f.
6. *Op. cit.*
7. See page 250.
8. "On the Origins of the Ego in Childhood," p. 93.

9. Fordham, New Developments in Analytical Psychology, pages 137–146.
10. "On the Origins of the Ego in Childhood," p. 95.
11. See page 120.
12. Genetic Field Theory of Ego Formation, pages 46–50.
13. Whitmont, "Magic and the Psychology of Compulsive States" and "The Magical Dimension in Transference and Counter-Transference."
14. Webster's Dictionary.
15. See pages 241–242.
16. van der Post, The Dark Eye in Africa and Venture to the Interior.
17. See page 43.
18. See pages 236–246.
19. Gebser, Ursprung und Gegenwart.
20. Psychologie des Weiblichen.
21. Practice of Psychotherapy, pars. 109–110.
22. Structure and Dynamics, pars. 773, 776, 777, 785, 787, 790.
23. Ginzberg, The Legends of the Bible, p. 30f.
24. Faust; author's translation.
25. See page 86.
26. See page
27. Structure and Dynamics, pars. 797, 798–800.
28. Memories, p. 325.
29. Ibid., p. 4.

CHAPTER 18
1. Civilization in Transition, p. 882.
2. From "Snow" from Complete Poems of Robert Frost. Copyright 1916 by Holt, Rinehart and Winston, Inc. Copyright 1944 by Robert Frost. Reprinted by permission of Holt, Rinehart and Winston, Inc.
3. Practice of Psychotherapy, par. 237.
4. See pages 42, 121.
5. Heyer, Seelenkunde im Umbruch der Zeit, p. 75.
6. Practice of Psychotherapy, par. 239.
7. Ibid., par. 399.
8. Ibid., par. 365.
9. Ibid., par. 82.
10. Jung, Psychology and Religion, par. 530.

Bibliography

ABENHEIMER, K. M. "The Ego as Subject," in *The Reality of the Psyche*. New York: C. G. Jung Foundation, 1968.

ADLER, GERHARD. *Studies in Analytical Psychology*. New York: C. G. Jung Foundation, 1966.

BALDWIN, JAMES. *Another Country*. New York: Dial Press, 1962.

BENNET, E. A. "The Double," in *Studien zur Analytischen Psychologie C. G. Jungs*, Vol. 1. Zurich: Rascher Verlag, 1955.

BITTER, WILHELM, ed. *Meditation in Religion und Psychotherapie*. Stuttgart: Ernst Klett Verlag, 1958.

BOSS, MEDARD. *The Analysis of Dreams*. New York: Philosophical Library, 1958.

BRELAND, KELLER and MARIAN. "The Misbehavior of Organisms." *American Psychologist*, Vol. 16, No. 11 (November 1961), pp. 681–684.

BRUNNER-TRAUT, EMMA. "Pharao und Jesus als Söhne Gottes." *Antaios*, Vol. 2, No. 3 (September 1960), pp. 266–284.

BUBER, MARTIN. *Hasidism*. New York: Philosophical Library, 1948.

———. "Religion und modernes Denken." *Merkur*, Vol. 2, No. 48 (February 1952), pp. 101–120.

CASSIRER, ERNST. *An Essay on Man*. New Haven: Yale University Press, 1944.

Columbia Encyclopedia, 3rd ed. New York: Columbia University Press, 1963.

COOMARASWAMY, ANANDA K. *Hinduism and Buddhism*. New York: Philosophical Library, n.d.

CROSSMAN, RICHARD (Ed.). *The God that Failed*. New York: Harper & Row, 1949.

ELIADE, MIRCEA. *Images and Symbols*. New York: Sheed and Ward, 1965.

———. *Myths, Dreams and Mysteries*. New York: Harper & Bros., 1960.

ELLIS, HAVELOCK. *Studies in the Psychology of Sex*. New York: Random House, 1936.

ELWORTHY, FREDERICK THOMAS. *The Evil Eye*. New York: Julian Press, 1958.

ENGEL, WERNER H. "Reflections on the Psychiatric Consequences of Persecution." *American Journal of Psychotherapy*, Vol. 26, No. 2 (April 1962), pages 191–203.

EVOLA, JULIUS. *Metaphysik des Sexus*. Stuttgart: Klett, 1962.

FIERZ-DAVID, LINDA. "Frauen als Weckerinnen seelischen Lebens," in *Kulturelle Bedeutung der Komplexen Psychologie*. Berlin: Julius Springer,

————. Psychologische Betrachtungen zu der Freskenfolge der Villa Dei Misteri in Pompeji. Zurich: privately printed, 1957.

FORDHAM, MICHAEL. New Developments in Analytical Psychology. London: Routledge & Kegan Paul, 1957.

————. "On the Origins of the Ego in Childhood," in Studien zur analytischen Psychologie C. G. Jungs, Vol. 1. Zurich: Rascher Verlag, 1955.

————. "The Relation of the Ego to the Self." The British Journal of Medical Psychology, Vol. XXXVII (1964), pp. 89–102.

FREUD, SIGMUND. The Standard Edition of the Complete Psychological Works of Sigmund Freud. London: The Hogarth Press and the Institute of Psycho-Analysis; New York: Basic Books; especially the following:

Vol. IV: The Interpretation of Dreams (First Part). 1953

Vol. XVII: An Infantile Neurosis and Other Works. 1955.

Vol. XXII: New Introductory Lectures on Psycho-Analysis and Other Works. 1964.

Vol. XXIII: Moses and Monotheism, An Outline of Psycho-Analysis and Other Works. 1964.

FROST, ROBERT. Complete Poems of Robert Frost. New York: Modern Library, 1946.

GEBSER, JEAN. Ursprung und Gegenwart. Stuttgart: Deutsche Verlagsanstalt, 1949.

GIBRAN, KAHLIL. The Prophet. New York: Knopf, 1923.

GINZBERG, LOUIS. The Legends of the Bible. New York: Simon & Schuster, 1956.

GOETHE, JOHANN WOLFGANG VON. Faust. Translated by G. M. Priest. New York: Knopf, 1941.

————. "Morphologie," in Sämmtliche Werke, Vol. 14. Stuttgart: I. G. Cotta, 1874.

GOLLANCZ, VICTOR. (Ed.). Man and God. Boston: Houghton Mifflin, 1951.

GRAFTON, SAMUEL. "The Tense Generation." Look, Vol. 27, No. 17 (August 27, 1963), pp. 17–23.

GRAVES, ROBERT. Man Does, Woman Is. New York: Doubleday, 1964.

GUARDINI, ROMANO. Zu Rainer Maria Rilkes Deutung des Daseins. Bern: Verlag A. Francke, 1946.

HARDING, M. ESTHER. The Way of All Women. New York: C. G. Jung Foundation, 1970.

————. Woman's Mysteries, Ancient and Modern. New York: Pantheon Books, 1955.

HEYER, GUSTAV RICHARD. Seelenkunde im Umbrich der Zeit. Stuttgart: Hans Huber Verlag, 1964.

————. Vom Kraftfeld der Seele. Zurich: Origa Verlag, 1949.

I Ching, or Book of Changes, translated by R. Wilhelm and C. F. Baynes, copyright © 1950, 1967 by the Bollingen Foundation. Princeton: Princeton University Press (Bollingen Series XIX), 1967.

JACOBI, JOLANDE. Complex/Archetype/Symbol in the Psychology of C. G.

Jung. Princeton: Princeton University Press (Bollingen Series LVII), 1959.

JAFFÉ, ANIELA. *Der Mythus vom Sinn im Werk von C. G. Jung.* Zurich: Rascher Verlag, 1967.

JUNG, C. G. *The Collected Works of C. G. Jung.* Princeton: Princeton University Press (Bollingen Series XX); London: Routledge & Kegan Paul; especially the following:

Vol. 3. *The Psychogenesis of Mental Disease.* 1960.
Vol. 5. *Symbols of Transformation.* 1956.
Vol. 7. *Two Essays on Analytical Psychology.* 1953.
Vol. 8. *The Structure and Dynamics of the Psyche.* 1960.
Vol. 9. Part 1. *The Archetypes and the Collective Unconscious.* 1959.
Vol. 9. Part 2. *Aion.* 1959.
Vol. 10. *Civilization in Transition.* 1964.
Vol. 11. *Psychology and Religion: West and East.* 1958.
Vol. 12. *Psychology and Alchemy.* 1955.
Vol. 14. *Mysterium Coniunctionis.* 1965.
Vol. 16. *The Practice of Psychotherapy.* 1954.
Vol. 17. *The Development of Personality.* 1954.

——. *Aion: Untersuchungen zur Symbolgeschichte.* Zurich: Rascher Verlag. 1951.

——. "The Interpretation of Visions." *Spring,* 1960, pp. 106–148.

——. *Memories, Dreams, Reflections.* New York: Pantheon Books, 1962.

——. *Modern Man in Search of a Soul.* New York: Harcourt, Brace & Company, 1933.

——. *Psychological Types.* New York: Harcourt, Brace & Company, 1923.

——. "Reply to Buber." *Spring,* 1957, pp. 1–9.

——. *Studies in Word Association.* New York: Moffat, Yard & Co., 1919.

KERÉNYI, KARL. *The Gods of the Greeks.* London: Thames & Hudson, 1951.

KOESTLER, ARTHUR. *The God that Failed.* See Crossman.

——. *The Invisible Writing:* being the second volume of *Arrow in the Blue.* New York: Macmillan, 1954.

LANDIS, J. C., ed. *The Dybbuk and Other Great Yiddish Plays.* New York: Bantam Books, 1966.

LIFTON, ROBERT JAY. *Thought Reform and the Psychology of Totalism.* New York: W. W. Norton, 1961.

LORENZ, KONRAD. *On Aggression.* New York: Harcourt Brace and World, 1963.

MARJASCH, SONJA. "The 'I' in Dreams." *Spring,* 1966, pp. 60–75.

NEUMANN, ERICH. "Narcissism, Normal Self-Formation, and the Primary Relation to the Mother." *Spring,* 1966, pp. 81–106.

——. *Der Schöpferische Mensch.* Zurich: Rhein-Verlag, 1959.

——. "The Significance of the Genetic Aspect for Analytical Psychology," in *Current Trends in Analytical Psychology,* edited by Gerhard Adler. London: Tavistock Publications, 1961.

——. *Psychologie des Weiblichen.* Vol. 2 of *Umkreisung der Mitte.* Zurich: Rascher Verlag, 1953.

PIAGET, JEAN. *Language and Thought of the Child*. New York: Humanities Press, 1959.

Poetic Edda. Translated by Henry Adams Bellows. New York: American-Scandinavian Foundation, 1923.

PORTMANN, ADOLF. *Biologie und Geist*. Zurich: Rhein-Verlag, 1956.

SAINT AUGUSTINE. *Confessions*.

SCHRÖDINGER, ERWIN. *Science and Humanism*. Cambridge (England): Cambridge University Press, 1961.

—— and others. *On Modern Physics*. New York: Clarkson N. Potter, 1961.

SETHE, KURT HEINRICH, ed. *Die alt-aegyptischen Pyramidentexte*. 4 Vols. Leipzig: J. C. Hinrichs, 1908–22.

SINNOTT, EDMUND W. *Cell and Psyche*. Chapel Hill: University of North Carolina Press, 1950.

SPITZ, RENÉ. *A Genetic Field Theory of Ego Formation*. New York: International Universities Press, 1959.

——. "Hospitalism," in *The Psychoanalytic Study of the Child*, Vol. 1. New York: International Universities Press, 1945.

THIGPEN, CORBETT H. and H. H. CLECKLEY. *The Three Faces of Eve*. New York: McGraw Hill, 1957.

ÜXKÜLL, JAKOB VON. "A Stroll Through the Worlds of Animals and Men," in *Instinctive Behavior*, translated and edited by Claire H. Schiller. New York: International Universities Press, 1957.

VAN DER POST, LAURENS. *The Dark Eye in Africa*. New York: Morrow, 1955.

——. *Venture to the Interior*. New York: Morrow, 1951.

WHITMONT, EDWARD C. "Magic and the Psychology of Compulsive States." *Journal of Analytical Psychology*, Vol. 2, No. 1 (January 1957), pp. 3–32.

——. "The Magical Dimension in Transference and Counter-Transference," in *Current Trends in Analytical Psychology*, edited by Gerhard Adler. London: Tavistock, 1961.

WOLFF, TONI. "Structural Forms of the Feminine Psyche." Zurich: privately printed, 1956.

Index

Lightning Source UK Ltd.
Milton Keynes UK
UKOW02f0225141216
289883UK00001B/201/P